PSYCHOANALYTIC COUPLE THERAPY

The Library of Couple and Family Psychoanalysis

Series Editors: Susanna Abse, Christopher Clulow, Brett Kahr, David Scharff

Other titles in the series:

Sex, Attachment, and Couple Psychotherapy: Psychoanalytic Perspectives
edited by Christopher Clulow

How Couple Relationships Shape Our World: Clinical Practice, Research, and Policy Perspectives
edited by Andrew Balfour, Mary Morgan, and Christopher Vincent

What Makes Us Stay Together? Attachment and the Outcomes of Couple Relationships
by Rosetta Castellano, Patrizia Velotti, and Giulio Cesare Zavattini

PSYCHOANALYTIC COUPLE THERAPY
Foundations of Theory and Practice

Edited by
David E. Scharff and Jill Savege Scharff

with the collaboration of
*David Hewison, Christel Buss-Twachtmann
and Janine Wanlass*

A collaboration of The International Psychotherapy Institute and
The Tavistock Centre for Couple Relationships

KARNAC

First published in 2014 by
Karnac Books Ltd
118 Finchley Road
London NW3 5HT

Copyright © 2014 to David E. Scharff and Jill Savege Scharff for the edited collection, and to the individual authors for their contributions.

The rights of the contributors to be identified as the authors of this work have been asserted in accordance with §§ 77 and 78 of the Copyright Design and Patents Act 1988.

All rights reserved. No part of this publication may be reproduced, stored in a retrieval system, or transmitted, in any form or by any means, electronic, mechanical, photocopying, recording, or otherwise, without the prior written permission of the publisher.

British Library Cataloguing in Publication Data

A C.I.P. for this book is available from the British Library

ISBN-13: 978-1-78220-012-3

Typeset by V Publishing Solutions Pvt Ltd., Chennai, India

Printed in Great Britain

www.karnacbooks.com

CONTENTS

ABOUT THE EDITORS AND CONTRIBUTORS ix

SERIES EDITOR'S FOREWORD xiii
Brett Kahr

PREFACE AND ACKNOWLEDGEMENTS xvii

PART I: FUNDAMENTAL PRINCIPLES OF PSYCHOANALYTIC COUPLE THERAPY

CHAPTER ONE
An overview of psychodynamic couple therapy 3
David E. Scharff and Jill Savege Scharff

CHAPTER TWO
Shared unconscious phantasy in couples 25
David Hewison

CHAPTER THREE
Intimacy and the couple—the long and winding road 35
Susanna Abse

CHAPTER FOUR
Attachment, affect regulation, and couple psychotherapy 44
Christopher Clulow

CHAPTER FIVE
Aggression in couples: an object relations primer 59
David E. Scharff

CHAPTER SIX
Getting back to or getting back at: understanding overt aggression in couple relationships 71
Christopher Vincent

CHAPTER SEVEN
Responding to the clinical needs of same-sex couples 81
Damian McCann

CHAPTER EIGHT
The selfdyad in the dynamic organisation of the couple 91
Richard M. Zeitner

CHAPTER NINE
Dreams in analytic couple therapy 101
Jill Savege Scharff and David E. Scharff

CHAPTER TEN
Why can being a creative couple be so difficult to achieve? The impact of early anxieties on relating 116
Mary Morgan

PART II: ASSESSMENT AND TREATMENT

CHAPTER ELEVEN
The couple state of mind and some aspects of the setting in couple psychotherapy 125
Mary Morgan

CHAPTER TWELVE
Establishing a therapeutic relationship in analytic couple therapy 131
Jill Savege Scharff

CHAPTER THIRTEEN
The triangular field of couple containment 148
Carl Bagnini

CHAPTER FOURTEEN
Projection, introjection, intrusive identification, adhesive identification 158
David Hewison

CHAPTER FIFTEEN
Negotiating individual and joint transferences in couple therapy 170
James L. Poulton

CHAPTER SIXTEEN
Narcissism in a couple with a cocaine-addicted partner 180
Carl Bagnini

CHAPTER SEVENTEEN
The dream space in analytic couple therapy 190
Tamar Kichli Borochovsky

CHAPTER EIGHTEEN
Clinical narrative and discussion: a couple who lost joy 201
Pierre Cachia and Jill Savege Scharff

PART III: UNDERSTANDING AND TREATING SEXUAL ISSUES

CHAPTER NINETEEN
How development structures sexual relationships 215
David E. Scharff

CHAPTER TWENTY
Assessing the sexual relationship 228
Jane Seymour

CHAPTER TWENTY-ONE
Addressing sexual issues in couple therapy 237
Norma Caruso

CHAPTER TWENTY-TWO
Unconscious meanings and consequences of abortion in the life of couples 246
Yolanda de Varela

CHAPTER TWENTY-THREE
Working with affairs 254
David E. Scharff

PART IV: SPECIAL TOPICS

CHAPTER TWENTY-FOUR
The couple as parents: the role of children in couple treatment 269
Janine Wanlass

CHAPTER TWENTY-FIVE
Divorce and parenting wars   279
Kate Scharff

CHAPTER TWENTY-SIX
Trauma in the couple   295
Jill Savege Scharff

CHAPTER TWENTY-SEVEN
Treating intergenerational trauma: the bomb that exploded me continues
    to blow up my family   303
Hanni Mann-Shalvi

CHAPTER TWENTY-EIGHT
But my partner "is" the problem: addressing addiction, mood disorders,
    and psychiatric illness in psychoanalytic couple treatment   310
Janine Wanlass

CHAPTER TWENTY-NINE
The ending of couple therapy with a couple who recovered joy   323
Pierre Cachia and Jill Savege Scharff

EPILOGUE   335

INDEX   337

ABOUT THE EDITORS AND CONTRIBUTORS

Susanna Abse is Senior Couple Psychoanalytic Psychotherapist and CEO of The Tavistock Centre for Couple Relationships (TCCR), London, UK. She is a full member and past Vice Chair of the British Society of Couple Psychotherapists and Counsellors. Recently, she has co-developed a new mentalization-based intervention for parents in destructive conflict over parenting issues, many of them post-separation. She is the author of several articles and papers on clinical work and on family policy in the UK.

Carl Bagnini, L.C.S.W., B.C.D., private practice, Port Washington, NY; Founding and Senior Faculty Member, The International Psychotherapy Institute (IPI) in Chevy Chase, MD and Long Island, NY; Clinical faculty, Adelphi University's Derner Institute for Advanced Psychological Studies and New York University's Post-Master Certificate Program in Child & Family Therapy; Clinical Supervisor, Yeshiva University's Ferkauf Graduate Program in Clinical Psychology. His new book, *Keeping Couples in Treatment: Working from Surface to Depth* is published by Jason Aronson.

Christel Buss-Twachtmann, BSc, Dip. Mar. Psych, member, British Society for Couple Psychotherapy and Counselling; Clinician and former Director of Training, Tavistock Centre for Couple Relationships. For two years, she co-organized the international course "Foundations of Couple Psychotherapy" on which this book is based.

Pierre Cachia is a counselling psychologist, individual psychotherapist and couple psychoanalytic psychotherapist in private practice; clinical staff member and tutor on the Postgraduate Diploma in Individual and Couple Counselling at the Tavistock Centre for Couple Relationships;

staff member on the Doctorate in Counselling and Psychotherapeutic Psychology, University of Surrey.

Norma Caruso, Psy.D., is a clinical psychologist in private practice in Richmond, Virginia; Associate Clinical Professor of Psychiatry, Medical College of Virginia; faculty, International Psychotherapy Institute; sex therapist, certified by the American Association of Sexuality Educators, Counselors and Therapists. She has published several articles on the evaluation and treatment of sexual dysfunction in couples.

Christopher Clulow, Ph.D., is Senior Fellow and former Director of the Tavistock Centre for Couple Relationships, editorial advisor for the international journal *Sexual and Relationship Therapy*, editorial board member for *Couple and Family Psychoanalysis*, and has published extensively on marriage, partnerships, parenthood and couple psychotherapy. Author and editor, he most recently edited *Sex, Attachment and Couple Psychotherapy: Psychoanalytic Perspectives*. He maintains a private clinical and training practice in St. Albans, England.

David Hewison, D.Cpl.Psych.Psych., is a consultant couple psychoanalytic psychotherapist and the Head of Research at the Tavistock Centre for Couple Relationships in London. He is a developmentally trained Jungian Analyst and has developed an integrative model of brief couple therapy for treating depression for the National Health Service. Author of many papers on psychoanalytic and Jungian themes, he teaches internationally.

Tamar Kichli-Borochovsky is an accredited marital and family therapist and certified bibliotherapist. She has a Master's Degree from Haifa University and is presently in a doctoral program. She is a student in the Tel Aviv affiliate of IPI's international couple psychotherapy course. Tamar provides family and marital therapy privately and supervises bibliotherapy students at Haifa University. Her book *Rehabilitation Stories* is in publication.

Hanni Mann-Shalvi, Ph.D., a graduate of the Hebrew University of Jerusalem, is the Director of the International Institute for Psychoanalytic Couple and Family Therapy Training in Israel, which is affiliated with IPI; adjunct faculty to the Couple, Child and Family Program of IPI. She teaches at the Hebrew University, and is a board member of the International Association of Couple and Family Psychoanalysis. She has a private practice in Tel Aviv of individual and couple psychoanalysis, psychotherapy, and supervision.

Damian McCann is a couple psychoanalytic psychotherapist at TCCR and a consultant family and systemic psychotherapist in the NHS. He is a clinical associate of Pink Therapy Services, where he delivers training on the Diploma in Gender and Sexual Diversities. His clinical doctorate in Systemic Psychotherapy explored violence and abuse in couple relationships of gay men. He has extensive clinical experience with same-sex couples.

Mary Morgan is a consultant couple psychoanalytic psychotherapist, psychoanalyst, and member of the British Psychoanalytical Society; Head of the MA in Couple Psychoanalytic

Psychotherapy at TCCR; and a member of the International Psychoanalytic Association's Psychoanalytic Perspectives of Families and Couples Working Group. She has published widely on couple psychoanalytic therapy. She has developed couple psychotherapy trainings in several countries, including Sweden and the USA.

James Poulton, Ph.D., is a psychologist in private practice in Salt Lake City, Adjunct Professor in Psychology at the University of Utah, and faculty member of IPI. He is the author of *Object Relations and Relationality in Couple Therapy*.

David E. Scharff, M.D., is former Director and Chair of the Board of IPI; Honorary Fellow, TCCR; Honorary Member, British Society of Couple Psychotherapists and Counsellors; Chair, the International Psychoanalytical Association's Couple and Family Working Group; former Vice-President, International Association for Couple and Family Psychoanalysis. He is author and editor of thirty books and numerous articles, most recently, with Jill Savege Scharff, *The Interpersonal Unconscious*, and with Sverre Varvin, *Psychoanalysis in China*.

Jill Savege Scharff, M.D., is co-Founder and former co-Director of the International Psychotherapy Institute (IPI); Founding Chair of the International Institute for Psychoanalytic Training at IPI; Clinical Professor of Psychiatry, Georgetown University, Washington DC; Honorary Fellow, TCCR; Honorary Member, British Society of Couple Psychotherapists and Counsellors; Author and editor of twenty-five books and numerous articles, including *New Paradigms for Treating Relationships* and *The Interpersonal Unconscious* with David E. Scharff, and most recently *Psychoanalysis Online*.

Kate Scharff, M.S.W., is a clinical social worker with children, couples, and families. In addition to her general psychotherapy practice, her work focuses on multi-disciplinary alternatives to traditional adversarial models of separation and divorce. She is a founder of the Collaborative Practice Center of Greater Washington, author of *Therapy Demystified: An Insiders Guide to Getting the Right Help*, and co-author of *Navigating Emotional Currents in Collaborative Divorce: A Guide to Enlightened Team Practice*.

Jane Seymour is an experienced psychosexual therapist, couples counsellor, and former Head of TCCR's MSc in Psychosexual and Relationship Therapy. She works as a therapist, supervisor, and trainer and has a private practice in South London.

Yolanda de Varela, Ph.D., is a member of the International Psychoanalytical Association and training analyst in Panama. Founding faculty of IPI and founder of IPI Panama. She has published numerous articles and has a private practice in adult psychoanalysis and couple therapy.

Christopher Vincent is a couple psychoanalytic psychotherapist in private practice, a visiting lecturer at The Tavistock Centre for Couple Relationships and a researcher looking at the impact of a diagnosis of Huntington's Disease on couple relationships. With Mary Morgan and

Andrew Balfour, he recently edited *How Couples Shape Our World: Clinical Practice, Research and Social Policy Perspectives*.

Janine Wanlass, Ph.D., is a psychologist and psychoanalyst practising in Salt Lake City, Utah. She is Professor and former Director of the Master of Science in Professional Counselling Program at Westminster College. She serves on the national faculty of the International Psychotherapy Institute (IPI) in Chevy Chase, Maryland, where she chairs the Couple, Child and Family Program, and is on the faculty of the International Institute for Psychoanalytic Training at IPI.

Richard M. Zeitner, Ph.D., is the Director and Training and Supervising Analyst of the Greater Kansas City Psychoanalytic Institute. He is Clinical Assistant Professor of the University of Missouri Kansas City School of Medicine and Adjunct Faculty Member of IPI. He is the author of *Self Within Marriage: The Foundation of Lasting Relationships*.

SERIES EDITOR'S FOREWORD

When, many years ago, I became a student at the Tavistock Marital Studies Institute, to train in "psychoanalytical marital psychotherapy", I had the privilege of learning from some of Great Britain's most experienced practitioners. Although my fellow trainees and I enjoyed highly stimulating clinical and academic seminars, I must confess, somewhat shamefacedly, that during the entire length of the five-year training, our tutors never assigned us an entire book to read! Of course, we devoured scads of articles and chapters, many written by our distinguished teachers themselves, and all of them truly excellent. But we never had to read a *whole* book, because at that time, we had nothing that really served as a comprehensive textbook true and proper. Naturally, I supplemented the required reading by ploughing through literally hundreds of volumes on psychotherapy and psychoanalysis and psychopathology, but I did so in my "spare time", and never as part of the training itself. Oh how I wish that I could have read *Psychoanalytic Couple Therapy: Foundations of Theory and Practice* back then. If I had done so, I suspect that my internal map of the complex terrain of couple psychoanalytical practice might have become much clearer much sooner!

This new book, edited by David Scharff and Jill Savege Scharff, cherished leaders in our field, with the collaboration of three extremely accomplished practitioner-teachers of couple psychoanalysis—David Hewison and Christel Buss-Twachtmann of the Tavistock Centre for Couple Relationships (T.C.C.R.), and Janine Wanlass of the International Psychotherapy Institute (I.P.I.)—represents a masterstroke. Although mental health professionals have published countless books on "couple therapy" over the last half-century, this newest arrival deserves pride of place on our bedside tables as the most comprehensive, the most rigorous, and the most readable, and written, moreover, with the profundity of understanding offered by the psychoanalytical lens. I predict that within a very short time *Psychoanalytic Couple Therapy: Foundations of Theory and Practice* will become the standard textbook for our profession, and deservedly so.

Throughout their long and distinguished career, Dr. David Scharff and Dr. Jill Savege Scharff have pioneered the field of couple and family psychoanalysis, in addition to their many contributions to the fields of individual psychoanalysis and psychosexual therapy. Not only have the Scharffs broken new ground by mapping out the field in both an expansive and a detailed manner, but they have accomplished the impossible by producing a brace of books and chapters and essays not only for the experienced clinician but, also, for the fledgling trainee. As dedicated, longstanding practitioners and educators, the Scharffs know how to write for a multiplicity of audiences, and they do so brilliantly.

Reference works in the mental health field frequently adopt a very pedestrian, or even condescending, style, reducing complex and nuanced ideas into simple formulae, but this carefully prepared and lovingly edited tome avoids all of those traditional pitfalls. In spite of the fact that all twenty of the expert contributors have a wealth of clinical experience in the couple psychoanalytical arena, none write in a stodgy or bombastic style; therefore, one derives great pleasure from reading this book, in spite of its potential heft. Perhaps the great approachability and accessibility of this text derives from the fact that all of the authors know such a great deal about the creation of partnerships, not least the partnership between a writer and a reader. Indeed, in their "Preface and Acknowledgements", the Scharffs refer to their audience as "fellow travellers" (p. xvi)—an editorial state of mind which characterises the twenty-nine chapters and the "Epilogue" which follow, covering every stage of the treatment process from assessment to termination.

The eminent contributors to this volume invite the readers on a truly fulfilling journey through the very foundations of the field; and the first section, on "Fundament Principles of Psychoanalytic Couple Therapy", boasts many excellent contributions from some of the real "stars" of our profession. The Scharffs themselves set the tone in a masterful chapter which provides an overview of the entire terrain with admirable breadth and depth, followed by truly engaging chapters by distinguished colleagues on such diverse subjects as the struggles with intimacy and aggression, the function of unconscious phantasy in the couple, the role of attachment, the obstacles to creativity, the use of dream analysis, and the particular needs of the same-sex couple. The second section, on "Assessment and Treatment", brims with delicious reflections on a diverse range of topics from establishing contact and the couple's state of mind, to the role of triangulation, defence mechanisms, the transference, the dangers of narcissism, and the restoration of joy.

The editors could well have ended the book at this point, because they have already given us so many meaty chapters to digest. But as pioneers in speaking frankly about sexuality in psychoanalytical treatment with couples and among psychoanalytical professionals as well, the editors have also provided a third section, on "Understanding and Treating Sexual Issues", which includes chapters on such key themes as, *inter alia*, the assessment of sexual struggles and the extramarital affair. The fourth and final section of the book, "Special Topics", covers the role of parenting, the impact of divorce on couples and on their children, the consequences of trauma, psychiatric illness, as well as termination. In the "Epilogue", David Scharff and Jill Savege Scharff share their lifelong enthusiasm for the field of couple mental health, encouraging all of us to contribute increasingly to this vital area of psychological work.

Not only does *Psychoanalytic Couple Therapy: Foundations of Theory and Practice* survey and extend the entire landscape of the profession, but its very construction also reveals how much creativity can emerge when couples—even mental health couples—work in expansive partnerships. For this book could not have appeared without the Scharffs' pro-social, pro-coupling stance. As young psychiatrists, the Scharffs undertook postgraduate training at the Tavistock Clinic, back in the 1970s, and since that time have maintained a rich relationship with colleagues at the Tavistock Centre for Couple Relationships. Indeed, the Tavistock Centre for Couple Relationships bestowed upon both David Scharff and Jill Savege Scharff the high distinction of its title of Honorary Fellow; and subsequently, the British Society of Couple Psychotherapists and Counsellors—the Professional Association of the Tavistock Centre for Couple Relationships—appointed each of the Scharffs as an Honorary Member—a rare honour indeed—in recognition of their unique contributions to the field.

The Scharffs have long facilitated the development of couple collaborations among mental health professionals and among mental health organisations; and this book represents not only David Scharff's pioneering work in international video-conferencing and in the creation of international summer schools, co-chaired with Janine Wanlass from the United States and by Caroline Medawar and Catriona Wrottesley from Great Britain but, also, the culmination of the comprehensive course on couple psychotherapy designed by David Scharff, Christel Buss-Twachtmann, David Hewison, and Janine Wanlass, and authorised by Susanna Abse, the Chief Executive Officer of T.C.C.R. This vital collaborative work has also included regular visits to London by the Scharffs and their American colleagues, and reciprocal visits to I.P.I. by T.C.C.R. staff, all resulting in a stimulating transatlantic programme of Anglo-American collaboration. Consequently, *Psychoanalytic Couple Therapy: Foundations of Theory and Practice*, represents a true coupling, not only of two institutions but, also of two nations.

At a time in human history when we witness couplings collapsing all around us, the Scharffs and their colleagues have devoted themselves to the creation of couples, to the repair of couples, and to the enrichment of couples. Those of us who have worked for many years in the field of couple mental health, as well as those of us just beginning to do so, owe a deep debt to Dr. David Scharff and to Dr. Jill Savege Scharff and to their many collaborators at both the International Psychotherapy Institute and at the Tavistock Centre for Couple Relationships for having bequeathed to us such a rich work which provides a truly secure base for future growth and maturation.

Professor Brett Kahr
London

PREFACE AND ACKNOWLEDGEMENTS

David E. Scharff and Jill Savege Scharff

Psychoanalytic couple therapy dates back sixty-five years to the founding of the pioneering Family Discussion Bureau by Enid Balint and her colleagues, an entity that gave rise to the Institute of Marital Studies, and continues to break new ground in clinical innovation and research, now under its current banner, Tavistock Centre for Couple Relationships (TCCR). As young psychiatrists in training at the Tavistock Centre forty years ago, we were inspired by colleagues at the clinic and at the institute—Henry Dicks, Henry Ezriel, Bob Gosling, Hyatt Williams, Sally Box, and Anton Obholzer. Twenty years ago, with a group of American colleagues, we founded the International Psychotherapy Institute (IPI) in Washington DC, USA, a psychoanalytic learning community, and invited our valued British colleagues to teach and learn with us there. In 2008 David E. Scharff introduced the idea for a course in psychoanalytic couple therapy in collaboration between IPI and TCCR. David Hewison of TCCR, Janine Wanlass of IPI and David E. Scharff designed and implemented the first offering of the course. Later, Christel Buss-Twachtmann took over the leadership of the course at TCCR, and, since her retirement, Catriona Wrottesley stepped in. The partnership has now expanded to include sponsorship and participation by the British Society of Couple Psychotherapists and Counsellors (BSCPC), currently chaired by Liz Hamlin.

This book aims to give students and practitioners a foundation for the practice of psychoanalytic psychotherapy with couples in the tradition of these institutions. The chapters are drawn from various lectures and workshops of the IPI/TCCR course occurring from 2009 to 2012. The participants of the course meet twice a month by video link connecting students and faculty in live-time in Washington DC, London, Salt Lake City, Long Island, Indianapolis, Taiwan, Panama, and Israel. Other students call in by telephone from all over the US and the world. This creates a large group seminar with an exciting mix of cultures and contributors, which has enriched thinking for everyone. That is not to say that there is agreement among all of the contributors of every theoretical position, but we do have agreement about the core theories and competences, knowledge and experience with which to ready the clinician for the practice of analytic couple therapy.

The core ideas are drawn from modern psychoanalysis: the centrality of unconscious organisation and fantasy; mechanisms of unconscious communication; the continuing influence of early life and object relations in the functioning of individuals and couples; the role of therapists as containers of anxiety; the importance of transference and countertransference; the role of sexuality in the life of couples; the disorganising effects on couples of early trauma or of trauma during adulthood; and the use of interpretation to help the spouses or partners grow in understanding and relating to each other.

Beyond these core ideas, many aspects of theory have had to be expanded and modified to fit the needs of couples and make couple therapy a truly psychoanalytic undertaking. We have had to explore the way the couple forms a special group, one that is powered as much by small group dynamics as by the issues of the two individuals who form the partnership. Theories of development have evolved in the last years to focus on early patterns of attachment. We track the ways these affect couples and then play out in the life of the children, who in turn influence the couple. We begin to see how the couple's shared organisation influences the personality of each of the partners who form the couple, and causes the couple to become stuck in dysfunctional patterns or supports them to grow. We want to know what promotes a couple's potential for intimacy and creativity, and what can sap it, from problems in early attachments to unbridled aggression. What role does couple sexuality play in promoting or disrupting intimacy, and why do certain early problems prove so recalcitrant to growth-promoting efforts?

These questions about fundamental processes of individual and couple growth are aimed at helping us as clinicians in the pressurised cockpit with the couples who seek our help. Sometimes, rarely, the sailing is smooth. Other times, most times, there are bumps and detours in the road. Most of this book is devoted to the clinical challenges of growing and maintaining a couple state of mind, acting as a container, accessing our countertransference, and finding ways to speak to couples about matters that are often difficult to speak of and harder yet to hear. We address the bastions that couples form, intended to protect their life together but unfortunately creating various kinds of impasse. These bastions arise from an inevitable mixture of individual developmental issues, traumas, losses, wishes, and fears generated in the course of the couple's unique partnership, and therefore cause pain when mentioned and probed. How much of an impasse belongs to one of the partners and how much to the pair? We find it intriguing to figure out how each partner contributes separately and together to the couple dynamic and how they can work together with us to create a path forward to a healthy couple relationship.

To this end, this book addresses basic theory, clinical approaches from beginning to end of treatment, and special topics. Part I explores foundational ideas. David and Jill Scharff give an overview of psychoanalytic couple therapy, including the integration of ideas from chaos theory, attachment research, and trauma theory. David Hewison reviews and illustrates the concept of shared unconscious phantasy. Susanna Abse looks at issues of intimacy, while Chris Clulow shares his deep interest in attachment theory and its application in couple therapy to understanding and treating couples. David E. Scharff reviews theories of aggression and its management, followed by Chris Vincent's close inspection of aggression in a couple. In the last four chapters in this section, Damian McCann discusses central issues in working therapeutically with gay and lesbian couples, Richard Zeitner describes the selfdyad in couples, Jill and David E. Scharff outline and illustrate principles of dream work in couple therapy, and Mary Morgan describes the creative couple and the impediments to creativity.

Part II opens up the work of assessment and treatment. Mary Morgan begins by exploring the couple state of mind and its value to couples and the therapists who work with them. Jill Savege Scharff talks about how to establish a therapeutic relationship, Carl Bagnini discusses containment in the triangular field that constitutes couple therapy, David Hewison examines the complexity of shifting projections, and James Poulton describes his way of negotiating joint and individual transferences. Then Carl Bagnini's second chapter examines the problem of narcissism in a couple with cocaine addiction. Tamar Kichli Borochovsky looks at a particular constellation of dream work with an Israeli couple, and the section closes with a chapter giving close process examination of a clinical narrative of couple therapy by Pierre Cachia in discussion with Jill Scharff.

In Part III, we approach the role of sexuality and sexual issues in couple therapy. David E. Scharff describes developmental issues in the life cycle that support intimacy and sexual relating. Chapters by Jane Seymour, Norma Caruso and Yolanda de Varela address the importance of sexuality in the life of couples from various points of view, focusing on specific issues that arise and describing methods for treating them, and David E. Scharff looks at aspects of infidelity and its management in the therapeutic relationship.

Each couple dynamic is unique. Partners coming together from disparate family and social cultures create their own unique culture. The variety in presentation, dynamic, and culture is infinite. We do well to have a diverse armamentarium, a wide awareness of issues and situations. In Part IV Janine Wanlass addresses the challenge to the couple of parenthood. Kate Scharff introduces us to some modern developments in the legal and psychological aspects of divorce. Jill Scharff and Hanni Mann-Shalvi discuss the disorganising and organising effects of trauma in the couple and in the culture. In her second chapter, Janine Wanlass discusses the complications that psychiatric illness and substance abuse bring to couple relationships and therapy. Jill Scharff and Pierre Cachia reprise the therapy they presented in Part III as they consider of the task of ending therapy after a successful treatment. We end with a brief epilogue on the nature of our work with couples.

We are grateful to many people without whom this book would not be and without whom it would be considerably less than it is. Beyond the chapter authors, and the many others at TCCR and IPI who contributed to the course, Susanna Abse, Brett Kahr and Liz Hamlin for TCCR and the British Society for Couple Psychotherapists and Counsellors have been invaluable in their support of our shared project, as has Geoff Anderson, director of IPI, and Anna Innes, IPI's beloved administrator, who keeps our project going, and Janine Wanlass, Chair of IPI's Child Couple and Family Program, who also manages our video technology from the hub at Westminster College in Salt Lake City. We are grateful to the participants of the program for their patience with a sometimes shaky video conference and telephone connection across the globe, and for their engaging discussion of the issues being presented. They give vitality to the teaching and learning of the video conference and to the material we present here. Thanks to all of them, and to you as readers and fellow travellers who work to make ideas like the ones we present here useful to couples around the world.

Acknowledgements

We gratefully acknowledge the following for permission to reprint chapters, images and modifications of previously printed material in this volume.

Chapter One by David and Jill Scharff was modified from Scharff, D. & Savege Scharff, J. (2007). Psychodynamic couple therapy. In: G. Gabbard, J. Beck & J. Holmes (Eds.), *The Oxford Textbook of Psychotherapy* (pp. 67–75). Oxford: Oxford University Press.
    By permission of Oxford University Press.

In Chapter Three, the translation of the thirteenth century poem *Married Love* by Kuan Tao-Sheng is used with permission of New Directions Publishing Company. The photographic images in this chapter are used through purchase of images and rights.

Chapters Five, Eighteen, and Twenty-Nine, all written for this volume, have been previously published in *Couple and Family Psychoanalysis* and are reprinted here by permission of the publisher, Karnac.

Portions of Chapter Twenty-One, by Norma Caruso, previously appeared in two articles:
    Caruso, N. (2006). A troubled marriage in sex therapy. In: J. S. Scharff & D. E. Scharff (Eds.), *New Paradigms for Treating Relationships* (pp. 385–396). Lanham: Jason Aronson. By permission, Jason Aronson Books and Rowman-Littlefield Publishing.
    Caruso, N. (2003). Object relations theory and technique applied to sex and marital therapy. *Journal of Applied Psychoanalytic Studies*, 5(3): 297–308. By license agreement with Springer Publishing for the journal.

We want to thank Oliver Rathbone and his team at Karnac including Kate Pearce and Rod Tweedy for their support and encouragement. Lastly we are grateful to the many couples, who in working with us to improve their relationships have taught us how to think about couples and how to communicate our understanding. In all the cases described in these chapters, the authors have either received permission from the couples, have disguised the identifying information to preserve confidentiality, or have created composites to represent the couple dynamics and cultures under discussion.

PART I

FUNDAMENTAL PRINCIPLES OF PSYCHOANALYTIC COUPLE THERAPY

CHAPTER ONE

An overview of psychodynamic couple therapy

David E. Scharff and Jill Savege Scharff

Psychodynamic couple therapy is an application of psychoanalytic theory. It draws on the psychotherapist's experience of dealing with relationships in individual, group, and family therapy. Psychodynamic couple therapists relate in depth and get firsthand exposure to couples' defences and anxieties, which they interpret to foster change. The most complete version of psychodynamic therapy is object relations couple therapy based on the use of transference and countertransference as central guidance mechanisms. Then the couple therapist is interpreting on the basis of emotional connection and not from a purely intellectual stance. Object relations couple therapy enables psychodynamic therapists to join with couples at the level of resonating unconscious processes to provide emotional holding and containment, with which the couple identifies. In this way they enhance the therapeutic potential of the couple. From inside shared experience, the object relations couple therapist interprets anxiety that has previously overwhelmed the couple, and so unblocks partners' capacity for generative coupling.

The development of couple therapy

Couple therapy developed predominantly from psychoanalysis in Great Britain and from family systems theory in the United States. At first the limitations of classical psychoanalytic theory and technique inhibited psychoanalysts from thinking about a couple as a treatment unit. In reaction to that inadequacy for dealing with more than one person at a time, family systems research developed. However, many of the early systems theorists were also analytically trained or had been analysed, and so psychoanalysis had an influence on systems theory contributions to family therapy, and its extension to couple therapy in the United States (J. Scharff &

D. Scharff, 2003). With wider access to object relations theory from psychoanalysis in Great Britain an enriched form of psychoanalysis readily applicable to couples emerged.

Until then, psychoanalytic theory had stressed the innate drives of sexuality and aggression (Freud, 1905). Freud made little reference to the effect of the actual behaviours of parents on children's development, unless abuse had occurred (Breuer & Freud, 1893–1895). True, Freud's later structural theory dealt with the role of identification with selected aspects of each parent in psychic structure formation, but these identifications were seen as resulting from the child's fantasy of family romance and aggression towards the rival, not from the parents' characters and parenting styles (Freud, 1923). It was as though children normally grow up uninfluenced by those they depend on until the Oedipus complex develops. Even then, the psychoanalytic focus was squarely on the inner life of the individual.

In the United States, family systems theorists understood that spouses became part of an interpersonal system, and then devised ways of changing the system. However, without an understanding of unconscious influence on behaviour they could not address the irrational forces driving that system. In addition, they remained more interested in family systems than in couple systems for many years.

In Great Britain

Object relations theory emerging in Great Britain was also an individual psychology, but since it was being developed to address the vicissitudes of the analyst-analysand relationship, it lent itself well to thinking about couples, as shown by Enid Balint and her colleagues and students at the Family Discussion Bureau of the Tavistock Centre. As object relations theory continued to develop in Great Britain, it provided the theoretical foundation needed for the psychodynamic exploration of marital dynamics being explored at the Tavistock in what was now called the Tavistock Institute of Marital Studies in the 1950s (Pincus, 1955). Then in 1957, it was the publication of Henry Dicks's (1967) landmark text, *Marital Tensions*, integrating Fairbairn's theory of endopsychic structure and Klein's concept of projective identification that gave the crucial boost to the development of a clinically useful couple therapy. At that time, two therapists in the Adult Department of the Tavistock Clinic treated a married couple by one of them treating the husband while the other treated the wife, and then reported on their sessions at a shared meeting with a consultant. The team could then see how the individual psychic structures of marital partners affect one another. This observation led Dicks to realise that the psychic structures interact at conscious and unconscious levels through the central mechanism of projective identification to form a "joint marital personality," different from, and greater than, the personality of either spouse. In this way, partners rediscover lost aspects of themselves through the relationship with the other. Later, Dicks and his colleagues realised that it was more efficient for a single therapist to experience the couple's interaction first-hand, and couple therapy as we know it today had arrived (Dicks, personal communication).

In America

The next boost to couple therapy came from psychoanalysis in South America where modern concepts of transference and countertransference were being analysed in detail. Racker (1968) thought that countertransference was the analyst's unconscious reception of a transference communication from the patient through projective identification. He said that this countertransference might be of two types, concordant or complementary. The concordant identification is one in which the analyst resonates with a part of the patient's ego or object. The complementary identification is one in which the analyst resonates with a part of the patient's object. Let's say that the patient who was abused by his father feels easily humiliated by aggressive men in authority positions. He feels like a worm in front of the analyst whom he glorifies, and he defends against this feeling of weakness and insignificance by boasting about his income. If the analyst feels envious and impoverished in comparison, he is identifying with the patient's ego (concordant identification). If the analyst responds by puncturing the boastful claims, he is identifying with the patient's object derived from his experience with his father (complementary identification). After Racker, analysts could understand their shifting countertransference responses as a reflection not just of the transference, but of the specific ego or object pole of the internal object relationship.

This insight from psychoanalysis deepened appreciation for the way that a relationship is constructed, each partner to the relationship resonating with aspects of projective identifications to a greater or lesser degree. Applying this insight to the couple relationship between intimate partners, couple therapists could better understand how partners treated one another. They also had a way of using their unique responses to each couple to understand how the partners connected with their therapist.

In North America in the 1960s, Zinner and Shapiro (1972) went against the systems theory mainstream to study the family systems of troubled adolescents in relation to their individual psychic structures, using Dicks's ideas as the explanatory linking concept. Focusing on the parents as a couple Zinner (1976) extended Dicks's ideas on marital interaction to explore marital issues as a source of disruption to adolescent development. Their research findings provided further support for the value of couple therapy. Another boost came in the 1970s from developments in the understanding and treatment of sexuality (Masters & Johnson, 1970; Kaplan, 1974; D. Scharff, 1982). Object relations theory of couple therapy now included an object relations approach to sexual intimacy (J. Scharff & D. Scharff, 1991). Furthermore, in the 1990s, research on attachment processes stemming from the pioneering work of Bowlby, revealed that early infant attachment bonds influence the attachment patterns of adults, which has a profound effect on the life of couples and on the attachment styles of their children. Several clinicians and researchers have applied infant and adult attachment concepts to study the complex attachment of couples (Clulow, 2000; Bartholomew, Henderson, & Dutton, 2000; Fisher & Crandall, 2000).

Theoretical basis of psychodynamic couple therapy

Fairbairn's model of psychic structure

Fairbairn held that the individual is organised by the fundamental need for relationships throughout life. The infant seeks a relationship with the mother (or primary caretakers) but inevitably meets with some disappointment, for example, when the mother cannot be available at all times or when the infant's distress is too great to be managed. The mother who is beckoning without being overly seductive, and who can set limits without being persecuting or overly rejecting infuses the infant's self with feelings of safety, plenty, love, and satisfaction. The mother who is tantalising, overfeeding, anxiously hovering, excessively care taking, or sexually seductive is exciting but overwhelming to the infant, who then feels anxious, needy, and longing for relief. The mother who is too depressed, exhausted, and angry to respond to her infant's needs has an infant who feels rejected, angry, and abandoned. The mother who gets it more or less right, has an infant who feels relaxed, satisfied and loved.

When a frustrating experience occurs, the infant takes into the mind, or introjects, the image of the mother as a somewhat unsatisfying internal object, whether of an exciting or rejecting sort. The infant's next response is to split off the unbearably unsatisfying aspects from the core of this rejecting internal object and repress them because they are too painful to be kept in consciousness. However, whenever a part of an object is split and repressed, a part of the ego or self that relates to it is also split off from the main core of the ego along with the object. This now repressed relationship between part of the ego and an internal object is characterised by an affect. The rejecting object is connected to affects of sadness and anger. The exciting object is connected to affects of longing and craving. Remaining in consciousness connected to the central ego is the ideal object characterised by affects of satisfaction.

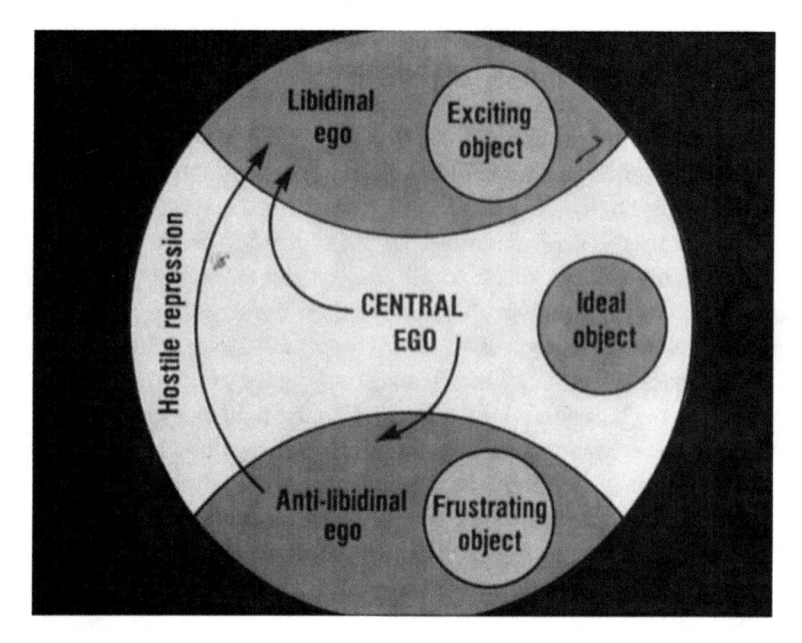

Figure 1. Fairbairn's model of psychic organisation. The central ego in relation to the ideal object is in conscious interaction with the caretaker. The central ego represses the split-off libidinal and anti-libidinal aspects of its experience along with corresponding parts of the ego and relevant affects that remain unconscious. The libidinal system is further repressed by the anti-libidinal system when anger predominates over longing as shown here, but the situation can reverse so that the libidinal system can act to further repress the anti-libidinal system when an excess of clinging serves to cover anger and rejection. (Copyright David E. Scharff reproduced courtesy of Jason Aronson.)

This produces three tiers of three-part structures in the self: central, rejecting and exciting internal object relationships in the ego, and within each internal object relationship, a part of the ego, the object, and the affect that binds them.

In health, these elements of object relations organisation are in internal dynamic flux, but in pathologically limited states, one or another element takes over at the expense of others in a relatively fixed way. So one person can be frozen into an angry rejecting stance towards others if dominated by rejecting object qualities; another can be fixed in an excited, seductive, and sexualised way of relating. In some trigger situations, one of these ordinarily buried ways of relating can take over in an automatic and repetitious way.

Klein and Bion's theory of projective and introjective identification

Klein proposed that people relate unconsciously and wordlessly by putting parts of themselves that feel dangerous or endangered into another person by projection. This unconscious mechanism characterises all intimate relationships beginning with the infant–parent relationship and continuing throughout life. Through facial gesture, vocal inflection, expressions of the eyes, and minute changes in body posture each of us continuously communicates subtle unconscious affective messages even while communicating a different message consciously, rationally, verbally. These affective messages are communicated from the right frontal lobe of the brain of one person to the right brain of another below the level of consciousness, but they fundamentally colour the reception of all communications (Schore, 2001). They transmit parts of oneself to the interior of the other person where they resonate with the recipient's unconscious organisation (a projective identification) and may evoke identification with the qualities of the projector. The recipient of a projective identification takes in aspects of the other person through introjective identification.

For instance, a child who fears his own anger will place it in his mother, identify her with his own anger, and then feel as afraid of her as he felt of his own temper. Or a weak wife who longs for strength, but also fears it, chooses a tyrannical husband whose power she regards with a mixture of fear and awe. A husband who is afraid that being sympathetic implies weakness locates tenderness in his wife or children, where he both demeans it and treasures it.

Bion (1967) described the continuous cycle of projective and introjective identification that occurs mutually between mother and infant. He studied the maternal process of containment, in which the parent's mind receives the unstructured anxieties of the child where they unconsciously resonate with the parent's mental structure, and the parent then feeds back more structured, detoxified understanding that in turn structures the child's mind. In this way, the child's growing mind is a product of affective and cognitive interaction with the parents. The same thing happens in couples: continuous feedback through cycles of projective and introjective identification is the mechanism for normal unconscious communication that is the basis for deep primary relationships. Bion (1961) also described valency, the spontaneous emotional clicking of strangers in a group setting, governed by fit between their unconscious needs. A couple is a special, small group of two who click as strangers and choose to become intimate, based on their unconscious needs.

Dicks

Dicks (1967) built his theory of marriage by integrating these elements from Fairbairn and Klein (to which we later added the contributions from Bion on valency and containment). Marriage is a state of continuous mutual projective identification. Interactions of couples can be understood both in terms of the conscious needs of each partner and in terms of shared unconscious assumptions and working agreements. Cultural elements are the most obvious determinants of marital choice—the sharing of backgrounds or values that are part of conscious mate selection—but Dicks's research showed that the long-term quality of a marriage is primarily determined by an unconscious fit between the internal object relations sets of each partner.

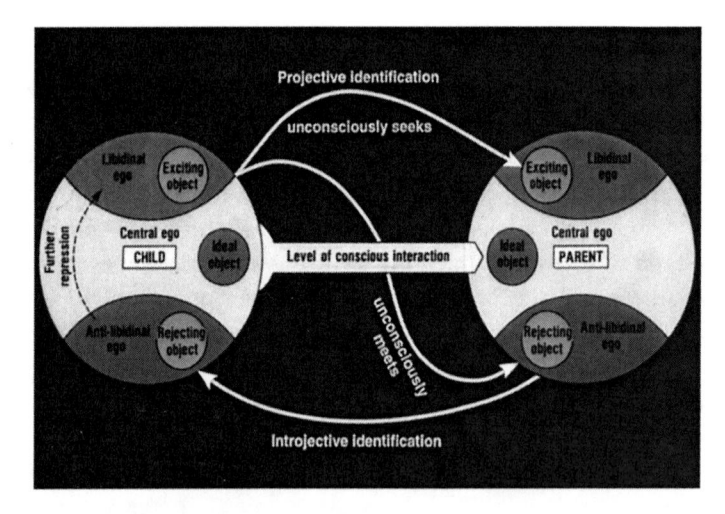

Figure 2. Projective and introjective identification in a marriage.

> Let's read this diagram of a couple relationship from the husband's point of view. A husband craves affection from an attractive but busy wife. He hopes she will long for him as he longs for her, but she is preoccupied and pushes him away. He responds by rejecting her before she can reject him and he squashes his feelings of love for her. To put this in technical terms, his exciting object relationship seeks to return from repression by projective identification with his wife's exciting object relationship. Instead, it is further repressed by her rejecting object relationship with which he identifies in self-defence. His rejecting object relationship is reinforced as a result and so increases the unconscious secondary repression of his exciting object relationship. His rejecting object is enhanced and his exciting object is crushed. In the marriage with healthy unconscious fit, his rejecting and exciting objects would have been modified and reintegrated into the central ego.

Winnicott's theory of the parent–infant relationship

To the foundation found in Dicks's integration of theories of Fairbairn and Klein, we have added other aspects. First, we have drawn from Winnicott's (1960) study of the infant–mother relationship (see Figure 3.) He described three basic elements, the environmental mother, the object mother, and the psychosomatic partnership. The environmental mother offers an "arms around" holding within which she positions the baby, providing a context for safety, security, a sense of well being, and growth. Within this "arms around" envelope, the object mother offers herself as a direct object for use by the baby in a "focused" relationship in which each incorporates the other as an internal object. There is a transitional zone between the contextual and the focused aspects of the infant–mother relationship. The psychosomatic partnership between parent and infant begins in pregnancy as a primarily somatic connection with minor psychological aspects based on the parents' fantasies of their unborn child and their imagined roles as parents. As the infant develops and becomes known as a person, the somatic element is subsumed in a psychological connection, which however, always retains vestiges of the original somatic one, and which therefore can lead to the somatising of psychological conflict. In later life the original psychosomatic partnership is the foundation of adolescent and adult sexual relationships (J. Scharff & D. Scharff, 1991; D. Scharff, 1982). In safety and intimacy enjoyed in the context of a committed sexual relationship, the partners experience a focused interpenetration of mind and body. They become each other's internal objects, drawing from internal object relationships that preceded their finding each other, and then modifying them in the light of new experience so as to build new internal organisations.

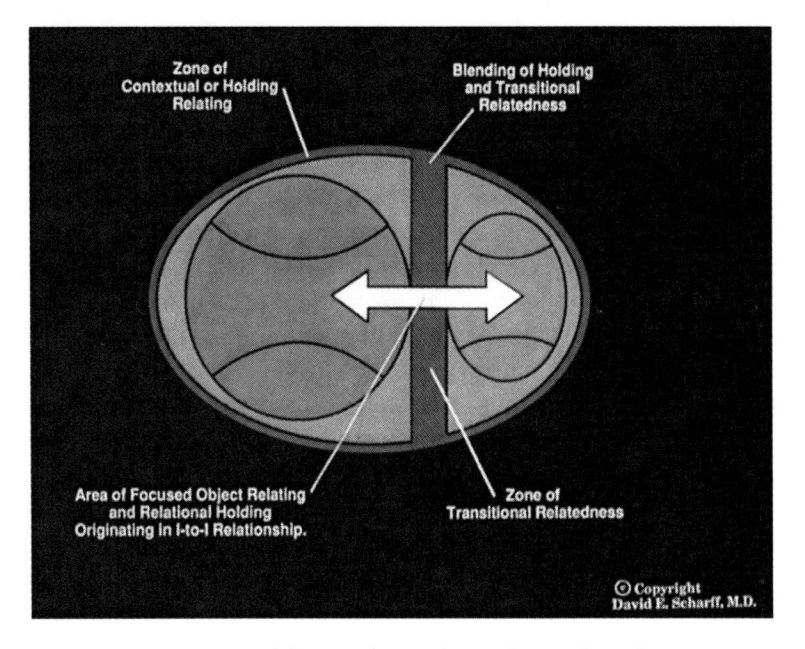

Figure 3. Winnicott's conception of the mother–infant relationship showing contextual holding, transitional space, and focused relating. Focused (or centered or I-to-I) relating occurs in and across the transitional space. Transitional space is in contact with both contextual (or arms-around) relating and focused relating, and is also the zone that blends the two. Transitional space is also the space between inside and outside world for the mother and for the infant, and the space of exchange between their individual inner worlds. Copyright David and Jill Scharff.

Attachment theory and couple therapy

Bowlby (1969, 1973, 1980) took an ethological approach to explore Fairbairn's proposition that relationships are the driving force in human motivation. Reviewing studies of mother–infant behaviour across many animal species, he found that all primate infants show instinctual behaviours—rooting, sucking, clinging, crying, and smiling—and that these behaviours had nothing to do with aggression release or sexual pleasure. In Bowlby's theory, these instinctual patterns had to do with ensuring protection, proximity, and emotional connectedness, and that when these needs for proximity were not met, pathology resulted. Bowlby's theory came to be called attachment theory.

Ainsworth and her colleagues developed a research model for use with humans to explore and refine this early attachment theory. They designed a test called the "Strange Situation" in which mother and baby are subjected to brief separations with and without a stranger present, and then study, score, and categorise the baby's reactions on reunion with the mother (Ainsworth, Blehar, Waters, & Wall, 1978). Infants' attachment style at a year can be classified into four groups: secure, anxious-insecure, avoidant-insecure, and disorganised/disoriented. If the baby treats the returning mother directly and confidently—even if the baby expresses angry protest at her absence—the attachment bond is coded as secure. If the baby clings, protests, and resists separating again, the coding is anxious-insecure; if the baby turns away and more or less shuns the mother, the coding is anxious-avoidant. If the infant moves away and then towards the mother, darts glances at her while avoiding her, and shows a chaotically rapid alternation of fear and need, the coding is disorganised/disoriented. This disorganised/disoriented group is associated with trauma and aggression perpetrated on the infant by the parent, or communicated to the infant unconsciously. It is of particular interest that an infant develops an attachment bond that is specific to each parent or caretaker. For instance, an infant can be securely attached with the mother and disorganised with the father.

Fonagy and colleagues (Fonagy, Gergely, Jurist, & Target, 2003) argued that attachment is not an end in itself but a context in which the self develops out of its relationships to others, a point of view similar to Sutherland (1990). They held that, within those relationships, an important variable is the mother's capacity to mirror her child's feelings and yet mark them as belonging to the child and not to herself. Her capacity to reflect upon and mentalize her infant's experience helps the child to read the feelings and intentions of others, discover and regulate affect experienced in interaction, and develop a sense of personal agency and selfhood.

Recently Main has developed a way of coding attachment styles in adults through analysis of their verbal narrative coherence as they describe their own histories (Main, 1995; Main & Solomon, 1987). Whether the content of these histories is secure or insecure is not the point. It is the style of the telling that determines the coding. An adult's attachment classification predicts the infant's attachment bond to that adult with a high degree of accuracy, even before the birth of the child.

Following these developments, researchers have begun to apply attachment theory to the study of couple dynamics. Clulow and his colleagues at the Tavistock Marital Studies Institute (now called the Tavistock Centre for Couple Relationships) have described complex attachments between couples (Clulow, 2000; Fisher & Crandall, 2000). Each partner provides an attachment object for the other while needing to be attached to the other. These patterns change with time and circumstance for a couple. Bartholomew and her colleagues have described various attachment patterns that correlate with healthy relationships and with those that are at risk for abuse or violence. For instance, a couple in which both parties code for secure attachment is at least risk, while a couple in which both partners show insecure, preoccupied, and anxious attachments is at greater risk, and the risk level is magnified when there are disorganised and fearful patterns (Bartholomew, Henderson, & Dutton, 2000).

Couples often experience distance or argument as a rejection that is analogous to the emotional separation that an infant feels. Similarly, they experience the interval between therapy sessions as a separation and reunion. This experience of the episodic nature of treatment mirrors the couple's own history of loss and reunion, and drives issues into the transference. This concurrence is then employed to advantage in couple therapy, as therapists interpret reactions to the frame of treatment in the light of the couple's previous experience.

Theory of transference and countertransference in couple therapy

Transference and countertransference are as central to psychodynamic couple therapy as they are to individual analytic therapy. To understand them, we refer to Winnicott's description of the environmental mother responsible for securing the context for safety and growth, and the object mother available to be used as the material for the child's world of inner objects. In the contextual transference a patient treats the therapist as a good understanding parent if the transference is positive, and as a misunderstanding, mismanaging parent if negative. In the contextual countertransference, the therapist feels taken for granted as a trusted benign parental object when things are going well, and treated with dismissal, suspicion or seduction if negative. In *the focused transference* a patient may treat her therapist as a critical mother, a cherished sibling or a seductive father—projections of discrete inner objects to which the patient's self relates. Or she may deal with her therapist as an ignorant child, greedy baby or irresponsible adolescent—hateful or craving parts of her self that she puts into the therapist. In the focused countertransference, the therapist feels treated in a certain specific way—hated, desired, attacked, or shunned—depending on the discrete ego or object pole of the inner object relationship being lived out through projective identification (J. Scharff & D. Scharff, 1991).

In the early phase of individual therapy, as the patient negotiates entry into the therapeutic space and establishes whether it is safe and secure, the contextual transference is central. As therapy evolves, and with increasing trust in the contextual transference, discrete focused transferences emerge. The therapist receives these discrete object transferences and resonates with them, the resulting countertransference providing access to the internal organisation of the patient and becoming the vehicle for their resolution (J. Scharff, 1992).

Similarly, in couple therapy, the contextual transference is important from the beginning, but it emanates not only from each partner individually, but more importantly from their holding of each other—that is from their shared environmental holding. Because the partners have a problem that leads to seeking help, by their own definition their shared holding has been insufficient. This deficit is further communicated to the therapist through their contextual transference. Figure 4 shows the transference situation and its origins in the contextual holding (which we sense in their joint marital personality) and through their centred holding (which is the sum of their patterned mutual projective identifications and use of each other as internal objects.) Together they project aspects of their separate and shared unconscious life into the therapist, who receives them as countertransference. While individual transferences certainly occur in couple therapy, we understand these principally as compensations for what each partner misses in the couple relationship. In treating couples, we use countertransference to understand deficits in the couple's shared holding that make it difficult for them to provide safety, meet each other's needs and contain anxiety (see below, example of evaluating a couple).

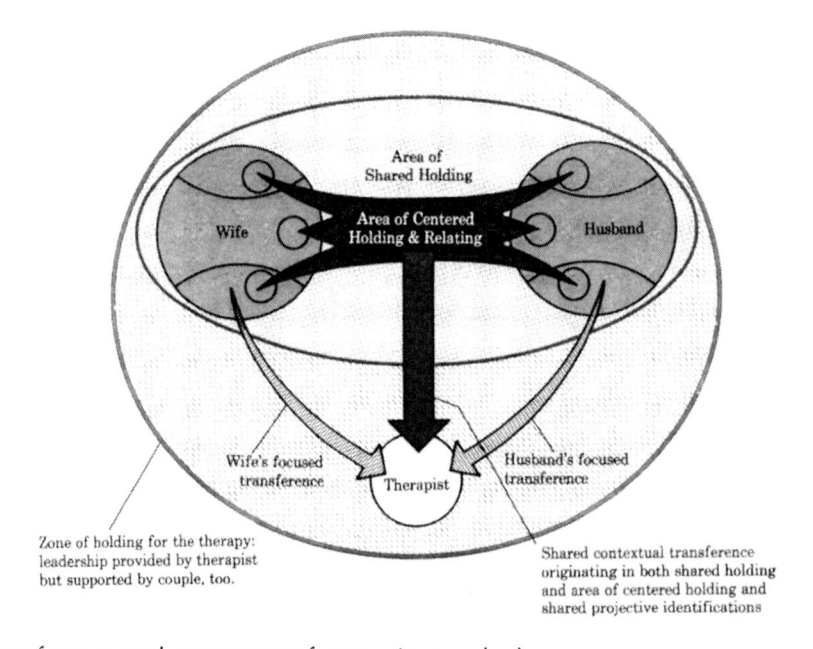

Figure 4. Transference and countertransference in couple therapy.

While focused transferences emanate from the individual partners, the most important source of couple transference is the shared contextual transference that conveys strengths and deficits in their shared holding capacity. Couple therapists' countertransference is most usefully interpreted as resonating with this area of transference. Copyright Jill and David Scharff.

The internal couple is an unconscious psychic structure consisting of two internal objects in relationship. It represents each person's accumulated experience and fantasies about couples—loving couples, hateful couples, couples with the impossibility of linking, couples who cannot differentiate, sexual, and asexual couples. Each therapist carries an internal couple, a constellation comprising the sum of his experiences growing up with couples, and an essential determinant of the therapist's countertransference to a couple. Any couple in therapy resonates unconsciously with a facet of the therapist's internal couple, and this is unique to that couple and that therapist.

Technique in couple assessment and therapy

The frame

In assessment and in subsequent therapy, couple therapists begin by setting a firm, but flexible frame bounded by frequency and length of sessions for an agreed-upon fee and maintained by a professional attitude that guarantees the couple confidentiality, respects ethical boundaries between therapist and couple, shows concern, interest, tact, and good timing. Couples' attempts to alter the frame are understood as communications about the holding provided by their couple relationship and their individual psychic structures in the present, and in their family of origin in the past.

Holding and containment

Couple therapists maintain a position of involved impartiality while creating a psychological space for work in which to offer safety and security (therapeutic holding) and begin the process of containment (mental receptivity, digestion, and unconscious resonance).

Following affect, gathering history, working with the unconscious

They look for aspects of object relations history, not by getting a preprogrammed history or a genogram, but by asking for history at moments of heightened affect so as to understand the here-and-now expression of early experience. In this way, history provides the context and language for understanding inner object relations and their effect on current interactions, both in therapy and in the couple's life. Couple therapists track affect in the session because it reveals split off object relations that are problematic for the couple.

Working with countertransference

Couple therapists use countertransference to detect transference that drives these core-affective moments. They analyse the feelings that are stirred in them by the couple they are treating and look for a match between their own responses and reactions the partners have now or in their families of origin. Responding to one member of the couple, the therapist arrived from inside his own experience at an idea of how that person's partner might be feeling. Resonating variously with a projected part of the ego or the object of one or another internal object relationship in wife or husband, over time therapists figure out the object relations set of each member of the couple by receiving mirror images in their own object relations set.

Working with dreams and fantasies

Work with dreams and fantasy is another avenue through which therapists reach the unconscious levels of the couple relationship. If a partner reports a fantasy, the therapist asks more about it and helps the partner share reactions and other fantasies. When a partner tells a dream in couple therapy, it is regarded as a communication from both partners, both of whose associations to the dream are valued. All elements are combined in arriving at understanding conveyed through tactful interpretation of defence, anxiety and inner object relations.

In assessment

In assessment, interpretations are tried out at several levels—from making links between memory and current experience, which the couple has kept apart, to making deeper interpretations about the defensive aspects of mutual unconscious projective identifications or the persistence of childhood patterns of interaction. This tests the couple's defences and their capacity for therapy. A formulation is then given to support the therapy recommendations. It is too soon to know much, and too soon to say all that is apparent to us in case it might be overwhelming. Nevertheless, enough must be said so that the couple can get a taste of therapy and decide if it will be helpful.

In therapy

In ongoing therapy, couple therapists continue their efforts to understand and interpret at moments of readiness. They offer continuing psychological holding and containment in a shared collaborative effort to promote growth and healing through understanding. Interpretation of conflict, defence, and understanding of basic anxieties take centre stage. Working through the issues over and over in different guises takes the couple into the late phase of therapy. By the time the partners are able to support each other, identify issues, share feelings, dreams, and fantasies, detect the unconscious factors that are interfering, and maintain an intimate bond, they are ready to terminate, equipped with skills for dealing with the developmental challenges that may come their way.

- Maintain the frame
- Hold attitude of involved impartiality
- Track the affect
- Take object relations history at core affective moments
- Assess attachment style
- Assess projective identificatory system
- Use countertransference to detect transference
- Integrate sex therapy
- Work with dreams and fantasies
- Interpret defensive patterns and sub-groupings
- Understand basic anxieties.

Figure 5. Techniques of couple therapy.

Example of an assessment with a couple

The following vignette illustrates the assessment process with a couple, in this case meeting with us as a co-therapy assessment team. A therapist working alone is equally likely to be effective, but for teaching purposes we have chosen a co-therapy example because it readily shows the effects of transference.

Assessing the couple's attachment style

Michelle and Lenny sought consultation because he wanted to get married and she wanted to break up. Their demeanour in the session was teasing, perverse, flippant, seductive, and yet highly entertaining. Michelle was taunting of Lenny, who appeared to delight in her no matter how she demeaned him. They explained that she was cruel only to him, and their friends did not enjoy their act, but as she said, "He does bring it out in me." When David E. Scharff asked why they were still together, Lenny, answered, "I'm the rock in the river, and I stay there while she runs up and down the river." He thought of himself as being steadfast like a rock, but she accused him of being immovable as a rock. Michelle claimed to have all the vitality for the couple, and while Lenny agreed that he got liveliness from her, he also saw her as flighty.

Michelle had an avoidant attachment style, while Lenny had an anxiously clinging one. Their projective identificatory system was stuck in a pattern in which he idealised her vitality and his steadfastness, while she held him in contempt for being stubbornly passive and for idealising her. Despite her contempt for his adoration, she desperately needed him to idealise her (since she did not love herself) and he needed her to bring him life.

Noting the projective identificatory system of the couple

Michelle's flamboyantly bright blue shirt with red, green, and yellow leaves met an echo in Lenny's blue polo shirt with faint yellow and green stripes and a touch of red. David, struck by the similarity and difference in their dress, asked about the shirts.

Michelle burst out laughing at the ridiculousness of his comment. She said, "It's a total coincidence! I bought that shirt for him. He would never buy it. It's not his personality; it's mine."

However Lenny said, "I like it, even tho I would probably buy the solids."

The shirts gave a vivid image of their system of mutual projective identification. Lenny had the more solid version of the colourful personality that he took in from the relationship with Michelle. She got stability from him even though she denigrated it as immovability. He got vitality from her, and tolerated her scorn as the price. Michelle said he came from an indulgent family that did not challenge him, while she came from a disorganised, intellectual family that felt special. Lenny added that in his family, he learned from his mother and sisters that men weren't good to women. He had grown up dedicated to setting that right.

Using transference and countertransference

As the session evolved, the therapists used the transference-countertransference exchange to understand and speak more effectively to the perverse quality of their relationship.

Jill Scharff noted that David had grown uncharacteristically quiet and seemed sleepy in comparison to her, much as Lenny seemed quiet compared to Michelle. She presumed that this difference between her and him was a countertransference response to the interior of the couple's relationship. She said aloud that she noticed that while she was quick to pick up on what was being said, he seemed uncharacteristically sleepy, perhaps responding to what was not being said. She said that she expected that his state of mind could be understood in a way that would allow more understanding of Michelle and Lenny's situation. That allowed David to shake himself back to a state of awareness and say what he had felt. He said that together Michelle's contradictions of his observations and Lenny's tolerance of her verbal abuse had defeated him—put him psychologically out of commission. Now, with Jill's supportive prompting, he was able to make this unconscious defeat conscious, and to say that Michelle's upbeat tone seemed to be the wrong music for the words she spoke about the death of the relationship. Michelle was quick to laugh off his comment that her words sounded like a dirge, but Lenny responded seriously. He said, "It's like the jazz bands at a New Orleans funeral."

Lenny's capacity to respond with another rich metaphor like this showed the emotional attunement and strength that must have been part of his appeal for Michelle, and encouraged us to predict a good capacity for work in ongoing therapy.

Asking about the couple's sexual intimacy

We asked directly about the couple's sexual life.

Michelle, nonplussed for the first time, said, "You talk about that, dear!"

It quickly emerged that Michelle hated sex because she hated her body, but Lenny's steadfast caring and careful handling had enabled her to tolerate intercourse for the first time in her life, while enjoying other aspects of sex. Her tone changed instantly as she described the situation: she still had vaginismus—tightness of the pelvic musculature that produced pain on penetration—and she was not orgasmic in intercourse, but she had learned to have orgasms in the shared situation. Gratefully and straightforwardly, she gave Lenny credit in this area.

This discussion filled in another piece of the puzzle. Sex secured their attachment. In this area, Lenny was a good enough object (like a rock) who could modify Michelle's rejection of sexual experience (like water running past it) so that sex could be a pleasure for both of them. We recommended an extended evaluation for understanding the dynamic of their pursuit and avoidance at the surface and their unconscious connectedness at emotional depth with a view to helping them decide whether to pursue couple therapy.

Integration of sex therapy techniques in couple therapy

Frank discussion of sexual functioning should be part of every couple evaluation. Matter-of-fact queries about sex from the beginning open a space for the frank discussion of sexual material as the therapeutic relationship deepens. Couples may accept superficially reassuring information about their sexual life at first, but later convey disappointment. They need their couple therapist to have a working knowledge of sexuality. Couple therapists must be fully informed on sexual development and dysfunction, sex research advances, and contemporary clinical approaches to extend those formulated by Masters and Johnson (1970), such as Kaplan's (1974) integration of behavioural sex therapy and psychodynamic couple therapy, and Scharff's (1982) developmental object relations approach to sexuality, sexual dysfunction, and sexual dysjunction in a couple's intimacy.

Couples' sexual difficulties derive from several areas: deficits in learning about sexual function—often because of cultural or family strictures concerning sex; problems in individual emotional development of one or both partners that produce difficulty in the sexual arena; and marital strain that takes its toll on a couple's sexual function. Life events and transitions— the moment of commitment or marriage, the birth of a first child or a child of one particular gender, adolescents leaving home, job loss, or the onset of menopause—may trigger anxieties that impinge on sexual function. Finally, physiologic factors interfere with sexual function: age, disease, or medication—especially psychotropic medications. Any of these factors that introduce difficulty in sex usually produce repercussions on the couple's overall relationship.

When sexual difficulty is the most significant feature of a couple's problem, or when it runs in parallel with overall difficulty and has not yielded to couple therapy, the couple therapist needs to use behavioural sex therapy techniques, integrated into the overall psychodynamic approach (Kaplan, 1974; Scharff & Scharff, 1991). The couple agrees to limit their sexual interaction to a graded series of exercises conducted in private. Exercises begin with nude massages, excluding breasts and genitals. Each session is reviewed with the therapist who looks for patterns of difficulty that provide an opportunity to work psychodynamically. Linking small failures in the exercises to the couple's overall difficulties and histories, the therapist interprets the underlying unconscious individual and couple issues, and integrates them in the subsequent assignments. Couples gradually move along the gradations of sexual exchange until they are ready for intercourse. Complete sexual function now has embedded in it both the therapist's contextual support and the therapist's collaborative effort to interpret themes that have precluded or inhibited sexual passion.

Working with dreams in couple therapy

Dreams offer partners a unique opportunity for working on unconscious communication inside the self and the couple's system. Dreams inform couples about the partners' internal self-and-object relations at the same time that they give important clues about the way each spouse uses the other as an external object. A dream from only one spouse obviously reflects the inner object relations of that one person, but told in couple therapy, that dream is regarded as a communication on behalf of the couple, and so it often leads to exploration of issues in both partners. When both partners report dreams, a richly interlocking texture of conscious and unconscious understanding is possible.

A clinical example of dream analysis in sex therapy

The following example illustrates both the course of sex therapy and the crucial role of dreams in helping a couple to move beyond therapeutic impasse. When working with dreams, couple therapists elicit the associations of both the dreamer and the partner and connect the elements of the dream to affect, personal history, sexual desire, and the intimate relationship.

Dr and Mrs T, both thirty-five, were referred to me (DES) after adopting an infant girl. Trying unsuccessfully to conceive during the preceding infertility evaluation, Dr T had experienced impotence occasionally. The couple's shared low sexual desire had become apparent to the social worker during the subsequent adoption evaluation. Dr T mentioned two events that he had found traumatic: He had been involved in boarding school homosexual encounters; and his father had suddenly left his mother seven years previously. Mrs T, who had older brothers, was pushed to be as athletic as the boys, which left her feeling shaky as a woman. In an individual session, I encouraged Dr T to tell his wife about his performance anxiety and erectile difficulty. Seeing them in a couple session, I said that they shared an avoidance of sexuality because of uneasiness about themselves as sexual people. I described how shared low sexual desire derived from their internal couples—his of a warring couple, and hers of a family repressing feminine sexuality. They agreed to my recommendation for psychodynamic sex therapy to treat the sexual difficulty itself and to explore and resolve their emotional distance.

Insecure and avoidant aspects of the couple's attachment had been projected into their sexual bond. Both of them were open and trusting. I felt good about them and I was hopeful for their progress. It was not long before I recognised that my hope for them was my countertransference to an excited object transference, and it would soon meet the usual fate of disappointment.

My bubble burst when Dr T found obstacles to scheduling our work. Frustrated, I confronted Dr T more insistently than Mrs T had done. He finally changed his schedule, and reported with a sense of relief that he had passed a crisis of commitment. He felt for the first time different from his father.

The early exercises went well as the couple relaxed into them. They felt a new investment in each other. But when genital stimulation was prescribed, Dr T continually reported feeling no arousal, and drew a blank. To help the couple move past the impasse, I looked to their unconscious. I asked Dr T if he had had any dreams. He promptly obliged:

> "I dreamt that a teacher I hardly knew at medical school came over and sat next to me. He was too arrogant to do that in real life. Last week I read that he had killed himself. We used to worry about suicide when my wife's brother was depressed but he didn't die. We also worried that her brother had organic causes for depression, just as I worry my impotence is organic."

I said that since Dr T could masturbate normally, his erectile function was not organically impaired. So we should look to the dream for understanding the source of his impotence.

Mrs T said, "I worry he doesn't find me attractive. I never feel sexy like a real woman. I was a runner who developed late and didn't menstruate until I was twenty-three. I think I got stuck at age sixteen."

I said that they both felt deficiencies about their bodies like most adolescents do, and that the dream showed that it felt like a life-or-death matter to them. The dream also suggested that they felt I was like an arrogant, unavailable medical school teacher, and could therefore not be trusted to be on their side.

The following exercise sessions were no different. Dr T felt no arousal even with genital stimulation, and actually lost arousal in masturbation exercises. I was losing hope for them. I thought, "Perhaps they were not treatable after all!" To put this in technical terms, I absorbed their doubts in my countertransference through my introjective identification, and so began to feel my hope for them "killed off." I now experienced them as a failed exciting internal couple. It crossed my mind that if they left treatment without improvement, I would be relieved. To use language identified with their metaphors, I felt "sick of treating them" and "had lost my desire" to help. Here, in resonance with my internal couple was a replay in my countertransference of their unconscious problem. I felt seduced by them as exciting objects, and then let down by the failure they also feared.

Then Dr T brought a second dream, assuring me it was unrelated to therapy:

> "I was standing with some people in a large room with our backs to the wall." We were going to be executed one by one. At first, I felt defeatist. I took off my jacket just as I did a moment ago here. I thought, "I hope they'll hurry." Then I thought, "I don't want to die. So, fight!" They were demonstrating killing us with carbon monoxide on a bed—which is how my old teacher killed himself. I asked to use the telephone and called my mother. There was no answer, but I just walked out the door of the room. I took off my shirt because it was a giveaway. It was 2 a.m. I began to run through a strip mall. A motorcycle cop caught up with me, but just then a bad guy came out and shot at him. The cop chased him and I got away.

Dr T's associations to the dream showed that the execution or asphyxiation that he feared was connected to the smothering anxiety of the sexual exercises that I assigned, for which he stripped, and which he carried out on a bed. When I said that the cop and the teacher he feared were standing for me, he said, "No doubt about that! I am beginning to realise I am afraid of being controlled by you and by my wife if she controls my penis." He said that the building in which he faced execution was like the boarding school he attended, leading us to talk about his pain on leaving home in adolescence. He explained that he had wanted away from his mother, but once he got to school he missed her and felt unprotected from the sexual teasing of older boys. He remembered that, as he left home, he suddenly realised that his parents had a sexual life.

In the dream, Dr T called his mother as he had done then when threatened by loneliness and homosexual seduction at boarding school. I realised that his resistance to therapy was a fearful reaction to me as a potentially seductive older boy and as a mother he might need too much.

Responding to Dr T's realisation that his parents had a sex life, Mrs T now said, "Well, they did have another child after you left, your sister, and we named our daughter after her. When I realised that my husband was afraid of me suffocating him in bed if I became sexual, I kept sex under wraps, which suited me anyway because I was so frightened of it. He would treat me as though I were a cop like his mother. We are both afraid of being sexual, and so we've been afraid of you, or rather of what we asked you to do for us. But I think I can stand my fright if my husband will try to stand his."

Mrs T's reluctance to engage sexually stemmed from her fear that being sexual would make her become a rejecting mother. Like her husband she was afraid of a controlling woman who emasculates her incompetent husband. Therapy addressed this shared internal couple and the unconscious fear it evoked.

In the exercises following this session, Dr T was easily aroused for the first time, and the treatment followed a rapidly successful course, to sexual satisfaction, and eventually to a much-desired pregnancy.

What broke the logjam? Dr and Mrs T recognised the dovetailing of their projective identifications. They revisited their adolescent anxieties about becoming sexual beings. They each found a critical parent in the transference and worked on it. They discovered that they were in the grip of a paralysed internal couple. Dr T allowed the image of his parents as a sexual couple to resurface, which gave him permission to be a sexual person and reassure his wife that she was desirable. The recovery of an unconscious sexual internal couple facilitated the actual couple's re-entry into the intimate life of the marriage. Given enough time, commitment, and a willingness to work with dreams and fantasies, many couples respond as well.

Challenges to the couple therapist

Working with trauma in couple therapy

Childhood physical abuse, sexual abuse, and traumatic medical intervention at a young age, significantly affect individual development by creating traumatic nuclei and gaps in the psyche. Adult survivors of trauma may visit trauma on their partners or avoid anything that might cause its recurrence. Sexual abuse will often—but not always—show up as sexual symptomatology in the couple, even if they have been able to have a relatively normal sexual life before marriage or early in the marriage (J. Scharff & D. Scharff, 1994). Adult trauma, too, will handicap couples, especially if it reawakens memories of childhood injury. Adults who were traumatised in childhood are at increased risk for adult trauma.

Tony and Theresa came to therapy after Tony lost his right arm and shoulder to amputation to abort a life-threatening infection in the upper arm following an injection there for asthma. Although his employer offered to support physical therapy and the fitting of a prosthetic arm, Tony resisted rehabilitation and became immobilised with depression. Theresa and he grew increasingly angry at each other over the next year. Exploring their anger, the therapist learned that in growing up, they had suffered physical violence. Each had taken the role of defending their siblings from physical attacks from their parents, and been hit frequently in the process. When they married, they had vowed never to fight, and now would go so far as to punch the wall and break their fists rather than strike each other. They would break a bone, or break up as a couple, rather than risk expressing anger directly, lest they lose all control and hurt each other.

The trauma experienced in adulthood brought this couple's shared history of childhood physical abuse to the forefront. Early in their marriage, their adult attachment seemed secure, but now trauma threatened to overwhelm their current recovery and brought out the old insecurity. Trauma to one partner can overwhelm the couple's holding and containment for one another. A therapist must spend time as witness to the trauma before it is possible to help the couple work in a symbolic, reparative way (J. Scharff & D. Scharff, 1994; D. Scharff, 2002).

Working with the difficult couple

The difficult couple is the one that the therapist dreads seeing. A therapist may be unable to tolerate silence, another cannot stand relentless fighting, yet another may be allergic to sweetness that masks hostility. Another type of difficult couple is the one in which one of the partners is sure that the other is being sided with by the therapist. The therapist who is committed to involved impartiality may feel extremely upset by accusations of unfairness and fail to interpret the sibling rivalries being fought out, probably because of painful feelings towards her parents over sibling issues of her own. Whatever specific form it takes, the difficult couple gets to the therapist's internal parental couple and stirs unease and sometimes despair (J. Scharff, 1992). The therapist's capacity for holding and containment is stretched to the limit. Only when the therapist is open to experiencing fully in the countertransference the hopelessness that underlies the couple's defence of being difficult is there some hope of recovery (Scharff & Scharff, 1991). On the other hand, sometimes the best course is to acknowledge a lack of fit and refer the couple. What may present a problem for one therapist may be easier for another. On the other hand the difficult couple may dump all their negativity with one therapist and appear to do well with the next one but in fact the partners have not developed the capacity to integrate good and bad objects.

Managing resistance to couple therapy

Sometimes one member of a couple does not want therapy, but it is usually possible to get the couple in for a single consultation session in which to work on the reasons for refusing treatment. The psychodynamic couple therapist does not use persuasion or paradoxical prescription to get the couple into treatment, but accepts that there must be a good reason for the resistance and tries to make it conscious and understandable so as to free the couple to make a choice based on a good experience of the value of reflection. Once a couple therapy contract is made, couple therapists work with the couple, not with the individual partners. They establish that way of working and hold to it as a standard from which to negotiate frequency, experiment with requests for individual sessions, and learn.

Working with the couple when there is an affair

The couple dealing with infidelity is filled with disappointment, envy, rage, and sadness. The first task of the couple therapist is to hold all the feelings that the marriage could not. Then she wants to know details of the affair because the attraction of the lover and the keeping of a secret contain important information about repressed object relations that cannot be expressed and contained within the marriage. Splitting good and bad objects between spouse and someone else is a major defence, and it does not stop with the end of the affair. Some couple therapists insist that the affair be stopped, on the grounds that they do not want to sanction a duplicitous life, but most therapists accept the marriage and its infidelity as the patient. They work to see whether the marriage is to continue, at which point the lover must indeed be renounced. Intimate partners cannot work on their relationship while one of them has another intimate partner. Even though the affair is a betrayal and a threat to the marriage, it is also an attempt to maintain the marriage by getting needs met elsewhere. Sometimes a partner reveals the secret to the therapist on the phone or in an individual session to which both partners have agreed. In this case it is best to acknowledge that a problem has arisen, and ask for more individual sessions to work it through. The therapist does not want to force a confession, but if the marriage is to continue in couple therapy, she learns about the meaning of the affair and the need for secrecy in individual terms, and works towards a planned revelation in the couple setting. Individual work like this may result in ending the couple therapy, or it may become a prelude to it.

Handling acute couple distress

Acute distress arises for instance when there is a sudden revelation of an affair, death of a newborn, suicide threat, acute psychotic reaction, and acute intoxication from substance abuse. Acute distress calls upon the couple therapist for an emergency appointment of sufficient length to assess the situation, give the couple time to express their distress, and let the therapist develop the necessary holding capacity and make the necessary arrangements—or refer to a colleague who can do so. Medication, removal of a violent member from the home, emergency care, and couple consultation may work together to avoid hospitalisation. Speed is essential for taking advantage of the healing potential of the crisis in the system. Enough time is necessary for demonstrating the possibility of understanding their overwhelming emotion, and a second appointment within the week should be confirmed before the couple leaves the session.

Termination

The couple in therapy has had some rehearsal for termination when ending each time-limited session and facing breaks in treatment due to illness, business commitments, or vacations. Couple therapists work with the couple's habitual way of dealing with separations in preparation for the final parting, for which the couple will be ready when the above goals have been met. The couple relives issues from earlier phases of the treatment, now with a greater capacity for expressing feelings, allowing difference, recovering from difficult moments, dealing with loss, respectfully confronting and understanding defensive positions, and mastering anxiety.

Table 1. Criteria for termination.

The therapeutic space has been internalised as a reasonably secure holding capacity
Unconscious projective identifications have been recognised, owned, and taken back
The capacity to work together as life partners is restored
Intimacy and sex is mutually gratifying
The holding environment extends to the family
The needs of each partner are separate and distinct
Or, the loss of the marriage is accepted, understood, and mourned.

References

Ainsworth, M. D. S., Blehar, M., Waters, E., & Wall, S. (1978). *Patterns of Attachment: A Psychological Study of the Strange Situation*. Hillsdale, NJ: Erlbaum.

Bannister, K. & Pincus, L. (1971). *Shared Phantasy in Marital Problems: Therapy in a Four-Person Relationship*. London: Tavistock Institute of Human Relations.

Bartholomew, K., Henderson, A., & Dutton, D. (2000). Insecure attachment and abusive relationships. In: C. Clulow (Ed.), *Adult Attachment and Couple Psychotherapy*, (pp. 43–61). London: Brunner/Routledge.

Bion, W. R. (1961). *Experiences in Groups and Other Papers*. London: Tavistock.

Bion, W. R. (1967). *Second Thoughts*. London: Heinemann.

Bowlby, J. (1969). *Attachment and Loss. Vol. 1: Attachment*. London: Hogarth.

Bowlby, J. (1973). *Attachment and Loss. Vol. 2: Separation: Anxiety and Anger*. London: Hogarth.

Bowlby, J. (1980). *Attachment and Loss. Vol. 3: Loss: Sadness and Depression*. London: Hogarth.

Breuer, J. & Freud, S. (1893–1895). Studies on hysteria. *S. E., 2*: 1–305. London: Hogarth.

Clulow, C. (Ed.) (2000). *Adult Attachment and Couple Psychotherapy*. London: Brunner/Routledge.

Dicks, H. V. (1967). *Marital Tensions: Clinical Studies Towards a Psychoanalytic Theory of Interaction*. London: Routledge and Kegan Paul.

Fisher, J. & Crandell, L. (2000). Patterns of relating in the couple. In: C. Clulow (Ed.), *Adult Attachment and Couple Psychotherapy* (pp. 15–27). London: Brunner/Routledge.

Fonagy, P., Gergely, G., Jurist, E. L., & Target, M. (2002). *Affect Regulation, Mentalization, and the Development of the Self*. New York: Other Press. Reprinted Karnac, 2004.

Freud, S. (1905). Three essays on the theory of sexuality. *S. E., 7*: 135–243. London: Hogarth.

Freud, S. (1923). The ego and the id. *S. E., 19*: 3–66. London: Hogarth.

Kaplan, H. S. (1974). *The New Sex Therapy*. New York: Brunner/Mazel.

Main, M. (1995). Recent studies in attachment: overview, with selected implications for clinical work. In: S. Goldberg, R. Muir & J. Kerr (Eds.), *Attachment Theory: Social, Developmental, and Clinical Perspectives* (pp. 407–474). Hillsdale, NJ: Analytic Press.

Main, M. & Solomon, J. (1987). Discovery of an insecure disorganized/disoriented attachment pattern: procedures, findings and implications for the classifications of behaviour. In: M. Yogman & T. Brazelton (Eds.), *Affective Development in Infancy* (pp. 95–124). Norwood, NJ: Ablex.

Masters, W. H. & Johnson, V. E. (1970). *Human Sexual Inadequacy*. Boston: Little, Brown.

Pincus, L. (Ed.) (1955). *Marriage: Studies in Emotional Conflict and Growth*. London: Methuen.

Racker, H. (1968). *Transference and Countertransference*. New York: International Universities Press.

Scharff, D. E. (1982). *The Sexual Relationship: An Object Relations View of Sex and the Family*. London: Routledge. Reprinted 1998: Northvale, NJ: Jason Aronson.

Scharff, D. E. (2002). The interpersonal sexual tie to the traumatic object. In: J. S. Scharff & S. Tsigounis (Eds.), *Self Hatred in Psychoanalysis* (pp. 47–68). London: Routledge.

Scharff, J. (1992). *Projective and Introjective Identification and The Use of the Therapist's Self*. Northvale, NJ: Jason Aronson.

Scharff, J. S. & Scharff, D. E. (1991). *Object Relations Couple Therapy*. Northvale, NJ: Jason Aronson.

Scharff, J. S. & Scharff, D. E. (1994). *Object Relations Therapy of Physical and Sexual Trauma*. Northvale, NJ: Jason Aronson.

Scharff, J. S. & Scharff, D. E. (2003). Object-relations and psychodynamic approaches to couple and family therapy. In: T. Sexton, G. Weeks, & M. Robbins, (Eds.), *Handbook of Family Therapy* (pp. 59–81). New York and Hove, Sussex: Routledge.

Schore, A. N. (2001). The right brain as the neurobiological substratum of Freud's dynamic unconscious. In: D. E. Scharff, (Ed.), *The Psychoanalytic Century: Freud's Legacy for the Future* (pp. 61–88). New York: Other Press.

Sutherland, J. D. (1990). Reminiscences. In: J. S. Scharff (Ed.), *The Autonomous Self: The Work of John D. Sutherland* (pp. 392–423). Northvale, NJ: Jason Aronson.

Winnicott, D. W. (1960). The theory of the parent–infant relationship. *International Journal of Psycho-Analysis, 41*: 585–595.

Zinner, J. (1976). The implications of projective identification for marital interaction. In: H. Grunebaum & J. Christ (Eds.), *Contemporary Marriage: Structure, Dynamics, and Therapy* (pp. 293–308). Boston: Little, Brown.

Zinner, J. & Shapiro, R. (1972). Projective identification as a mode of perception and behavior in families of adolescents. *International Journal of Psycho-Analysis, 53*: 523–530.

CHAPTER TWO

Shared unconscious phantasy in couples

David Hewison

In this chapter, I will present a historical review of the development of ideas about unconscious phantasy in individuals and in couples. I will look at the real and spurious distinctions between fantasy and phantasy and the argument about when in human life unconscious phantasy begins. Unconscious phantasies operating in a couple's way of relating are defended against by various symptomatic interactions, all of them preferable to a feared catastrophe. I will look at one example of defence against catastrophe—infidelity.

Fantasy or phantasy?

"Unconscious phantasy" is, firstly, a debated expression even before its nature as a concept is gone into: it is the result of an attempt in the late 1920s and 1930s by Freud's English translator, James Strachey, to render into adequate English, two German terms used by Freud: the noun "Die Phantasie" and the verb "phantasieren". These terms were not coined by Freud, but themselves have a complicated and rich history in European thought—a history which Freud was aware of, but the subtleties of which do not always make themselves heard in the English translation. Strachey was attempting to distinguish between something capricious and whimsical, and something more imaginative and visionary. In this he was following the different strands of meaning that Plato's "phantasia" and "phantasthein", purely mental activities with no connection with external reality, had evolved into through the process of adoption and translation from the Greek to the Latin and thence into the European languages. Strachey wanted to capture the "technical psychological phenomenon", as he put it (Strachey, 1966). The difficulty is that Freud's German term means "the imagination, its contents and the creative activity which animates it" (Laplanche & Pontalis, 1973, p. 314). "Freud", as Laplanche and Pontalis say, "exploited these different connotations of the common German usage". The German

"Phantasie" and "phantasieren" were used by writers familiar to the young Freud—"Goethe, Schiller, Hoffman, Tieck, Lessing, Fontaine, and Heine ... to refer to creativity, but also to what happens in dreams, madness or when one falls in love" (Steiner, 2003, p. 3). These, of course, are not simply Strachey's "technical psychological phenomena".

Following from Freud, Susan Isaacs (1948) distinguished fantasy and phantasy in her own way. She said that phantasy is "the primary content of unconscious mental processes" (Issacs, 1948, p. 84) whereas fantasy refers to conscious daydreams, and fictions. Laplanche and Pontalis (1973) pointed out a problem with her approach in that Freud doesn't use phantasy and fantasy in the way Isaacs assumes Freud does. Phantasy in the Freudian sense is somewhere between a wish/drive and memory. Freud located it somewhere between the Pleasure Principle and the Reality Principle. Babies have to manage the gap between what they want and what they can have. But Freud (1918) also introduced two other terms—"Urphantasien" (primal phantasies) and "Nachträglichkeit" (deferred action also called après-coup in French, namely something that happens after the event). Some phantasies are unconscious and have always been so—that is, they are not the product of repression from consciousness—and can only be known about by the effect upon them of deferred action, a re-working in the present of what was experienced in the past in such a way that the re-working has a psychic impact which the original did not. These are images that are with us when we are born, part of our phylogenetic inheritance as a species—images of penis, womb, intercourse, breast, babies, are triggered when we try to make sense of life. We innately make sense of our parents as being in intercourse even though we have not actually seen this.

When a wife brings a memory to her couple therapy session, are we listening to a true event or a primal phantasy that happens to take this form? This question was first raised around incest reports. Are they phantasies or are they memories? For instance, thinking about the Wolfman's situation, Freud (1918) said that the important thing in the Wolfman's complex was not that he had seen his parents making love at the age of one and a half but that he remembered it at the age of four and a half, at which point he knew what it meant and felt traumatised by it.

When does unconscious phantasy arise?

The "Controversial Discussions" in London, shortly after Freud and Anna Freud tried to settle in, or muscle in, to the British Psychoanalytic Society in London turned into a debate by Anna Freud and her followers, and Klein and her followers; a debate between whether unconscious phantasy refers to something later or something earlier in human development (King & Steiner, 1991). Contemporary Freudians in the UK think of phantasy as related to the past unconscious and the present unconscious (Sandler & Sandler, 2003). They have a sense that earliest aspects of a child's life exist behind a repression barrier so they think that when working with a young child they are working with regulation of the child's current emotional state arising from phantasies of the present unconscious. Kleinians think of phantasy as very early, active, and ubiquitous. For Klein (1936) and her followers, unconscious phantasy is a way of dealing with the death drive, so that the baby can survive internal and external persecution. Kleinians think that phantasies begin right away at the beginning of life and that they take form in relation to what it means to have a body. We are in effect a psychosomatic alimentary canal, relating in a biting taking in or spitting out, digesting, keeping it in or shitting it out and attacking someone with it.

The idea of the baby having a mind that is like a digestive system is at the base of the Kleinian concept of phantasy. So the young child manages the impact of sexual intercourse as an oral event, a biting, chewing up event, that the child must later learn is a good thing, as it becomes a genital event in phantasy.

Money-Kyrle (1971) had an idea that as human beings we are struggling all the time with the supreme goodness of the breast, the supreme goodness of parental intercourse, and the inescapability of time. If we accept the goodness of the breast, we can accept that we did not make ourselves, we do not have omnipotent control over life, and we grow older and die. It is particularly important for couples to know that we are mortal. If they have an understanding of the goodness of the breast, they have access to good creativity, and can enjoy being together even though the body is fading and the partner is not quite the person we fell in love with. All relationships must be conducted around these three immutable facts of life. In us there is gratitude that our parents got together and bore us. This can be denied but can never be got away from.

According to the key Kleinian theorist, Susan Isaacs, "phantasy is (in the first instance) the mental corollary, the psychic representative, of instinct. And there is no impulse, no instinctual urge or response which is not experienced as unconscious phantasy" (Issacs, 1948, p. 83). It is simply there. It is in us. One problem with this idea is that it gives rise to the fantasy of a theory of everything. Unconscious phantasy in her definition also includes defensive processes: Projection, introjection, omnipotent denial, and splitting, all experienced in embodied form. It has been accused of covering too much. So contemporary Kleinians attempt to make a distinction between types of fantasises. For instance Hanna Segal (2003) points to the difference between daydreams (fantasies) and imagination (phantasy). Daydreams are "as if" phenomena based on the pleasure principle, hallucination, and the denial of reality. For instance we can imagine ourselves as superman, not limited by our bodies and gender. Imagination, on the other hand, is a "what if" idea of what could be, and what will it be like. It is not omnipotent and can be put to the test as it is based on the reality principle and the demands of the depressive position. You can imagine seeing a couple who imagine doing anything they want and having a perfect relationship, and they refuse to admit that they are not like that, or their life is not like that, as if life should be the way they imagine. They are not grounded in reality and have not faced the limits of themselves and therefore cannot move on unless in therapy they become able to face their disappointment and to tolerate feeling sad.

Jungians tend to use "fantasy" as imagination because they believe imagination itself is a primary activity, part of being human, so that a special term of "phantasy" is unnecessary. The archetypal layer of fantasy corresponds to and approximates to Freud's unrepressed unconscious. Jung's definition of an archetypal image as "the self-portrait of instinct" (Jung, 1948, para. 277) is nearly identical to Isaacs' definition of unconscious phantasy above: an image linking psyche and soma underlying all mental processes. There is nothing that isn't based around an archetypal image. Kleinian and Jungian theories make use of a repetitive and persistent image or scene as both a structuring element of, and content within, the mind of both infants and adults, linking mental and physical experiences. Both see the mind as existing of combinations of elements from within it and elements from outside that structure it. The only difference is that for Kleinians the innate "scenes" are fewer. For Jungians there is an infinite number of scenes. We can say then, that the idea of unconscious phantasy, or its very near equivalent, is ubiquitous. Versions of it are found in all the depth psychologies (though there are debates about how to make use of it clinically—see Colman, 2005). It structures experience, makes sense of it for us. We use our unconscious phantasies to make sense of our relationships and they simultaneously structure our relationships.

A couple version of unconscious relating

As analytic couple therapists we look at the way each spouse's internal structure shapes, and is shaped by, interaction with each other. We are interested in the structure and process of unconscious relating to the self and the other, and we see a couple version of this unconscious relating specific to each couple. Lily Pincus and her colleagues wrote in the book that she edited *Marriage: Studies in Emotional Conflict and Growth* (Pincus, 1960) that in every spouse or partner we note the presence in the adult of childhood phantasies that correspond to the same or the opposite phantasy in the partner. In 1960, the writers had not reached the awareness of these phantasies being "shared".

After 1965, it was realised that there is an "unconscious agreement between the partners to maintain mutual misperceptions as a defence against the recognition of their underlying problems" (Woodhouse, 1965, p. 5). This defence against realising what is going on in the couple prevents development. The couple comes into therapy because this defence didn't work or damaged the couple. It was Bannister and Pincus in *Shared Phantasy in Marital Problems* who developed ideas about how phantasy is shared. Shared phantasy is based on the projective and introjective systems of each of the couple. The spouses are doing something to each other. Bannister and Pincus put it this way:

> Into marriage each partner brings conscious and unconscious drives, attitudes and needs which are partly acceptable and partly unacceptable to himself. Those attitudes or drives, which each has difficulty in accepting in himself, each may try to attribute to a partner. The more at war with himself an individual is, the more of himself he may project, and the more dependent he may become on the container of his projections. In marriage, the relationship with the partner who is thus invaded then partly becomes a relationship with oneself, and the partner ceases to exist as an individual in his own right. (Bannister & Pincus, 1965, pp. 61–62)

In other words, there is a form of unconscious relating in which distinctions between partners dissolve and you end up having a narcissistic relationship with yourself. They continue:

> Within the marriage relationship these projections and identifications must be a mutual process; each partner is to some degree a willing receptacle for the unwanted parts of the other ... Where the pattern of defences is excessively fragile or too rigid, each partner may cling to a false image of himself and the other, and reality-testing, which makes for growth and development, becomes impossible. (Bannister & Pincus, 1965, p. 62)

We see this where one spouse refuses to hear the other spouse's description of himself or indeed to recognise how he is being related to.

Bannister and Pincus conclude, "The partners' shared illusions may then become a paralysing bond which keeps them together in pain and frustration. Shared phantasies and illusions exist in all marriages—but in those with less anxiety and more flexibility, the collusive interaction between the partners will be modified by the changing demands of life experience" (Bannister & Pincus, 1965, p. 62).

Each spouse is required to play a part that needs to be kept to for various reasons that it will be our task to understand. Sometimes we ask a couple, "Why did you get together? What was the attraction?" Some couples have an idea of what it was, but there is a longer story behind it as you unpick it. Other couples cannot articulate it at all, other than saying it was meant to be: "This is the one!" They can't understand why the other suddenly became a bastard. These couples make no link between the current state of conflict and the initial stage of rapture because the choice to be together was filled with denial of something the other must go along with instantaneously. Later the couple has a crisis in order to make sense of their relationship, of the structure and function of processes that underlie their unconscious relating. As analytic therapists, we are not interested in helping couples become happier, more productive, better parents: we are interested only in their way of unconscious relating.

In a book by Clulow and Cudmore (1985): *Marital Therapy—an inside view*, it was very clear that a couple shares a system that does something to each other and to the couple. By 1985, this notion of the couple as a shared psychological system was well established; this included the idea of a shared defence, as each partner in the marriage acts to confirm and support the projections of the other. In other words: the shared unconscious phantasy gives rise to shared defences. One of the couples they worked with, Mr and Mrs Johnson, could not allow for any differentiation because they feared if that happened they themselves would fall apart and so would their marriage. Mr and Mrs Johnson's shared defence was based on shared anxiety about the survival of their relationship, a shared anxiety which itself was dependent upon a shared phantasy that their marriage "would not survive the kind of separateness which permitted each to know about and express their different feelings and needs" (Clulow & Cudmore, 1985, p. 45).

In the 1990s, Ruszczynski (1993) talked about attachment in couples in his book *Theory and Practice of the Tavistock Institute of Marital Studies*. He said that the couple's unconscious attachment to each other is made up of "shared internal phantasies and shared defences" (Ruszczynski, 1993, p. 9), and that if there is not sufficient flexibility in each of the couple's sense of self and other, these shared phantasies and illusions "will become defining and restricting characteristics of their relationship" (Ruszczynski, 1993, p. 9). He suggested that because of this the relationship itself is an unconscious phantasy. This phantasy will "become the focus for the couple psychotherapist's therapeutic intervention. In this sense, the patient for the couple psychotherapist is the couple's relationship—*the interaction between the two partners*—rather than either or both of the individuals" (Ruszczynski, 1993, p. 9).

James Fisher (1995, 1999), another psychoanalytic couple therapist in the UK, has contributed more to our understanding of shared unconscious phantasy in couples. He has made use of Donald Meltzer's (1983) idea of thought as a kind of ongoing dream-life in which we relate through our phantasies to our own emotional life and that of others. Fisher suggests that clinical work can be understood as being invited into a couple's unconscious processing of their life, and he has asked: when we speak of a couple's unconscious phantasy, are we talking about a dream or a nightmare? When we attend to the symbolic detail of an interaction between a couple retold in the session, he suggests we can find it helpful to wonder whether we are dealing with the replay of infantile content (essentially something from the couple's past object relations) or are we in the middle of a kind of process of symbolisation of current emotional conflicts more akin to the work that goes on in dreaming? In his later work, Fisher (1999) echoes some of the concerns about the over-application of the concept of unconscious phantasy by describing the dangers of looking too hard for a shared unconscious phantasy in the couple material. If we therapists do this as a matter of course we will simply be translating all that they say into something that it isn't quite, potentially leaving the couple bereft of an understanding Other in the person of the therapist, and missing the story that they (repeatedly) bring. For Fisher, the idea of unconscious phantasy is simply to alert us to the fact that more may be going on than we, or the couple, currently comprehend, rather than to show us exactly what to look for.

Defences against catastrophe

As analytic couple therapists, we often meet couples who cannot do anything other than separate. Frequently we find that they have been confused about whether emotional separation is the same as physical separation. They divorce because they can't conceive of being emotionally separate and still remain in the relationship. They aim to convince us of why they should part. It can be hard for the therapist to hang on to the idea that this is internal to them, rather than something that needs to be externalised and brought-about. On the other hand, when separating or being more separate is viewed as a catastrophe, the couple stays together in a co-dependent way to avoid a disaster. If, for example, a couple have both come from families in which their families' histories of having children has been disastrous (say their mother became depressed at birth or a parent suffered a bereavement, or one twin was rapacious and the other was sickly) an idea gets running in them that children are disastrous and they get together with someone who does not want to have children. Then other desires for children stir, or their sexual life becomes frustrated, and they get frustrated with each other—something disastrous begins to happen. Still this is better than the feared catastrophe of getting pregnant and all hell breaking loose. The symptom has within it the very catastrophe they are trying to avoid. This brings us back to what brings a couple together in the beginning. It may be the shared avoidance of a calamity.

Henry Ezriel (1956) derived an idea from his work with groups that we apply in couple work. He described the required relationship as a defence against the feared relationship as a defence against the catastrophe that the couple is trying to avoid. There's a conflict between the pressures in the couple and the attempted solution to their problems. Our work as clinicians may become uncomfortable when we try to help a couple understand their extreme distress as we may require them to be in even greater extreme pain and distress.

Infidelity

Let's think of the catastrophe of infidelity. It takes three people to have an affair. The impetus does not lie only in the person who is unfaithful. The affair has a purpose for the relationship as well as for the individuals. For couples whose parents had damaging affairs, the anxiety about remaining only in a twosome is that they may outdo their parents in an oedipal triumph. Couples who vow, as a result, that there will be no affair are the most likely to have an affair. They cannot have in mind an imaginative "what if?" question about the impact of the affair on the self, the partner, and the marriage. They can only repeat the infidelity as a way of trying to understand their parents' situation and their own unconscious way of relating in light of that. When it happens, it is difficult for the betrayed one to focus on how much the relationship means to them. Without that focus it is hard to reflect on what they might have done to contribute to the betrayal, by current behaviour or by choosing to couple with the spouse as someone who would do this—possibly even relying on them to do it. The person who is in touch with the blow wants to counterattack, claim victim status, and blame the third party for causing the problem. That person finds it hard to recover reliance on the basic goodness of the marriage. For some couples infidelities are an attempt to bring a different emotional quality into the relationship, or into themselves. It is useful to understand what the third party is like. Doing so might reveal a poignant longing for a certain type of experience that may have been there as an attribute of the couple in the beginning but got lost, or never developed. The danger of affairs as attempts at development is that they are explosive and damaging. We have to ask why the couple couldn't find a less dangerous way to bring in this longing and, at the same time, realise that not everything can be achieved in one relationship. Affairs, after all, can be the start of something new.

The third party may not be an adult lover but a child who dominates his mother and is felt as an aggressive attack on the couple. The third party may be a husband's preoccupying relationship with a computer, or a walled-off individual fantasy life, or devotion to an ideal from adolescence, or pornographic images instead of having a sexual life with his partner. The question needs to be asked: what is he getting from the second life in his sexual relationship with his lover or with his computer that he isn't getting from his wife? To give an example of the potential complication of this, in 2008 a UK couple got divorced because both had avatars and online role-playing fantasy lives with each other until one day the wife's online character discovered the husband's character having an affair with another character (Morris, 2008). This was cause for divorce proceedings as if his betrayal had been exactly the same as by an affair with a live woman. Catastrophes come in different forms, some anti-developmental and some developmental. Understanding them is quite a task.

How to understand a couple's shared unconscious phantasy

We do not treat the spouses as separate, as two individuals, but as two intimately related people in a couple relationship. We focus on the way that each spouse relates to the marriage in conscious ways, and then we explore the level of unconscious relating. One of the ways of getting to understand the shared unconscious phantasy is to look at the shared defence, the marital fit and the onset of the problems. The therapist's countertransference can at times be the main indicator of it. The contrast between this and the couple's defensive strategies can be powerful because the strategy of each partner is complementary and together this strengthens the defensive position of each of them. This is a universal phenomenon—neither just good nor just bad in itself. A necessary binding link is most evident in situations where couples are free to choose each other—something has to keep them together rather than choosing someone else. It is when this collusive pattern becomes overburdened, generally by life events such as parental death, job loss, infidelities, illness, miscarriage, still-birth, and so on, that the potential benefits of the unconscious fit between the partners in the couple can become a liability.

Shared defences may themselves be part of the couple's shared unconscious phantasy system—that is, the couple unconsciously enact a phantasised scenario that is designed to protect them from the repetition and/or enactment of other feared relational scenarios. Although strictly speaking unconscious phantasy refers to the phantasy of a relationship, in the practice of couple therapy it is often focused on the couple's unconscious beliefs about intimate relationships and the consequences felt to ensue from particular forms of relationship. Since shared unconscious phantasy refers to the couple's unconscious image of what a couple relationship is like, should be like or should not be like, this concept bridges (or even encompasses) the concepts of marital fit and shared defence. It is not an easy concept to pin down and different clinicians will emphasise different elements of it.

As part of a research project at the Tavistock Centre for Couple Relationships (Hewison, 2003) we asked couple therapists to describe their understanding of shared unconscious phantasy. Their responses variously emphasised cognitive, systemic, imaginative, or general elements. When trying to address the concept of unconscious phantasy, some analytic couple therapists emphasised the cognitive element of the concept by referring to knowledge or belief of a particular thing or experience: whether these be intercourse, intimate relationship, trauma, or the ways in which trauma has been responded to. This links to Freud's (1918) phylogenetic inheritance as well as the Sandlers' (2003) notion of the present unconscious that seeks equilibrium. Others talked about unconscious phantasy as a "system", a repetitive "leitmotiv" which structures the choice of partner and the kind of relationship they have. It does this either by being enacted or by being defended against. The structuring elements link it to both an archetypal view, and a Kleinian one. When its imaginative elements were described, it was felt that together with the defences it makes up a system of phantasised scenarios acting together or against each other, and so is related to the couple's image of what a couple is. This has links to images of the parental intercourse (the primal scene) in psychoanalytic theory as well as the "coniunctio" in Jungian theory. Others thought of unconscious phantasy in a more general sense as something that is not entirely shared (i.e., is a coming together of something that each of the couple has separately) but which is "collusive", "congruent" or "complementary", bringing about conflict if one partner begins to change.

In summary: shared unconscious phantasy has many facets and has many layers. It acts intrapsychically and interpersonally. It bridges or encompasses "marital fit" and "shared defence". It is affected by external events. It is recreated in the transference relationship and is mainly known clinically through the countertransference. We work with it by focusing on the relationship, not the individual. We keep the couple in mind. We note how the partners relate to each other and to their marriage, and how a couple relates to us.

How do we access shared unconscious phantasy in our clinical work with couples? We can attend to the following questions:

1. What attracted them to each other?
2. What was the unconscious choice and how did it serve each of them?
3. What was the projective system and couple fit?
4. When and why did it stop serving them well, why now?
5. What are the links to individual histories?
6. What shared unconscious image of a couple have they developed from within and without?

In effect, we need to answer the question: "which version of unconscious phantasy is at play at this moment, what is its content, in what way is it shared, what are the psychic processes that make it shared, and why are we seeing it now?". Shared unconscious phantasy is part of a couple's ordinary life, underlying mutual attraction and enabling them to bind together. Ultimately, when we access it in therapy, it is also the vehicle for change.

References

Bannister, K. & Pincus, L. (1965). *Shared Phantasy in Marital Problems: Therapy in a Four-person Relationship*. London: Institute of Marital Studies.

Clulow, C. & Cudmore, L. (1985). *Marital Therapy: An Inside View*. Aberdeen: Aberdeen University Press.

Colman, W. (2005). Sexual metaphor and the language of unconscious phantasy. *Journal of Analytical Psychology, 50*: 641–660.

Ezriel, H. (1956). Experimentation within the psycho-analytic session. *British Journal for the Philosophy of Science, 7*: 29–48.

Fisher, J. (1995). Identity and intimacy in the couple: three kinds of identification. In: J. Fisher & S. Ruszczynski (Eds.), *Intrusiveness and Intimacy in the Couple*. (pp. 74–104). London: Karnac Books.

Fisher, J. (1999). *The Uninvited Guest: Emerging from Narcissism towards Marriage*. London: Karnac.

Freud, S. (1911). Formulations on the two principles of mental functioning. *S. E., 12*: 218–226. London: Hogarth.

Freud, S. (1918). From the history of an infantile neurosis. *S. E., 17*: 3–123. London: Hogarth.

Hewison, D. (2003). *Conceptualising Audit in Couple Psychoanalytic Psychotherapy*. Unpublished doctoral dissertation. Tavistock Marital Studies Institute & University of East London.

Isaacs, S. (1948). The nature and function of phantasy. *International Journal of Psycho-Analysis, 29*: 73–97.

Jung, C. G. (1948). Instinct and the unconscious. *The Structure and Dynamics of the Psyche, Collected Works 8*, London: Routledge and Kegan Paul (1969). pp. 129–138.

King, P. & Steiner, R. (1991). *The Freud-Klein Controversies 1941–1945*. London: Tavistock/Routledge.

Klein, M. (1936). Weaning. *The Writings of Melanie Klein, Volume 1: Love, Guilt and Reparation* (pp. 290–305). London: Hogarth. (1975).

Laplanche, J. & Pontalis, J. -B. (1973). *The Language of Psycho-Analysis*. London: Hogarth.

Meltzer, D. (1983). *Dream Life: A Re-Examination of the Psycho-Analytical Theory and Technique*. Perthshire: Clunie Press.

Money-Kyrle, R. (1971). The aim of psychoanalysis. *International Journal of Psycho-Analysis, 52*: 103–106.

Morris, S. (2008). Second Life affair leads to real life divorce. *The Guardian* 13th November. www.guardian.co.uk/technology/2008/nov/13/second-life-divorce. Last accessed 10th August, 2013.

Pincus, L., (Ed.) (1960). *Marriage: Studies in Emotional Conflict and Growth.* London: Institute of Marital Studies.

Ruszczynski, S. (1993). The theory and practice of the Tavistock Institute of Marital Studies. In: S. Ruszczynski (Ed.), *Psychotherapy with Couples: Theory and Practice at the Tavistock Institute of Marital Studies* (pp. 3–23). London: Karnac.

Sandler, A. -M. & Sandler, J. (2003). Phantasy and its transformations: a contemporary Freudian view. In: R. Steiner (Ed.), *Unconscious Phantasy* (pp. 77–88). London: Karnac.

Segal, H. (2003). Imagination, play and art. In: R. Steiner (Ed.), *Unconscious Phantasy* (pp. 211–221). London: Karnac.

Steiner, R. (2003). *Unconscious Phantasy.* London: Karnac.

Strachey, J. (1966). Notes on some technical terms whose translation call for comment. *Standard Edition 1.* London: Hogarth.

Woodhouse, D. (1965). Introduction. In: K. Bannister & L. Pincus (Eds.), *Shared Phantasy in Marital Problems: Therapy in a Four-person Relationship* (pp. 5–7). London: Institute of Marital Studies.

CHAPTER THREE

Intimacy and the couple—the long and winding road

Susanna Abse

Married love

By Kuan Tao-Sheng 13th Century AD Chinese painter, calligrapher, and poet.

> You and I
> Have so much love
> That it
> Burns like fire,
> In which we bake a lump of clay
> Moulded into a figure of you
> And a figure of me.
> Then we take both of them,
> And break them into pieces,
> And mix the pieces with water,
> And mould again a figure of you,
> And a figure of me.
> I am in your clay
> You are in my clay
> In life we share a single quilt.
> In death we will share one coffin.

Most couple therapists would agree that intimacy is a key part of any satisfactory relationship and that the drive for intimacy is compelling, leading us to make, break, and reform relationships throughout our life. Despite this passionate quest, the actual definition of intimacy is nearly as intangible as the experience itself. This paradox makes the search for intimacy rather like the search for the pot of gold at the end of the rainbow—elusive, exciting, and with a sense that when the rainbow fleetingly appears, it seems almost within reach. But as the famous Irish folktale reminds us, searching for the pot of gold at the end of the rainbow is based on a bit of trickery—there really is no end to a rainbow. The way the physics work, rainbows are actually full circles—only the horizon gets in the way of seeing the full circle.

This reaching for an illusion is perhaps what hampers couples in their search for intimacy and it is possible that real intimacy is only ever discovered once the search for the pot of gold and its accompanying idealisation has come to an end.

Below are two images of couples, one of a young couple naked and in passionate embrace, and the other of an elderly couple sharing a private moment. I have shown these pictures to hundreds of people over the last several years asking which they find most intimate and my research has shown the people unanimously choose the older couple. Why might that be? What do we see in the faces of the older couple that is missing from the overt sexuality of the younger?

Though it is certainly difficult to define intimacy, it is reasonable to try and outline some of its core components. One model of intimacy (Reis & Patrick, 1994; Reis & Shaver, 1988) describes intimacy as the product of transactional, interpersonal processes in which self-disclosure and partner responsiveness are key components. In this view, intimacy develops through a dynamic process whereby an individual discloses personal information, thoughts, and feelings to a partner and receives a response that is experienced as understanding, validating, and caring. Further it seems that intimacy accrues across repeated interactions over time. As individuals introject their experience of these interactions, they form general representations that reflect the degree to which the relationship is intimate and meaningful (Reis, 1994).

An intimate relationship for instance, is likely to include some sense that each partner believes themself to be known and understood. It is also true that intimate relationships will frequently include mutual shared pleasures, whether those are sexual or quite ordinary and every day,

Figure 1. Naked young couple in intimate embrace.
Image © Sean Nel/Shutterstock.

Figure 2. Elderly couple sharing a private moment.
Image © Lucian Coman/Shutterstock

like taking the dog for a walk! And a sense of safety and security which allows for dependency is also surely a pre-requisite? Couples who feel intimate are likely to be comfortable in showing their vulnerability and feel their openness is recognised and reciprocated, and most importantly, accepted. Finally, perhaps deep intimacy needs a shared historical narrative of experience—the older couple are so compellingly more intimate than the younger, because the viewer senses that they have a mutual set of lived experiences which informs the way they see the world and the way in which they share that view.

Is then the exciting experience of falling in love not real intimacy but merely a chimera? Or perhaps the early passion of sexual love leads to a misunderstanding, where sexual passion and romantic sentiments are confused with intimacy? But perhaps intimacy is not a fixed state but rather a journey between two people, which fluctuates, deepens, and shallows as external life circumstances and internal world preoccupations fluctuate too. The older couple in the picture are far along this journey and though we may fantasise that that they are now fixed in a contented intimate state, this is no more real than the fleeting intimacy of a young couple in passionate embrace.

Intimacy therefore is something that comes and goes; it is no more a permanent state than any other human pleasure. However, repeated satisfactory interpersonal experiences between couples through a lifetime together, will build inside them an internal object that can be turned to in need, operating within the individual as a container and processor of experience (Colman, 1993).

This internal object or "couple container" is vital for intimacy because without a shared space where feelings can be experienced and managed a couple cannot truly become known to each other. Without this emotional knowledge, the couple fall back to a type of relating that is suffused with phantasy, where assumptions and beliefs predominate (Morgan, 2010). These assumptions and beliefs commonly pertain to the individual's dominant object relationships, their transference to each other and their resulting use of each other in re-enacting patterns of relationship generated from childhood experience.

The beginnings of most love affairs are characterised by feelings of oneness; one purpose of this symbiosis is the protection of the self through omnipotent phantasy. "If we are one—you can't hurt me. If we are the same, locked forever in a loving embrace, you will never leave me." The newer the relationship and the fewer the real experiences of positive transactions, the more the need for the phantasy of merger and the protection of this omnipotent defence. In healthy relationships, adult partners, go through a gradual disillusionment and separation process. The partner stops being the ideal phantasy object but becomes a real other and whilst there is a painful loss of the idyllic state of oneness it is compensated for by the benefits of inter-subjectivity.

Human beings seem programmed to search for this symbiosis, but conversely this drive and longing is balanced by the drive and longing for autonomy—the sweet sticky postcoital embrace usually ends with the longing for sleep—an activity that requires a withdrawal into the self. At its simplest, people want blissful merger, but they also want their lover to stop leaning on their arm, particularly when they start to suffer from pins and needles!

However, as in the illustration below, some couples driven by catastrophic anxieties, never fully give up the omnipotent phantasy of merger or in response to threatening life events, regress to a symbiotic state.

> Mr and Mrs B's need for attunement was so great that most of their energy was directed towards maintaining a perfect fit. Their primitive anxieties were alleviated by their habit of constantly touching, stroking, and holding each other. They once told us that their need to touch was so great that they sometimes wondered if they would manage to get from the downstairs reception to our consulting room without physical contact and joked that if they went missing in this way we might find them "snuggling" in a cupboard somewhere. In the same session they described their relationship as being a leaking lifeboat in a dangerous sea. Later in the therapy Mrs B said she felt like one of the baby monkeys clinging to a bit of cloth for comfort in those experiments she'd seen on T.V. She felt she had to hang on to Mr B at all costs; it was a matter of survival.
>
> To maintain this perfect attunement and the resulting relief from fears of disintegration all desire had to be denied, all evidence of individuality hated, all wanting repudiated. In the case of Mr and Mrs B they told us they had never had an argument, that they fitted perfectly like a hand in a glove.
>
> If there was only one roll left for breakfast, Mr B would want the top and Mrs B would want the bottom of it. It worked perfectly and nothing ever needed negotiating.

Winnicott describes the importance of the mother's ability to merge with her infant. Without this merger which implies an almost perfect adaptation to the babies' needs, the baby cannot achieve the most basic step in development, that of "going on being". At this most early phase, the infant has only two possibilities: "Being and annihilation". Non adaptation and attunement to the babies' needs is felt as impingement and produces anxiety about extinction. Further, in his paper "Transitional objects and transitional phenomenon" Winnicott describes omnipotence as a necessary defence for the fragile ego of the infant; an illusion of power that the mother needs to support. The infant, in reality is utterly impotent, so is driven to create a protective phantasy of being one with the mother and having control of the breast.

Melanie Klein also explored the infant's need for omnipotent phantasy, which is closely related to the stage she called the paranoid-schizoid position. Object relatedness in the paranoid-schizoid mode is predominately in the form of projective identification (Klein, 1946). Projective identification is a mechanism in which an aspect of the self (which is threatened or threatening) can, in phantasy, be attributed to another person. This ridding of parts of the self, aims to bolster the infant's fragile sense of omnipotent control by the evacuation of experience that threatens the integrity of the self. In couples, projective identification leads to interpersonal enactments which reinforce the original phantasy, where partners through unconscious pressure, find themselves full of feelings which only in part belong to them. Whilst projective identification is an early psychological process and one of the more primitive defence mechanisms, it is also thought to be the basis out of which more mature psychological processes like empathy and intuition are formed.

It is ironic therefore that the use of projective identification, greatly limits the capacity for intimacy, as it hampers real contact between the couple. Through attributing parts of the self to their partner, this omnipotent defensive use of projective identification leads to a confusion of self/other boundaries where each partner's perception of the other is distorted by projective identification. In this situation, another kind of merger occurs, but rather than a blissful union with the ideal object, this merger is based on identity diffusion and confusion,

Projective identification however is not always about omnipotent control of the object, sometimes it is about communication (Bion, 1962) and is used as an unconscious way of sharing unprocessed feelings. This phenomenon is closely linked to empathy because in this situation, the momentary confusions of self/other are used to foster understanding between partners, not to rid the self of unwanted aspects. It is interesting to note that research in neuroscience (Gallese, 2003) has shown that when we empathise with someone we activate the same neural systems as the other, thereby momentarily replicating their experience. To be intimate, however, probably involves the capacity to both momentarily identify with the experience of the other, whilst at the same time being separate. This separation allows for an interpersonal experience of recognition and acceptance and one cannot feel truly recognised and accepted without this little distance.

But returning to the question of merger and symbiosis, it seems that the greater the anxiety about survival, the more completely the phantasy of merger is held to, with the result that the capacity to acknowledge and tolerate difference between partners is severely limited. In the illustration below, traumatic events between the partners had pushed them towards a mode of relating which was dominated by projections, which avoided difference and which starved both of the intimate experiences they longed for.

The couple and their presenting problem

Mark and Polly a couple in their early thirties were in couple therapy for nearly four years.

They decided that they needed help following Polly's confession that she had had an affair seven years earlier with her husband's best friend. This affair had lasted for a few months but the guilt and shame of this event seemed to have been secretly carried by Polly ever since. Mark was utterly devastated by this revelation and fell into a deep, hopeless depression, which alternated with unmanageable rages, where he would threaten to kill his friend.

The flavour of that first consultation predicted the pattern of their way of relating to me and each other for the next two years. Every session, Mark and Polly would arrive, settle down and Polly would report carefully and quite cheerfully on Mark's state of mind. She would tell me how he had been, speak on his behalf, facilitate his communication in the session if he seemed stuck, and endlessly reassure him of her continuing fidelity and loyalty.

Whilst on the surface, this behaviour of Polly's seemed caring and concerned; my prevailing countertransference towards her was of irritation as Mark veered between paranoid fantasies, impotent rage, and deep despair that he would never be able to get over this appalling betrayal. He would complain endlessly about Polly's behaviour, demanding that she come home early from nights out with her friends or asking her not to wear makeup or any kind of clothes that enhanced her sexual attractiveness.

Their histories and why they chose each other

Mark's childhood was painful to listen to. The oldest son of a war photographer, now dead, who had been an abusive violent man, terrorised the family and regularly and ritually beat the children and his wife. Mark's passionate hatred for both his parents was quite disconcerting and he described in a bitter voice, how his mother would collapse into depressions and despair when his father was away at work. At these times, Mark, the eldest son would be left as a little adult supporting her and his sisters despite being small himself. On father's return, the couple would lock the children into their rooms whilst they re-connected in what Mark believed were long sado/masochistic sexual encounters. Mark particularly hated his mother for her weakness in continuing to stay married to this violent abuser and I interpreted the betrayal that Mark felt because despite his fervent caring, mother dumped him for father each time he returned home.

Polly, on the other hand, found it difficult to say much about her own history. She described a happy childhood with one younger sister. She was she told me, particularly close to her father when young, though that had changed after her parents divorced when she was in her mid teens. This event was the only trauma or difficulty she could begin to describe and there was a feeling that the divorce was utterly mysterious to her and did not connect up in any way in her mind with this glorious and contented childhood.

Session after session Mark would either speak incoherently about his fear of going mad or weep uncontrollably as he talked about his childhood or how betrayed he felt by Polly, whilst all the while she would try and soothe and placate him, looking strangely anxious, guilty, and terrified.

I had a terrible sense that nothing was ever going to change, Mark seemed to become more and more controlling of Polly and she in turn seemed to disappear as the tyranny of his angry sadness dominated their relationship. At the heart of this interaction, the couple avoided any emotional contact, whether this related to the grief they both felt about their damaged relationship, or whether it related to the terrible anger they felt with each other.

Making sense of the interlocking fears and preoccupations this couple shared was by no means easy, not least because Polly seemed to know so little about her emotional life, let alone the detailed experiences of her childhood.

In part of course perhaps this was the very reason for Polly's choice of Mark as her partner? Mark was fully preoccupied with his emotional pain and in particular his sense of having been used and indeed abused by his parents. I speculated that the central theme that Mark returned to over and over again of feeling used and betrayed in all his relationships, echoed not only his own childhood experience, but also somehow linked to Polly's childhood situation too?

Indeed, this theme of one person using another ruthlessly was played out in the here and now between the couple in front of my eyes. Mark omnipotently demanded endless reassurance and compliant soothing from Polly, and as this occurred, both of them were oblivious to Polly's own pain and distress and oblivious to the way Polly played this role of "carer" so well.

As the therapy progressed and Polly became more emotionally available, her own childhood situation, so clear in the enactment between the couple, was confirmed and she became able to tell me about her own mother's depressions. She described how her mother who would withdraw into angry despair, threatened to kill herself or kill her husband, and how Polly would feel hostage to this behaviour and responsible for managing, protecting, and preserving her mother. She began to explore the terrifying anxiety that overcame her when she sensed her mother was about to descend into one of her rages and how these rages were quickly followed by her mother's depressive withdrawal into her bedroom, which would leave little Polly, frightened, alone, and confused.

Exploring this, it became clearer that Polly's fear of catastrophic abandonment created a powerful need in her to create a phantasy of omnipotent merger in which she believes herself to be in control of Mark's state of mind. Whilst this was clearly a repetition of a childhood experience with mother, the anxiety this provoked was mitigated by her belief that she was at least, in part, in control.

The projective system at work

But of course, this sense of responsibility that Polly felt for Mark and her mother must somewhere leave her with very angry and unhappy feelings. In the sessions these were notably absent, because though clearly anxious, her predominant manner was of concern, with a relentless positivity that bore little relation to the reality of the situation. In contrast, Mark was frantic with anger and it became slowly clearer that this imbalance was a result of projective identification.

Gradually, I came to understand how Polly projected into Mark all her depression and anger about her own experience of misuse and betrayal, and that this projection into Mark left him with, not only his own angry feelings, but also Polly's. This phenomenon is sometimes called "double dosing" in which one partner is carrying feelings for both, leaving the other, Polly, relatively functioning. But the projective system in this couple went both ways because whilst Polly rids herself of the experience of betrayal, Mark rids himself and projects into Polly a part of himself that feels responsible and guilty with a resulting need to repair and care—feelings that he had also experienced for his mother in childhood. In this way Mark leaves Polly with all the responsibility for his wellbeing and he feels free of concern for her—the one who betrayed him.

At this point in the therapy, I was able to explore with them their shared childhood experiences, where both of them had felt responsible for a damaged and damaging mother, and where both of them had felt their own survival to be dependent on keeping mother alive and functioning.

In this way, the couple were deeply interlinked with gross confusions between self and other. They need each other desperately and are psychically enmeshed by their shared unconscious preoccupations, but because the feelings are split and projected, the couple have no way of really helping each other with these terrible fears.

The journey from self/other confusion to real intimacy and healing?

We all may have a tendency to daydream but I suspect poets, more often than most, migrate temporarily to imaginative other worlds. As Keats said, "Thou art a dreaming thing" (Keats, 1819, p. 435). In addition, poets seem to have an enlarged empathic capacity, to the point of confusion between self and other. A therapist needs to be alert and attuned, but not more than momentarily at one with the patient. The therapist needs to hold a little distance—a sympathetic and sensitive distance certainly, but still a distance in order to be helpful to the patient. John Keats, however, could not only identify himself with a bird pecking at the gravel outside his window but he could, he confessed, feel himself unified with a billiard ball "in its own roundness, smoothness and very volubility & the rapidity of its motion" (Bate, 1963, p. 261). No wonder he took flight from the traumas of medicine. That poetic capacity to empathise was not peculiar to Keats. Other poets, too, seem to have been blessed and cursed that same way. The great German poet, Rainer Maria Rilke, related how he would worry about a piece of soap left behind in his hotel room lest it might become lonely.

The journey from merger and self/other confusion towards real intimacy is a hard road. For Polly and Mark, it meant they had to own their painful and difficult feelings for themselves and when Mark was able to own and manage his feelings, his concern for Polly returned. The sense that he had been reliving frightening and unbearable experiences of childhood began to recede and Polly once again began to be real to him, as a person with her own difficult story and needs. Correspondingly, Polly too, seeing Mark more contained by the therapy, began to step away from her anxious caring role, thus freeing her to relate to Mark more realistically. But of course giving up the omnipotent phantasy that she was in control of Mark's feelings, meant that Polly had to own her own depression and anger and this was a difficult and long process. She battled Mark and me in avoiding her own pain but when it finally broke it was tragic and moving for us all. This emergence of a more "real" Polly further pushed Mark out of his narcissistic preoccupation with his own mental state and the couple began to really relate to each other openly and honestly.

Therapists know when they are in the presence of something truthful; when their patients allow themselves to be truly known, when they are authentic and actively vulnerable. For therapists working with couples, seeing that process alive not just between the therapist and the patient but between the couple too is a particularly moving experience.

The process of building greater intimacy between a couple involves helping them have a more real understanding of each other and through that understanding they are in a better position to gain a more empathic perspective of their own and their partner's role in the shared difficulties. Beyond building a sense of greater mutual understanding is the need for acceptance, which in turn fosters an emotional context more conducive to intimacy and collaboration. Over time these repeated experiences of mutual empathy and acceptance lead to the creation of a containing object; an object which is introjected and called "our relationship".

References

Bate, W. J. (1963). *John Keats*. Cambridge, MA: Harvard University Press.

Bion, W. R. (1962). *Learning from Experience*. London: Heinemann.

Colman, W. (1993). Marriage as a psychological container. In: S. Ruszczynski (Ed.), *Psychotherapy with Couples: Theory and Practice at the Tavistock Institute of Marital Studies* (pp. 70–96). London: Karnac.

Gallese, V. (2003). The roots of empathy: The shared manifold hypothesis and the neural basis of intersubjectivity. *Psychopathology, 36*, 4: 171–180.

Keats, J. (1819). The Fall of Hyperion: A Dream. *John Keats, The Complete Poems*. London: Penguin Classics (1988).

Klein, M. (1946). Notes on some schizoid mechanisms. *International Journal of Psycho-Analysis, 27*: 99–110.

Laurenceau, J. P., Feldman Barrett, L., & Pietromonaco, P. R. (1998). Intimacy as an interpersonal process: the importance of self-disclosure, partner disclosure, and perceived partner responsiveness in interpersonal exchanges. *Journal of Personality and Social Psychology, 74*, 5: 1238–1251.

Morgan, M. (2010). Unconscious beliefs about being a couple. *The Journal of the Northern California Society for Psychoanalytic Psychology, 14*, 1: 36–55.

Reis, H. T. (1994). Domains of experience: investigating relationship processes from three perspectives. In: R. Erber & R. Gilmore (Eds.), *Theoretical Frameworks in Personal Relationships* (pp. 87–110). Hillsdale, NJ: Lawrence Erlbaum.

Reis, H. T. & Patrick, B. C. (1996). Attachment and intimacy: Component processes. In: E. T. Higgins & A. W. Kruglanski (Eds.), *Social Psychology: Handbook of Basic Principles*, (pp. 523–563). New York: Guilford Press.

Reis, H. T. & Shaver, P. (1988). Intimacy as an interpersonal process. In: S. Duck (Ed.), *Handbook of Personal Relationships* (pp. 367–389). Chichester, England: Wiley.

Winnicott, D. W. (1953). Transitional objects and transitional phenomena *International Journal of Psychoanalysis, 34*: 89–97.

Winnicott, D. W. (1960). The theory of parent–infant relationship. *International Journal of Psychoanalysis, 41*: 585–595.

CHAPTER FOUR

Attachment, affect regulation, and couple psychotherapy

Christopher Clulow

Psychotherapy might be defined as the application of developmental psychology to understanding and changing problematic ways of relating—to ourselves and to others. The aim of this chapter is to apply to the field of couple psychotherapy insights originating from perspectives that have enhanced our understanding of human development, paying particular attention to attachment theory.

Attachment theory

For Bowlby, the author of attachment theory, humans were innately social animals, motivated from birth to seek and maintain connection with others. It was through these connections—relationships—that development occurred. Combining ethology (the biologically based study of animal behaviour) with psychoanalysis (the clinically based study of unconscious processes) Bowlby asserted that what happened within the archetypal couple of mother and infant helped to shape patterns of relating in adult life. In consequence it had huge significance for the mental health of communities. Physical proximity and syntonic emotional responsiveness were what infants needed most from those who cared for them to protect them from painful or threatening experiences, and to instill in them a sense of security (Bowlby, 1969, 1973). This sense of security provided the foundations for good relationships in adulthood. Without it, experiences of separation and loss might turn out to be psychopathogenic (Bowlby, 1980). The central tenet of his theory remains as robust as ever: it is through relationships that we absorb our sense of security as human beings, our potential for development, and the kernel of our sense of self—a self that is essentially relational. It is also through relationships that we learn to regulate our own emotional states and to be alive to those of others.

Bowlby defined attachment in very precise terms as a motivational and affect regulating behavioural system:

> ... any form of behaviour that results in a person attaining or maintaining proximity to some other clearly identified individual who is conceived as better able to cope with the world. It is most obvious whenever the person is frightened, fatigued or sick, and is assuaged by comforting and caregiving ... for a person to know that an attachment figure is available and responsive gives him a strong and pervasive feeling of security, and so encourages him to value and continue the relationship. (Bowlby, 1988, pp. 26–27)

While attachment behaviour was most marked and visible in infancy and early childhood, Bowlby was clear that it could be triggered throughout a person's lifetime when he felt threatened or anxious. It is clear that in these terms not only parents but also partners and therapists have the potential to become attachment figures for those who turn to them for help. Patterns of relating in the original couple of mother and infant may also transfer to patterns of relating in adult couple and psychotherapy relationships (C. Clulow, 2001).

Affect regulation and attachment security

Affect regulation and attachment are linked in a circular manner: the experience of affect regulation contributes to the forming of attachment, and a central function of attachment is to regulate affect. Neurobiological research has shown us how important early parent–infant relationships are for developing the capacity of the brain to regulate emotions triggered by sensory stimuli arising from within the body and from the external environment (McGilchrist, 2012).

To talk of the brain as if it were a singular entity may be misleading, since we know that the brain is lateralised into two halves, each of which processes information in different ways. The right hemisphere of the brain is dominant in the first two years of life, before the capacity for language and symbolism comes on stream. At this stage of development, and, indeed, throughout life, it specialises in processing implicit information contained in facial expressions, vocal inflection, touch, and other sensory signals.

From two to three months onwards, when the visual area of the occipital cortex has developed sufficiently for the infant to focus on and follow objects in the environment, the mother's face and eyes are tracked with growing intensity. Her gaze conveys affective information that triggers biochemical changes in the infant's body responsible for developing and structuring neural connections in the brain. When she smiles and coos in response to her baby's half-formed smiles and sounds she amplifies the positive affective bond between them. This pleasurable exchange further excites her baby, activating the sympathetic nervous system and releasing endorphins associated with pleasurable arousal. This often becomes visible in the infant's behaviour, for example, in the uncoordinated waving of arms and kicking of legs. If the excitement becomes too intense her infant may break visual contact and turn away. His mother, picking up on this sign of hyper-arousal, will pull back from her role as stimulator and calm their interaction. When he re-engages with her she will cue into his signals and reactivate the cycle of playful arousal between them. When things go well these largely unconscious, emotionally synchronised and regulated interactions, repeated over time, enable the infant to forge a secure attachment to his mother or other primary caregiver (Schore, 2003b).

While attuned mother–infant interactions result in regulated affective states that lay the foundations for secure attachment, misattunement can result in dysregulated states and insecure attachment. A mother who is depressed, anxious, or for other reasons unresponsive to her infant, may fall short in cuing into her infant's unprocessed emotional states, or "vitality affects" (Stern, 1985). Showing little emotion, and blocking the approaches of her infant, she may provoke protest and distress. If this pattern is consistently repeated over time the result may be a child, and later adult, who shows little emotion and avoids approaching others because of the expected response of rejection or neglect. The need for others, and protest at their unavailability, does not go away; it simply disappears from conscious awareness. Turning away from them offers some protection against painful feelings, and might also serve unconsciously to punish them ("you're as unimportant to me as I feel I am to you"). Avoiding eye and other contact becomes a self-calming strategy that aims to deal with the disappointed hope of receiving a soothing response from others. The parasympathetic nervous system involved in down-regulating activity, affect and interest takes precedence over the sympathetic nervous system that drives excitement and arousal. Over-controlled behaviour, low expressed emotion and excessive self-reliance characterise this way of being in the world. Repeated over time, this can result in the sculpting of neural pathways to support such internalised patterns and the down-regulating of affective states.

In contrast, a mother who over-stimulates her infant but shows little capacity for offering a syntonic calming response when his affective state becomes over-excited provides few opportunities for learning about regulating emotions. The combination of unregulated arousal and inconsistent responsiveness serves to leave him in an anxious state, constantly scanning her face, reading her moods and gauging his own emotional state in response to hers. The process of playing and exploring the world independently of her becomes inhibited. A pattern develops in which the child, and later adult, excessively depends on others to know about and regulate emotional states, states that may be over-animated to engage and maintain the attention of others. The ability to self-calm in stressful situations, to self-regulate emotions, remains underdeveloped. Here the bias is towards activating the sympathetic nervous system and deactivating the parasympathetic system. Over time, this may result in the kind of dendritic sculpting associated with under-controlled and impulsive personalities that externalise and up-regulate affective states as an unconscious means of recruiting others into regulating their emotions for them.

These two "organised" patterns of insecure attachment (organised in the sense that they provide strategies for being with others in less than optimal emotional circumstances) help the developing child and later adult in dealing with feeling emotionally out of step with others: they can either be avoided or pursued. More complex is the dilemma resulting from a mother who frightens or is frightened by her infant, or who offers no protection from other threatening experiences. What then follows is an overload of sensory stimulus that sends the sympathetic nervous system into overdrive—a kind of over-vigilant, fight/flight response to alarm. If this fails to restore emotional equilibrium the parasympathetic system takes over, shutting the organism's responses down in a frozen state of dissociation: a retreat from the terrors of the world. Dissociation is evident not only in infants who have been exposed to the over-arousal of repeated trauma or abuse, but also to the under-arousal associated with extreme neglect (Schore, 2003a).

Regulated—and dysregulated—affective experiences between infants and caregivers become imprinted and stored in early procedural memory, outside consciousness. They constitute a model of the relational world that influences non-conscious expectations of future relationships. More than this, they shape the way neural connections are patterned in the infant's brain—growing and pruning dendritic pathways and firing synaptic connections triggered by environmental stimulus. Through the caregiving relationship a mother thereby "downloads" her own affect regulating processes into her infant's brain her own affect regulating processes. By the time her infant is a year old, this will have become installed as an internal representation of self-other relationships, something that Bowlby (1980) described as an "internal working model". The parallel with electronic communication implied by the term "downloading" is an imperfect one, for infants play a part in shaping their parents' responses; internal working models are shaped by relationships and not one-way transfers of information.

Bowlby described the function of internal working models in the following terms:

> Every situation we meet with in life is construed in terms of the representational models we have of the world about us and of ourselves. Information reaching us through our sense organs is selected and interpreted in terms of those models, its significance for us and those we care for is evaluated in terms of them, and plans of action executed with those models in mind. *On how we interpret and evaluate each situation, moreover, turns also how we feel.* (Bowlby, 1980, p. 229)

The crucial function of internal working models (highlighted by the sentence I have italicised) is to achieve and maintain an internal sense of security through regulating affect. The stress associated with a mismatch between inner world assumptions and outer world experience is not simply a matter of cognitive dissonance but also of affective dysregulation. The (unconscious) choice facing an individual in this position is whether to restore equilibrium through engaging with others and the otherness they present (a kind of reality testing that has the potential to encourage development), or retreating from such engagement because the threat is too great (deploying defences). Bowlby saw the task of psychotherapy as creating the conditions in which individuals might engage with others to review their internal working models in order that they might become better adapted to their environment (Bowlby, 1988).

In the course of normal development, the "downloading" of affect regulating capacity from mother to infant takes place initially at a pre-verbal level. The mother modulates her infant's emotional states by tracking and staying attuned to them. As he moves into his second year her role extends beyond being an auxiliary presence that augments his experience to one that incorporates a more prominent socialising function. This is achieved through disruptions in their symbiotic state of emotional attunement, which introduce for the infant the stress of being in an emotionally dysregulated state. While the sense of being merged with an attuned mother intoxicates the developing toddler with his own faculties and capacities—an identification that generates an illusion of omnipotence—he can separate from her, explore the universe around him, extend his achievements and return to her in an excited state that she will reciprocate his pride and confidence. When she does not, the dysjunction between his experience and her response can feel like a narcissistic blow, challenging the illusion of their fused emotional state. This asynchrony between a self-admiring mental state and the awareness of another's negative appraisal is stressful. From around the age of eighteen months it can elicit feelings of shame—a primary emotion in the socialising process. Here, eyes are averted and excitement drops in the face of a reproving other. Shame functions as an arousal blocker, a down-regulator of the heightened emotional states of elation and grandiosity (Schore, 1994).

Breaks in affective synchrony are made tolerable when a mother does not leave her infant in a dysregulated state but restores the emotional connection between them. The rupture is then repaired, restoring a sense of emotional balance and relational synchronicity. Through successful outcomes to repeated experiences of relational disruption the infant learns to tolerate affective dysregulation and to ingest a confident expectation that it can be repaired and learned from. Subsequent breaks in emotional connection become less stressful, allowing greater fluidity and spontaneity into the relationship. This hopeful outcome is a sign of secure attachment. Insecure attachment is associated with less fluidity in relationships, more anxiety about and vigilance towards potential ruptures, or, conversely, a rigid disconnection from those who might initiate them.

Child development research has provided us with graphic evidence of these processes. Close examinations of infants' responses to being separated from and then reunited with their mothers show how linked their behaviour is to the behaviour of their caregivers. It is as if, from the outset, infants are using their attachment figures to regulate their own emotional states through figuring out the emotional states of their parents. Repeated encounters create patterns that can become visible in the behaviour of children (Ainsworth, Blehar, Waters, & Wall, 1978) and adults (Clulow, 2003), patterns that can later be captured in the ways people talk about their early family experiences (Hesse, 1999). Bodily arousal, behavioural enactments and linguistic representations all provide windows into the unconscious. They convey the degrees of internal freedom people have to explore and evaluate themselves in their environment, and the extent to which others can be relied upon to help them establish and maintain a sense of emotional equilibrium in the process.

Affect regulation and the adult couple

Part of a mother's affect-regulating capacity with her infant comes from her own emotional security, allowing her to know about and monitor her feelings as they are evoked by the relationship she has with her infant. In this she can be assisted by her attachment to significant others in her life, and especially, if she is in a couple relationship, her partner. Indirectly, as well as directly, a secure inter-parental relationship contributes to an infant's growing sense of security. Moreover, the parental couple can offer an affect regulating experience for each of the partners that is different from that which they grew up with, and so offers a potential buffer against the intergenerational transmission of insecure patterns of attachment. Here is an argument for supporting couple as well as parent-child relationships when seeking to promote the wellbeing of children (Balfour, Morgan, & Vincent, 2012; Cowan & Pape Cowan, 2009; Schulz, Kline Pruett, Kerig, & Parke, 2010).

If couple relationships contribute to the attachment security of children, what might be drawn from this understanding of the processes by which they internalise a capacity to regulate their own emotions that is relevant to adult partnerships? Are there parallels that can be drawn with processes operating in the attachment, caregiving, sexual and interest sharing systems that constitute adult romantic relationships?

Attempts to explore these questions from an attachment perspective suggest that the processes can be remarkably similar, but with one significant difference: symmetry. Secure adult partnerships are symmetrical in terms of the fluid and bi-directional ways partners relate to each other when under stress: for example, their freedom to give as well as receive care from each other, their awareness of their own and each other's emotional states, and their mutual capacity to repair ruptures when the emotional connection between them has been broken (Crowell & Treboux, 2001; Fisher & Crandell, 2001; Gottman, 1999). Insecure partnerships, in contrast, retain some of the asymmetrical features of parent–infant relationships. At the dismissing end of the approach-avoidance spectrum they are characterised by minimising expressions of affect and the significance of others who might be turned to for help. At the other, preoccupied, end of the spectrum, they are characterised by maximising expressions of affect to avoid the feared catastrophic significance of ruptures to emotional connection. In both cases, maintaining a sense of emotional connection can be fraught with difficulty. In the first, excessive self-reliance diminishes the potential of relationships to mend emotional fences; in the second, over-reliance on others discourages the development of self-regulation to restore emotional equilibrium.

It will be apparent that secure partnerships are likely to be more resilient than insecure partnerships when facing stress. Balancing a capacity for self-regulation with a confidence about approaching others for help increases a couple's capacity for meeting challenges without overtaxing the resources of their partnership. In contrast, partners who avoid seeking help from each other, or unconsciously recruit their "other half" to do this for them, may end up feeling isolated and overburdened when under pressure. Unconsciously they might rely on their body to signal the help they need, for example, through psychosomatic illness. Alternatively, those who rely too much on others to regulate their affective states may place an intolerable burden on their partnership. Either way, a rigid response may interfere with a much-needed adaptation. It is then that couples run into difficulties and may find their way to a therapist.

Affect regulation and couple psychotherapy

What pointers might be drawn from the preceding summary of processes involved in affect regulation and the development of attachment that might inform psychotherapeutic practice with couples? In answering this we might link the knowledge emerging from developmental psychology and neuroscience with Winnicott's seminal concept of maternal "mirroring" (Winnicott, 1974).

Winnicott proposed that infants discover their own emotional experience in their mother's face, because what she looks like is related to what she sees in her infant's face. Not only does the mother provide her infant with physical, bodily holding, she also "holds" her infant's affective experience, and so contributes to shaping her infant's existential sense of self: "When I look

I am seen, therefore I exist" (Winnicott, 1967, p. 114). His description of the therapeutic process was very much in terms of maternal mirroring:

> This glimpse of the baby's and child's seeing the self in the mother's face, and afterwards in a mirror, gives a way of looking at analysis and at the psychotherapeutic task. Psychotherapy is not making clever and apt interpretations; by and large it is a long term giving back what the patient brings. It is a complex derivative of the face that reflects what is there to be seen. (Winnicott, 1967, p. 117)

Throughout life we turn to relationships, as well as art, religion, and theatre, to mirror and give form to our emotional experience—we search, as do infants, for resonance (Wright, 2009). Psychotherapy similarly offers a relationship to provide resonance and give form to unprocessed emotional experience (Beebe & Lachmann, 2002).

Mirroring is a less than perfect term for what goes on between mothers and infants in either parenting or psychotherapeutic contexts except, perhaps, in its pathological form. It captures insufficiently the two-way co-construction of the mirroring process and implies that the mother offers an exact, if reverse, reflection of the infant's expression. It restricts the medium of holding and reflecting experience to facial expression when tracking changes in excitement and arousal, something that infant researchers have extended to other pre-verbal forms of communication (for example, the earliest language of "motherese" and the tactile contact involved in holding and being held—experiences that are evident in infant and romantic couple relationships alike). From Winnicott's perspective, what the mother does, in the best of all worlds, is to read accurately the cues of her baby and to respond in ways that are in tune with the baby's internal state, but not in ways that replicate it. When her responses are in tune with the infant's gestures they have been described as "contingent", but what she also does is to "mark" (differentiate) her responses, so that a distinction is drawn between what belongs to her and what belongs to her baby (Fonagy, Gergely, & Target, 2002; Gergely & Watson, 1996). Her success or otherwise in accurately reading and appropriately bounding that experience has been associated with different patterns of attachment. Secure attachment is associated with contingent and appropriately marked responses; insecure dismissing attachment with marked (differentiated) responses that lack contingency; insecure preoccupied attachment with contingent but unmarked (undifferentiated) responses (Holmes, 2001).

Clinical Example

How might this play out in couple psychotherapy? Let me introduce you to a couple, whom I'll call Tamsin and Tom.

Tamsin is an attractive mother of a five-year-old boy. Tom is her go-getting businessman husband. They came for help because they were arguing a lot. The immediate trigger had been an argument over Tamsin's mother, who occasionally minded their children and whom Tom was highly critical of.

Rather than take a full history I prefer to start with what couples bring, and I look for the core emotional experience that underlies their complaint. So I asked about their experience of becoming parents and heard about the considerable pressures they were under juggling parenting and work commitments. In telling me they catalogued how they had felt either let down or criticised by those to whom they had turned to for help and support. This, along with other material about parent figures with shortcomings, left me feeling I must approach with caution how I offered myself to them in order not to join the line of people whom they felt had either been critical of or disappointing to them. The main thrust of my comments at this first meeting was to be generally supportive, saying that it sounded as if they had their hands full at the moment (contingent mirroring), much of what they were saying seemed to be concerned with them becoming parents (contingency with some marking), but I included one main couple interpretation that I hoped resonated with their shared emotional experience: it sounded as if each felt abandoned by the other in managing the pressures on them (marking with some contingency). I said nothing at this stage about their fear of being criticised or disappointed by those they turned to for help, including myself, which my countertransference was alerting me to.

When they came back for a follow-up consultation they told me that they had appreciated being listened to rather than advised, and that they wanted to have more sessions. Tamsin then described an ongoing problem she had with her mother, a woman she found it difficult to connect with. She said she would tell her mother what was going on in her life but felt that she either didn't listen or tended to be critical. She got annoyed when she found that her mother would subsequently tell her friends things she had told her, as if to boast about her, but never seemed to react much to her, or to offer her positive affirmation. She said her father was a much more rewarding person to talk to but someone who tended to stay in the background of family life.

Listening to this, Tom waded in saying that Tamsin's mother was indeed a very self-preoccupied woman, and that Tamsin needed to protect herself from her and not get caught up in her agenda. While he appreciated the childcare support she sometimes offered them, he felt she could sometimes stir things up between him and Tamsin when she handled their child in ways they didn't like. His response prompted Tamsin to become tearful. I asked what her tears meant, puzzled because Tom seemed to be echoing some of her sentiments. She said she didn't like her husband wading in like this because he painted a picture of her relationship with her mother as being worse than it was. She said Tom didn't recognise that she still needed something from her mother, and her tears were of frustration with him for not understanding this. She knew she was frustrated by her mother, and having become a mother herself was more than ever aware of what she longed for and had missed from her own mother. But she needed to protect her from Tom's criticism.

What seemed to have gone wrong in this exchange was that while Tom had picked up on and responded contingently to Tamsin's frustration with her mother, he had added some of his own frustration with parent figures (i.e., his response had not been adequately marked), so Tamsin was left with an experience of something alien or incomplete being attributed to her that she needed to resist. In attachment terms I thought Tamsin was describing a relationship with her mother that was on the preoccupied side of secure. She was describing an ambivalent involved relationship that continued to make her angry, and there was some indication of role reversal and projection in her wish to protect her mother from the anger and criticism that she attributed to Tom but also felt in herself. It seemed that Tom could then become either the non-understanding or the appropriating maternal object against whose intrusions Tamsin needed to protest against and protect herself from.

I was concerned that the relationship between Tamsin and her mother should not become the exclusive focus of attention, leaving Tom and their relationship out of the picture. So picking up the maternal relationship theme in terms of them as a couple I suggested that while Tamsin might feel she had to protect her own experience from being intruded upon by keeping Tom out, Tom's experience seemed to be that of an outsider trying to get in, and that this pattern might be connected with their experience of having become parents themselves. They recognised this as being a familiar pattern between them, Tom feeling particularly acutely that Tamsin shut him out as a father. This was a particularly sensitive matter for him as he did not want to repeat the family patterns he had grown up with, where his father was an outsider from whom he felt estranged and abandoned to become a "mummy's boy" at home.

Given the connections between preoccupied states of mind and enmeshed patterns of relating, where there is a tendency to define different relationships as if they are "psychically equivalent" (Fonagy & Target, 1997), my energy in this session was on establishing boundaries. I asserted that Tamsin's relationship with her mother was her business and not Tom's, and that managing their son was their business as a couple and not that of Tamsin's mother. Establishing this distinction, and supporting it, seemed to me to be a way of conveying that I understood Tamsin's anxiety that others might define her experience, and Tom's of feeling shut out, and that I wanted to reinforce the boundary defining them as a couple. This can be seen as contingent marking for them as a couple: cuing into a key area of their shared anxiety but reflecting back something that gave definition to what could become for them a diffused, undifferentiated experience. They both took encouragement from my drawing these distinctions, alleviating some of my anxiety that by coming in strongly about boundaries I might be the one to be perceived as defining and hence intruding upon their experience.

However the concept of mirroring is operationalised, it is clear that an important part of the therapist's role is to be an auxiliary presence to assist couples in managing their affective experience, to act as a container for unmetabolised emotional states, and to help them find an emotional equilibrium that enables both partners to feel secure with each other. When feeling insecure, anxiety closes down a person's capacity to attend reflectively either to themselves or to their partner. Couples seeking help are usually anxious because of a sensed threat to their relationship with their primary figure of attachment—their partner. So how can the therapist be this auxiliary presence and overcome the obstacle that attachment anxiety places in the way of restoring a sense of security? Here are eight attributes that might help couple therapists address this challenge:

1. The therapist as the "safe haven" and "secure base"

Bowlby's description of the key role a parent plays in providing someone to whom a child can turn when feeling frightened or distressed (safe haven), but who also provides a platform and motivation to explore (secure base), maps well on to attachment conceptions of the therapist's role. The basic requirement of any psychotherapy is to provide a safe, predictable, encouraging environment, a framework within which behaviour, feelings and experience can be engaged with and reflected upon. Every successful therapeutic endeavour relies upon the building of an alliance between patient and therapist founded on trust and a shared understanding of what they are trying to achieve together. The therapeutic "frame" and "alliance" are essential to both "safe haven" and "secure base" functions, enabling learning to follow from experience and enhancing a sense of competence and confidence. In this process the therapist's role is not to explain, but to encourage exploration—as Bowlby said to his patients: "You know, you tell me" (Bowlby, 1988, p. 151). Whatever transpires from the relationship will be something that has been jointly created, with both patient and therapist standing to learn from the encounter.

In promoting exploration parents do not only calm anxiety by acting as a "safe haven", they actively stimulate positive emotions and are involved in the pleasurable exchanges generated by the achievement of their infants. This aspect of affect regulation may be overlooked in the therapeutic process. Because emotional intensity in sessions often clusters around painful feelings, the therapist's attention is most likely to be directed towards down-regulating affect, containing anxiety and restoring a sense of safety. But it might be worth remembering how exploration can be facilitated by actively stimulating affective arousal, and by amplifying emotions.

Strange as it may seem, establishing a secure base is not only a prerequisite for the therapeutic process but also a measure of its outcome. Enhancing the capacity of a relationship to act as a secure base—whether between partners or in their relationship with their therapist(s)—can be described as a goal of therapy. Once this has been achieved the developmental process may continue with or without the help of a third party.

2. The couple as the therapist's patient

For couple psychotherapists there is an additional aspect to functioning as a "safe haven" and "secure base", which is vital to the success of the endeavour. The "patient", while including each of the partners as individuals, is primarily the relationship between them. An objective of couple psychotherapy is to develop the capacity of that relationship to contain the partners (Colman, 1993): in attachment terms to enable their relationship to become a safe haven and secure base for each of them. Maintaining this focus requires an evenly balanced attention to be paid to the triangle made up by each of the partners and their relationship together as a couple, and for tracking what might account for any loss of balance in attention. This requires of the therapist a capacity to move between the dyadic mind-set that features so much in attachment thinking and the triangular relational configurations that can generate rivalrous and competitive anxieties. It involves a sense of security in moving beyond choosing to focus on *either* the individual *or* the relationship to incorporating each of the partners *and* the relationship they create together as a couple.

3. The therapist as the repairer of affective ruptures

In maintaining this balance there will inevitably be breaks in the emotional connection established with the partners. Rather than seeing this as a constraint in the therapeutic process it may be the very means by which this and the couple's relationship develops. The aim of the therapist is not to achieve a state of detached neutrality, but to encourage emotional engagement and to make it safe. Identifying and recovering from "mistakes" is an authentic way of bringing about change. Regulating affect through weathering emotional disconnections requires the ability to feel and to think when tracking the affective course of a session.

4. The therapist as a "mirror"

As we have seen, attachment theory pays special attention to the developmental significance of the first two years of life in learning to regulate affect, a period during which attachment security is developed through the non-verbal cues and responses of others. It is also a period in which the infant is struggling to recognise experiences emanating from his body as well as the world outside. The mother helps in this process by being receptive to emotional signals, unconsciously attuning to their significance and providing a response that gives form, and ultimately recognition, to the infant's self, a self that is first experienced as embodied emotion.

Drawing the parallel between maternal mirroring and the role of therapists, as I have done, implies that non-verbal cues and responses will be of particular significance when communicating about emotional experience. Facial expression, tone of voice, body posture, heart rate, and other sensory communicators become channels through which affective signals are transmitted and received. These are not subject to conscious control, but they are open to being experienced and thought about by an attuned caregiver. In applying this to the couple therapist's role approaches will vary between focusing on mirroring of affect between the partners (Clulow, 2010) and in relation to the shared emotional climate generated in the session (Clulow, 2007).

5. The therapist as "corpus callosum"

Being available to unconscious intersubjective communications requires therapists to attend to their own affective and bodily states, for it is here that non-verbal signals are most likely to register. When emotions are embodied it may be that this is where attention must first be focused, encouraging an awareness of bodily states—a "bottom up" approach to containing affect—before linking this with a "top-down" interpretative approach that relies on higher levels of cortical functioning. Neuropsychoanalysts tell us that embodied emotions are transmitted unconsciously between people via the right hemispheres of brains, by-passing language and other forms of symbolic processing.

Transference and countertransference communications are also thought to be the product of right brain interconnectivity, providing opportunities for therapists to make the link between what is experienced and what is known about, often by offering a name for the experience and a context within which it might be understood. This can be a differentiating as well as connecting function (distinguishing between the self and its representation as an object of transference), performed in the service of integration. In neurobiological terms it is as if the therapist acts as a corpus callosum, the tissue connecting right and left hemispheres of the brain that acts both to inhibit the transfer of data (protecting each hemisphere from being flooded by the other and allowing them to perform their different functions) while also, paradoxically, allowing communication between the two. This enables the holistic processing of the right brain and the narrower abstracted focus of left brain processing to be both differentiated and connected. The psychiatrist and philosopher Ian McGilchrist quotes from a Hindu text to describe the paradoxical significance of the role of the corpus callosum for the two hemispheres of the brain (for "heart" he would substitute "brain"): "In the space within the heart lies the controller of all ... He is the bridge that serves as the boundary to keep the different worlds apart" (McGilchrist, 2012, p. 213). Encouraging this process has been described in the attachment canon as "mentalization" (Fonagy, Gergely, Jurist, & Target, 2002).

6. The therapist as decoder

Psychoanalysis is often referred to as "the talking cure", implying that language is central to the mechanism that makes it work. While neuropsychoanalysts suggest that it might be time to rename the process as "the communication cure" (Schore, 2012), language can convey affect and anxiety unconsciously, as do non-verbal forms of communication. The Adult Attachment Interview (AAI) is perhaps the best known illustration of this (George, Kaplan, & Main, 1985), a research instrument specifically designed to "surprise the unconscious" and tap into a person's state of mind with regard to attachment—their internal working models. What therapists can take from this procedure is the potential of language not simply to convey information (content), nor, more subtly, to conceal emotions within a narrative framework that relies on interpretation to be uncovered (hermeneutics), but also to reveal states of mind through the syntax, coherence, and manner of the discourse. This perspective allows language itself to be thought of as a form of affect regulation, denying access or coercing others into the emotional world of the speaker. Variants of the AAI have been developed for use with couples (Alexandrov, Cowan, & Cowan, 2005; J. A. Crowell & Waters, 2005), and therapists might want to consider what scope there is for using these directly as part of the therapeutic process.

7. The therapist as narrative builder

We have already seen that Bowlby regarded the process of accessing and reworking the internal representational worlds of patients as lying at the heart of psychotherapy, and I have emphasised the function of these as regulators of affect. Cognitive therapists work on the assumption that if you change the way you think you can change the way you feel. Attachment therapists are more likely to reverse that equation, seeing the accessing and reprocessing of affective experience as the key to effecting change. Whatever approach is adopted, the telling and retelling of life experiences with an attachment figure—someone who is interested, respected, and has the capacity to tune into affective content—paves the way for freeing expression, revising narrative structure and telling a different story. Since stories provide frameworks of meaning they serve to regulate affect. Revising stories allows for the revision of meanings that help regulate emotional states (Holmes, 2010).

With couples this process involves both partners, and therapists will differ in how they manage this dual dimension of reprocessing feelings through narrative. Emotion-focused therapists are likely to position themselves primarily as consultants to the couple, encouraging the partners to speak directly to each other about their feelings (Johnson, 2004). Psychoanalytically-orientated therapists may focus primarily on the transference of each partner to the other and to their therapist, and on the therapist's countertransference to the individuals and the relationship they have created (Ruszczynski, 1993). Relational psychoanalysts might privilege group process, attending to the intersubjective experience jointly created by the couple and their therapist from whatever primary source (Poulton, 2013), and all will vary in terms of privileging current and past "stories". Whichever approach is taken, the affective focus comprises the common core, and reworking narratives plays a part in regulating unprocessed emotion.

8. The therapist as the environment

Bowlby's insistence that the internal world of the infant, and later the adult, resulted not from innate unconscious phantasies but from real life experiences has especial resonance for couple therapists. The environment can place extreme pressures on the best of couple relationships—poverty, illness, bereavement, and other events originating from outside the couple can destabilise their emotional balance, however flexible and reciprocal their relationship together might be. The cultural revolution in sexual and gender assumptions that has taken place in the western world over the past fifty years has transformed assumptions underpinning couple relationships. They may need attention in their own right, and not just as externalisations of the internal theatre of object relations that every couple brings to therapy.

We therapists, too, are part of the couple's environment, as well as being potential transferential objects for them. Be we black, white, male, female, rich, poor, secure, insecure, partnered, parents, single, gay, bi-sexual, or whatever combination of these and other descriptors, we serve as reminders of environmental realities that provide external as well as internal reference points. If the unconscious is interpersonal, as all the evidence indicates that it is (Scharff & Savege Scharff, 2011), then it is also likely to be social, cultural, and political. What implications this has for attachment-informed psychotherapy with couples is to be discovered in each case, but implications there will be.

References

Ainsworth, M. D. S., Blehar, M., Waters, E., & Wall, S. (1978). *Patterns of Attachment: A Psychological Study of the Strange Situation*. Hillsdale, NJ: Lawrence Erlbaum.

Alexandrov, E. O., Cowan, P. A., & Cowan, C. P. (2005). Couple attachment and the quality of marital relationships: Method and concept in the validation of the new couple attachment interview and coding system. *Attachment and Human Development, 7,* 2: 123–152.

Balfour, A., Morgan, M., & Vincent, C. (Eds.) (2012). *How Couple Relationships Shape Our World. Clinical Practice, Research and Policy Perspectives*. London: Karnac.

Beebe, B., & Lachmann, F. (2002). *Infant Research and Adult Treatment: Co-constructing Interactions*. Hillsdale, NJ: Analytic Press.

Bowlby, J. (1969). *Attachment and Loss: Attachment (Vol. 1)*. London: Hogarth.

Bowlby, J. (1973). *Attachment and Loss: Separation (Vol. 2)*. London: Hogarth.

Bowlby, J. (1980). *Attachment and Loss: Loss, Sadness and Depression (Vol. 3)*. London: Hogarth.

Bowlby, J. (1988). *A Secure Base: Clinical Applications of Attachment Theory*. London: Routledge.

Clulow, C. (2003). An attachment perspective on reunions in couple psychoanalytic psychotherapy. *Journal of Applied Psychoanalytic Studies, 5,* 3: 269–282.

Clulow, C. (Ed.) (2001). *Adult Attachment and Couple Psychotherapy. The 'Secure Base' in Practice and Research*. London: Brunner-Routledge.

Clulow, C. (2007). Can attachment theory help define what is mutative in couple psychoanalytic psychotherapy? In: M. Ludlam & V. Nyberg (Eds.), *Couple attachments. Theoretical and clinical studies* (pp. 207–220). London: Karnac.

Clulow, C. (2010). Attachment perspectives on couple functioning and couples interventions. In: M. S. Schulz, M. Kline Pruett, P. K. Kerig & R. D. Parke (Eds.), *Strengthening Couple Relationships for Optimal Child Development. Lessons from Research and Intervention* (pp. 149–161). Washington: American Psychological Association.

Colman, W. (1993). Marriage as a psychological container. In: S. Ruszczynski (Ed.), *Psychotherapy with Couples. Theory and Practice at the Tavistock Institute of Marital Studies* (pp. 70–96). London: Karnac.

Cowan, P., & Pape Cowan, C. (2009). Couple relationships: A missing link between adult attachment and children's outcomes. Introduction to the special issue. *Attachment and Human Development, 11,* 1: 1–4.

Crowell, J., & Treboux, D. (2001). Attachment Security in Adult Partnerships. In: C. Clulow (Ed.), *Adult Attachment and Couple Psychotherapy. The 'Secure Base' in Practice and Research* (pp. 28–42). London: Brunner-Routledge.

Crowell, J. A., & Waters, E. (2005). Attachment representations, secure-base behaviour, and the evolution of adult relationships. The Stony Brook Adult Relationship Project. In: K. E. Grossman, K. Grossman & E. Waters (Eds.), *Attachment from Infancy to Adulthood. The Major Longitudinal Studies* (pp. 223–244). New York: Guilford Press.

Fisher, J., & Crandell, L. (2001). Patterns of relating in the couple. In: C. Clulow (Ed.), *Adult Attachment and Couple Psychotherapy. The 'Secure Base' in Practice and Research* (pp. 15–27). London: Brunner-Routledge.

Fonagy, P., & Target, M. (1997). Attachment and reflective function: Their role in self-organisation. *Development and Psychopathology, 9*: 679–700.

Fonagy, P., Gergely, G. Jurist, E. L., & Target, M. (2002). *Affect Regulation, Mentalization, and the Development of the Self*. New York: Other Press. Reprinted Karnac, 2004.

George, C., Kaplan, N., & Main, M. (1985). *The Adult Attachment Interview*. Unpublished manuscript, University of California at Berkeley. Berkeley: University of California.

Gergely, G., & Watson, J. (1996). The social bio-feedback theory of parental affect-mirroring. *International Journal of Psycho-Analysis, 77*: 181–212.

Gottman, J. M. (1999). *The Marriage Clinic. A Scientifically Based Marital Therapy*. New York: Norton.

Hesse, E. (1999). The Adult Attachment Interview: historical and current perspectives. In: J. Cassidy & P. Shaver (Eds.), *Handbook of Attachment: Theory, Research, and Clinical Applications* (pp. 395–433). New York: Guilford.

Holmes, J. (2001). *The Search for the Secure Base. Attachment Theory and Psychotherapy*. London: Brunner-Routledge.

Holmes, J. (2010). *Exploring in Security. Towards an Attachment-informed Psychoanalytic Psychotherapy*. London: Routledge.

Johnson, S. (2004). *The Practice of Emotionally Focused Couple Therapy. Creating Connections* (2nd edition). New York: Brunner-Routledge.

McGilchrist, I. (2012). *The Master and his Emissary. The Divided Brain and the Making of the Western World*. (2nd edition). New Haven: Yale University Press.

Poulton, J. L. (2013). *Object Relations and Relationality in Couple Therapy. Exploring the Middle Ground*. New York: Jason Aronson.

Ruszczynski, S. (Ed.) (1993). *Psychotherapy with Couples*. London: Karnac.
Scharff, D. E., & Savege Scharff, J. (2011). *The Interpersonal Unconscious*. New York: Jason Aronson.
Schore, A. N. (1994). *Affect Regulation and the Origin of the Self*. Hillsdale, New Jersey: Lawrence Erlbaum Associates.
Schore, A. N. (2003a). *Affect Dysregulation and Disorders of the Self*. New York: Norton.
Schore, A. N. (2003b). *Affect Regulation and the Repair of the Self*. New York: Norton.
Schore, A. N. (2012). *The Science of the Art of Psychotherapy*. New York: Norton.
Schulz, M. S., Kline Pruett, M., Kerig, P. K., & Parke, R. D. (Eds.) (2010). *Strengthening Couple Relationships for Optimal Child Development. Lessons from Research and Intervention*. Washington: American Psychological Association.
Stern, D. (1985). *The Interpersonal World of the Infant*. New York: Basic Books.
Winnicott, D. W. (1967). Mirror-role of mother and family in child development. In: D. W. Winnicott (Ed.), (1971) *Playing and Reality* (pp. 111–118). London: Tavistock.
Wright, K. (2009). *Mirroring and Attunement. Self-realization in Psychoanalysis and Art*. Hove: Routledge.

CHAPTER FIVE

Aggression in couples: an object relations primer

David E. Scharff

Aggression in couples presents the clinician with some of our most difficult clinical problems. There have been some useful recent contributions to understanding violence and aggressiveness in couples, but they have not focused on the origins of aggression (Monguzzi, 2011; Ruszczynski, 2010, 2012). To understand aggression and the mental and physical violence that shows up in symptomatic couples, I begin with the developmental origins of aggression. Then I look at the way this is expressed in ordinary and problematic couples, and finally I provide some guidelines for understanding and treating symptomatically aggressive couples.

From the outset, I want to acknowledge that the psychoanalytic study of aggression is a complicated, rich field about which a great deal has been written. This contribution is only what its title suggests, a primer, and cannot do justice to the full range of valuable contributions in the literature or all the complexities of thought the subject warrants. This article is intended as an outline, a guide that might organise a way of thinking and working clinically, and therefore must remain open to accusations both of bias and incompleteness. I beg the reader's indulgence in this. My hope is that the synthesis of a few of the important trends in the field will offer some clarity for the practitioner early in her experience.

Two basic kinds of aggression

As I see it, two basic kinds of aggression are present from the beginning of life. First, there is what we might call "benign aggression" that provides the energy for the child to explore, to move towards novel experience, to take care of herself, and to be curious. Second, there is the kind of "reactive aggression", which can be for good purposes, or can become malignant, and that comes in reaction to obstacles or rejection. It is involved in self-defence, but in extreme cases of neglect, impingement or abuse, this goes beyond self-defence. When the need for this kind of reactive aggression is prolonged and extreme, it can lead to the development of an aggressive personality in which it co-opts benign aggression and becomes the be-all-and-end-all of personal motivation, leading to a malignantly angry and destructive personality.

Freud and Klein: the death instinct

Freud's theory of the life and death instincts (1923) put forward the view that aggression was primary, innate, and fundamentally destructive. Melanie Klein (1957) developed this idea further, holding that the child was born with an excess of innate aggression because of the death instinct. Therefore the child unconsciously felt a need to do something about this internal threat, and handled it through projective identification. This is to say that the child, unconsciously perceiving this internal threat from her own inborn aggression and hatred, offloaded the dangerous aggression into the mother, then identified her as characterised by that very aggression, and therefore a threat to the child. Rosenfeld (1971) gave an elegant addition to Freud's and Klein's ideas in describing varieties of fusion of the life and death instincts in narcissistic personalities characterised by aggression, and the example of those narcissistic personalities who are characterised by in internal mafia-like gang that usurps personality.

This chapter, however, is an attempt to go beyond what many feel are the limitations of basing a theory of aggression on the idea of instincts together with the complexities of the idea of fusion and defusion of instincts, that marks Rosenfeld's way of fitting Freud's ideas to developmental considerations. The idea that aggression is based on a death instinct, and in a perpetual clash with the sexual or life instincts, diminishes the role of relationships in shaping aggression throughout life. Moreover, it is the role of relationships that I feel is not only in the forefront in the development and expression of aggression, but that is most crucial in the clinical practice of couple therapy.

Fairbairn: internalisation of aggressive relationships

Where does aggression come from as the child grows if it is not simply a matter of inborn instincts? Ronald Fairbairn (Fairbairn, 1952; Scharff & Birtles, 1994) believed that the child was born without innate aggression. He thought that what organised the child was the innate need for relationships, and although there were instincts or drives, he believed they only took on meaning by the shaping that relationships gave them. Aggression was instantiated as a result of inevitable disappointments in the availability of the people on whom the child relied, and with whom the child needed a relationship of love and concern. Fairbairn believed that when the child encountered these inevitable disappointments, she took in, or introjected, the disappointing aspects of relationships in a manner that began the process of structuring the mind, split off the most painful of these relationships, and buried them through repression.

This led to a model of psychic organisation, in which parts of self and parts of the internal object were related through emotional links, and in which the affective link of the aggressive internal object constellation was one of sadness, frustration, disappointment, and anger. This internal object relations constellation (which he termed the internal saboteur or anti-libidinal object relationship) could attack the self from inside. It was modelled on a couple: an internal object attacking a part of the self to which it was tied. But then this internal pair also had the potential to attack other part-object organisations of the self. For instance, the angry, anti-libidinal object constellation can attack the whole self, or could attack the part of the self that longs for love. In either case, the angry, destructive part of the self comes to dominate the personality, either for the time being, or more thoroughly over time.

Kernberg (1992) extended Fairbairn's ideas on the way love and hate form the affective links between repressed internal self-object structures. Rage characterises the full and often unbridled expression of the aggressive continuum, just as full erotic love is the highest expression of the continuum of libidinal affects. These affects form both the links and the motivational structures of internal object constellations. The affects are what give a sense of meaning to relationships.

Fairbairn (1943) developed another theory that is critical to many of our clinical cases with individuals, couples, and families. This is the "moral defence," a formulation developed in answer to the question, "Why do children with abusive parents tend to blame themselves for the abuse?" The answer, he said, is that the child unconsciously believes that:

> It is better to be a sinner in a world ruled by God than to live in a world ruled by the devil. A sinner in a world ruled by God may be bad: but there is always a certain sense of security to be derived from the fact that the world around is good—'God's in His heaven—All's right with the world!'; and in any case there is always a hope of redemption. In a world ruled by the Devil the individual may escape the badness of being a sinner; but he is bad because the world around him is bad. Further, he can have no sense of security and no hope of redemption. The only prospect is one of death and destruction. (Fairbairn, 1943, pp. 66–67)

If the world is fundamentally good, then even if the child is bad, there is hope for redemption and forgiveness. If the world is fundamentally bad, then even being good offers no hope. Therefore the child opts for hope.

Fairbairn also (1958) disputed the view that malignant organisations of the kind Klein had described occurred under the aegis of a death instinct and an inborn excess of aggression. He suggested that his view of aggression, as generated by the internal persecuting object relationship that had formed in the face of actual rejection and mistreatment, offered a better understanding. However, he noted, a patient characterised by excessive aggression could well appear, clinically, as though she had been born with an excess malignant aggression, thereby covering up the role of disappointment in the formation of such presentations.

Winnicott's synthesis

Winnicott's (1970) view on aggression helps to resolve the controversy between whether humans are born with an excess of aggression, or whether it develops solely in reaction to disappointment and mistreatment. Winnicott held that the child had two fundamental kinds of aggression. First there is normal, benign aggression necessary for exploration and growth, the kind that powers curiosity and mastery. With this aggression, the child uses the relationship with the mother (and parents) "ruthlessly"—that is to say, without being concerned for the wellbeing of the mother. For her part, the ordinary mother allows this use of her without retaliation, understanding intuitively that her child must use her to grow.

Secondly, Winnicott proposed, there is reactive aggression that comes, as Fairbairn had said, in response to disappointment, frustration, or mistreatment. Although every child also has a component of this reactive aggression, it is the hypertrophy of this aspect of aggression, that is, anger, hatred, and the malignant ruthlessness that we associate with destructiveness and violence in relationships. I note, however, that just as benign aggression that is fundamental to the process of growth for the child builds a relational link to the parents, so reactive or malignant aggression also builds an angry, destructive link to the object, and this can become a major feature of personality when the disappointment, rejection, and mistreatment have been severe and prolonged. In practice, the clinical differentiation between benign and malignant aggression may not be so easy, as in the example of an adolescent whose normal aggression is deployed in promoting her independence, and who abuses her parents as though that were necessary to achieve autonomy. It is as if the adolescent feels she will only be able to leave home over her parents' dead bodies.

More recently, Glasser (1998) has categorised two types of aggression, especially violence, somewhat differently. "Self-Protective Violence", the type closely related to an animal hunting prey, is unrelated to an internal sense of treating other people as actual persons. They are felt to be more like inhuman objects of personal aims related to self-protection. "Sado-Masochistic Violence", on the other hand, is always aimed at another person. It is involved in the quality (and sexualisation) of the relationship with that person, both externally and internally, insomuch as that person represents an internal object. This differentiation is close to that of Winnicott, in that what Glasser calls self-protective violence may not be associated with a history of mistreatment. But Glasser's categorisation is also different, because it addresses violence rather than aggression itself.

Neuroscience and interpersonal aspects of development

To expand our investigation of the origins of aggression, I now turn to the findings of neuroscience. One of the first things a child does when confronted with incoming information about relationships is to monitor them for danger. The right amygdala, a small walnut-shaped structure, is the seat of this process, monitoring all incoming stimuli for signs of danger (Schore, 2003). When there is significant danger from early relationships, this function hypertrophies and becomes more automatic and pervasive. Ordinarily, in the arms of positive early relationships, the review of the amygdala's process by higher centres, especially the right orbito-frontal cortex (the part of the brain over the right eye), dampens down the tendency to see everything as potentially dangerous. When there has been a high titre of danger, these higher regions do not grow optimally. Then two things happen. First, reflexive responses to danger that originate in the amygdala come to predominate. Second, hypothalamic functions to stress produce high circulating levels of cortisol that condition persons for stress.

Interpersonally, the abused child has parents or relationships with other adults who treat him aggressively. He learns that danger is intrinsic in intimate interpersonal relations. This might be conveyed by pervasive aggressive patterns with shouting, hitting, or—even more confusing—rapid alternation between seductive and punitive treatment. It might be signalled through parents' anger with each other, lack of parental limit-setting on sibling aggression or on the child's own aggression, or through beatings or sexual abuse. Or it may be that there is a penetrating atmosphere of aggression because the parents fight with each other, even though no one actually shouts at or hits the child. In short, there is a range of overly aggressive settings and behaviours that convey to the child the pervasiveness of danger in the interpersonal environment. The child's fantasy elaboration of these external situations has a great deal to do with the extent of her perception of threat in the family setting, or in other important settings.

To return to the contributions of neuroscience, let us look at mirror neurons (Gallese, 2003). These cells are located next to motor neurons in the motor cortex. They fire when an individual carries out an action, for instance taking a drink from a glass. But they also fire when he sees or hears another person do the same action. They are the single-cell basis for learning by seeing and by imitation. The ramifications of the mirror neuron system are complex, with higher-level centres modifying the simple firing of neurons in response to observation. Nevertheless, the existence of mirror neurons establishes that human beings (and other animals) are born to learn through observation and that infants learn emotions from seeing them in the people they are close to.

Therefore, when early interaction is aggressively tinged, the child takes deeply into herself the aggressive mental organisations that cause such behaviour and emotional communication. Then when this child grows up to have adult couple and family relationships, the tendency to recreate such relationships is built deeply into her. There is a tendency to pair up with a partner who can respond to and share this kind of organisation. Such couples do not only find resonating mirror neuron systems in each other, but also, through mutual projective identification, they build resonating cycles of aggression that continue to reinforce and magnify this way of relating. As such couples build various kinds of oscillating cycles of aggression, they reinforce—at both brain and psychological levels—the original tendency to find and recreate aggressive relationships.

Bion's container/contained model

There are, of course, mitigating forces in development. Bion's (1970) model of the container/contained describes in theoretical terms how the parent's mind takes in the primitive and unstructured experience of the child, transforms it into more manageable form, and feeds it back to the child in a metabolised form. What we are dealing with here is the balance between aggression that can be transformed and contained, and that which is beyond the capacity of parents and their children to digest and contain. The child needs the parents to modulate her normal developmental aggression in this way, to keep it focused on growth needs, and to blend it with a growing capacity to be concerned for others. Without this, the untamed tendency for aggression to usurp the capacity for love and concern can become an undisciplined growth of developmental needs.

Affect regulation

Fonagy and his colleagues (2003) have shown us that one central role of the early attachment relationship is the process of affect regulation. In the beginning, the infant has strong emotions that on his own, he cannot soothe or understand. It is the role of the attachment figures to take in these unprocessed emotions, tolerate them through the parents' containment, and then pass them back to the infant as calmer, more regulated, and both more tolerable and manageable. In the case of anger and aggression, the mother can absorb the aggression, let it resonate inside herself intuitively and, through her unconscious understanding, get an idea of what it means emotionally. Then she is in a position to feed it back to the infant through "down-regulation," that is by adding understanding, and calming words and tones, that gradually, over the early months and years, make the aggression tolerable and susceptible of being given meaning. This process is applicable to couples: What is raw and not understood between them—perhaps amygdala-driven rage—in the augmented containment of therapy can be taken in by the therapist, tolerated and understood, and fed back, both with down-regulation and with enhanced meaning.

Some types of aggressive partnerships

The degree to which early experiences might lead to later aggression varies. But in general, poor regulation of early aggression leads to incapacity of the growing child to regulate aggression. This is exacerbated when there is an experience of trauma and neglect in early life, leading to impaired containment, that is, a defective capacity to deal with disappointment and frustration, and a tendency to seek out more traumatic experience or traumatising relationships in later life. When this happens, partners tend to see each other as posing danger; this is all the more so in the closeness of intimate relationships, and they fear retraumatisation as a result of being in an intimate couple relationship.

Aggressive partnerships are of varying kinds. Some might be ones with cycles of mounting aggression. Others may result in the couple protectively distancing themselves from each other to avoid a feared destructiveness. Still others may be characterised by long periods of calm marked by sudden outbursts of aggression. Each has to be understood in the contexts of the development of the individuals who form the couple, of the nature of the relationship they have formed, and of the way the couple invokes the aggression that troubles them.

For instance, a severely traumatised man grew up in a climate of violence in which his father beat his mother and sisters. This man hit his wife without remorse. In identification with his father, he felt she needed to be kept in line. Also in identification with his father, he unconsciously felt she could be dangerous to him, but consciously, he took it for granted that it was his duty to beat her into correct behaviour and obedience. Such women need physical protection if they seek our help, but many of the women come from similarly violent backgrounds, and unconsciously feel they deserve the aggressive treatment they get.

Another kind of example comes from those couples in whom there are cycles of the husband's violent outbursts followed by remorse. Typically, the wife forgives such a man, who behaves in a compliant and tender way until the next outburst, followed by another round of remorse and repentance. These couples, too, have grown up in climates of violence, and also present danger that requires protection. I should say that while I am using examples of aggression by husbands, there is a minority group of couples in which wives are physically violent, and husbands take the punishment.

Aggression forms a link between all such couples. We are used to thinking of the way love or sex binds intimate partners. For these aggressive couples, hatred or violence holds the same function, dominating couples' minds as violence does in a country at war. The couples may have other versions of internal organisation too—loving ones perhaps—but the ones that bring them to couple psychotherapy are the warring states of mind, a model of couple relationships that puts aggression in the forefront.

Monguzzi (2011), has explored aspects of anger and aggression in couple therapy from an intersubjective standpoint. He regards the symptomatic expression of aggression in couples as a lack of reflective mentalizing capacity, best understood in the clinical encounter through the empathic resonance on the part of the therapist who, perforce, must become involved inside her mind in an interpersonal cycle of the aggression—must fall ill with the couple's illness (J. Scharff & D. Scharff, 1998). Countertransference thus becomes the sine qua non of understanding, and therefore the instrument from which interpretive action flows in order to repair and enhance the couple's capacity individually to self-regulate and mutually to regulate aggressive affects, and accompanying violent affects, that disturb their relationship.

Ruszczynski (2010, 2012), who has published widely on sado-masochism, violence, and perversion in couples, has described couples who are pervasively dominated by aggression as enacting a form of disordered relating that is characterised by an inability to mentalize and a lack of symbolic function leading to reflexive acts of psychic and/or physical violence. These behaviours become patterns of relating, much of the time but especially at times of strain and regression to more primitive ways of handling emotional impasse. In the face of such emotional violence that is carried into the consulting room, the clinician has to sustain her own reflective function, and indeed to elevate her capacity into an empathy for the couple's situation of inner impossibility, all in order to feedback to the couple the detoxifying understanding and capacity for reflection that slowly leads to new, non-violent ways of function.

The role of social attitudes

Society's attitudes towards violence play a role in its promulgation. Some cultural attitudes even support its use. Western culture, until the last century, supported a man's right to mistreat his wife as he chose. Today we witness such prejudice against women still in various sub-cultures. Some fundamentalist religions continue to hold that men's dominance over women is God-given and not to be questioned. Prejudice against women leads to the mistreatment of wives, including violence in marriage, to neglect or infanticide of girl children, and to keeping women in inferior positions in the family. My point is that the social climate of prejudice can support or minimise the use of aggression in relationships, as we see in the differences among cultural attitudes toward women and wives. When the social climate is dominated by brutality, as in times of war, poverty, or brutal governance, the tendency for aggression to be expressed in intimate relationships grows. It is only slowly that the social systems of the world have responded to these inequities. In the West, laws protecting women and children, and promoting their equality have developed over the last two hundred years. In China, these changes are a product of the last fifty to seventy-five years, and we see evidence in daily news reports that reforms have yet to begin many other places in the world.

Assessing couple aggression

When we see these couples in psychotherapy, the first dimension we want to assess is the amount, the modes of expression, and danger posed by aggression. Is their aggression violent physically, or "merely" a matter of continual arguing and hurling words at each other? Is it constant or intermittent? Is it the only mood for the partners, or is it a troubling interruption to an otherwise loving relationship?

The second point of assessment is the reaction to aggressive expression. Reactions within the couples characterised by outsized aggression within their relationship vary widely. Is there self-justification without remorse, or is there regret and remorse. Does the offending partner want to change, or does he regard himself as justified? And is it one or both partners who offend?

Then we want to assess whether there is a capacity in one or both partners to reflect psychologically on the causes of the aggression. Can the partners move towards seeing their own role in the generation of aggressive or violent ways of relating? Even better, can they work together over time to see how the difficulties and disappointments in their relationship have led them to substitute aggression for love and respect? In the best case, the couple moves, with our help, to work together to grow this kind of understanding. In some cases, one partner has more psychological-mindedness than the other, but can help the other to move in that direction. In a worst-case scenario, neither partner is willing or has the capacity to use insight to change the way they relate. That does not automatically mean we cannot help, but it means we are reduced to behavioural prescriptions, or to the hope that something will seep in from our benign stance and understanding that will detoxify the situation, even without the psychological support of the couple.

Often work with the couple begins with therapist's observation that what makes their relationship toxic are the threats that anger and aggression will be forthcoming—even at those times that violence or aggressive outbursts are not actually happening. Because the spouse feels a general lack of safety, she is always on guard for danger, even when it is not actually present. She has to protect herself. It may be that she holds herself at an emotional distance, or that she feigns compliance to demands to ward off anger, or that she develops a masochistic stance. The intermittent or constant threat of angry outbursts or violence kills love in one way or another.

The exception is the couple who are dominated by a sado-masochistic bond in which the violence and suffering are also exciting. This can be a major theme in those couples who also express regret for the aggression. In others, however, so long as the sado-masochistic bond is working for them, they do not seek our help. I cannot here do justice to this large topic. Dealing with the sexually sado-masochistic couple is beyond the scope of this primer, but we have to take note that for many couples for whom physical aggression plays a role in their relationship, there is an eroticisation of aggression that draws them to it, even in the absence of sexual sado-masochism. When this is present, the couple's attraction to violence, sadism, and suffering has to be a central part of therapeutic exploration.

Once we have assessed the capacity for new understanding and flexibility in a couple, we might turn to ask about the backgrounds that have led the couple to this state of aggression. How aggressive or violent were their families as they grew up? Were they yelled at regularly, beaten, abused physically or sexually? Did they live in situations of social violence such as severe prejudice, violent ghettoes, or war?

Then we want to assess two other dimensions. How encapsulated is the aggressive organisation in each of the partners? In cases of severe trauma, it is likely that one or both have encapsulated traumatic internal object organisations so that they are often well beyond conscious reach. That is to say, aggressive internal object constellations may be walled off, away from everyday awareness, only to burst into expression when provoked, and then disappear again, as though these violent organisations never existed.

That leads to another assessment issue about the couple's interaction: How much provocation is there in the couple's relationship? Sometimes, it is one partner who provokes and the other who is openly aggressive, but in many aggressive couples, partners take turns in provoking and responding. These couples are dominated by their shared aggressive, antilibidinal object relations constellations, but they take turns which of them is the victim and which the actively aggressive partner. In all these couples, one or both partners use projective identification—the unconscious transmission of aggression to the other—to portray the other as the one who expresses the aggression openly. For example, a husband unconsciously puts his victim-self into his wife, and she puts her unconscious aggressor into him. This is the common pattern of the sado-masochistic couple, bound together by the cycles of aggression.

Defences against aggression

Some couples, deeply troubled by aggression, handle things quite differently, building a wall against open expression of anger and physical violence. Bion thought of this organisation as being so armed against aggression that it was essentially erased from the mind. He represented a positive mental representation of aggression as "+H", and a mental organisation that erased it as "-H." (Bion, 1962) Here we see a couple who unconsciously share a "-H" mentality. For instance, one couple told me that each of them had been subject to physical abuse growing up. The husband was beaten by his father when he failed to protect his sisters, and he saw his drunken father beat his mother many times. The wife, the youngest of several children, saw her older siblings beaten by her mother, and often threw herself between her mother and the others, suffering such injuries as a cracked skull for her efforts to defend them. Early on, this couple made a pact never to hit each other or their children. Instead, in their determination to be the opposite of their abusing parents, they built a wall between themselves. In their refusal to physically express anger—which was inevitably there—they each hit walls with their fists, occasionally breaking their knuckles in the process. Their form of discipline with their two sons was to say to them, "Go hold a wall." That meant that the child would go stand with his head against the wall until regaining control. The worst damage to this couple's relationship was the wall they unwittingly built between themselves. Over time, the emotional wall grew so that they could no longer breach it. This couple altruistically protected each other from the danger each felt to lie within themselves, and they thereby tried to protect their couple relationship. But inevitably, what is suppressed and repressed comes back nevertheless to haunt the relationship through depression, hopelessness, the growing distance between them and the outbursts when anger could no longer be denied (Fairbairn, 1943).

Clinical management of marital violence

The first thing we do to treat violence in relationships is to set limits. We cannot treat a relationship that is still in danger from actual physical violence; safety comes first. When the couple can stop the physical aggression, we can proceed. When they cannot, then the abused spouse needs literal protection: separation from the abusing partner, a temporary or permanent shelter or new home, and perhaps legal restraining orders.

When there is anger, but no physical aggression, or when the couple can stop the literal abuse, psychotherapy can begin. We work towards helping each partner and the two together understand their role in the cycles of aggression and/or violence, balancing our view, remaining neutral in that we are on the side of each partner, against only the destructiveness they have shared. We try to understand the sources of outsize aggression in their early years, aggression and trauma in their social environment and in their daily life, and sources of anger in their intimate life together. We help the aggressor or aggressors understand when and why this is the only response available, but, equally, we look to help the partner who provokes and off-loads the anger to own up to his/her part in the cycle.

Underneath all of these patterns of aggression, there are common fundamental factors that trigger anger and aggression. There is always a substratum of danger to both partners, of hurt and injury, sadness and disappointment. There is always some quality of hopelessness about whether there can be a better way of responding or a better way of life. Underneath all of this, is a mutual feeling of being unloved and unlovable that the partners share, and that, at the most fundamental level, powers the substitution of anger and aggression for love and tenderness.

The role of the therapist's countertransference

We work by attempting to absorb the violence and hatred in the couple's relationship into the sessions and into ourselves. We ask the couple to collaborate with us by bringing their disappointments, fights, and misunderstandings into the sessions, and as we do so, and if things are going well, they decrease in intensity and frequency in their everyday life. In this way, in our work, we are exposed to these aggressive forces. But more than that: we take them inside our own experience. Through the countertransference, we invite their excessively aggressive bond to infect us, and as it does, we work within ourselves to understand and detoxify it, and then to move it from wordless emotional experience within us to being something we can think about and therefore talk about with them. It is usually a painful inner experience for the therapist. But it is this process—using ourselves as therapeutic instruments through a willingness to tolerate, live with, and transform aggression—that we convey new possibilities to the couple. The ways of talking to them and of being with them are those that training and experience have made possible. Doing this, over and over again, builds their trust in us over time. It is this trust—in us and in the process of therapy—that couples draw on to build an increased capacity for trust in each other.

A final example

A young couple came because the wife complained that her husband's rigidity, his refusal to take her wishes or distress seriously, and his outbursts of anger including two episodes of shoving her, were intolerable. She had no thought that she contributed to their difficulty, but hoped that psychotherapy could fix him. He came reluctantly, having no idea of how or whether psychotherapy worked. In a series of interviews with me and my co-therapist, Janine Wanlass, over five days, we learned that the husband was ashamed and remorseful about his behaviour, which he thought was inexcusable and incomprehensible. He had no idea why he had reacted so badly, and he told us, without any prompting, that the angry expressions, and especially all physical violence, had to stop.

We learned that the husband had grown up with a father who denigrated women, and who continued to insist that his mother take care of the father in a way that demeaned her. The wife had grown up with a father she adored, but who also denigrated women, and who had struck her mother on many occasions. We understood that there were social attitudes that contributed to the attitude of demeaning women that therefore supported these behaviours. While both partners, in their current life, wished to treat each other differently than their parents had, these old identifications broke through at times of stress, and had come to dominate their relationship.

As the interviews progressed, we began to see how the wife provoked her husband, putting him down in identification with her own self-centred father, and emasculating him, as a kind of unconscious revenge on her father. Seeing how that part of the couple's pattern worked, we could begin to see how the husband's reactive aggression and withdrawal created a cycle of occasional, but extremely destructive, aggression that was further destroying the potential for a loving relationship in the couple.

Surprisingly, we found that the insights we could offer the couple were much easier for the husband to take in than for the wife. What began as a picture of rigidity in the husband and a seeking for answers by the wife, evolved into an underlying picture of openness in the husband and rigidity in the wife. It was a beginning. At the close of the evaluation, the husband said that going beyond the outbursts now seemed possible. We were moved when, in the closing moments of our consultation, he turned to his wife and said, "I think if we slow things down, we can understand more and make things better. I didn't understand this idea of therapy when we came, but now I think I do. I think it can really help us." That was enough for her to become a bit more trusting, and to allow space and time for more growth.

In our work, in the best of times, we get chances like this. It is what we hope and work for. It does not always happen this way with couples, but more often than not, we find ways to give them new chances to find love where hate had predominated. It is what keeps us going.

References

Bion, W. R. (1962). *Learning from Experience*. London: Heinemann.
Bion, W. R. (1970). *Attention and Interpretation*. London: Heinemann.
Glasser, M. (1998). On violence: A preliminary communication. *International Journal of Psycho-Analysis*, 79: 887–902.
Klein, M. (1957). *Envy and Gratitude*. London: Tavistock.
Kernberg, O. F. (1992). *Aggression in Personality Disorders and Perversions*. New Haven: Yale.
Fairbairn, W. R. D. (1943). [1990] The repression and return of bad objects (with special reference to the "War Neuroses"). In: *Psychoanalytic Studies of the Personality* (pp. 59–81). London: Routledge and Kegan Paul.

Fairbairn, W. R. D. (1952). [1990] *Psychoanalytic Studies of the Personality*. London: Routledge and Kegan Paul.

Fairbairn, W. R. D. (1958). [1994] On the nature and aims of psychoanalytical treatment. In: D. E. Scharff & E. F. Birtles (Eds.), *From Instinct to Self: Selected Papers of W. R. D. Fairbairn. Vol 1* (pp. 74–92). Northvale, NJ: Jason Aronson.

Fonagy, P., Gergely, G., Jurist, E. L., & Target, M. (2002). *Affect Regulation, Mentalization, and the Development of the Self*. New York: Other Press. Reprinted Karnac, 2004.

Freud, S. (1923). *The Ego and the Id. S. E., 19*: 3–66. London: Hogarth.

Gallese, V. (2003). The manifold nature of interpersonal relations: The quest for a common mechanism. *Philosophical Transactions of the Royal Society of London Biological Sciences, 358*: 517–528. London: The Royal Society.

Monguzzi, F. (2011). Anger and aggressiveness in couple therapy: Some clinical considerations from an intersubjective perspective. *Couple and Family Psychoanalysis, 2, 1*: 210–221.

Rosenfeld, H. (1971). A clinical approach to the psychoanalytic theory of the life and death instinct. *International Journal of Psycho-Analysis, 52*: 169–178.

Ruszczynski, S. (2010). The problem of certain psychic realities: aggression and violence as perverse solutions. In: D. Morgan & S. Ruszczynski (Eds.), *Lectures on Violence, Perversion and Delinquency* (pp. 23–42). London: Karnac.

Ruszczynski, S. (2012). Personality Disorder: A diagnosis of disordered relating. *Couple and Family Psychoanalysis, 2, 1*: 133–148.

Scharff, D. E. & Birtles, E. F. (Eds.) (1994). *From Instinct to Self: Selected Papers of W. R. D. Fairbairn. Vol 1*. Northvale, NJ: Jason Aronson.

Scharff, D. E. & Scharff, J. S. (1998). *Object Relations Individual Therapy*. Northvale, NJ: Jason Aronson.

Schore, A. N. (2003). *Affect Regulation and the Repair of the Self*. New York: Norton.

Winnicott, D. W. (1970). *Playing and Reality*. London: Tavistock.

CHAPTER SIX

Getting back to or getting back at: understanding overt aggression in couple relationships

Christopher Vincent

Background

In our 1980s study of British family courts' welfare officers and their clients, we observed that, in many of the intransigent post divorce disputes about childcare arrangements, it was unclear whether the continuing arguments between parents were serving the purpose of "getting back to or getting back at" each other (Clulow & Vincent, 1987, p. 211). That is, we were uncertain whether the highly angry interactions we were witnessing functioned to punish a former partner, or were an attempt to get back into a closer relationship, or were a confused amalgam of both objectives.

Most of the litigating couples we worked with were an exceptionally contentious group of parents and, as we reported, "Psychological survival was at stake for these parents. A petition for divorce could have the impact of a declaration of war, following which the world was divided into friends and foes" (Clulow & Vincent, 1987, p. 209). For these parents overt aggression was manifest through a number of channels often starting with the original divorce petition which, in a very high proportion of cases, cited the "unreasonable behaviour" of the respondent. In this way the "blame game" was started and could be continued through subsequent applications to the court for different remedies. For example, variation in childcare arrangements was the most likely reason for our involvement as welfare officers-come-researchers, but we were also aware of ongoing and often parallel proceedings to ban ex-partners from the former matrimonial home, to seek orders to prevent molestation and to seek variation in financial affairs. In these proceedings accusations by the aggrieved parent of unreasonably aggressive behaviour or domestic violence were often the reasons for seeking the eviction of a partner from the matrimonial home or asking the Court to make orders preventing further harassment. Moreover, the initiation of legal proceedings, whatever its justification, was often experienced as an aggressive act itself since it invariably threatened to destabilise established patterns of living, financial wellbeing and childcare arrangements.

Since completing that project I have sustained a clinical interest in work with couples who are either anticipating or going through the processes of separation and divorce (Vincent, 1995, 2012). My work is now outside the Family Court system and based in private practice where the angry couples I meet are mostly at an early stage in the processes of separation and, indeed, many decide through the course of couple work not to continue down that path. In this work, the phrase "getting back at or getting back to" has continued to come into my mind as a helpful explanation of the ambiguities that lie at the heart of couples who remain very angry with each other yet appear unable either to separate satisfactorily or to give up the fight. Understanding this interaction in order to intervene in helpful ways is very difficult. The experience of sitting with couples who argue with each other can produce a rising crescendo of accusation and counter-accusation so that thoughtful reflection of what the other is saying is batted away as if words were offensive missiles. The experience of being unable to think clearly is as much a problem for the therapist as it appears to be for the clients. Following each partner's conflicting story and being pulled in opposite directions is invariably demanding for the therapist but intervening to break up the pattern is necessary in order to see whether accusatory and defensive narratives can be temporarily relinquished and "cease fire" conditions established as the forerunner to different and more thoughtful ways of relating, without prejudice to whether the couple decide to separate or stay together.

There is a powerful case for couple therapists giving careful thought and attention to these situations and the dynamics that underlie them. It is estimated, for example, that in the UK at least one in five women and one in ten men will experience domestic violence (Walby & Allen, 2004) and, although it is judged that there remains a significant under-reporting of this crime, the largest couple counselling organisation in the UK, Relate, claims that a third of their clients has experienced some form of domestic violence or abuse (Relate, 2011).

These findings are crucially important for counsellors and psychotherapists who work with couples for they confirm the very high probability that issues around domestic violence, or, at least, very angry interaction will arise either at the point of initial assessment or, more commonly in my experience, as the work progresses and clients feel more able to disclose and address aggressive behaviours. In these unhappy circumstances the welfare of both the adults and any children they may have can be seriously threatened (Jones & Bunston, 2012). It is, therefore, incumbent on couple therapists to think deeply about the nature and meaning of angry interactions and the implications this understanding carries for ways of responding and intervening (Monguzzi, 2011). As a starting point, how is it possible to understand the meaning and origins of aggressive or violent behaviour?

A complex field

In the first place, defining what we mean by angry or aggressive behaviour is a difficult task ranging from what might be thought about as "healthy" anger at one extreme to "unhealthy" anger at the other. Much has been written about the healthy function of anger as an important component of seeking individuation and freedom from oppressive relationships (Zulueta, 1993). Winnicott captured this in his much repeated words, "If society is in danger, it is not because of man's aggressiveness but because of the repression of personal aggressiveness in individuals" (Winnicott, 1958, p. 204). The anger of the adolescent can be understood, in part, as the fuel that drives his bid for separation from his family and which underpins his experiment to claim an emerging adult identity, however frail that identity may be. It is also true that anger may be a necessary component of relinquishing a bad or failing marriage as was the case of a man in our divorce study who said somewhat sadly that, in relation to the ex-wife he did not want to lose, "I have to hate her to let her go" (Clulow, 2012). Similarly, victims of persecuting partners who want to leave a destructive relationship but lack the emotional resources to go, have to muster some healthy, life asserting anger to find ways of breaking free. In these circumstances, we might say that anger is part of the solvent releasing the glue binding people together.

But anger may also have less creative or developmental aspects and can have thoroughly destructive, violent and, even, deadly consequences. These negative aspects of aggression have received attention from philosophers, theologians, and psychologists for thousands of years and, in their thinking there has been a strong and recurring proposal that aggression in its negative aspects is programmed into our nature. St Augustine's doctrine of original sin is an early example of this approach. Chadwick, one of his most valued modern translators puts his position thus:

> Augustine's diagnosis of the human condition is sombre. Since Adam's fall no human being has come into the world without a perverted self-love, without an ignorance beyond that natural to childhood, and without a radically disordered emotional life. Man's love is turned away from God to the inferior and creaturely, so that he finds his love gravitating down to lust; his anger (even when justified) passing into hatred; his sadness into self pity; even compassion at others' misfortunes … is easily mixed with a tiny element of horrifying satisfaction, a schadenfreude which, when detected, makes one despise oneself. (Chadwick, 2009, p. 152)

According to Augustine, man can only redeem himself through finding God again on a long and painful spiritual journey through life.

It is perhaps significant that some of the writers who have argued that destructive aggression is genetically programmed have witnessed man's behaviour at its most violent and destructive. The English political philosopher Thomas Hobbes published his Leviathan in 1651 during the English civil war. He argued that man needed a sovereign authority with a monopoly of the use of force to save people from the evils of the "state of nature" by which he meant that individuals would otherwise pursue their own selfish ends through violent means; "Hereby it is manifest, that during the time men live without a common power to keep them in awe, they are in that condition which is called war; and such a war, as is of every man, against every man" (Hobbes, 1651, p. 143). Hobbes felt that the only check on man's violent self interest was the constraining influence of society's institutions.

Whereas Hobbes thought that man's aggression could only be checked by social structures external to the self, Freud, writing more than two centuries later, held the view that limitation on innate aggression is something that is managed internally within the self. In his later theorising first outlined in *Beyond The Pleasure Principle* (Freud, 1920), and written in the shadow of the Great War's ending, Freud argues that life involves the struggle between competing instincts; "Our views have from the very first been dualistic, and today they are even more definitely dualistic than before- ... we describe the opposition as being, not between ego-instincts and sexual instincts but between life instincts and death instincts" (Freud, 1920, p. 53). By life instincts Freud meant those impulses towards creativity and building complexity into life while, by the death instinct, he meant those impulses to reduce complex structures into their fundamental elements or building blocks. He thought of the death instinct as something that we are inclined to turn inwardly against ourselves as in those behaviours like masochism where attacks on the self dominate. But he suggested that interpersonal aggression emerges when these destructive impulses are turned outward towards others as in sadistic aggression.

Freud's theory of a competing set of instincts seems on the face of it a promising theory to explain the ambiguities inherent in the phrase "getting back to or getting back at". Might it be that "getting back to" a partner captures the creative wish to reassert something complex and good while the notion of "getting back at" with its connotation of punishment is an expression of the death instinct?

Some may find the explanatory power of the life and death instincts helpful so long as these two concepts are understood as metaphors capturing some of the phenomenological intent of those who are arguing. In certain situations the wish to get back to a partner can have a creative, or at least benign element to it if the motivation is to re-establish a previously well functioning relationship while the wish to get back at a partner can often feel as if real hatred and the wish to destroy the other lies behind the wish to punish.

However, for our purposes, the theory of the death instinct as defined by Freud has the major weakness that aggression is only associated with destructive or negative outcomes. Storr (1968) concluded that so long as Freud held onto the notion that the aim of all instincts is to rid the body of all tension and to achieve a state of satiated bliss, he could see no place for aggression stimulating the body as would arise when appropriate power needs to be dispensed to achieve specific aims such as having a healthy domestic row. The idea that aggression might be a means towards achieving a healthy outcome was not countenanced by Freud and, therefore, he would not allow the possibility of any positive intent co-existing with negative intent in the behaviour that we might label as "getting back at".

The value of attachment theory

Bowlby's attachment theory developed from observing the behaviour of young children particularly as they managed separations and reunions with their primary caretakers. Building on his pioneering study of institutionalised children (Bowlby, 1953), his observational studies with James and Joyce Robertson clearly illustrated the functional importance of aggression for the young child in both protesting about a rupture in his relationship with his primary caretaker and the important role it plays in reclaiming the proximity of that person. Anxiety, anger, and punishment can be observed in the distressed state of any toddler who has temporarily lost a needed contact with their caretaking adult, and the effectiveness of these behaviours will be observed in those children whose caretakers respond appropriately by returning and allowing the toddler to be reassured and resume play.

Wind forward into adult years and Bowlby (1988) could see that similar processes can operate between adults. In healthy adult relationships anger can function to re-establish a link with a close partner who is emotionally or physically absent. The angry plea is heard as a signal of distress (even though it may well have strong accusatory elements contained within it) and the absent partner, who is able to identify with the distress within the message and tolerate the blame, can respond in a thoughtful and compassionate way. One might say that in these situations there is a triumph of the wish to "get back to" over the need to punish as in "getting back at" the absent partner. Anger in these circumstances acts as a catalyst to re-glue the relationship.

But this is not always the case and the reverse may apply so that the angry bid may elicit an equally angry response in which empathic identification is absent and a spiralling argument may follow culminating in aggressive and violent behaviour. Bowlby thought that "violence ... can be understood as the distorted and exaggerated version of behaviour that is potentially functional" (Bowlby, 1953, p. 81) but which in its distorted shape is failing to have any productive effect. What is it that differentiates those circumstances where anger may have a positive outcome from those where it may become entrenched into a "self maintaining pattern of social interaction and emotional regulation"? (Shaver & Clark, 1994, p. 119).

The reasons why some partnerships are unable to use anger in productive ways and resort to partner abuse are helpfully elaborated by Bartholomew, Henderson and Dutton (2001). They suggest that there are particular combinations of adult attachment styles that are particularly associated with partner abuse. Using the four attachment patterns of secure, dismissing, preoccupied and fearful, they found that:

- Across studies the preoccupied pattern was, for both men and women, strongly associated with the receipt and perpetration of abuse.
- For men the fearfulness pattern was strongly associated with the receipt and perpetration of abuse and was most strongly associated with male violence.
- Most abuse is bi-directional in nature notwithstanding the fact that men are physically stronger than women and inflict more severe injuries.
- There was a high degree of similarity between the experience of men and women in abusive relationships which called into question the sufficiency of a patriarchal model of relationships to explain couple violence.
- Jealousy and fear of separation or abandonment are common triggers for abusive episodes, a finding echoed by Feeney and Monin (2008).

In their analysis Bartholomew and colleagues note that the four attachment patterns can be located on two intersecting axes that record how individuals regard themselves and regard their partner. Secure individuals have a high self regard and also rate their partners highly. Dismissing individuals have a high self regard and low regard for their partners. In the two categories which appear to be most vulnerable to experiencing abuse, preoccupied individuals have a high regard for their partners but a low self regard which tends to result in an over dependency on their partners whereas fearful individuals have both low self regard and low regard for their partners which results in a fear of intimacy particularly linked to past and expected experiences of rejection. By linking attachment patterns to ideas about the self, Bartholomew and colleagues make explicit the links between attachment behaviour and subjective ideas about identity and the self.

This seems to me to be a vital link for clinicians because, in my experience, when couples argue or are violent there is a powerful sense that both feel that their sense of self and the integrity of their current and prior experience is being questioned and attacked. Typically in a row, each partner describes their shared experience in diametrically opposed ways and, in doing so, insists that the other's experience and feelings are wrong and dangerously wrong. This is what was meant at the beginning of this chapter when referring to psychological survival being at stake for the divorcing couples we worked with. Under these conditions it is not surprising that individuals feel hurt and misrepresented, thus fuelling the wish to blame and "get back at" but anger can be expressed in such a way which seeks to change their partners' opinions to more closely resemble their own so that some restitution of the former relationship can develop; there may be a drive "to get back to" the pre-existing relationship however deeply hidden this aim may be in words and behaviour that look like "getting back at" the other. These ambiguities were palpable in the couple work I will now describe.

Failure to connect?

Robert and Sally came to consult me at the suggestion of Robert's therapist who had thought that a couple focus was needed to help with his acknowledged problem in managing his anger. Both were in their late forties and were unmarried although they had been living together for three years. Robert had not been married before and Sally had divorced her husband some time before she and Robert met. Neither had children.

The problem they both agreed was that Robert got into periodical rages with Sally about every six months. He felt terribly about these states and wanted to do anything he could to overcome them. When I asked them both at our first meeting to give me an example of a particular row, they told me about the previous weekend when Robert had become furious with Sally for not taking responsibility for her own financial affairs, presenting as he saw it a helpless inability to get her mind around on-line banking and leaving him to act for her. As we looked more closely at this particular row, it became clear that what exasperated Robert was his perception of Sally's failing to meet him halfway and instead retreating from properly engaging with him over this particular financial task. In the argument, Robert's sense of Sally not joining with him made him feel initially anxious and then progressively angry, feeling that an unfair burden was resting on his shoulders. Sally's counter-claim was that Robert's instant anger frightened her and drove her into a distant and self-protective stance.

This pattern of Sally retreating in the face of Robert's frightening crescendo of anger was the underlying dynamic that characterised many of the arguments we came to talk about. In seeking to understand their genesis it was unclear, as is often the case in spiralling arguments, what was cause and what was effect. Did Sally's retreat provoke Robert's anger or was his anger the cause of her retreat? Might it be both at different times and over different matters? Their family histories explained something of this dynamic process.

Robert was one of two children, his sister being a few years older. He was sent to boarding school from a young age and hated it. He was frequently home sick, and had a recurring anxiety about the welfare of his parents. They were both keen cruising sailors and, when he was away at school, he had recurring anxieties that, in their weekend cruises afloat, their boat would founder and he would become orphaned. Robert recognised that this very clear and explicit childhood anxiety captured an important truth about the way that he thinks about and reacts to people close to him now that he is an adult. He often talked about the importance of sustaining relationships with important people in his life and of feeling very anxious if these relationships are threatened in any way. More particularly he recognised that when he feels Sally to be distant from him or drawing away emotionally he gets anxious. This anxiety turns to a sort of panic and he can then become angry.

Sally was the only girl among four boys. Her father's short temper and irascibility was a strong influence over her family upbringing. He had been harshly treated as a prisoner of war by the Japanese and the family understood that it was this experience that contributed to his unpredictable fits of anger. Sally commented that all the family tiptoed around him and it is reasonable to assume that, as a result, she developed a particular susceptibility to retreating into her own shell when confronted by what felt like incomprehensible and frightening male aggression.

From the brief sketch of their family backgrounds, it was not difficult to conclude that Robert and Sally's primary emotional defences are mutually reinforcing. When made anxious in an interpersonal situation Robert moves towards the person he cares about, seeking reassurance that they and he will survive. By contrast Sally's first line of defence is to retreat from contact with anyone whose behaviour frightens her. It is not difficult to see that these individual defences contribute to a couple dynamic where the impulse to get close is matched by an impulse to move away, thus creating an interaction where, at those moments, neither is able to reassure or contain the other's anxieties. There is a failure to connect emotionally in certain high stress situations.

In our work together we were able to identify times when stress between them might be particularly acute. Points of reunion, which took different forms, were among these. For example, the end of the working day was identified as one potential point of conflict when Sally would complain that Robert was unable to leave his work behind him so that their time together was sacrificed to his business calls. Unpacking this specific niggle opened up a broader set of questions about whether they could prioritise their relationship as a couple over separate individual interests and concerns. This exploration saw them both consciously making great efforts to give each other time and consideration, so that an expanded area of shared activities began to emerge that they felt good about.

However, just over a year into their therapy a particularly angry and violent argument took place between them. They had both had busy weeks and Sally had been away for two or three nights visiting friends. She had returned to their house on Friday evening feeling tired and sad. She wanted to stay in, put her feet up and relax. Robert had contacted her and invited her to join him and a group of friends in a local pub for their regular end of week drink. Sally declined the invitation saying that she was tired, which left Robert disappointed. Later he phoned again and she did come to the pub for a brief drink but excused herself from going on with the group for a meal in a local restaurant. Robert was again miffed by her withdrawal and, on his return later in the evening, expressed his hurt by sleeping in a spare bedroom. The following day they were due to attend a summer garden party which involved a good hour's drive. From waking up to arriving at the party neither initiated any real conversation, it being obvious that the previous evening's misunderstandings had created an angry and withdrawn atmosphere between them.

They did not speak at the party and Robert became progressively more upset at seeing Sally enjoy herself and appearing to flirt with an unattached man. Fuelled by alcohol, Robert hit this man and he and Sally retreated by taxi to a hotel room where a very violent row ensued which was ended by Sally calling the police who arrested Robert and detained him overnight. Sally decided not to press criminal charges and they turned up to see me three days later. Before the meeting, Sally had emailed me twice to outline some of the problem and to tell me that Robert remained in a very angry state.

It is possible to see in this very distressing episode a magnification of the dynamic problem we had previously identified and sought to remedy. A physical reunion, at the end of the week when both had lead separate busy lives, had not been possible because of their different ways of relaxing and recharging their batteries. Sally had wanted to relax and recover on her own while Robert had wanted to engage socially with others and to have involved Sally in his end of week celebration.

In the sessions after the distressing argument they were subdued, shocked, and concerned at the awfulness of what had happened and the potentially catastrophic consequences for them both. They both wondered about whether the partnership should end, but their presence together suggested that this was not what was wanted. They insisted they wanted to go forward together but never to repeat anything like their recent row. In this discussion I also made it clear that I could not continue working with them if violence re-emerged, thus adding some weight to the urgency of really understanding what had taken place and to do something about it.

They talked a lot about the background feelings which fed into the traumatic flare up. Sally felt that in recent times she had not felt cherished by Robert, which shocked and surprised him because he felt he had made strides in putting her first ahead of his intrusive work demands. He felt that she did not want to be with him, and would really like to be living in the area she had visited in the week before the flare up where some of her dearest friends lived. Sally countered that this was far from the truth and was happy living in Robert's home patch where she now feels settled.

There is much that could be discussed about this material and I have omitted more that would contextualise and make sense of it. But it does convey, I think, the struggle Sally and Robert had at that time to maintain a sense of connection with each other particularly when they had experienced a separation. For Robert the events of Friday evening left him feeling rejected in spite of his bid to "get back to" Sally. Her refusal to join him took place in a context where she had not been feeling cherished by him of late, and she felt that her "sadness" was better resolved by being on her own. Whether Sally consciously thought about it or not, one can detect in her decision to be on her own an angry or at least disappointed feeling which might represent a wish to "get back at" Robert. Subsequently their physical distancing and refusal to speak to one another may have had many layers of latent meaning, but it seems reasonable that both were "getting back at" each other through the "silent treatment".

Their accounts of what happened at the party were diametrically different, but both agreed that they were not together as a "couple" and that this contributed to the violence that then followed. The accusation that Sally flirted was vehemently denied, but put alongside Robert's feeling that Sally would prefer to live near her old friends than live with him and Sally's anger at the priority Robert can give to his business over their joint interests points to their shared fear that they could come second best to other individuals and interests. This can be a miserable experience where one can feel lonely, belittled, and humiliated. Perhaps the angry denigration of each other, whether expressed in words or through physical violence, is a primitive way of communicating those feelings that has been impossible through other means. If this is true then there is complex way in which "getting back at" through punishing a partner is a communicative act and can be understood as a perverse way of "getting back to".

Two years after this traumatic event Sally and Robert remain together and continue to see me. There has been no repetition of the violence and I think it is fair to say that they have drawn from their experience in creative ways and are more established as a couple.

Final thoughts

It is perhaps self-evident that much domestic violence takes place within a couple context. However in some quarters it has not followed that treatment should focus on the couple as an interactive system. For those clinicians and organisations that see the problem arising from patriarchal male abuse and an imbalance in domestic power relations (for example, Women's Aid Federation England, 1996), there has been a call to focus on male perpetrators often using anger management programmes.

Bartholomew and colleagues' work shows that causative factors are often more complex than a focus on one partner would suggest, and that it is important to take into account the contribution of both partners to their shared difficulties. This is not to suggest that all relationships where anger dominates the relationship are healthy or sustainable. There will be some couples where it is in everyone's interest, children included, that the relationship ends. Campbell makes the point that a feature of a sadistic relationship is that in a sadistic attack the relationship to the object must be preserved, not eliminated (Campbell, 2011). There will be many sadistic partners who seek to reconstitute the relationship with the conscious or unconscious expectation that the abuse will continue.

I am suggesting that one way of identifying those relationships that can survive angry and, at worst, abusive behaviour is where there can be a positive outcome to therapist interventions that address the often concealed wishes to reconstitute the relationship as it existed before the anger erupted. To do this requires being able to weave together comments and interpretations that address the "getting back at" with the "getting back to". The challenge in addressing both motivations is that the therapist has to identify and comment upon the vulnerable, confused, and needy aspects of both partners that lie behind the angry, omnipotent, and excited aspects of blame and violence.

If such interpretations resonate in ways that produce a reduction in anger and facilitate genuine and consistent demonstrations of care and concern, then there is hope that the couple focus is justified. Sally and Robert were able to do that and their relationship is significantly more robust as a result. I would like to thank Robert and Sally who have read this heavily disguised account of their experiences in this chapter and have generously consented to its publication.

References

Bartholomew, K., Henderson, A., & Dutton, D. (2001). Insecure attachment and abusive intimate relationships. In: C. Clulow (Ed.), *Adult Attachment and Couple Psychotherapy: The Secure Base in Practice and Research* (pp. 43–61). London: Brunner-Routledge.

Bowlby, J. (1953). *Child Care and The Growth of Love*. Harmondsworth, England: Penguin Books.

Bowlby, J. (1988). *A Secure Base: Clinical Applications of Attachment Theory*. London: Routledge.

Campbell, D. (2011). The nature and function of aggression. In: P. Williams (Ed.), *Aggression: From Fantasy to Action*, (pp. 1–22). Psychoanalytic Ideas Series. London: Karnac.

Chadwick, H. (2009). *Augustine of Hippo: A Life*. Oxford: Oxford University Press.

Clulow, C. (2012). Personal communication.

Clulow, C. & Vincent, C. (1987). *In The Child's Best Interests: Divorce Court Welfare and the Search for a Settlement*. London: Tavistock.

Feeney, B. C. & Monin, J. K. (2008). An attachment-theoretical perspective on divorce. In: J. Cassidy & P. R. Shaver (Eds.), *Handbook of Attachment: Theory, Research and Clinical Applications*, 2nd edition (pp. 934–957). New York: Guilford Press.

Freud, S. (1920). *Beyond The Pleasure Principle, S. E., 18*. London: Hogarth.

Hobbes, T. (1651). Leviathan. In: J. Plamenatz (Ed.), *The Natural Condition of Mankind as Concerning Their Felicity and Misery* (pp. 141–145). The Fontana Library, 1962. London: William Collins and Sons.

Jones, S. & Bunston, W. (2012). The original couple: enabling mothers and infants to think about what destroys as well as engenders love, when there has been intimate couple violence, *Couple and Family Psychoanalysis*, 2: Autumn 2012, 215–232.

Monguzzi, F. (2011). Anger and aggressiveness in couple therapy: some clinical considerations for an intersubjective perspective, *Couple and Family Psychoanalysis*, 2: Autumn 2011, 210–221.

Relate, (2011). Comment on Domestic Violence Review, press release, December 14th, www.relate.org.uk

Shaver, P. R. & Clark, C. L. (1994). The psychodynamics of romantic attachment. In: J. S. Masling & R. F. Bronstein (Eds.), *Empirical Perspectives on Object Relations Theories* (pp. 105–156). Washington DC: American Psychological Association.

Storr, A. (1968). *Human Aggression*. Harmondsworth, England: Penguin Books.

Walby, S. & Allen, J. (2004). Domestic violence, sexual assault and stalking: findings from the British Crime Survey, Home Office Research study 276, Home Office Research Development and Statistics Directorate.

Vincent, C. (1995). Consulting to divorcing couples, *Family Law, Dec.*, 25: 678–681.

Vincent, C. (2012). Commentary on working therapeutically with high conflict divorces. In: A. Balfour, M. Morgan & C. Vincent (Eds.), *How Couples Shape Our World: Clinical Practice, Research and Social Policy Perspectives* (pp. 159–168). London: Karnac.

Winnicott, D. W. (1958). *Collected Papers: Through Paediatrics to Psychoanalysis*. London: Tavistock.

Women's Aid Federation of England (1996). Domestic violence: service provision, policy research, findings and statistics. WAFE: Bristol.

Zulueta, F. de. (1993). *From Pain to Violence: The Traumatic Roots of Destructiveness*. London: Whurr.

CHAPTER SEVEN

Responding to the clinical needs of same-sex couples

Damian McCann

Development in thinking about same-sex couples within the field of psychoanalysis is still very much in its infancy. Moreover, the continued reliance on heteronormative thinking as a guide to practice with lesbian and gay couples raises fundamental questions concerning our understanding and management of difference, as well as exposing practitioners and their professional bodies to the charge of homo-ignorance. This chapter aims to raise awareness of the clinical needs of same-sex couples as a means of increasing sensitivity and responsiveness when engaging psychotherapeutically with lesbians and gay men presenting for therapy.

The chapter begins with a brief consideration of the ways in which the psychoanalytic profession is responding to the challenges of theory and practice with lesbians and gay men. This is followed by an examination of working with difference, the ways in which unconscious processes affect the couple dynamic and the impact of this on the therapeutic relationship. Specific attention is paid to gender role socialisation, as a way of highlighting the particular qualities and differences within and between lesbian and gay couple relationships, and the chapter ends with an exploration of therapist factors.

Challenges to psychoanalytic thinking and practice

Historically, psychoanalytically informed practitioners have obscured the lives of lesbians and gay men in the language of pathology, immaturity, and immorality (Gus, 2008). Underscoring this point, Ellis (2010) suggests that psychoanalytic theorising of homosexuality has restricted itself to interpretations regarding the internal world, where pre-oedipal fixation and oedipal conflicts were believed to be the cause of homosexuality. Unfortunately, those holding such beliefs have wittingly or unwittingly tended towards a directive suggestive approach

(Mitchell, 1981) interpreting away from same-sex attraction, since analytic theory presupposes a heterosexual norm (Barden, 2011).

Thankfully, a great deal of reparative work within the profession is now taking place, as one professional body after another has been forced to "come out" and state its position regarding psychotherapeutic work with lesbians and gay men. For instance, in 1991, the American Psychoanalytic Association issued a statement opposing and deploring public and private discrimination against male and female homosexual oriented individuals. In 1999, it went one step further in regard to reparative therapy, stating that "same gender sexual orientation cannot be assumed to represent a deficit in personality development or the expression of psychopathology", a view also endorsed by the British Psychoanalytic Council who, in 2011, made its own statement opposing "discrimination on the basis of sexual orientation" and asserting the belief that it does not accept a homosexual orientation as evidence of "disturbance of the mind or in development".

Given these powerful statements, there is clearly some urgency in terms of considering how, as psychoanalytically informed couple psychotherapists, we think about and respond to lesbians and gay men presenting for couple's therapy. Moreover, adopting an object relations approach obliges us to stop thinking in terms of individuals in isolation but to see them as interacting with others in the environment (Ruszczynski, 1993). In that regard, within the therapeutic relationship, the therapist's own conscious and unconscious beliefs, feelings and conflicts, provide a particular reference point when working with lesbian and gay couples, since they also have an influence on the form and direction of the therapeutic process. It is therefore vital that we closely attend to the specificities of same-sex couple relationships as well as our own internal responses to these in order that the therapeutic encounter is authentic, safe, and effective.

Respecting difference

Although universal issues exist for all couples, heteronormative thinking conveniently ignores difference and disappears the cultural specificities that shape and give meaning to lesbian and gay lifestyles and relationships. For instance, Connolly (2004) suggests that same-sex couples present quite distinct clinical concerns arising out of the impact of homophobia, heterosexism and indeed the internalisation of both. Without a clear understanding of the workings of these pernicious influences, both on the individuals and the couple relationship itself, therapists attempting to work with such couples may find themselves on the receiving end of an awkward and uncomfortable encounter without knowing anything about the part they played in the very creation of this dynamic. Worse still, therapists who fail to take account of difference may even be adding to the problems the couple have brought to therapy, since the heterosexual lens through which they are engaging with the lesbian or gay couple, only serves to reinforce the couple's sense of otherness and adds to their ongoing struggle to validate their own relationship.

In other words, because of the existence of heterosexism, homophobia, and internalised homophobia, lesbians and gay men are forced to claim a socially stigmatised existence. Therapists working with such individuals and couples must therefore recognise that they are working with people at the edge of a culture in which definitions of relationship and family have essentially excluded them (Knudson-Martin & Laughlin, 2005). This external ambivalence towards same-sex couples is believed to exert a destabilising influence on the couple relationship itself and some believe that this accounts for the increased relational ambiguity shown by such couples (Green & Mitchell, 2002). This ambiguity often manifests itself in the two individuals struggling to establish the relationship and in creating appropriate boundaries around which the relationship will grow, simply because, like those around them, there is a question as to the legitimacy or value of such relationships. Therefore, questions asked of same-sex couples in therapy, particularly those implying pathology or deficiency, may well tap into a reservoir of self and relational doubt within the couple and serve to increase their sense of inadequacy, confusion, and despair. In view of this, therapists must consider their own transferences to the material same-sex couples bring for exploration if they are to unconsciously avoid alienating such couples or damaging the therapeutic relationship.

Working with unconscious processes

D'Ercole (2008) emphasises the importance in clinical work with same-sex couples of attending to internalised experiences relating to feelings of difference. This is because negative social attitudes are believed to produce internal conflicts within the individual, manifest in feelings of guilt, alienation, confusion, hostility, etc. This internalised homophobia needs careful "working through" in order to help the individuals develop identity cohesion and integration, since, for some, the development of a false self keeps others at bay. However, the splitting that is necessary for survival can be acted out within the couple relationship itself and threaten its very foundation. For instance, one of the participants recruited for my doctoral research (exploring the meaning and impact of violence and abuse within the couple relationships of gay men) spoke of a partner who was struggling to manage his sexuality. Unable to reconcile his same-sex attraction with his lived reality, he violently projected his anger and rage into the partner, as if he were literally trying to kill-off his own sexuality through this means. Masters (2008) also reminds us that for many gay men, internalised homophobia can be lost to conscious retrieval and instead morph into self destructive ways of life that seem natural and familiar. An important implication of this for therapy is that individuals and couples may not be open to exploring the meaning of such behaviours and may defend against this by questioning the therapist's own value systems that lead them to pursue certain aspects of behaviour in the individual or couple.

Hertzmann (2011) links the role of cultural and societal attitudes in relation to homosexuality to that of superego functioning, the notion of a prohibitive and restrictive internal agent acting against full expression of one's sexuality. This is because "internalized homophobia, functioning as an unconscious introject, acts as a host for aggressive aspects of the superego potentially resulting in a very punitive attitude towards the homosexuality of the self and of others" (Hertzmann, 2011, p. 350). This may, in part, explain a couple's negative transference towards the therapist, since the therapist is experienced by the couple as representing the problematic superego function, in that the therapist's presence and psychotherapeutic stance are experienced as a judgmental and an intrusive presence that provokes a hostile reaction towards the therapist. The ability to speak to this emerging and problematic dynamic from an "as if" position, for example, it may feel to you that it is as if I am judging you, or, I wonder if you feel that there is something I am not fully understanding about your situation, may help free the couple and therapist from this particular stranglehold, and prevent the couple from prematurely ending therapy. Hertzmann (2011) provides useful examples of the kinds of therapeutic impasse which can result from this particular aspect of internalised homophobia. Nevertheless, it is important to acknowledge that working with internalised homophobia, whatever its route or form, is a technically challenging task, since so much is held in the unconscious. Not only can it take time to reach, but when it is brought to consciousness, it can evoke powerful feelings in the couple or between the couple and the therapist.

Extending the thinking further in regard to considering the workings of unconscious processes, Vaughan (2008) helpfully draws attention to the discordance between parents' internal representations of their child and the child's own self representation, which, in terms of homosexuality, may also result in feelings of alienation, something which is further reinforced by a negative and rejecting external world. This sense of discordance may actually limit a lesbian or gay male's capacity to trust his or her objects, which, in time, could lead to further conflict within the couple relationship as they attempt to affirm their connection. What I am suggesting here is that the early faulty coupling between a lesbian daughter or gay son and their primary caregiver, may exert an unconscious force on the current couple relationship and throw up fundamental questions about the authenticity of the couple fit. Again, being able to work with this sense of "wrongness" within the individual or couple relationship itself may help the couple become more conscious as to the ways in which love, hate, and ambivalence operate and are managed by a couple.

A further source of potential strain for lesbian and gay couples is that of relating to the internal parental couple, since, in common with their heterosexual counterparts, what lesbians and gay men actually internalise is, by and large, a model of heterosexual pairing. To some extent, this conundrum accounts for some of the differences in lifestyle and patterns of relating which lesbians and gay male couples have evolved; since in the absence of external validation and appropriate role models, same-sex couples have been forced to create their own. However, the models of relating which they have evolved have often been a source of scrutiny, since in not conforming to accepted heterosexual standards or mores, same-sex relationships are often judged as deficient in one way or another. The recent publication guidelines for psychologists working therapeutically with sexual and gender minority clients (2012) suggests that there has been an over reliance on heterosexual marriage and fixed binary views of sexuality, as a way of making sense of and responding to the needs of same-sex couples.

It is also possible that internalised homophobia has a bearing on unconscious couple choice, in that, a partner who is "out" finds herself teaming up with a partner who is not, and then finds herself reacting to the partner who is struggling to "come out" by expressing frustration and anger. At the same time, the partner who is struggling to "come out" has unconsciously chosen someone who has conquered this developmental challenge, perhaps with the hope that she would be supportive and empathic, only to find another version of a negatively reactive external force. However, in the face of pressure brought to bear by the partner who is "out", we now find the one who is not withdrawing further in the face of this "stage discrepancy", which is then experienced as a threat to the relationship. It is noticeable in my own clinical work with lesbian and gay couples how differences between the partners, whether in terms of age, money, a previous marriage, etc., become a source of frustration and pain rather than something more nurturing and developmental.

Case example

Jenny and Martha have been living together for the past two years and now seek therapy because of conflict within their relationship. The conflict is linked to Jenny's mounting criticism of Martha's extremely close relationship to her mother and sister, which Jenny feels is interfering with the development of their couple relationship. Although Martha's mother and sister appear to be at ease with her lesbianism and are supportive, Jenny feels excluded and suspicious. A recurring theme in her arguments with Martha is that her mother and sister will only really be happy when she settles down with a man. It is of note that Martha's father left the family home when Martha was eight-years-old and, as he now lives some distance away with his new partner, Martha has had little or no contact with him over the years.

The conflict between Jenny and Martha has reached something of a crisis in the light of Martha's decision to have a child. It has recently transpired that Martha has identified a donor. She is also keen for this donor to have an ongoing role in her child's life. Jenny, although open to the possibility of Martha having a child, once again feels excluded from the process and questions whether Martha is having this child for herself or whether it is something which they, as a couple, can share.

One of the obvious tensions in this couple's presentation is the fact that Jenny is estranged from her family of origin who struggled to accept her lesbianism and who seemed to focus their attention instead towards Jenny's younger brother. As a consequence, Jenny left home as soon as she could and worked hard at establishing her independence. When Jenny met Martha she felt that she had finally met someone with whom she could share her life, so she is now bitter with disappointment.

Although this case example raises a number of issues, I particularly wish to focus on the unconscious couple fit, since both of these women appear to have chosen their contrasting counterpart. Jenny is clearly looking to Martha for the kind of connection she felt was missing in her own life, namely the idea of a close and accepting family, whereas Martha has chosen a partner who has managed a degree of separateness from her family, a far cry from Martha's experience. In addition, the projective system appears to be threatening the base of their relationship, as Jenny projects her unresolved feelings about her family's rejection of her lesbianism onto Martha, whilst at the same time feeling rejected and excluded as she did in her family of origin. Martha, by privileging her relationship with the male donor over her relationship with Jenny, appears to be communicating something about her ambivalence about being in a relationship with another woman, and is leaving Jenny feeling unwelcome. In addition, Martha is also attempting to make amends for a father who abandoned her as a child by ensuring the donor's ongoing involvement in her child's life, whilst unconsciously exposing Jenny to the kind of rejection Martha must have felt when her father left for another woman.

Faced with this presentation, the therapeutic task will be one of helping these two women explore the possibility of becoming a couple. For Jenny it is a case of finding a way in. For Martha it seems to be about creating a space for Jenny in her life. The extent to which they feel comfortable exploring their lesbianism and the meaning of their connection will have far reaching consequences for their relationship. Whilst they continue to enact unresolved childhood traumas and shy away from the specific developmental challenge of embracing a same-sex couple relationship, with or without a child, they will likely remain as separate individuals within a couple relationship.

The impact of gender

Therapists working with lesbian and gay couples must also be alive to the impact of gender and the ways in which this consciously and unconsciously affects the couple dynamic. For instance, there is a body of thinking which draws attention to processes relating to gender role socialisation, which are believed to account for differences in patterns of relating between lesbian and gay male couples and between same-sex and heterosexual couple relationships. A particular example of this thinking is the belief that, because of gender role socialisation, lesbians appear to prize a love relationship above all else, whereas gay men (and indeed many heterosexual men) do not. Tunnell & Greenan (2004) believe that because gay male couples violate some of society's strongest prohibitions about gender role behaviour, the form and pattern of relationships for gay men will differ from heterosexual and lesbian couple relationships. Indeed, Boyle (1993) found that the rule of cohabitation and sexual exclusivity is lower in gay male couple relationships compared with that of lesbian relationships.

However, therapists confronted with such differences in their practice have historically lacked curiosity about the meaning or value of such differences and have instead constructed theories that have pathologised both the individual and the couple relationship itself. Here I am referring to the concerning idea in the field which holds with the belief that lesbians, as a whole, are fused (unable to tolerate difference) and that gay men, as a whole, are polymorphously perverse (unable to tolerate intimacy). It is worrying that some therapists, relying on heteronormative thinking, utilise heterosexual privilege to view and treat same-sex couples as an inferior version of heterosexual pairing. This is most evident when therapists search for the male within a lesbian couple relationship and look for the female within a gay male couple relationship. This reliance on rigid gender dichotomies as a signpost of supposed healthy development robs both the therapist and the couple of an exploration of the uniqueness and meaning of male times two and female times two, and so the values and strengths of such pairings are lost.

In view of this, I am arguing that lesbian and gay couples need space and encouragement to explore the meaning and uniqueness of their particular couple dynamics, but that they can only do so if the therapist is also on board. Indeed, Lesser (2002) asks us to consider the kind and style of attachment our developmental theories value as "normal", the style of relationship that is considered valid, that is, monogamous, long-term, emotionally intimate relationships, as opposed to polygamous arrangements, or relationship structures that question the need for attraction and sexual passion always to be linked together. Instead we need to use our theories to help us explore for ourselves and the couples we see, some of the tensions which exist in finding true meeting points rather than defensive splits.

To illustrate the point, I wish to look at the somewhat contentious area within psychoanalytic circles regarding open relationships, since these appear to raise particular questions and anxieties about the nature of these relationships, particularly in regard to the unconscious couple fit. Generally speaking, open relationships are not usually viewed as a preferable or viable alternative to long-term monogamous relationships (despite the fact that many long-term monogamous relationships are non-sexual), since open relationships often require a degree of splitting (i.e., of sex and emotion) that is felt to be anti-developmental. However, there is evidence that confirms that non-monogamy in and of itself does not create problems for gay male couples provided they are able to openly negotiate this. In fact, research conducted by Spears & Lowen (2010) suggests that non-monogamy is a viable option. For the couples they interviewed, it actually increased the trust between the partners, resulted in more forthright communication and personal growth, although they did acknowledge that this comes with some risks and the need for ongoing maintenance. However, this warrants further exploration since Greenan & Tunnell (2003) suggest that although, intellectually, open relationships can have great appeal and often represent a rejection of the majority culture by gay men, the lack of boundaries inherent in these relationships can challenge a couple's ability to create an identity. Also, open boundaries around sex may actually exacerbate and reinforce the problems of relational ambiguity.

Case example

Larry and Peter, a longstanding couple, have successful careers and a home that reflects their shared interests. On the face of it, they appear to have a collaborative and committed relationship, although they have come to therapy in response to Peter's discovery that Larry has been having sex outside of their relationship. Peter feels betrayed, as he thought that they were in a monogamous relationship, and so he is looking to therapy as a setting in which they can restore their relationship.

From the outset, Peter makes it clear that he is serious about leaving unless Larry is willing to be monogamous. This all or nothing feel to the presentation goes to the heart of the couple's struggle and represents a fundamental split and developmental challenge to their relationship. For instance, Larry feels that their relationship has been stagnating for some time, and highlights the fact that they have not had sex together for a number of years. He says that when he has tried to talk about this, Peter usually becomes defensive. Although raising the issue seems to bring them closer for a time, it does not actually result in them having sex. Larry also feels that despite having sex outside of their relationship, he is open to exploring possibilities within the relationship if Peter will let him. Peter, however, is only concerned with extracting an agreement from Larry that he will not have sex outside of the relationship. Larry feels Peter is missing the point and feels invested in keeping the conversation going, as he clearly wants something more developmental.

Drawing on Colman's (1993) thinking relating to marriage as a psychological container, it seems important to consider the question as to whether open relationships represent a breakdown in the container or whether they actually represent a container for gay men, since it may allow them to remain within a long-term committed relationship. Colman speaks of a fundamental tension inherent in marriage between, on the one hand, the autonomous development of the individual and, on the other hand, the allegiance to the shared world of the partnership. Given that the tension between autonomy and independence, on the one hand, and commitment and dependence, on the other, can never be resolved, I wonder if open relationships represent an avoidance of the disillusionments that each of the partners in a couple relationship have to negotiate on the way to establishing a satisfactory and fulfilling relationship. Or, as I suggested earlier, open relationships may signal an acceptance of the disillusionment and a moving on—especially since the so-called container must be able to contain the tension that arises from the need of the individuals to develop outside the relationship as well as within. Whilst acknowledging the tensions inherent in these positions, the therapeutic relationship itself and indeed the therapy setting also acts as a useful container in its own right, in that it offers the possibility of exploring the nature of the boundaries within the couple relationship. However, the therapist's own relationship to this exploration must also form part of the thinking.

It should be clear by now that what is going on in the therapist and what the therapist brings to the therapeutic endeavour when working with lesbians and gay men is of particular importance. This is especially so, given the damage wrought by psychoanalysts relying on theories drawn from heteronormative thinking when undertaking therapy with a population that they knew little about or even wanted to know. This reinforces the need for therapists to dig deep in order to better equip themselves for the task of understanding and embracing difference. I will end the chapter with a consideration of factors that therapists need to consider when working with same-sex couples.

Therapist factors

King et al., (2007) in their systematic review of psychotherapy services for gay and lesbian clients in the UK, found that a therapist's attitudes, knowledge and practice were more important than their sexual orientation. Drescher (1999) urges a move away from etiology, which has been an analytic preoccupation with homosexuality, towards a search for meaning. Put another way, there is a need for therapists to suspend judgment and to adopt more curiosity when working with lesbian and gay couples. This inevitably demands an exploration of the therapist's own beliefs and values and the impact of these on the therapeutic encounter. After all, the intersubjective field is alive with transference and countertransference material, and whilst it is vital to stay close to the language and meaning the couples attach to their relationship, it is equally important that we therapists pay close attention to that which gets activated in us. Masters (2008), for instance, highlights the fact that when gay patients describe their sexual activities in sessions, it can create a host of countertransferences regardless of the gender or sexual orientation of the therapist. "At times we may find ourselves intrigued, disgusted, envious, and, yes, even sexually excited" (Masters, 2008, p. 376).

Although the therapist's individual analysis affords some protection, there is a question as to whether it goes far enough in encouraging a meaningful exploration of the therapist's own gender and sexuality. In addition, I wonder what the context might be for therapists to feel motivated to do this work, since without it, questions arise as to how far the therapist is equipped to help the couples they see plumb the depths they need to go to if they are to understand fully the nature of internalised homophobia and the impact of gender and sexuality on their relational dynamics.

Another question that arises when working with lesbian and gay couples is the extent to which the boundaries that inform the work with heterosexual couples needs to be adjusted when working with same-sex couples. One obvious challenge comes from therapists needing to consider how transparent and "out" they may be with a population who have had to endure a lifetime of hiding and avoidance in order to survive. Although aware of the complexities relating to self disclosure in psychoanalytic work with couples, I do believe that therapists working with same-sex couples need to consider the implications of non-disclosure and how they would work non-defensively when they receive a challenge to their therapeutic stance and position. For instance Falco (1991) says, "I have chosen in my practice to always indicate my sexual orientation when a client asks me directly (which gay clients almost always do and non-gay clients rarely do). I do this because I believe it is therapeutic for the client to know this, and because it facilitates modeling" (Falco, 1991, p. 53). At the same time, Falco also searches out the meaning of the client's enquiry. However, ultimately as therapists we have a responsibility to properly attend to the specific demands of our work with lesbian and gay couples if we and our profession are to grow and move forward.

Conclusion

I have highlighted a number of factors specific to lesbian and gay relationships that therapists need to consider when undertaking psychotherapeutic work with this population. I placed particular emphasis on the need for therapists to attend to their own transference reactions to lesbian and gay lifestyles, patterns of relating and the relationship between gender and sexuality, since a reliance on heteronormative thinking as a basis for practice runs the risk of further alienating this client group. In situations where therapists working with same-sex couples feel out of their depth or at the limits of their experience, consultation and supervision are an obvious source of support, but only if consultants and supervisors have themselves considered the issues. Ultimately, we must be prepared to refer on if, for whatever reason, we are not open or equipped to deal with the issues that lesbian and gay male couples present. It is no longer acceptable to rely on generic skills, interpret our way out of situations, or assume that it is all countertransference material. The profession has been called to account. Now it is time for its practitioners to take note and step up to this challenging but rewarding task.

References

Barden, N. (2011). Disrupting Oedipus: The legacy of the Sphinx. *Psychoanalytic Psychotherapy, 25,* 4: 324–345.
Boyle, M. (1993). Sexual dysfunction or heterosexual dysfunction? *Feminism in Psychology,* 3: 73–78.
Guidelines and Literature Review for Psychologists Working Therapeutically with Sexual and Gender Minority Clients. (2012). The British Psychological Society.
Colman, W. (1993). Marriage as a psychological container. In S. Ruszczynski (Ed.), *Psychotherapy with Couples* (pp. 70–96). London: Karnac.
Connolly, C. M. (2004). Clinical issues with same-sex couples: A review of the literature. In: J. J. Bigner & J. L. Wetchler (Eds.), *Relationship Therapy with Same-Sex Couples* (pp. 3–26). New York: Haworth Press.

D'Ercole, A. (2008). Homosexuality and psychoanalysis lll: Clinical perspectives. *Journal of Gay and Lesbian Mental Health, 12, 4*: 368–371.

Drescher, J. (1999). Attending to sexual compulsivity in a gay man. Paper presentation at William Alanson White Institute's Conference on "Hungers and Compulsions".

Ellis, M. L. & O'Connor, N. (2010). *Questioning Identities: Philosophy in Psychoanalytic Practice*. London: Karnac.

Falco, K. L. (1991). *Psychotherapy with Lesbian Clients: Theory into Practice*. New York: Brunner/Mazel.

Green, R. J. & Mitchell, V. (2002). Gay and lesbian couples in therapy: Homophobia, relational ambiguity and social support. In: A. S. Gurman & N. S. Jacobson (Eds.), *Clinical Handbook of Couple Therapy* (3rd edition) (pp. 546–568). New York: Guildford Press.

Greenan, D. E. & Tunnell, G. (2003). *Couple Therapy with Gay Men*. New York: Guildford Press.

Gus, J. R. (2008). Homosexuality and psychoanalysis lll: Clinical perspectives. *Journal of Gay & Lesbian Mental Health, 12, 4*: 361–368.

Hertzman, L. (2011). Lesbian and gay couple relationships: When internalized homophobia gets in the way of couple creativity. *Psychoanalytic Psychotherapy, 25, 4*: 342–360.

King, M., Semlyen, J., Killepsy, H., Nazareth, I., & Osborn, D. (2007). A systematic review of research on counselling and psychotherapy for lesbian, gay, bisexual and transgender people. British Association for Counselling and Psychotherapy.

Knudson-Martin, K. & Laughlin, M. J. (2005). Gender and sexual orientation in family therapy: towards a post-gender approach. *Family Relations, 54, 1*: 101–115.

Lesser, R. C. (2002). Notes in an elegiac mode on Stephen Mitchell's papers on homosexuality. *Studies in Gender and Sexuality, 3, 1*: 111–120.

Masters, S. (2008). Homosexuality and psychoanalysis lll: Clinical perspectives. *Journal of Gay and Lesbian Mental Health, 12, 4*: 373–378.

Mitchell, S. A. (1981). The psychoanalytic treatment of homosexuality: Some technical considerations. *International Review of Psychoanalysis, 8*: 63–80.

Ruszczynski, S. (1993). *Psychotherapy with Couples*. London: Karnac.

Spears, B. & Lowen, L. (2010). Beyond monogamy: Lessons from long-term male couples in non-monogamous relationships. www.thecouplestudy.com.

Tunnell, S. C. & Greenan, D. E. (2004). Clinical issues in gay male couples. *Journal of Couple and Relationship Therapy, 3, 2/3*: 13–26.

Vaughan, S. C. (2008). Homosexuality and psychoanalysis ll: Theoretical perspectives. *Journal of Gay & Lesbian Mental Health, 12, 4*: 327–337.

CHAPTER EIGHT

The selfdyad in the dynamic organisation of the couple

Richard M. Zeitner

With the increase in the demand for couple treatment and couple therapy training throughout the United States and Great Britain, there has also been a corresponding increase in the variety of psychotherapeutic strategies deriving from the literature pertaining to couple and family treatments (personal communications, Clulow, 2012; D. Scharff, 2011). These included those that are psychoanalytically oriented and those that are non-psychoanalytically based.

Although I use the word "strategies", I am including in this a corresponding expansion of interest in understanding the functioning and the psychodynamics of the intimate permanent partnership—the couple. However, in spite of this expansion of interest in treating the couple, ironically, the therapy of the couple relationship remains one of the most difficult clinical enterprises—an area of practice throughout the mental health disciplines that is frequently over simplified and sometimes misunderstood. Even the term "marriage counselling" or the recommendation to "go see a marriage counsellor," in my mind, frequently carries with it a simplistic connotation, suggesting implicitly that a couple, for example, that may have been having severe and longstanding difficulties in relating, even when the couple problem represents a significant contributor to a mental illness in one partner, after getting some good old fashioned advice on how to solve these problems, might possibly do a little better. The implication, however unfortunately, is often that the couple therapy is ancillary or palliative, and that the real "cure" will emanate from the medication prescribed and/or the individual treatment.

Furthermore, most training programmes today still focus on an individual model of treatment, ranging from psychiatric training programmes, clinical and counselling doctoral programmes, through the various social work and other counselling training regimens. If there is any training in couple and family therapy it usually consists of one or two courses, and if fortunate, some minimal supervision on a case or two. Couple therapy, unfortunately then remains the stepchild in most training programmes at the graduate level, and if additional training is desired, it must usually be obtained at the post-graduate level, such as that offered at the International Psychotherapy Institute and at the Tavistock Centre for Couple Relationships. Besides the relative scarcity of formal training in couple and family treatments at the graduate level, there are other psychologically based as well as economic reasons for the infrequency with which couple therapy is recommended and practiced, many of which I have described in previous writings (Zeitner, 2003; 2012).

The field of psychoanalytic couple therapy then deserves more research, theoretical writing, as well as more well-trained psychotherapists who are competent to practice in this area, and especially those clinicians who are able to move flexibly between couple and individual therapies, knowing how and when to implement which therapy with which clients and under what conditions. This prescriptive way of practising psychoanalytically is unfortunately still rare today. It is instead more usual for psychoanalytically oriented clinicians to practice individual psychotherapy, more comfortably focusing on the individual patient and the dyad of the therapist and patient through the vicissitudes of transference and countertransference, while not so easily recognising the potential and often the need for couple therapy. When a couple consultation is either directly asked for by the patient, or instead its need becomes glaringly apparent to the therapist because, for example, the focus of the individual treatment has become centred on the couple's problems, the referral for couple therapy may now be made. It is not that this decision for a referral is ill conceived or inappropriate, but in fact it is often most appropriate, however late.

What I have found quite often while supervising other therapists, or when a patient has consulted me after having been in individual psychotherapy with another therapist for months or even years, and who now has quite clear, conscious, and well-articulated concerns about his or her intimate partnership (and who unfortunately has had the same prevailing concerns throughout the individual therapy) is that the patient has actually addressed his relationship issues within the individual treatment, but with little or no improvement. Thus frequently, the individual therapy has moved into a primarily supportive realm, rather than exploratory, but with no accompanying structural change within the couple's relationship—the very arena in which the individual patient's difficulties have been waged. The supportive therapy may have been sustaining and helpful, but for the individual patient only, while leaving the intricate dynamic organisation of the couple relationship relatively untouched and unmodified, while at high risk for further deterioration, especially when the individual therapy comes to an end.

The selfdyad as a bridge between the individual and couple

For the purpose of this chapter I wish to focus on one aspect of the couple which, in my way of thinking has been underemphasised by individual therapists most certainly, but even by couple therapists, when if given increasing theoretical and practical emphasis in training programmes and supervision at the graduate and post-graduate levels, might eventually yield an increased number of those who more comfortably practice in the field of psychoanalytic couple therapy. Previously I have commented on the conceptual leap that is required when moving from a psychological understanding of the individual in treatment to understanding the couple and its intricate dynamics. I contend that the difficulties that are inherent in making this paradigmatic shift at least in part account for the relatively fewer psychoanalytic practitioners who comfortably work with both the individual patient and with the couple, and who can flexibly execute the dosage and timing for using combined therapies.

Here I will attempt to provide an understanding of a concept pertaining to the couple—one that bridges the gap between individual and couple therapy—a construct that I have called the "selfdyad". My ideas about the selfdyad and its importance for understanding the couple theoretically and clinically are not entirely unique. Perhaps what is most important about this concept is that "I" consider it to be at the heart of understanding the couple, and that its centrality, including the careful focus on exploring its dynamics within the couple's treatment, is the very instrument that provides the clinician his leverage in assisting the couple toward growth and improvement of the relationship.

Although I have expanded the concept, consider it indispensible for couple therapy, and will provide some technical guidelines in the form of clinical vignettes to illustrate its use within the treatment process, the person who is credited with having first discovered its precursor, the joint marital personality, is Henry Dicks, a British clinician, who practiced and conducted couple research at the Tavistock Clinic. In his 1993 book that was first published in 1967, *Marital Tensions: Clinical Studies Toward a Psychological Theory of Interaction*, Dicks first described the intimate partnership (at that time called "marriage") as being founded on the basis of an unconscious fit between the two partners' individual personalities, described in Fairbairn's system of endopsychic psychology as consisting of both partners' conscious and unconscious internal object relationship systems (Dicks, 1993).

Dicks emphasised that for an intimate couple or marriage to develop, that an "unconscious complementariness" (Dicks, 1993, p. 69) must first occur, usually beginning in the courting phase of the partnership, in which the partners first note, (most usually unconsciously) and then further create an intimate connection that is based upon a way in which each individual experiences the other as if he or she were part of the self.

This is an intricate process involving perceptions of the other that are at first consciously experienced as appealing or attractive traits and features, but which unconsciously represent qualities of the self and/or internal object relationship scripts that have been repressed, lost, or undeveloped. As the relationship progresses, assuming that the boundaries of the self of both partners remain sufficiently permeable and flexible such that communication occurs in a manner that is primarily reality based, (with a minimum of perceptual distortion of qualities of the other) a consolidation of roles then forms for the partners. Henceforth, the role relationships and responsiveness to the other will function synchronistically, now allowing both partners to experience "lost aspects of their primary object relationships" (Dicks, 1993, p. 69) through both conscious and unconscious communication, fitting together like a hand in glove. Now the partner is experienced as part of the self, creating an experiential revision of the self through the shared intimacy, or more specifically, through the co-created "selfdyad". Here I note that the formation of an intimate partnership most often represents a creative solution for both partners—a function of a developmental transition from "isolation" into "intimacy", all preparing for an entry into those stages of adult life that will ultimately follow (Erikson, 1950). The dynamic mechanism to account for this transformative process, and that which is inherent to this intimate communication, is that of projective identification, a concept well known to analytically informed therapists but whose theoretical discussion is beyond the scope of this chapter.

David and Jill Scharff have described a prerequisite for the formation of the joint marital personality as involving a "blurring of boundaries between self and other", (J. Scharff & D. Scharff, 1991, p. 47) although I prefer to conceptualise this process in systemic terms which seem less "pathologised", by describing the partners as having or developing an essential permeability and flexibility of self boundaries. Furthermore, these features of self boundaries must be maintained throughout the partnership for the couple to continue experiencing through the intimate connection those qualities of self and internal object relations that have been repressed, lost, or otherwise disavowed.

There are many couples who come for treatment, for instance, where one partner's complaints centres on the difficulty he or she has in "communicating" with the other, which in the course of treatment comes to be understood as a way in which the boundaries of the selves have become impermeable. Here one partner presses for more closeness, (often called "more communication") while the other partner correspondingly closes off even more, sometimes withdrawing in anxiety and accompanying isolation. Of course, the more impermeable these self boundaries become, intimacy progressively wanes as frustration mounts for both. It is here that the first partner then often becomes even more anxious, pursuing, and cajoling, while escalating his/her attempts to get the other to respond. In its more chronic form is the couple that comes for treatment when the pattern of interaction and the self boundaries have already become fixed and rigid, while communication and intimacy have become nearly non-existent.

The selfdyad as an expansion of the joint marital personality

The reader may wonder then what is added in the reconceptualisation of the joint marital personality, now called the selfdyad. Within the consulting room I have been repeatedly struck by a characteristic manner in which troubled couples present for treatment. These complaints about the marriage and/or the partner frequently carry an unconscious message or an echo, as it were, of something that is missing, to which one or both partners feel entitled, but also deprived of. Although this presentation is sometimes well disguised, it is nearly always present. Unconsciously then, within the frustration, anger, deadness, disappointment, or other dysphoric experiences pertaining to the relationship and the partner is the wish, the cry, if not the demand, to have what one was originally promised—implicitly perhaps—that that very crucial part of the self that was originally lost, repressed, undeveloped, or disavowed through development, will ultimately be provided by the partner, now creating an intersubjective space for a revised and more complete sense of self.

It is here in my conceptualisation of the selfdyad as a reformulation of the joint marital personality that I call upon some of the more contemporary theoretical ideas of Heinz Kohut and self psychology, utilising these concepts as supplementary and additive, rather than supplanting an object relational perspective. Furthermore, these expansions, I believe, have significant implications for working with couples by adding to our armamentarium of available techniques within the consulting room (Kohut, 1971, 1977).

First briefly, I will expand a conceptual base to these self psychological additives in preparation for describing some of the technical interventions that can assist the clinician in her work with the couple, using more here and now interventions, in addition to those directed more to the then and there—the latter exemplified by the construct of projective identification and other interventions that are geared to exploring the past. The reader will note that "selfdyad" is unhyphenated, carrying by implication, a reference to, if not an alliance with Kohut's selfobject, which is also unhyphenated. For Kohut the selfobject refers to one's experience of another individual as part of the self, but always in the service of providing or fulfilling a need for the self. According to Kohut there is a continuum from those selfobjects that are more archaic to those that are considered to be more mature. Importantly, selfobjects are fundamental to all close and intimate relationships, including many "helping" relationships throughout the entire lifespan.

In making his theoretical and technical contributions, Kohut focused mostly on understanding the analytic process, differentiating three forms of transferences which came to be known as mirror, idealising, and twinship or alterego transferences. He theorised that these transferential experiences were essential in the analytic process for the patient to develop a cohesive and stable sense of self, and furthermore, that they were rooted in earlier developmental epochs between the mother and her infant, their vicissitudes either facilitating or impeding the child's developing sense of self. Essential for the establishment of these selfobject transferences, which Kohut considered to be potentially mutative for the patient, is the analyst's ability to provide empathy and understanding for the patient's self experience, expressed within the relationship with the patient, and through the interpretations and all other interventions occurring within the analytic experience. Self psychological theory has over time been extrapolated from the analytic consulting room by demonstrating that variations of these transference experiences, including the presence of empathy for the other, are inherent to many of the helping relationships, including those of student and mentor, as well as most, if not all intimate relationships throughout the lifespan, without which the self within that relationship risks losing its cohesion, sometimes shriveling, and even possibly collapsing.

What is added then to Dicks's joint marital personality, by reformulating the concept into the selfdyad, is that for the couple to remain intimate and loving, including maintaining the very projective identifications that were at one time fundamental to the couple's original unconscious "pact", including the conscious and unconscious roles that were originally agreed upon and assigned to one another—is that this joint intersubjective construction, the selfdyad, must continue to provide selfobject experiences for the partners, while affirming the part of the self that has come to be experienced within and through the self of the other. I contend that variations of these features of affirmative relating are fundamentally mirroring, idealising, and twinship at their core. Other authors have expanded Kohut's ideas pertaining to selfobject transferences by describing derivative mechanisms by attempting to understand the dynamics occurring between intimate partners as they affirm those essential needs for both the formation and the continuation of the intimate partnership—those ranging from the mother–infant bond to the adult intimate couple (Ringstrom, 1994; Stolorow, Brandchaft & Atwood, 1987; Winnicott, 1965; & Wolf, 1988).

The selfdyad fracture

Before introducing clinical material to illustrate the selfdyad as a central construct in working with the couple, a word must be said about the ways the therapist is able to recognise the selfdyad breach. As stated, at the core of the plea for clinical assistance with the couple's relationship is always the implication of no longer having what at one time was experienced within the relationship, or was at least promised, whether the problem is represented as an extramarital affair, anger at the partner for his poor parenting, feeling controlled and stultified, experiencing a lack of support for one's autonomy, sexual disappointment, or even the vapid cry for better communication. Here the therapist must always recognise the unconscious expression of a need which was at one time provided by the partner, if not in reality, then at least through an implied promise for its eventual fulfillment. Now because of its failure to be provided, which is usually accompanied by painful expressions of affective states represented as complaints and unhappiness with the partner, the therapist is able to hear the failure of selfobject relating. It is in the exploration of the selfdyad, by investigating its origins and its vicissitudes, including a careful exploration of those unconscious needs that were at one time present in the couple's "in love" subjectivity, along with its periodic successes throughout the history of the partnership, where important discoveries will be made about each partner's original selfobject vulnerabilities—those needs that the partner implicitly "promised" to provide, but which are now withheld.

These painful affective states, although played out in a myriad of ways in the consulting room, fundamentally represent what is frequently considered to be one of Kohut's most original contributions to our field. According to Kohut, when the self experiences injury, narcissistic rage is unleashed, which then provides the beginning point for a wide range of subsequent experiences, including the potential for destructive behaviors that may follow, all represented within a constellation of aggression, hurt, anger, and disappointment. Furthermore, many, if not all of these reactions and behaviours are subsequently experienced by the partner as a threatened sense of self, carrying with it the potential for a further loss of its vitality and cohesion.

This conceptualisation of narcissistic rage, I think, accounts for many of the complicating aspects of couple therapy, one of which is the frequent observation that individuals within their problematic relationships often perpetuate their attacks on the other through variations of revenge and retaliation, thus continuing what seem to be endless cycles of destructive projective identification. From this perspective these cyclical and problematic interactions, which are often ignited by criticism and anger, or sometimes simply an expressed wish for the partner to be different, often evoke in the partner the very reaction that is most unwanted. These behaviours can be seen as the partner's effort, albeit usually futile, to acquire what was at one time promised, but which is now experienced as denied. Here narcissistic rage and its unique representation can be seen as the individual's attempt to restore the selfdyad and its capacity to provide crucial selfobject relating, which in the beginning of the relationship was experienced as fulfilled.

A model for treatment

Within this section I will provide a bulleted model for the goals of treatment, which summarises the foregoing ideas pertaining to the selfdyad and its centrality in the organisation of the intimate couple. In some ways this model for working is not unique, as I believe that well-conducted psychodynamically oriented couple therapy may always incorporate some aspect of this roadmap, although not necessarily conceptualised by the therapist in the way that I describe it. Furthermore, this structure, I hope, is general and superordinate enough where many kinds of interventions can be incorporated, depending upon the therapist's personal style of working and the special needs of the patient-couple. The range of appropriate interventions, I contend, is then wide. It may include interpretations and reconstructions of a more familiar sort—those that are perhaps best known to the psychoanalytically informed clinician, clarifications, reflections, and empathic statements about internal experience, questions, but also teaching and edifying comments, the providing of support and structure, corrective remarks, the giving of assignments, and even behavioural/prescriptive interventions. What is essential to this way of working, however, is an understanding of the selfdyad by exploring and highlighting for the couple the ways in which its original selfobject functions are no longer provided, but which must now be restored or remodeled in some manner.

The following guidelines for the therapy process then are presented as scaffolding upon which many kinds of interventions can then be applied, all in the service of assisting the couple toward a revision of the selfdyad into a more affirming and functioning unit.

- To restore or remodel the selfdyad such that the selves of both partners are more fully supported and affirmed within the relationship.
- By enhancing the couple's selfobject functioning.
- Through interpretation and other necessary interventions, including the historical investigation of the dynamic origins of the selfdyad.
- While showing the couple how their original desires and needs for transformation were at one time repaired or solved by creating a unique partnership—the selfdyad.
- With a partner who at one time provided a complementary part of the self and essential affirmation through selfobject functioning.

A case of sexual disjunction: Teresa and Edward

Sexual disjunctions, the chronic disagreement on the frequency or preferred sexual activities can appear with such salience for the couple that one or both partners can experience an erosion of the self, and even a collapse of the self. Teresa and Edward, a couple in their thirties called for a consultation expressing considerable urgency to be seen. Teresa had become dissatisfied with Edward's incessant demands for sex, while simultaneously becoming afraid of his anger at those times she asserted herself by refusing him. Prior to marriage both Edward and Teresa had essentially agreed on most sexual matters. As time went on, however, Edward's requests seemed to turn into demands, while Teresa began to feel that these demands now represented "something compulsive, like a sexual addiction". Here Teresa added, "Edward, sometimes it seems like you are a machine … It's like I'm not there with you … it's weird … like you are masturbating … sometimes he doesn't even ejaculate …" What prompted the initial consultation was Edward's verbal and nearly physical tirade against her, presaged, however, by months of incessant arguing about issues that centred around power, control, anger, and mutuality.

Early in their marriage Edward and Teresa had a mutually satisfying sexual relationship, with a quality and a frequency upon which they both agreed. Struck by Teresa's depiction of Edward's sexual advances as "something compulsive … it's like I'm not there … like you are masturbating …" which sounded vaguely dissociative, I invited Edward to tell me about the disappointment he had been experiencing in their sexual relationship. Clearly for Edward the changes in their sexual relationship seemed to represent a betrayal of their original "agreement". Tentatively at first, but then gradually picking up the tempo, Edward began to speak shamefully about his background. He had been raised in an isolated rural area in a commune in which it was customary for the adult males to have multiple sexual partners, some of whom were referred to as wives. Edward's mother was one of four wives. Edward's father was a respected but also feared leader of the community, and one whom Edward also feared.

Within the community it was common practice for both boys and girls to be recruited into a kind of "sexual indoctrination", where they were required to have sex with the male leaders of the organisation. Edward too had been indoctrinated. But his mother, to whom Edward had been quite close, and who was known to be an ardent opponent of these practices, secretly arranged for Edward, at age fifteen, to escape from the community to live with an aunt and uncle who would ultimately raise him. It was later at college when Edward and Teresa first met, Teresa being the first person to whom Edward would tell his story. Edward swore her to secrecy that the details of his life would never be revealed. His background was never again discussed, as they established their lives together in a way that was at first mutually fulfilling, including sexually.

Teresa grew up as a first born child, having three younger brothers. She was raised in an intact family, her mother recently dying of complications related to her long-standing multiple sclerosis. Because of her mother's crippling illness, Teresa had been a parentified child, the main caretaker of her younger siblings, her mother, and her father. She recalled, somewhat stoically, that she had no childhood and virtually no teenage years as a result. It was here that she said, "But I don't resent it because it gave me a real sense of responsibility and purpose, including what it means to care for others". Her statement resounded within me, as it already provided crucial insight about her needs to be needed, while also representing a disavowal of her own needs for individuation and autonomy.

Couple therapy was recommended, supplemented by individual sessions for both in which we were able to eventually work through Edward's sexual trauma. Through the course of therapy we explored his shame, as well as his anger toward his father for the aggression and assault upon him. Furthermore, we were able to learn that within the regressive atmosphere of the sexual relationship with his wife, there was now a return of the repressed (Fairbairn, 1944), in which forcing Teresa into intercourse became a present day revision of the force that was once inflicted upon him. Now he treated Teresa as he had once been treated, with no freedom for the autonomous expression of her self needs.

Through patient and careful work Teresa came to accept her disavowed needs for self expression, which had been previously rationalised by her as appropriately teaching her "responsibility and purpose". Through their co-constructed selfdyad, Teresa had been able to locate her needy self within Edward—the part of her that had been lost in childhood, including those adolescent experiences that foreshadowed individuation and a development of personal agency.

Here we can observe that Edward and Teresa's selfdyad had been founded on an unconscious agreement that Teresa would take care of Edward, as she sensed early in their relationship his profound sense of vulnerability and his need for her affirming presence. Similarly, Edward located within Teresa a part of his self that required rescue by a loving and sacrificing woman who would once again protect his masculinity by complying with all his sexual demands.

Finally, I will say a word about specific techniques used in working with Edward and Teresa. Although the outcome of their treatment was generally positive, yielding what I felt was a good long-term prognosis, the actual ingredients of the work were not without complication. There were several occasions, for example, when Edward experienced more disorganised functioning during the times that he was recalling and working through the details of his sexual trauma. Here I often provided considerable direct support of Edward, while I also encouraged and even coached Teresa in providing the necessary support for Edward's self functioning. There were other times that I encouraged and structured ways for them to interact at home with one another, while at the same time I steered them away from too quickly resuming their sexual relationship, intending to protect their intimacy before they had sufficiently worked through their respective issues and regained a sense of safety with one another. Similarly, there were times that I confronted Edward about his controlling qualities, while actively interpreting the residue of his aggressive and abusive father. On other occasions, often at times the couple appeared stuck, regressed, and sometimes mutually hopeless, I moved into a more didactic-educative mode in which I spoke, sometimes quasi lecturing, about the fundamental importance of the expression of self needs in marriage, to assist them in better supporting each other's autonomy without resentment.

In summary, we know that it is always easier to speak about theory, principles, and the techniques of our therapies, than it is to implement them with consistent skill within the consulting room. The selfdyad, provides a construct that integrates existing psychoanalytic ideas, especially those from an object relations perspective with those from a self psychological perspective. Furthermore, I believe that it is invaluable as a way of organising and understanding what occurs within the complex internal network of the couple's intimacy, not simply in the beginning of the relationship, but continuing throughout the partnership while insuring the vitality and the enriching qualities of the relationship for both individuals.

References

Dicks, H. (1993). *Marital Tensions: Clinical Studies Toward a Psychological Theory of Interaction*. London: Karnac. (Original work published in 1967.)
Erikson, E. (1950). *Childhood and Society*. NewYork: W. W. Norton.
Fairbairn, W. R. D. (1944). Endopsychic structure considered in terms of object-relationships. *International Journal of Psychoanalysis*, 25: 70–93.
Kohut, H. (1971). *The Analysis of the Self*. New York: International Universities Press.
Kohut, H. (1977). *The Restoration of the Self*. New York: International Universities Press.
Ringstrom, P. (1994). An intersubjective approach to conjoint therapy. In: A. Goldberg (Ed.), *A Decade of Progress, Progress in Self Psychology*. Vol. 10 (pp. 159–182). Hillsdale, NJ: Analytic Press.
Scharff, D. E. & Scharff, J. (1991). *Object Relations Couple Therapy*. Northvale, NJ: Jason Aronson.
Scharff, D. E. & Scharff, J. S. (2011). *The Interpersonal Unconscious*. Northvale, NJ: Jason Aronson.

Stolorow, R., Brandchaft, B. & Atwood, G. (1987). *Psychoanalytic Treatment: An Intersubjective Approach.* Hillsdale, NJ: Analytic Press.

Winnicott, D. W. (1965). *The Maturational Process and the Facilitating Environment.* New York: International Universities Press.

Wolf, E. (1988). *Treating the Self.* New York: Guilford.

Zeitner, R. M. (2003). Obstacles for the psychoanalyst in the practice of couple therapy. *Psychoanalytic Psychology,* 20, 2: 348–362.

Zeitner, R. M. (2012). *Self Within Marriage: The Foundation for Lasting Relationships.* New York: Routledge.

CHAPTER NINE

Dreams in analytic couple therapy

Jill Savege Scharff and David E. Scharff

Consulting to and supervising recently trained individual psychotherapists, we have found that many of them have heard that the dream is the royal road to the unconscious. Yet they do not know how to work with dreams, even though there are many thoughtful papers on the subject, beginning with Freud's *Interpretation of Dreams* (1900b). Little wonder then that analytic couple therapists may not know how to work with dreams in couple therapy. They tend to focus on the context of the couple relationship, the projective identificatory system of the relationship, the roots of its dynamics traced to family history, and the expression of mother–infant and oedipal dynamics in the couple's intimate life. Preferring these routes to understanding unconscious dynamics, analytic couple therapists too often overlook the analysis of dreams because they do not realise its power to "turn a page" in the couple's treatment (Quinodoz, 2002) and its value in treating sexual, marital, and family trauma issues (D. Scharff & J. Scharff 1991, 2004; J. Scharff & D. Scharff, 1994).

So we will go back to the beginning and extrapolate from individual dream interpretation and mechanisms of dream construction drawn from Freud, and then move on to an object relations approach to the functions of dreaming and principles of dream interpretation. We will pay particular attention to couples' resistances to having, reporting, and working with dreams and we will give equal importance to their therapists' resistances to engaging in dream interpretation in analytic couple therapy. We will conclude with a clinical illustration taken from David E. Scharff's work with the Smith couple in analytic couple therapy.

Dreams from before Freud to object relations

In the early twentieth century dream analysis was synonymous with psychoanalysis. In the twenty-first century however, the topic of dream analysis has taken a back seat. Dreams have gone from having an overvalued, exceptional position and being subjected to a rather deadly, painstaking analysis to being mentioned only in passing, and more recently being commonly totally neglected (Greenson, 1993). Admittedly there are many ways to reach understanding of unconscious processes, for instance by focusing on projective identification, intersubjectivity, here-and-now enactments, and psychosomatic and conversion phenomena. But dream interpretation is particularly useful on the path to truth and breakthrough. It remains the cornerstone of analytic work. Dreams provide access to preconscious wish fulfillment and unconscious conflict. They are powerfully evocative of passion and creativity (Sharpe, 1937). Yet not all couples are willing to bring in their dreams for shared work and not all therapists are eager to encourage dream work. Losing access to dreams is a major loss in analytic couple therapy. So it is worthwhile to consider the resistance to dream work.

Resistance to working with dreams in analytic couple therapy

Resistance to dreaming may occur at various levels. There may be resistance to remembering a dream, or reporting a dream that is remembered, or associating to a dream that is reported. Resistance may lie in the couple, the individual dreamer, the partner of the dreamer, or in the couple therapist. We need to name the resistance and work to understand its source and interpret the underlying anxiety about engaging in analytic couple therapy. Those who claim not to remember dreams, or indeed not to have dreams at all, may be so traumatised that the dream space has collapsed. Some may simply not want to be open, while others may actively hold dreams in contempt. For instance one husband believed that dreaming was child's play, material of no evidentiary value. He resisted the psychic reality of the dream. The individual or the partners who have dreams but do not report them may have calculated that it is better to keep silent about dreams that might reveal conflict in the couple or with the therapist, or a specific fantasy that must be denied. Those who tell dreams but do not contribute their associations are more likely resistant to a specific insight that is hinted at in the dream or to a transference that is about to emerge. The couple may be resisting the possibility of progress in the treatment because of fear of change and growth and wishes to hold on to the therapist in preference to terminating and functioning independently as a couple. They may resist a profusion of dreams as they do the possibility of overwhelming sexual passion. The commonest source of resistance, shared by patient, couple and therapist, is the fear of deepening engagement in the transference-countertransference dialectic. If we can make these resistances conscious, we may help the couple gain access to their dream life, and to its value in therapy.

Therapists' resistances to working with dreams

Resistance to dream work lies not only in the couple, but may also arise in the therapist. Our resistance to working with dreams is manifest in various levels of our dream work. We may be totally unable to remember the dream because the manifest content alone has been too much for us to hold in mind. If we have not been trained to work with dreams, we may remember the story of the dream, but may not know what to do with what follows. We may be unable or unwilling to listen to and gather associations that will lead us to the latent content of the dream. When the dream has a strong impact and hits too close to home, we may be unable to detect and use our countertransference to help us reach deeper into the dream experience. Then it is useful to review the nature of our resistance and what it protects us from. We turn to the work of Meltzer (1984) who drew attention to various fears that may afflict therapists who avoid working with dreams: Fear of invasion, fear of confusion, and fear of impotence.

Fear of invasion

The moment that a patient or couple announces that they have had a dream, a sense of excitement builds about what will be revealed. As the dream is told, a feeling of intimacy develops and adds to the excitement about what will be created in the collaboration of dreamer, partner, and therapist. There is a sense of anticipation. Powerful images are projected in the telling, and these may be profoundly upsetting or even paralysing to the therapist who feels anxious about the content, the manner of telling, and the ability to contain the experience.

Fear of confusion

The dream is in essence a puzzle. Its manifest content is disjointed, nonsensical, and fantastical. It is usually not a coherent narrative, but one that skips about from image to image. Even if the surface narrative seems coherent, the underlying meaning may not be. The therapist may become anxious about feeling that he cannot solve the puzzle. He feels confused, perhaps overwhelmed. This can occur because the therapist does not know how to listen to the dream by cueing in to the unconscious theme revealed in the couple's associations. Instead he focuses compulsively on each element, trying to wrest the latent meaning from the manifest content. It may simply be too soon for the dream to reveal its meaning to the couple or to the therapist because the therapeutic relationship is not ready to deal with the hidden reality of the latent content of the dream.

Fear of impotence

When the meaning of a dream remains obscure, the therapist may feel inept, weak, ignorant, or guilty. The therapist who is afraid of feeling impotent wants to avoid this anxious reaction when she is faced with an apparently nonsensical dream. She wants to feel in control of the powerful longings and fears that members of a couple feel toward each other and toward her. At the next level, the therapist's facility with dream interpretation may penetrate the unconscious but fail to convince the couple of the meaning of their dream communication. Again the therapist feels inept. To maintain control, she discourages the sharing of dreams, which only impoverishes the therapeutic potential of the session and paradoxically actually does render her impotent.

Facing these fears is the first step towards understanding why a couple is not working with dreams. To build confidence in proceeding with dream interpretation, we need to return to study the first principles of dream interpretation, beginning with Freud.

Principles of dream interpretation

Before Freud, dreams had been thought to consist of a series of symbols of universal meaning. Dreams were analysed according to a code in which each element had a particular significance. We might call this the decoding approach to dreams. Freud brought to dream interpretation a dynamic approach. He used the psychology of neuroses and hysteria to understand dreams and at the same time he used interpretation of dreams to understand neuroses and hysteria. When bringing his own and his individual patient's dreams under self-examination, he too might assign meaning to certain elements. For instance, in the Dora case, he assumed that a jewel box represented female genitalia (Freud, 1905). However, he extended the explanatory power of dream interpretation by including Dora's associations to key elements in the dream in order to reveal the personal significance of the dream.

Freud was insistent that a dream cannot be properly analysed in isolation. Even with full access to the associations, the analyst who arrives at an easy interpretation of the dream's apparent meaning must accept that beyond that there is darkness. Each dream is part of a process of discovery, and no interpretation is ever complete. Remembering this is reassuring to the therapist in moments of puzzlement over a dream. Still, we need more knowledge to guide our understanding of dream communication, and so turn to the basics of dream construction (Freud, 1900c).

A dream is a final common pathway for denied desire and fear of desire to reach consciousness and be acknowledged and dealt with. But to meet the demands of the censor, the path must be hard to follow. The manifest content of the dream reported to us has many elements woven into a story or series of images that may hide the latent content. Whether it seems easy to follow or not, the dream has been constructed using a series of mechanisms to provide an outlet for the dream thoughts connected to the repressed desires and conflicts over them, and at the same time keep them disguised. The main mechanisms are condensation and displacement, reversal and symbolisation. Then the question is "What lies behind this manifest content, and what mechanisms have led to the construction of this simple narrative?"

Mechanisms of dream construction

Condensation

In condensation, the dream-thoughts are compressed into a few elements, each one connected to extensive dream thoughts in the broad categories of wish and fear, the choice of each element being multiply determined. Let's imagine that a forty-two-year-old mother of two children begins to tell a dream set in a railway station. She has dreamed that she is too late to catch a train and awakes terribly anxious about it even though she could still catch the bus. This scenario could connect to dream thoughts of fear of separation, wish to leave her husband, wish to reconnect with her older child who has left home, wish for travel to unknown destinations, longing to return home, wish to run away from situations or unconscious conflict—or all of these and many more, all compressed into one multiply determined scene. We cannot tell what the dream is about until we have connected the manifest content to the latent conflict.

Composition and identification to create a composite figure or collective figures

A composite dream figure represents disagreeable or arousing aspects of two or more figures that have these aspects in common and are difficult to confront individually. Say that in the dream the woman asks the stationmaster for a refund, and then yells at him when he rudely ignores her. The figure of the stationmaster may be a composite of her feelings for her father, her husband, and her male couple therapist.

Collective dream figures express the same common element. The collective figure obscures the identity of the particular person whose disagreeable or arousing aspect is the source of the dreamer's conflict. For instance a number of passengers might all express disapproval at the woman's outburst, the action of the collective figure of a group of passengers representing transference to the feared disapproval of one important person, the couple therapist who is a stickler for beginning a session on time.

Displacement, distortion, and disguise

Because of censorship of unacceptable wishes that must be denied, indifferent experiences with a "*weak* charge of intensity" substitute for psychically significant unacceptable ones with an intense charge (Freud, 1900a, p. 177). For example, the woman of forty-two who already has teenaged children and who dreams of missing the bus may have displaced anxiety about a missed period and the accompanying fear of a problem pregnancy, which she has unconsciously displaced onto a minor issue so as not to worry herself and her husband consciously about the possibility of having to face the responsibilities of having a late baby, or she may be reluctant to face the end of her reproductive years. If the dreamer were a woman with no children, the dream might express her feeling that she has missed the opportunity for motherhood (the train) even though her other option of work outside the house is adequate for a fulfilled life (the bus).

Reversal

The opposite of the feared wish is presented instead of the feared wish itself. The dream denies the wish to avoid the journey. Say that the woman realises that she is naked on the platform. She notices the horror on the faces of other women passengers and feels shame. The dream process has reversed her wish to exhibit herself and her repressed homosexual desire to be loved and admired by a woman, a desire that she had to deny because she wanted to remain with her husband.

Symbolisation

An object is selected to represent a repressed sexual wish. For instance, the speed and noise of the train might refer to the rush to orgasm, the length of the train to the penis, the tunnel to the vagina, and so on. I say "might" because symbols do not carry universal meaning. The same symbols may or may not carry the same meaning from one dream to another in the same person. The meaning of a symbol to one member of a couple may or may not have the same meaning to the spouse.

Dramatisation

The narrative of the dream is enacted in the telling of it. For example the woman who dreamt of missing her train arrives late to her session and talks fast as if to catch up, but she beats around the bush and misses the opportunity to have a full, satisfactory experience.

Functions of dreams and dreaming

Before Freud, the purpose of a dream was widely thought to be predictive. The Biblical figure Joseph has a dream that warns of famine. With each element of the dream imagery given a symbolic value, the dream was thought to provide a vision of the future that determined political and personal decisions. Freud saw things differently. For Freud, a dream is a compromise between an infantile wish that seeks expression and reality that opposes it. The dream evacuates overload of drive pressure and repairs the damage from encroachment by daily eruptions of psychic tension caused by the threat of reawakened infantile conflict that seeks to return from repression. In this way, it provides a bridge between body and mind, but it also links past and present.

Freud said that dreaming is necessary to protect sleep and allow the body to rest and recover from the strains of the day (Freud, 1900b). Following this line of thought, Palombo (1978) added that dreaming allows for the daily sorting of experience so that it can be connected to prior experience and to long-term memory. Anzieu thought that the dream protects the sleeping psyche by creating a psychic envelope for the daily refurbishing of the executive part of the mind (Anzieu, 1993). Anzieu also described the dream as a membrane or a film on which images are developed. These images plug the holes caused by daily eruptions that puncture the membrane, and they reweave what has come unraveled in the daytime. According to Gamill (1993), the dream provides a shield against the pain of unsatisfied infantile desires and residues from the experiences of the day. The dream brings imaginary satisfaction to id, ego and superego. He thinks of the dream as a nightly partner, a relic of the taking in of goodness and comfort from the breast.

Fairbairn said that dreams, like shorts of a longer film, give a picture of the whole personality (Fairbairn, 1952). For Fairbairn, the structure of the dream reveals the structure of the personality. Segal (1993) agreed with that view, and added that each dream is also a part of the working through in analysis. Bion (1962) looked at dreams from a different vertex than Freud. Whereas Freud thought of dreams as a set of mental mechanisms, such as condensation and displacement, used by the sleeping mind to present conflict in a disguised way that could permit access to conscious elaboration, Bion thought that dreaming allowed conscious experience to move into the unconscious level where it could undergo psychological work (Ogden, 2004a). We think that dreaming delivers communications about conflict and experience to various levels of the self for conscious and unconscious individual and joint elaboration by significant others such as intimate partners or therapists. We see a dream as an interpersonal event of conscious and unconscious proportions, a comment on work already done and a way to move forward to new areas of exploration in couple therapy.

Drawing from Fairbairn and Segal, we think that dream images run like animated film sequences that are reviewed, rewound, edited, and projected when shown in the telling to an individual therapist, or to an intimate partner, or to a couple therapist in analytic couple therapy. Dreams are expressions of the link among dreamer and significant others and couple therapist. This link evolves in the process of dreaming and in the telling, associating to, and interpreting of the dream (D. Scharff & J. Scharff, 2011).

Dynamic approaches to dream work: decoding, hunting, unraveling, reverie, and gathering

In antiquity, the *decoding* approach read the dream elements as universally accepted signs of what was to come. In Freud's dynamic approach, he looked for the individual significance of each element of a dream and its connection to the individual dream thoughts in the present and infantile wishes from the past. We might call this a *hunting* approach. Freud noted all the elements of a dream and any fragments of dreams. He used the day residue to connect to the manifest content of the dream, and worked from superficial associations to deep associations. He noted the degree of incoherence or coherence of the dream. He sometimes asked the patient to repeat the dream, and then he attended to small differences in the re-telling so as to detect weak spots in the dream's capacity to disguise the latent content. He knew that no dream interpretation was ever complete, and so he often revisited dreams, or continued analysing one dream at length over time (Freud, 1900a).

It was Greenson (1993) who emphasised that the dream itself is an association to what has gone before. He thought of the dream as the free-est of associations. Analysing the dream looks beyond the story and imagery of the dream (the manifest content) to the form, the manner of its telling, and the associations in order to detect the latent content (consisting of affect, conflict, and childhood memories). We look for what is hidden, how it is hidden, and why it must be hidden. We might think of this as the *unraveling* approach. Contemporary object relations theorists approach dream analysis by entering a state of dreaming while awake. The analyst listens to his own dream as a way of receiving the patient's dream and understanding it (Bion, 1962; Ogden, 2004a; Ferro, 2009). We might regard this as the *reverie* approach.

When we listen to dreams we drift with the dream, sometimes taking notes, sometimes not. Sometimes it becomes the focus of the session, sometimes not. We usually do not ask for associations. We believe that whatever topics the patient turns to next are the associations to the dream, no matter how disconnected from the dream they appear to be. So we simply wait to see what comes next. We also notice what comes to mind from previous sessions and earlier dreams as we listen to the session in which the present dream appears. We call this the *gathering* approach. In our work with couples, we employ the same general approach, except that in this case we listen to the dream as a product of the relationship in treatment, and we work with associations from both partners.

Working with dreams in analytic couple therapy

Working with individuals in analysis, Freud found that "the interpretation of dreams is the royal road to a knowledge of the unconscious activities of the mind" (Freud, 1900c, p. 608). Dream analysis reveals underlying conflict and makes it available for interpretation and understanding. In couple therapy, that royal road is a dual carriageway. Working with spouses or intimate partners in couple therapy, we hold that the individual's dream is a product of the couple and of their relationship with their therapist. We begin with the individual's dream and accept that individual's associations as we would in individual therapy. Then we wait for, look for, or ask for, the partner's associations, not to interpret the dream as an individual production, but to build a shared experience of the dream. We understand it as a communication between and from the couple, not just an individual production. We use the dream to arrive at shared insight about the couple, the individual partners, and their relationship to the therapist.

We connect the dream to the present-day setting and current ways of thinking about experience, and we also explore its connection to the past that cannot be left behind. In the present role relationships displayed in the dream, we see the past imagoes. We are always looking beyond the manifest content to the latent content, and we do this by gathering associations and tuning in to unconscious themes in the associations. We may have a hunch as to what the dream is about. If so, it makes sense to go with our intuition, and then look for corroborating elements. We attend to the details. We resonate with the senses shown in the dream, and evoked in us—sight, sound, smell, touch, colour, tone, and feeling. As Sharpe (1937) puts it, we need to emotionally inhabit the dream. We also examine various dream elements and deconstruct the processes of condensation, displacement, symbolisation, and so on by which they have been created, in order to understand what they represent. We look for dramatisation of the dream, that is to say we may notice that the couple's behaviour around the telling of the dream in the session enacts the theme of the dream. We look at our countertransference as we ask ourselves, "What does this dream bring to mind? How does the dream make me feel?"

We also note the effect of the dream on us, and ask ourselves various questions about that as we try to deduce the unconscious purpose that the dream serves. Does the dream appear to be a gift of love, a criticism, a contradiction that proves us wrong? Does it seek to avert our wrath by placating us? Does it try to satisfy an imagined demand from us, or to put a demand on us? Is the dream a diversion, an entertainment to fill the hour and keep us from our devotion to the task of analysing the couple relationship? Does the dreamer present a compact dream that requires patient unpacking, or a long disconnected story that defeats memory and constricts the time for associations? Does the dream provide another angle on the couple's life and move the therapy process forward or does it seem to be a way of avoiding everyday reality? Does the individual's dream function to the benefit of the couple, or does its length, content, and manner of telling exclude the partner's associations and obliterate the couple, as if to redefine couple therapy as an individual treatment? Sometimes the couple will withhold a dream they both know about until the end of the session, when it is too late to work on it. This is frustrating for the eager therapist, much as the mother feels when a toddler withholds a urethral or fecal product. The exercise of power over the therapist is a way of controlling fear. The dream may represent potency of a urethral or anal nature, as a defence against, or prelude to, discussion of sexual potency in the couple relationship.

Clinical example

Sandy and Mike Smith asked David E. Scharff to work with them in analytic couple therapy. They had each been in individual therapy with good therapists, but their relationship had not improved, and they worried that they might face divorce. David will now describe his work with them.

Mike and Sandy Smith are in their mid thirties, both professionals, with two children, a girl age four and a half and a boy age two. Mike is extremely anxious and compulsive, and frequently puts Sandy down for failing to carry through on something or check on things—like feeding the fish. Sandy has lost feelings for Mike.

Sandy came to the marriage from a family of three, with one brother and a handicapped sister all living with her divorced mother. Mike came from a family of three boys, with overbearing parents. Mike's mother doted on him, but her criticism and denigration of Sandy and of her other sons left even her idealised son Mike anxious lest she turn on him. Sandy, a high achiever, nevertheless could not earn her mother-in-law's respect. In relation to her, Sandy felt as she had done as a teenager when she could not get her own mother's respect for her academic and athletic success because of her mother's preoccupation with Sandy's handicapped sister.

Over the first five months of therapy, Mike did improve his side of the marriage. He became better around the house, less absent, and less inclined to take her for granted. Despite these changes, Sandy's anger at him hardened over the months and did not yield to interpretation. I wondered if this was a stuck feature of her depression. I suggested that she consider a trial of medication, which she reluctantly agreed to. However, within a few days of going on an anti-depressant of the selective serotonin reuptake inhibitor class, she suddenly became acutely suicidal for the first time in her life, with a recurrent urge to drive off a bridge. She called me and her psychopharmacologist, stopped the medication, and immediately was no longer suicidal. Obviously Sandy had had a biochemical reaction to the medication, but coincidentally the angry fix on Mike now became amenable to interpretation. Fortunately Sandy had a dream that showed me the unconscious dynamic at work at that time in the marriage and in the transference:

> I was at home with Mike. He had his dead grandmother propped up in the living room. He said that he had to leave, and I should stay with her. While he was gone the dead grandmother, who was just a stuffed sack figure, opened her eyes. I wanted to say to somebody, "But she opened her eyes!" Mike came back, and I said to him, "You don't believe me, but she's not dead." Then he dragged the dead grandmother into the bedroom, and I went, too, and he left again. The furniture was arranged so I couldn't get out of the room even though the room wasn't locked. The dead grandmother opened her eyes again and smirked at me. I didn't want to be with this "not-dead dead person." I kept telling him and he wouldn't believe me, and then Mike's brother came in, and said, "*I believe you, even though she's only doing

it to you, and I know she won't open her eyes when I'm here. But I believe you." I was very grateful to Mike's brother for believing me, but Mike was on the run and had left.

Sandy said that Mike often left her with his mother during visits and that he cannot believe how awful she is to Sandy. Mike said that his mother apparently does things to Sandy that she does not do when he is there and does not do to him. I said that Mike's mother is the dead mummy that Sandy gets locked in with while he runs free of it. I wondered what kind of death grip on Mike's mother could account for a destructive feeling that is reversed in her doting on Mike and unleashed in tormenting Sandy. Sandy added that the image of the dead grandmother also echoed her suicidal feelings, disembodied ideas of driving off a bridge, which Mike could not believe.

The dream seemed to say that Mike didn't believe Sandy about her experience with his mother, the deadness of her feelings for him, and the reaction to medication I had arranged for. I said that the dream also expressed the feeling that, having sent Sandy for medication, I did not believe her descriptions of life with Mike, and so I had left her with the threat of emotional death in a relationship she was locked into.

This dream has plenty of symbolism to keep its meaning hidden, but it is also somewhat transparent to Mike and Sandy because of the therapy that preceded it, and so it makes sense to them on the surface as a story about the effect of Mike's mother on their relationship. Sandy associates to the dream first in an easy, non-resistant way, and then Mike joins in to augment her association. In this way the couple inhabits the dream. Then the therapist is able to join in the conversation about the role of the mother and link it to the couple's shared experience of deadness and destructiveness. Linking the day residue of the behaviour of Mike's actual mother with their shared internal object relationships and the unconscious links between them leads to further associations to Sandy's recent experience with Mike and, in the transference, to me.

In the beginning of the session a few weeks later, we discussed Mike's wish to have another child and Sandy's fear of it at her age because her younger sister, born when her mother was older, is handicapped. Sandy said that the family they have is intact with two healthy children, so why tempt fate? Then she told her dream:

> Mike and I are in a new house. Two of his top teeth fell out. I said, "There's a hot stuff dentist in the neighbourhood. Put your teeth in milk." Meanwhile, we went to sleep, and nearly all of Mike's top teeth fell out. Mike was unfazed about the loss of his teeth, but mine were all falling out too, until there were only two left. I was panicky and said, "Mike we have to find a dentist to put my teeth back." He said, "OK. The dentist is eating out at a restaurant." We drove to the restaurant in a place like the Outer Banks with the restaurant over the water. As we were walking towards it I fell in some yucky water. I managed to keep my last two teeth in though. We went in and found the dentist, and he agreed to help me with my teeth—after he finished dinner. I looked at Mike and said, "The new house we're living in has mould that rots my teeth out. We have to move."

In association, the couple talked about looking for a new house. Sandy took the dream loss of her teeth as a sign they shouldn't move. Mike said, "The old house isn't happy, so Sandy looks for a new house, or reorganises the rooms in the current house." (Interpreting the house as a symbol for their relationship, Mike collaborates in decoding the symbolic elements of the dream.)

I said that in the dream, Sandy felt afraid that she was losing her bite. (Here David is interpreting the teeth as a symbol of aggression). Mike said that recently when Sandy was screaming at him for not speaking up against his mother who was trying to impose a visit on them, she had apologised quickly and calmed down. She agreed that it was wrong to scream. Mike then blamed her for not speaking up and not helping him to stop giving in to his parents. (Both Sandy and Mike are giving further associations to the dream, showing that they are not in a resistant phase, but are adding to our shared capacity to understand the emotional content of the dream.) I said the dream was about both of them losing their ability to speak up. I noticed that when Sandy lost her teeth, she also lost interest in Mike's dental emergency, and was only able to look at her own distress. (Here is Sandy's narcissistic preoccupation dramatised within the couple relationship.) Sandy agreed that in the dream and in life when she panics, she's so worried about falling apart, she can't think about him. (Sandy again adds to David's interpretation, exhibiting trust in the treatment and using the exchange to inhabit the conflict that is shown in the dream.)

I said that I was the hotshot dentist, taking care of myself and my own oral needs before helping them (David interprets the transference significance of the dentist, drawing partly on his countertransference feeling that he obviously values the dream so much that they may feel he may care more about dreams than about them.) But in fact, they continue to say, they did talk it over and pulled things together by themselves this time.

Looking back on the session, Mike's losing his teeth brings to mind an image of toothless gums, which connects the dream to Mike's wish for another child. The falling out of the perfect set of teeth connects to Sandy's fear that another pregnancy would bring disorder, loss, and bodily ruin to the child and to the family. (David did not see this at the time of the session—an example of something still hidden in the dream and of things incompletely understood in any session or, indeed, in any treatment.)

In the next session, Sandy said the interpretation about the bite and loss of her sense of self had helped more than anything she could remember. She had another opportunity to lose her temper and her mind this week, but had held things together and was pleased that she could. Then Mike was able to be more responsive to her as well.

While the interpretation about the bite was not the only way of understanding the dream, it had spoken to an important issue in a way the couple could take in. So it had been part of the evolving link of the therapy that was moving things forward.

Four months later, Mike felt less anxious, and Sandy's anger had diminished. Mike reported a recurrent dream, which this time had a different ending. Although the relationship is improved, the dream shows that it is not enough.

> I'm going through replicas of old girlfriends and I have to find the person to marry. I go through one after another and they're not right, and I'm panicked that no one would seem right. Usually at the end of the dream I find Sandy and she is the right one, but this time I didn't find Sandy, so nobody was right.

I asked Mike for thoughts, and he said, "Sandy and I are getting along. We do what we have to do. Everything is going smoothly, but I don't feel loved."

Sandy said, "Mike, you were sick this week, and maybe I didn't fuss over you enough. I wonder if that felt bad to you."

Mike said, "No, I was very happy with how you treated me. I was glad you didn't really carp on it. I worry you will be critical if I get a virus when others don't catch it, or you'll get mad, say if I take too long to do something."

Sandy said, "Well, it's hard for you to feel loved when there's been so much anxiety and stress."

I said that I thought the dream was raising the question of whether each of them, not just Mike, felt loved. (David picks up on the theme of feeling unloved that speaks for both of them and that he has come to feel is central to the remaining work of couple therapy.)

Sandy said, "You know what made me very happy this week? He was home yesterday, and he said, 'I'm gonna do some of those jobs that have been sitting there waiting to be done.' He did them and that really made me feel cared about. That's when I feel more loving." She began to cry as she said, "I don't feel loved myself. I feel sometimes he's resentful or that he's only doing things because I make him. So, I don't feel loved, but when he does something like that, just a little something, then I feel much more loving."

I said, "There's less anxiety and less pain in your life, and the survival of your marriage isn't threatened. Now, whether you each can feel more fully loved and loving becomes the main question about the future quality of your marriage. That's what the dream is bringing us to."

Following this dream, Sandy and Mike continued to explore the obstacles to love and worked at maintaining a loving relationship. Eight months later, feeling that their relationship was sufficiently improved, they were thinking of stopping couple therapy. Then Sandy had a dream:

> I was in a boat with the family, and I was thrown over the side into the water. I was holding our four-year-old son, and a little reef shark pulled at my elbow. I was afraid it would make me drop my son. I asked Mike for help, and he said, "I'll be there in a minute."

The word "shark", sounding so like "Scharff", is a reference to transference fear of being eaten alive by David as he pulls at Sandy to deal with the deepest painful things that might throw her into deep water and leave her unable to hold her family together. This dream also has to be understood in relation to the couple's considering termination. It refers to their fear that David will drop them into deep water and not help even though help may suddenly be needed.

I said to Mike and Sandy that through this dream, they could show me that they were thinking of ending therapy not only because they were substantially better, but also because therapy was eating away at them. They accepted this interpretation, got over their fear, and decided to continue in therapy. Another eight months later, Sandy and Mike showed further improvement. They were getting along well, dealing with only minor difficulties from which they could recover in discussion together between sessions.

Mike reported a dream.

> I was in the house and there was an intruder in the kitchen, a woman with a knife. I'm bigger than the woman, so I wrestle the knife away from her. Then she seems to disappear. Someone, probably Sandy, bought generic orange juice, but what I like is Tropicana. I explode and throw the orange juice on the ground.

Sandy said that it was amazing that she too had had a dream about an intruder:

> I had left the bed to get some sleep because Mike was snoring. He came in to see why I had left. Just as he woke me up, I had a dream about a shadowy intruder somewhere in the house. This is a dream I've had all my life. In this version, the intruder didn't seem threatening, but it is still an intruder. We couldn't find out who it was. The bedroom that I had moved to is what we call "our haunted bedroom" because there are strange noises in it, and we can never figure out where they're coming from.

In association, Mike said that the woman and the orange juice theme seemed connected to his feeling that his mother refused him nutrients and attention, and the knife to his mother's cutting style. When he's condescending to Sandy, he feels on the one hand that he's being like his mother and on the other hand that she, like his mother, is not meeting his needs. I said that the uncanny coincidence of Sandy's dream about an intruder shows that the two of them share this unconscious image of the intruding mother, and yet in both cases the intrusion is less threatening than before.

In these paired dreams, Sandy and Mike show that their unconscious link reflects shared images that non-defensively convey their remaining areas of vulnerability and their wishes for mutual support and understanding. The dreams show an enhanced capacity for useful condensation and symbolic representation. The thinness of the disguise in the construction of the dreams allows us to see Mike and Sandy's shared openness to exploration, and their trust in each other and in therapeutic process.

The following week the couple continued work on the dream. Suddenly, surprisingly, inexplicably, Sandy's mother took offence at something that happened over Sandy's handicapped sister, and cut off speaking to her children. The rejection hurt Sandy. Now she had only Mike to turn to. This incident, and the dreams, increased Sandy's need to recognise and understand the less evident cutting aspect of her own mother. Now we could see that both mothers—not only Mike's—could be self-centred and hurtful. When Sandy came up against the rejecting mother in Mike's mother and the hurtful potential in her own mother, as they re-emerged in Mike, he seemed to take on the rejecting mother for both of them.

Mike asked, "Do you know what my mother did last visit? She left a knife with the blade up on the kitchen counter where it could hurt someone, and although I asked her not to, she did it again."

Sandy said, "Don't you get it Mike? The knife was there in the visit, and then it was in your dream!"

I said, "Yes, your mother bothered you with her self-centred intrusiveness and unresponsiveness during the visit. That's how she cuts into you both. Those aspects of a rejecting mother are what you find in each other at times of hurt. You are now aware of how and why you may intrude on each other and hurt each other."

"That's it!" said Sandy. "Oh, I love this dream analysis stuff. It's really neat!"

In this final example, we see how the day residue that stimulated the choice of imagery in the dream emerges in the following session, and helps the couple explore the aspect of their link that has to do with emotional cutting. We also see that they have become so adept at conducting the analytic process, almost on their own, that they are now ready for a planned termination.

Conclusion

Dream analysis in couple therapy is the royal road to understanding both individual unconscious conflict and the interpersonal unconscious of the couple relationship. Dreams reveal the internal object relationship structures and their interpenetration in the joint marital personality. Dreams are bearers of the link to experiences in the families of origin through which unconscious and conscious patterns of behaviour and perception affect the couple. Dreams reveal the transference from each individual partner and from the couple as an entity. They reveal infantile elements in the transference. They elaborate on the theme of the work. They may provide a clue to a conscious secret or an unconscious trauma or disavowed idea. Ultimately, they both drive and document the evolution of growth in analytic couple therapy.

The dream is a touchstone to unconscious conflict. It brings to light present-day ramifications of preconscious thought and shows us the psychic unity of the preconscious and the unconscious. It conveys the evolution of the link between the partners and its expression among the partners, the couple, and therapist. It is a bridge between past and present, between body and mind, between individual and couple, between couple and therapist. Dreams reach into the unconscious underpinnings of individual emotional organisation, the affective structure of shared bonds, and the expression of various parts of the self that appear in relation to the loved one.

Rather than trying to be expert in dream interpretation, therapists will be more successful in work with dreams if we think of ourselves as interested listeners and facilitators of associations to the dream, not grand dream interpreters. Then we can enjoy a creative exploration and partnership with the couple as we look for clues that will lead to understanding. Above all, we relax into a dream state ourselves, a state in which we can access unconscious resonance with the themes of the dream and its relation to the therapeutic relationship and the process of the treatment.

References

Anzieu, D. (1993). The dream film. In: S. Flanders (Ed.), *The Dream Discourse Today* (pp. 137–150). London: Routledge.
Bion, W. R. (1962). *Learning from Experience*. London: Karnac.
Boyer, B. (1988). Thinking of the interview as if it were a dream. *Contemporary Psychoanalysis, 24*: 275–281.
Fairbairn, W. R. D. (1952). *Psychoanalytic Studies of the Personality*. London: Routledge.
Ferro, A. (2009). *Mind Works: Technique and Creativity in Psychoanalysis*. London: Routledge.
Freud, S. (1900a). Analysis of a specimen dream. *S. E., 4*: 106–120. London: Hogarth.

Freud, S. (1900b). *The Interpretation of Dreams. S. E., 4*: 1–338. London: Hogarth.
Freud, S. (1900c). The psychology of the dream processes. *S. E., 5*: 509–623. London: Hogarth.
Freud, S. (1905). Fragment of an analysis of a case of hysteria. *S. E., 7*: 3–112. London: Hogarth.
Gamill, J. (1993). Some reflections on analytic listening and the dream process. In: S. Flanders (Ed.), *The Dream Discourse Today* (pp. 127–136). London: Routledge.
Greenson, R. (1993). The exceptional position of the dream in psychoanalytic practice. In: S. Flanders (Ed.), *The Dream Discourse Today* (pp. 49–66). London: Routledge.
Meltzer, D. (1984). Resistance to dream analysis in patient and analyst. *Dream Life. A Re-examination of the Psychoanalytical Theory and Technique* (pp. 156–162). Perth, Scotland: Clunie Press, Roland Harris Trust. Reprinted Karnac, 2009.
Ogden, T. (2004a). An introduction to the reading of Bion. *International Journal of Psycho-Analysis, 85*: 285–300.
Ogden, T. H. (2004b). On holding and containing, being and dreaming. *International Journal of Psychoanalysis, 85, 6*: 1349–1364.
Palombo, S. R. (1978). *Dreaming and Memory: A New Information Processing Model*. New York: Basic Books.
Quinodoz, J. M. (2002). *Dreams That Turn over a Page*. Hove, East Sussex: Brunner Routledge.
Scharff, D. E. & Scharff, J. S. (1991). *Object Relations Couple Therapy*. Northvale, NJ: Jason Aronson.
Scharff, D. E. & Scharff, J. S. (2004). Using dreams in treating couple's sexual issues. *Psychoanalytic Inquiry, 24*: 468–482.
Scharff, D. E. & Scharff, J. S. (2011). *The Interpersonal Unconscious*. Lanham, MD: Jason Aronson.
Scharff, J. S. & Scharff, D. E. (1994). *Object Relations Therapy of Physical and Sexual Trauma*. Northvale, NJ: Jason Aronson.
Scharff, J. S. & Scharff, D. E. (2005). *The Primer of Object Relations 2nd Edition*. Lanham, MD: Jason Aronson.
Segal, H. (1993). The function of dreams. In: S. Flanders (Ed.), *The Dream Discourse Today* (pp. 100–107). London: Routledge.
Sharpe, E. (1937). *Dream Analysis*. New York: Norton.

CHAPTER TEN

Why can being a creative couple be so difficult to achieve? The impact of early anxieties on relating

Mary Morgan

Many couples struggle to relate in a creative way in which their relationship is potentially a resource to them, emotionally, cognitively, and physically. In order to function as a creative couple there needs to have been some favourable psychic development, particularly those developments in the early relationship to the primary object, oedipal development and adolescence. These developments come together later in a way that makes a creative couple relationship possible (Morgan, 2005).

Thought about in this way, one might see that the therapeutic challenge in working with couples is in helping the couple bring together and develop aspects that are there in some form, but have not yet come together in a way that allows a creative couple relationship. For other couples there are early difficulties in relating, especially in regard to the primary object, in which any intimacy is felt to be extremely difficult, even dangerous. The relationship to the primary object, usually the mother, is key, both because for most of us it is the only other relationship of such closeness prior to the intimate adult couple, and because this relationship at the earliest stage of psychic development is formative. It therefore functions as a crucial part of the template for later intimate relating. If, for example, the mother has been overly intrusive, projecting her own psychic contents into the infant or alternatively too distant and unavailable, the infant will carry this experience into later relationships. Even when the relationship to the primary object was good enough, other elements in later psychic development have to come together and lead to creative couple relating (See Morgan, 2005). For some, these elements have not developed sufficiently or exist in distorted and damaged ways, resulting in many difficulties for the adult including a most uncreative couple relationship. Such couples present a real challenge to the couple therapist. This chapter will offer a series of vignettes of work with such a couple.

I will begin by describing some of the salient features of the creative couple as I conceive it. It is primarily an internal capacity that reinforces the ability to be a creative couple in an external relationship. The individual has the sense of existing and functioning in the context of a relationship with another or others and experiences this as creative. This state of mind does not depend upon being in a relationship per se; whilst being part of a couple may be the desired state, not every individual chooses or achieves this. While the creative couple state of mind can be held by someone who is not in a couple, it is perhaps expressed most fully in the context of an actual intimate relationship.

In a creative couple, the relationship itself is continually being created by the couple's intercourse of every kind and at every level, as the different, or sometimes opposing, perspective of the other can be taken in to one's psyche and allowed to reside there where it mates with one's own experience to create something new. This creativity becomes possible because a state of mind has been achieved in which two minds, symbolised by the adult couple's "sexual intercourse", can come together and create a third—a new thought, perspective, or way of thinking symbolised by a "baby".

It is the outcome of the couple's intercourse that becomes a symbolic third and also provides the third position for the two individuals in the relationship. Thus the relationship is subjectively experienced as a resource, something the individuals have created and continue to create together, the whole being greater than the sum of the parts. The relationship is something the couple turns to in their minds and it functions as a container for the individuals (Colman, 1993). This is tremendously helpful to a couple who are having a difficult time together because there is, somewhere, the belief both that the relationship can stand it and that, while it may not be immediately apparent, an as yet unknown creative outcome to their difficulty is possible.

The couple I am going to describe illustrates two difficulties in relating: one is the level of anxiety they have about relating to another; the other is a difficulty with being able to be truly curious about each other. The capacity to relate to another with curiosity is fundamental to a creative couple state of mind.

The couple, Joe and Lucy, came to therapy because they wanted to start a family, but were unable to agree on the right time. They were in their late twenties and had been living together for a year.

For the first few months of therapy the couple took turns delivering monologues, anxious about whether their partner and I, as therapist, would hear them properly. If anyone interrupted, it felt devastating. I was reduced to providing a careful reiteration of what each had said, but it became problematic when I tried to put these two accounts together, as if this would annihilate them individually. The problem seemed to be that neither felt that taking in what the other had said might be valuable, not only to the other but also to themselves, as if it might transform something inside them and alter what they would say when it was their turn. Therefore, nothing one said changed the other. Furthermore, when one of them expressed a feeling, the other responded to it as an assaultive "statement of fact" that obliterated the other's feeling.

This lack of intercourse and curiosity had enormous implications for the couple's relationship. They both felt utterly unsupported by each other emotionally. Each found it hard to contain difficult feelings and felt left alone with them. It was also extremely difficult for them to think through any decisions because they could not explore what each other felt and bring their thoughts together. This, of course, linked to their presenting problem about when and if to start a family. When they tried talking about it, one of them might say, "I'm worried about how we'll manage financially". The other would take this as a negative, but there was no exploration of their financial situation, nor any thinking about it. It was as if this comment was simply taken as a "no!"

Sometimes it appeared as if the couple had no curiosity at all. Lucy said she wanted to know how Joe felt, for him to open up, as that would make her feel closer to him, and yet he was always complaining that she never asked him how he was, never the simplest enquiry about his day nor attention to him when he was obviously having a difficult time, for example, in his new job, which he longed for her to ask about. When she did talk about wanting to know how he felt, it seemed to be more her own narcissistic need. For him to open up and become vulnerable made her feel better, less isolated, but there was not really a sense of wanting to know him. He appeared less intrusive than she, more wounded and withdrawn, but he also expressed little curiosity.

So without the experience of being asked about, they resorted in a controlling way to trying to tell the other and me how they felt, as if they had to do this to establish a hold on reality. This was what they wanted to use the sessions for. Because of not letting each other in, and of unconsciously agreeing not to really try to know about each other, the same thing happened in the transference. Therefore, if a session focused on their relationship, things became tense and difficult because, in this parallel way, they feared letting me know about them and even letting themselves know about themselves.

Clinical vignette one: the primary object—a willfully misunderstanding object

A few months into the work, we could not do much about the sense of annihilation that came about with any kind of intercourse, but we were slowly able to begin to explore the way they felt the other got inside them and distorted their experience. They were talking about a shopping trip they had at the weekend, which seemed to have been frustrating and rather futile. As they both tried to describe their experience, I could see the way that each felt the other was projecting, not allowing the other to have a separate, different experience. Their dialogue deteriorated and became confused, as each seemed powerless to keep the other's projection from threatening their own experience.

I stopped listening to the account of the shopping trip in order to focus on this disturbing process. I realised I had a sense that if I tried to talk about the shopping trip, I would also inevitably be pushing another view into them that they would experience as distorting. I felt this countertransference illuminated something about the basic difficulty of their relating connected to their primary objects. There was no container that could help organise their experience, only another object projecting into them.

In "Attacks on Linking" (1959) and "On Arrogance" (1957), Bion describes the failure of the mother to detoxify the infant's experience as a catastrophe, not just because of the failure of projective identification, but because of the resulting establishment inside the infant of a willfully misunderstanding object with which the infant identifies. So something quite different gets set up—an ego-destructive superego. This affects the infant's normal curiosity upon which development depends.

This applies to what can then be such a complex problem in couples. Joe and Lucy were trying to get heard while at the same time trying to keep the other out. It became too threatening to take in what the other was feeling, as instead of being a loving thing, it felt like an attack—curiosity imbued with hate instead of love. So the couple's attempt to be heard by each other felt threatening. Opening communication channels made them feel vulnerable to unwanted projections. At times it was even more directly persecutory, because each felt the other was willfully misunderstanding.

Clinical vignette two: a defence against being curious

Another session started differently from usual, in that Lucy said she felt I had been unfair to her the previous week when I had asked whether she could hear Joe. But, she said, I had not asked him if he could hear her I reflected for a moment on whether I had been uneven-handed, but then I remembered that I had not addressed the same comment to him because at that moment, I had not felt it about him, but only about her. I then realised that what was important to them was that everything had to be fair, and had I made the same comment to him, it might have been fair but it would have been inaccurate—a poor, uncreative couple therapy interpretation. They did not feel I could comment to one of them while retaining a "couple state of mind" (2001). When I said to her that she felt it was more important to her that I was fair than it was that I convey what I really thought, it led to some understanding of this dynamic between them. Many times when one of them tried to talk to the other about something—for example how difficult one had found the other's anger—the partner would respond, "But you have to own your own anger!" Then the original anger, whoever had expressed it, never got explored. It felt like this attempt to put it back into the other rather than to own anything, to keep everything between them fair and equally poised, was an unconscious attempt to prevent any exploration.

I began to understand that I was never quite sure how they heard me. They seemed to respond to my voice. They often nodded or acknowledged what I said as helpful. However I was often not sure how much they could take in to make use of my interpretations. I felt they were constantly seeking validation rather than enquiring into things. They did not engage with an interpretation by agreeing, disagreeing, elaborating or associating to it. Then there was this kind of experience, as in this session, of finding that something I had said or not said had felt like an attack. They brought it back undigested, letting me know only how badly it had made them feel. It put me in touch with how most often they were not after developing understanding. Instead they needed to take control of their relationship so that it would feel safe and still. They were saying I hurt them, just by trying to understand. So the work was blocked by their feeling that curiosity and learning injured rather than helped.

Clinical vignette three: lack of safety

In another session following a break, Joe accused Lucy of denying things she had previously said. This made him mad. He also accused her of not responding to him when he told her he was upset. There was a crisis at work and he feared losing the job he had only just acquired. Lucy said she actually did not hear Joe sometimes, that he might say the words but she was distracted with something else like cooking dinner. She realised that when she was upset she sometimes said things she didn't mean, and then became defensive and denied she had said them. This session illustrated the unsafe atmosphere between them, in which things said in the heat of the moment could not be retracted. The more Lucy felt pinned down, the more defensive she became. Words, once spoken could easily become "things" that threatened. All this drove Joe mad. When they tried to listen to each other, they quickly became anxious. It was almost impossible to listen to the other's worries as it made them too anxious. Sharing anxiety felt like an attack, forcing unwelcome feelings into the other, like the mother Bion described who "could not tolerate experiencing such feelings and reacted either by denying them ingress, or alternatively by becoming a prey to the anxiety which resulted from introjection of the infant's feelings" (Bion, 1959, p. 313).

In this therapy, I had to pay attention continuously to trying to establish the setting as a safe place. It felt important to attend to breaks properly, and to take up any impingement on the frame. Progress made in sessions could easily fall apart after a day or two. After some time, Joe and Lucy were occasionally able to talk about things that happened between them. I tried to help them be interested in what went on inside each of them and between them, rather than simply having me hear their separate experiences. I linked this difficulty in taking in and retaining things to their problem with curiosity, not only about the object, but also about themselves.

Clinical vignette four: the primary object—the experience of evacuation

The couple's level of anxiety was illustrated in the following session. They had begun by trying to discuss how hard it was to talk. They felt so vulnerable if they were going to turn to each other for understanding that they had to "meet" and "check in" before they could begin. Joe felt Lucy did this by getting him to agree that they would talk at an appointed hour, sitting at the kitchen table without the radio on as it was most of the time. Lucy felt Joe would then try and move around the kitchen, making coffee or attending to something else, which made her feel as if she did not exist. She was left, sitting by herself, trying to listen to him but not being able to hear him properly, as if she were some kind of "listening machine" or a "listening bucket".

Lucy's expressions further illuminate the couple's difficulty taking something in. One was subject to the other's evacuation as if they were a bucket. This also reflected a dynamic between them and me. It was not exactly that I felt like a bucket, but I often felt that despite some progress in the session, they were not able to make use of it outside.

In contrast to couples like Joe and Lucy who fear intrusion in every exchange, in the creative couple each individual develops through exchange of thoughts and feelings. The capacities for thought and thinking inside an individual are enhanced by linking with and thinking with another. We see this in good couple relationships as well as between groups of well functioning colleagues, or when friends turn to each other for help.

Developmentally, this comes about as an outcome of the Oedipus complex through the experience of having had, and being able to make use of, an interested and understanding primary object that provides the basis for internalising a couple. Then the ongoing witnessing of the creativity of the parental couple further underpins the idea of a creative couple. In this later oedipal phase, the quality of seeing the parents manage uncertainties—not knowing, exchanging thoughts and feelings with one another and thinking things through—builds on the child's capacity for thought developed in relation to primary objects. This kind of internal couple, related to in love and hate through adolescence, eventually forms the basis for young adults' creative coupling.

The couple's early history and my experience with them suggested serious difficulties in relationship to their primary objects and couples. Joe described a very depressed mother who was distant and inaccessible to him. He said when he looked at her he felt there was "an invisible screen" between them and sometimes felt anxious about what was on the other side. His parents divorced when he was six and, as the only boy with two younger sisters, he felt he had to take on a parental role. He had virtually no contact with his father and found it difficult to separate from his mother, despite the lack of emotional contact.

Lucy's parents separated soon after her birth and intermittently came back together again for brief periods, but never for long enough for her to feel secure with them. The relationship between her parents continually broke down following verbal and sometimes physical hostility. Like Joe, Lucy found her mother preoccupied. She felt her mother never heard her properly and distorted what she communicated to her, often implying they were in agreement about things when they were not. Lucy said that even now she found it hard to distinguish her own thoughts and feelings from other peoples, especially Joe's.

For both Joe and Lucy, relating—having intercourse—did not feel safe. They were thus unable to build up an idea of a relationship as a symbolic third, nor did they have a relationship that could function as a third position to help them process differences, disagreements, frustrations, anger and hatred, with the hope that understanding might eventually come out of these struggles. They did not have the vantage point from which to see themselves with curiosity. A lot of the time they felt in a battle for survival, trying to find space to articulate their experience before the other took over.

In this state of mind, in which each felt desperation about being heard properly, it was difficult for them to hear, or be curious about what was going on between them. Such couples have difficulty seeing each other as separate, because one partner tries to control the other omnipotently in order to make them into the kind of object they need them to be. Or they try to impose their own version of reality on the other as if it were the only version. For life to be bearable, the individual tyrannises the other to ensure certain forms of behaviour. That Joe and Lucy were missing a fundamental belief in relationships as potentially benign and creative, affected not only the couple, but also the therapeutic endeavour based on such beliefs.

There are two areas that we might think about: containment and curiosity. This couple quickly became dependent on the therapy because, in a healthy way, they knew they needed a container and were able to respond to its offer by their therapist. Initially they may barely have sensed my being able to hear each of them reasonably accurately, despite also experiencing me as mishearing, unfair or even projecting into them. Nonetheless, therapy enabled them, over time, to build up a less fearful, less paranoid view of the other's interest. Therapy itself offered more safety than they had previously felt. So this allowed something to happen, but what? Gradually they were able to take inside the experience of my curiosity in them, in other words to allow and slowly appreciate a non-intrusive exploration inside them and their relationship.

There is an extra challenge for a couple coming to therapy that the individual patient may not have. In individual treatment we hope that our interest in our patients will stimulate interest in themselves, their inner world, what drives them to behave and relate in certain ways. In couple therapy we require this too, but in addition we need them to be interested in and curious about their partner. Otherwise it is hard to see how a relationship can develop. Perhaps one of the most creative things about couple therapy and the couple relationship is that this can work the other way around, too. If we help the partners in a couple relationship feel safe enough to risk becoming interested in each other, they may start to become curious about their own internal worlds.

In "The Emotional Experience of K", Fisher (2006) emphasises the role of curiosity in containment. Containment depends on a mother who is curious about her baby's physical and emotional wellbeing, who wants to "know" the baby. In Bion's terminology, this is the instinctive impulse 'K'. The mother must be able to bear being in touch with the baby's unbearable feelings with confidence that she has a mind that can process these states. Bion (1962) described this as the apparatus for thinking or alpha function. As Fisher puts it, "what Bion implies, but never quite says sufficiently clearly, is that the container does so by remaining a container-in-K, wanting to know and understand, not from an emotional distance, but by experiencing those emotions and yet retaining a K-state-of-mind" (Fisher, 2006, p. 1231). Where containment does not take place, a non-understanding object gets set up inside the infant, instead of an internal object that seeks to know and understand.

With Joe and Lucy's therapy, containment and curiosity slowly grew hand in hand. As the fragile therapeutic container strengthened, curiosity became possible, which in turn strengthened the container. Couples such as Joe and Lucy illustrate how much the capacity to relate as a creative couple is based on early development. When these developments have gone seriously awry, any later relationship will be affected. The couple therapist has painstaking work to do before relating can be experienced as potentially creative rather than persecutory.

References

Bion, W. R. (1957). On arrogance. In: W. R. Bion, (1967). *Second Thoughts* (pp. 65–85). New York: Jason Aronson.
Bion, W. R. (1959). Attacks on linking. *International Journal of Psycho-Analysis, 40*: 308–315.
Bion, W. R. (1962). *Learning from Experience*. London: Heinemann.
Colman, W. (1993). Marriage as a psychological container. In: S. Ruszczynski (Ed.), *Psychotherapy with Couples: Theory and Practice at the Tavistock Institute of Marital Studies* (pp. 70–96). London: Karnac.
Fisher, J. (2006). The emotional experience of K. *International Journal of Psycho-Analysis, 87*: 1221–1237.
Morgan, M. (2001). First contacts: the therapist's "couple state of mind" as a factor in the containment of couples seen for initial consultations. In: F. Grier (Ed.), *Brief Encounters with Couples* (pp. 17–32). London: Karnac.
Morgan, M. (2005). On being able to be a couple: the importance of a "creative couple" in psychic life. In: F. Grier (Ed.), *Oedipus and the Couple* (pp. 9–30). London: Karnac.

PART II

ASSESSMENT AND TREATMENT

CHAPTER ELEVEN

The couple state of mind and some aspects of the setting in couple psychotherapy

Mary Morgan

Psychoanalytic psychotherapy with couples requires a setting in which they feel held and their therapist is able to think. In discussing the nature of the setting, some of my thoughts are drawn from the fundamentals of psychoanalytic practice, while other aspects are specific to the couple psychoanalytic setting. The setting is primarily the analytic attitude and the couple state of mind of the therapist, but it also refers to the actual physical setting and arrangements in which the therapeutic process takes place. The two aspects are closely connected.

The couple state of mind

One of the most fundamental tools the couple therapist has is, I believe, a couple state of mind (Morgan, 2001). The couple therapist thinks of the couple's relationship as the patient (Ruszczynski, 1993) and this stance frames everything that goes on in the therapy. Thus the therapist is thinking about what kind of relationship the partners are creating and what unconscious phantasies and beliefs they have about being a couple. The therapist tries to hold a neutral position, in which, despite pressure from the partners to take sides, and sometimes a real sense inside herself that she is more sympathetic to one or the other, she is working with a relationship as a dynamic whole, an unconscious system in which each partner carries aspects for the other. These aspects can easily shift between them.

Although the therapist focuses on exploring and interpreting her understanding of the relationship, if her couple state of mind is firmly in place, there is freedom to focus on the individuals in the relationship, too. The point is that this is always done with the other partner and the relationship in mind. For example, if one partner is presented as the problem, the therapist will be thinking about what this means for the relationship, what function it serves unconsciously for each partner, and whether one of the partners is carrying something for both. It also affects the couple therapist's technique, so that if the therapist explores an issue with one partner, she will also be thinking about and exploring how the other partner feels, not just about the content being discussed but also about attention shifting to the other partner. For example how do the couple manage one of them getting their needs met in the session and the other not, even temporarily? Is it a relief to have the other focused on, or does it create feelings of abandonment or rivalry? And is there perhaps a belief that there is no room in the relationship for both their needs? In other words, if the couple state of mind is secure in the therapist, there is room for considerable freedom of movement between partners, the relationship and the therapist.

The therapist's couple state of mind is an important part of the couple psychoanalytic setting in another crucial way. Many couples who come for therapy do not have a sense of their relationship as an entity. They can see things from their own point of view, possibly at times from the other's point of view but not from a place where they can view the relationship and see what they are creating together. The therapist by holding a couple state of mind is continually bringing the relationship itself into focus, and is establishing a third position (Britton, 1989). If the therapy works, the couple state of mind, initially held by the therapist, becomes internalised by the couple. The space that has been opened by the therapist taking this third position becomes an aspect of the couple's relationship. This capacity in the couple to take a third position is one important aspect of a creative couple relationship which I have discussed elsewhere (See Chapter Ten and Morgan, 2005).

For some couples there is enormous resistance to taking this third position—so determined are they to lodge the problems in the other, and so far away are they from understanding that they are creating something together that needs to be understood. For other couples this feels like a welcome new thing, as they have never had a sense of a relationship as a third before. The therapist attending to it even in an initial consultation can feel its power, creating as it does more space for thinking as described by Britton (1989), and Ruszczynski in the marital triangle (2005).

The setting: physical, practical, and psychological

The couple state of mind is reflected in many aspects of the setting—both the physical and psychological setting—and in the practical arrangements. Psychoanalytic therapists try to create a setting that is as neutral as possible without being blank and cold. It needs to be a comfortable place for the couple and therapist without too many distractions. As Meltzer describes in *The Psychoanalytical Process*, "In order for this search for truth about the patient's mind to proceed, it is necessary that the setting should minimise those interferences with the unfolding and elaboration of his transference such as would be caused by the intrusion of external realities upon the setting" (Meltzer, 1967, p. xii).

In couple psychotherapy the therapist explores the transference in more than one dimension—the transference to the therapist and the transference relationship between the partners. In the latter situation the issue of neutrality is more complex, as the other partner is far from neutral. When one partner projects something into the other, it is not responded to from a position of neutrality, but often with the corresponding part of the projection or with a counter projection.

Couple therapy sessions can become complicated, confusing and even chaotic. Meltzer, in discussing the analytic setting states, "The secret is stability, and the key to stability is simplicity. Every analyst must work out for himself a simple style of analytical work, in time arrangements, financial agreement, room, clothing, modes of expression, demeanour. He must work well within the limits of his physical capacity and his mental tolerance. But also, in the process of discovery with a patient, he must find through his sensitivity the means of modulation required by that individual within the framework of his technique. In a word, he must *preside* over the setting in a way which permits the evolution of the patient's transference" (Meltzer, 1967, p. xiii). The stability of the setting supports the therapist in being able to make emotional contact with the couple and become properly attuned to the interior of the couple relationship. The couple therapist presides over the setting by maintaining a couple state of mind internally and reflecting this externally in the physical and practical arrangements of the therapy.

Working with a couple requires a different physical setting from individual analytic work. For example there needs to be two chairs, firm and comfortable, placed not too close or far away from the other so that both partners have room to feel both together and apart. Ideally they need to be at an equal proximity to the therapist's chair, facing slightly towards each other and the therapist. This creates a physical triangle in the room with the therapist as the third part of the triangle. Then the space between therapist and couple is a physical manifestation of the psychological triangular space I referred to earlier. It is also interesting that couples quite often attribute meaning to the chairs, sometimes owning a particular chair and not wanting to change with their partner from week to week. Others identify one chair as the "hot seat" because it is felt to be closer or further away from the therapist, even if it is not. Or they want the chair that is further inside the therapist's room, or closer to the door. The way the therapist sets up the consulting room conveys her attention in thinking about the couple, but also if set up in a clear and consistent way, the arrangement reveals the triangular oedipal dynamics that are often to the fore in couples work.

Charging a fee for the session relates to the couple's adult selves. Even those couples who are unable to pay very much, find it important to pay something. Not to pay anything might evoke feelings of being too dependent and childlike. In negotiating a fee with a couple it may be that one partner, the sole or major earner may offer to pay for both. Even where this is unavoidable, it is important to explore how this is experienced for each of them, and how it situates them emotionally in relation to the therapy. Couples often start treatment with one partner bringing the other. This might be reflected in the way the fee is negotiated. Ideally the fee should be both manageable and represent a genuine commitment to therapy. Paying for sessions the couple miss is sometimes a difficult issue, but apart from the needs of the therapist, it can, over time, feel containing to the couple that their session time is protected and regular even if they have to miss a session.

The minimisation of interferences is a greater challenge for the therapist in several ways. As already mentioned, one partner may have a particular impact on the other that mitigates what the therapist attempts to provide. Also unlike individual analysis in which the patient uses the couch and has a restricted view of the analyst, couple therapy is conducted sitting up facing the therapist, so that the real external characteristics of the therapist are more visible and possibly intrusive. The gender of the therapist may be of greater significance to the patient in couple therapy than in individual analytic work. For example, where the couple consists of a man and woman and the therapy is with a female therapist, the man can feel outnumbered, feeling the two women get together against him as the man. For same-sex couples, it can feel important to have a therapist of the same sex, while others prefer a therapist of the other sex, depending on the couple's issues. Whatever the situation, these issues of the therapist's gender are usually alive in couple's therapy, and need to be brought into the work.

A further issue where there are two therapists working conjointly, is that they have to work out their own style as a therapist couple, which may not always be easy, especially if there are differences between them theoretically or in status or experience. Where there are two therapists it is important to arrange regular time to meet together after the couple session so that counter-transference and projections that may get lodged in the therapist couple can be analysed.

Maintaining an analytic relationship with a couple can be just as hard as in individual work. It can be difficult to resist, if not an actual social relationship with the couple, then a social type of interaction. Temperley (1984) states, "This analysing stance, which runs painfully counter to the way both therapist and patient usually structure their relationships, is the setting for psychotherapy that I think is most fundamental. It is the most within one's control and also the most difficult to establish. All other aspects of setting are ways in which this basic psychological setting can be safeguarded and facilitated" (Temperley, 1984, p. 102). The therapist, by having an analytic stance, adopting a non-judgmental attitude, avoiding expressing a personal view and maintaining confidentiality, creates a particular and powerful kind of relationship with the couple.

In everyday life and social relationships it will be necessary much of the time for everyone to present what Winnicott called a "false self", a self that to some extent, however slightly, fits in with what's required socially. But therapy aims to provide the kind of setting in which aspects of the true self can emerge. This can also be thought about in terms of encouraging the relaxing of the usual censorship that we all put onto expressing our thoughts and feelings. Therapists attempt to create the kind of environment in which truer things are safe to express, because the usual social consequences of such frankness will not occur. In other words they will not be treated as social communications but as part of the work.

Both couple and therapist need a structure that has regular duration, a fixed time, frequency and place, with planned breaks. This is a crucial part of the containment and the boundary the therapist provides. The couple can then rely on something regular that starts and stops at a particular time, no matter what takes place within those times. Couples are usually seen once a week for one hour, though this may vary between fifty minutes to an hour and a half. In establishing the regular duration of the session, the therapist needs to think about what is a reasonable amount of time for the couple to be able to communicate something of what is happening, for the therapist to grasp something of the unconscious dynamics between the partners, and to put that back to them in a way that they can hear and take in while feeling contained. An important factor is consistency so that the setting becomes something that can be relied upon. If changes have to be made, we might make them in the break, although this does not necessarily reduce the impact. I remember a couple returning to therapy with my co-therapist and me after a summer break. The husband noticed with shock that the picture had changed on our consulting room wall. He then told us of a distressing argument he and his wife had at an art exhibition on holiday in Paris, and how this picture had come to his mind. At that moment it helped him to bring to mind a containing thinking space, which shows that the setting does not just exist in the analytic hour but exists symbolically inside the couple's minds between the sessions.

A clear boundary is important, because it makes it possible to see when the boundary is breached and then to think about it. Because in fact the perfect structure is an ideal, it does get broken by the therapist as well, hopefully not without considerable thought. For example with a clear boundary, it is possible to think about why one or both partners are late, what happens if one partner does not come, what happens if one partner makes contact in between the sessions, or why the therapist may act differently with a particular couple than her usual practice.

If the breaks in the therapy are planned enough in advance, the impact of the interruption can be thought about. If the sessions are consistent, then unplanned interruptions can be considered. The therapist works out what her usual practice is in this situation, for example to offer an alternative appointment if she has to cancel at short notice. Then it is possible to think about both what the couple do with this, and if the therapist does something different from usual, to consider what this change by the therapist might mean, for example an enactment of a powerful transference/countertransference dynamic.

How do couples experience the break between sessions? Sometimes the intensity of the couple interaction taken away from the session dominates the couple dynamics between the sessions. The couple may evoke the therapist, or the therapist's words to attack each other. With these couples the sessions can feel a week long experience without respite. Another way partners deal with the intensity of the sessions is to limit the experience of the session to the session itself, and have little emotional contact during the week between sessions. One such couple complained bitterly that it was possible to communicate with each other only within the sessions. Between sessions, her anger and his passivity would lead to a silent stalemate and absence of physical contact. The therapy then did feel like literally a once a week experience, which was frustrating for both therapist and couple, as it felt like a new beginning each week. The couple experienced a complete lack of containment in the couple relationship in daily life, and a parallel difficulty in using the containment of therapy except when the therapist was literally there with them. Over time, as the setting becomes established and the therapist is internalised as a symbolic third, the couple feel more contained between the sessions.

Many couple therapists will see the couple only if they attend together, since both partners being present is part of the frame. There are other good reasons for this, particularly that the partner who comes may volunteer information that is not to be shared with the partner, putting the therapist in the difficult position of holding a secret. This can happen just as easily with a phone call from one of the partners. The therapist can try to avoid this situation by establishing a rule that all information imparted by either individual to the therapist is to be shared with the other, but the individual can break the rule and make things awkward. Other therapists allow one of the individuals to attend if the other cannot, taking the view that the session is the frame, the couple pay for the session, and the therapist keeps this time and space for them and prefers to maintain the consistency of the meetings. The meaning of the absent partner, both for the present partner and the absent one the following week is then analysed.

A chapter like this on the setting can be read as a collection of rules or principles that have to be put in place. In fact, what I have tried to show is that the setting is primarily an internal phenomenon that is expressed in all practical aspects of the setting. In psychoanalytic work with couples I think that fundamental to the setting is the therapist's couple state of mind and analytic stance. One cannot overstate how important the setting is. The setting is introduced in initial assessment and gets fully established in the process of therapy. Assessment is fraught with difficulties and often the therapist feels overwhelmed by the distress and uncontained feelings of a couple in crisis. The task is complex: the need to gather information and make a formulation; the need for risk assessment; negotiating practicalities of time and fee. However I think that what is often not noticed by the therapist is the impact of approaching the couple with a couple state of mind and creating a different kind of space in which the relationship in all its facets can be brought forth and thought about. This is present in the way the therapist approaches the couple right from the beginning. The couple may be affected by a sensitive or challenging interpretation the therapist makes, but more than this, is affected by the couple analytic presence—the couple state of mind of the therapist that provides a very different kind of space for the relationship, and that gives each partner and the two of them together the hope that within this different kind of space what is going on between them can be understood.

References

Britton, R. (1989). The missing link: parental sexuality in the Oedipus complex. In: J. Steiner (Ed.), *The Oedipus Complex Today: Clinical Implications* (pp. 83–101). London: Karnac.

Meltzer, D. (1967). *The Psycho-analytical Process*. Perthshire, Scotland: Clunie Press.

Morgan, M. (2005a). First contacts: the therapist's 'couple state of mind' as a factor in the containment of couples seen for consultations. In: F. Grier (Ed.), *Oedipus and the Couple* (pp. 17–32). London: Karnac.

Morgan, M. (2005b). On being able to be a couple: the importance of a 'creative couple' in psychic life. In F. Grier (Ed.), *Oedipus and the Couple* (pp. 9–30). London: Karnac.

Ruszczynski, S. (1993). Thinking about and working with couples. *In Psychotherapy with Couples: Theory and Practice at the Tavistock Institute of Marital Studies* (pp. 197–217). London: Karnac.

Ruszczynski, S. (2005). Reflective space in the intimate couple relationship: 'the marital triangle'. In: F. Grier (Ed.), *Oedipus and the Couple* (pp. 31–47). London: Karnac.

Temperley, J. (1984). Settings for Psychotherapy, *British Journal of Psychotherapy 1, 2*: (pp. 101–111).

Winnicott, D. W. (1986). *Home is Where We Start From*. Harmondsworth: Penguin Books.

CHAPTER TWELVE

Establishing a therapeutic relationship in analytic couple therapy

Jill Savege Scharff

Establishing a therapeutic relationship is the first task that faces the analytic couple therapist. This task is of crucial importance. The therapist approaches the couple, not as two individuals meeting the therapist, but as a couple. The patient is the couple relationship, not the two spouses who comprise it. To deal with the couple, the therapist must enter a couple state of mind as she addresses the task of the first interview and hopes to move beyond assessment into couple therapy. She brings a background in theory, a tuning of her self as a sound therapeutic instrument from years in personal therapy or analysis, and a dedication to supervision, peer supervision, and process and review of her work. She brings care and concern, tact and timing, to the task. She builds the therapeutic relationship as the context for the in-depth work that will occur if the couple proceeds to ongoing therapy. When couple therapy begins, she continues to work on maintaining her connection to the couple, and uses it for her understanding. The therapeutic relationship is the frame for the work and the focus of the work. It must be maintained, and it must be analysed.

Beginning with the phone call

Establishing the therapeutic relationship starts on the phone before you even see the couple. One of the partners calls to request an appointment, and you want to return that call promptly. This shows respect for their feeling of urgency for help, and it connects you to the couple in good time, so that the desire for help does not extinguish for lack of response. If you do not have time to see them, or your office is inconvenient, you make a referral. It is best not to discuss presenting problems on the telephone but ask them to wait to meet in person. When you reach the couple, you want to offer them informed choice before commitment. So this is how I proceed.

I explain that we will meet for a single session at my full consultation fee, and at this session we can negotiate the fee for any further sessions. We can then decide whether to extend the consultation to a few sessions to allow for a more comprehensive assessment, after which I will give my recommendation, again giving them lots of choice as to whether to work with me or another colleague, and leaving them free to choose individual or family rather than couple therapy. We are not only assessing their needs, but also their suitability for analytic couple therapy.

The couple arrives for their first consultation. I meet them in the waiting room, already interested in whether they are on time or late, whether they are both present or one is missing. There is nothing to be gained from maintaining a totally neutral affect, walking silently up to them, and ushering them into the office. I bear in mind that this is an anxiety provoking moment as the spouses or partners cross over from the privacy of life to the unfamiliar consulting room. So I behave in a natural manner, greet them, and introduce myself. If only one is present, I explain that I do not begin until both have arrived. I begin my assessment. Do they look afraid, reluctant, or eager to see me? I note how they respond to my greeting in the waiting room, and how they enter my office. The office is furnished like a sitting room with a choice of upright chairs and comfortable sofa. I notice where the partners sit. Are they huddled together on the sofa? Do they occupy the two matching chairs? Or does one spread over the sofa while the other takes a distant chair?

I begin by asking for contact information. It's interesting to see which member of the couple answers or is asked to answer. I ask how the couple heard of me so that I know which of my colleagues to thank. I hand each member of the couple my business card and a brochure that explains the way the practice works, tells of my qualifications, and educational history. If there are any questions about my professional competence, I answer them. To me this information is public, and it pertains to the couple's developing confidence in this professional situation.

I discuss the fee that the couple can afford, and I explain that I charge for missed appointments. Other couple therapists in private practice may chooose to use a twenty-four-hour cancellation policy. Those who work in clinics obviously must follow the policy established by the clinic administration. My policy of charging for missed appointments is usual and customary among psychoanalysts in the United States but not surprisingly some couples object to this. They ask why they should pay for time in which they are not getting professional care? I explain that I am reserving that time for them. I am selling my time to relatively few couples on a long-term basis. I do not have a high volume practice with emergencies and a waiting list of people who can fill the time. I do however reschedule if I have enough notice, and I ask other patients if they are willing to switch an appointment time. All my couples know that this option is available and that they may be asked to accommodate another couple. This is an option, not a demand. This forthright response makes it clear from the start that this is a professional relationship with a business aspect that is not being denied. With these matters settled, we have begun to build a suitable environment for therapy. The point is to create a space that is safe for the couple, a private, comfortable, and well-bounded space that can become a safe psychological space. We set this up by our attitude of care concerning the arrangements. We offer a firm frame within which to work.

Some couples bend the frame. They cancel and reschedule. They fail to pay the bill. They come late. I do not enforce my policies in the consultation phase. I think of my frame as clear and firm but not rigid. I deal with attempts to bend the frame by interpretation. I want to see whether the couple can use the interpretive work. If interpretation cannot cope with the couple's attitude to the frame, it will be impossible to establish a therapeutic relationship. This is what we are assessing during consultation. Can this couple work with me in analytic couple therapy?

Now there is a choice as to what to say. I put it differently each time—"Over to you." "What would you like to tell me?" "What do you want to explore?" I never ask, "Who wants to start?" I wait and see. My opening remark establishes that I am interested, and that this is their space, a space for sharing and reflection, a space in which to express feelings and find words for them. I allow the couple to fill the space. I do this by listening to how the partners interact, how they get their points across. I look at their physical characteristics and the way they relate to each other as they engage with me. I note how they feel about seeing me. Do they seem reluctant? Are they excited and eager to speak? This attitude is not only about me, but dealing with me is an example of how they face strange situations and potentially difficult relationships in their families and social group.

It's no good relating to the couple like a blank screen analyst. Yet, you are non-directive and reflective. You follow the affect because it is a point of access to emotional connection. With your clinical skill you empathise with their emotional situation and enter with them into the conflict that it reflects. Perhaps you are seeing a core affective exchange—a situation in which early relationship difficulties come to life in the present moment with each other and with you. I seem to do very little. I am simply being there, listening, responding, and noting how the session affects me. Leaving things open in this way is an advanced clinical skill but it is good to start with that intention. I tell students, "Go in and try not to do too much." When you work in a clinic you may have to fill out an assessment form, but I advise filling it out after the interview, not before.

You want to engage the couple in an enquiring stance. You want them to think about what they expect out of life. How do they think of themselves as a couple, and what are their plans for the future. How do they think about having children? Contemplating a family changes their view of themselves as a couple. We are interested in their everyday life, in whatever they want to tell us. It is our job to make something of that, to use it as the vehicle for exploring their conflicts, hopes, fears, and wishes. We are interested in the context in which they live and work. We want to understand how they are placed within the generations and in their society. By our few comments, we convey a reflective, inquiring frame of mind focused on the couple relationship.

As couple therapists, we are not there to keep the couple together. We are there to help the couple think about itself, and what it needs and wants, and what its individual members need and want. The couple relationship is about supporting the differentiation of each of the members and this personal growth comes back to enrich the couple and any children they may raise. You are there to be used as a transference object, an object of use for the couple. You don't have to behave as a blank screen to draw the transference. Transference is already established between the members of a couple. It is more active in their dyad than it is between them and you. They have a projective identificatory system already. They know each other better than you can know them. They have an intimate bond. You are excluded from it, at least at first. That can be frustrating but it is less frightening than being drawn in prematurely.

The feelings you experience in relation to a couple who agree to work with you are complicated. You can feel hurt and useless if you are totally kept out by their intense bond. You feel privileged to be invited in—and possibly anxious and guilty. You may feel like a child overexcited by the privilege. We tend to defend ourselves from this painful oedipal feeling, each of us in individually unique ways. Some people defend themselves by never seeing couples! But if you can stand it for a few sessions, then you can work on your discomfort and rework your oedipal adjustment. Some couples need a longer session than others. You customise the length of the session to suit the couple. It is a matter of negotiation between the couple's need and one's own.

So far I have addressed the practicalities of the arrangements that make the therapeutic relationship possible. But what we do is not simply a matter of technical considerations. The way we make these arrangements is a reflection of our stance toward the couple and the therapeutic relationship we intend to offer. That stance is based on an ethical, respectful, enquiring attitude of care and concern, and also on theory. The stance from which analytic couple therapists such as the authors of this book build a therapeutic relationship is by applying object relations theory. We have fleshed out the theory at length in various chapters. For now, here is the briefest summary.

We use Fairbairn's understanding of personality as a system of internal object relationships. We see the way the partners behave toward each other, each one identified with a rejecting or exciting object, as a display of their individual object relations. We find Klein's concept of projective identification helpful in thinking about how couples may split good and bad experience and deal with guilt and reparation to heal their couple relationship when it takes a battering from splitting. We use Henry Dicks' integration of Fairbairn's endopsychic situation and Klein's projective identification to understand how the partners have formed a couple and find lost parts of themselves in the other spouse whom they then attack or cherish according to whether the projected part of the self has been cherished or attacked. We work on helping the partners take back their projective identification into each other.

From Winnicott comes the concept of the environmental mother and the object mother. In analytic couple therapy, we offer ourselves as a safe environmental mother by attention to the frame, and then we offer ourselves as an object mother they can use and abuse ruthlessly. From Bion we take the concept of containment. While listening and observing and trying not to do too much, we are sitting with anxiety without reacting, jumping in, interrupting, or ending the session early. We are learning to hold anxiety and give it back to the couple in a more manageable way so that they have the experience of using thought to transform distress. We also see Bion's concepts of dependency, flight/fight and pairing at work in couples each a small group of two, already engaged in pairing, hopefully of a creative sort, and yet the fact they need to seek help speaks to the destructive aspect of their pairing. One may be unduly dependent on the other, or both may depend too much on families with whom they are enmeshed.

Clinical example

A couple in their late twenties had had many problems when living together at Harvard, and broke up. Nevertheless, they continued to love each other, and married even though none of the problems had been resolved. Rose left a good job to join Winston and is as yet unemployed, while Winston is working in a vintage car repair shop, which he enjoys but at which he does not earn as much if he had a job commensurate with his educational level. Winston and Rose were referred to me by Rose's individual therapist at a local reduced fee clinic. I was asked to assess whether analytic couple therapy were indicated and could help them solve their ambivalence. The interview took place at a military facility on video for teaching purposes (to which the couple kindly agreed) and at no cost to them. I did not meet them in a waiting room, but in a studio. They were already seated and miked when I arrived to begin the interview. This is an unusual setting for a couple assessment. Nevertheless once the strange setting has been acknowledged, they and we settle in to work as if in a consulting room.

As I say good morning, and invite them to be seated, I notice their appearance. They are dressed in nice casual clothes like graduate students. Winston's hair is short and reddish, hers is long and dark. Rose is of Asian descent, probably Japanese I think, and has a very still, perhaps sad face. Rose looks to Winston to take the lead, and so I see only the side of her face. Winston smiles affably but his pale blue eyes dart from side to side as if he is on the look-out for trouble. I am alert to the need to connect with each of them, and for me it may be easier to do so with Winston because I have trouble reading the expression on the Rose's face. I listen as Winston begins by saying that he and Rose met at Harvard, broke up because of unresolved difficulties, and then had got back together with some trepidation and had married two weeks ago! The session continues, now addressing their fears and their conflict over work and intimacy.

Conflict over work and intimacy

WINSTON: I should say that she didn't want to have any further contact with me. But, nevertheless here we are, together again.

JSS: What reason did she have to be hesitant about it?

WINSTON: Some relationships end amicably by mutual consent, ah, I don't know, but in any event, in ours, I'd say she suffered a lot more than I did, from the separation. It was, at least it was, it was a question of careers in a certain sense—not so much business although I suppose that it was that in part, but a choice of life's purpose ...

JSS: I'm not sure what you mean.

WINSTON: Well, the career was mutual, and incompatible.

JSS: Maybe you should tell me what careers you're talking about, because there's a certain sense of mystery as you're talking.

ROSE: Well, it's not really a career. I think calling it a career is sort of yuppifying it. I think it's more a life's ...

WINSTON: A calling.

ROSE: A calling. I certainly saw it as a religious calling, pertaining to a religious calling at the time.

WINSTON: Hmmm.
ROSE: It was a life style—ah. Well, what it was, was, Winston wanted to be very politically active to the extent that political activity became the central focus of his life, uhm, and the relationship no longer mattered. In reacting to that I sort of went to the other extreme and thought that for me all I wanted was the relationship and that nothing else mattered. I think intellectually, another part was that I always thought intellectually we were very compatible, which, considering the school we went to … ah …
WINSTON: I don't know how compatible we were with the rest of the people who went there …
ROSE: Yeah because uhm, what I thought, well, what I really enjoyed about the relationship while we were in school was that we could sort of get together to laugh at everybody else, or find some aspect of intellectual commonality that sort of set us apart from other people. In a sense, it was us against everybody else.
JSS: Hmmm.
ROSE: And it was, it was very nice to feel that way.
JSS: Now, then, what about the political activity? Was that relating to a political belief that you also share, or that divides you?
WINSTON: I really don't think it was the belief or the ideology—I think it was the time and the fact and the perception that the cause came before the person.
JSS: Hmmm.
WINSTON: So, I mean, I don't think it was a question of an ideology that Rose opposed, uhm, per se, but the way it was carried out …
JSS: Is it one that you support, or you just—people can think differently and that's fine.
ROSE: Yeah, it's one I support intellectually, and did even then. But the manifestations of it, of Winston's work for it, ah, I couldn't …
JSS: The way it took him over?
ROSE: Right, and the amount of time he spent on it, uhm.
JSS: Now, can you tell me what the cause is, so I can understand it?
WINSTON: The cause, well, generally the rubric is progressive causes. And concretely: At the time it was political education. Selling a newspaper, holding events, and much of it was very self-absorbed.

This couple has a heavily intellectual defence. I, who teach the value of not doing too much, had to keep asking questions. I had to push for enough information to understand the nature of the political activity and the behaviours that upset them. In this chapter I am writing about how to establish a therapeutic relationship, but in this case I found it hard to join with the couple. Once I pointed out how the man especially was keeping me at bay, the woman became able to speak. So then I got a more complete picture of their issues and their relationship. I noted their preference to get together to laugh at others, and I felt that I had now become one of the others. I felt anxious. I felt stupid, forced to ask specific questions to get past the obfuscation and the cryptic intellectual language that operated like a brick wall to keep me out. I began to think that their working together to exclude me (and others) is what enabled them to be a couple. I noted that they are collaborating now in such a way that the man is doing to the woman what they as a couple had done to others. So, although I felt stupid and not the best analytic couple therapist that I could be, I was able to keep thinking and working on my experience.

Feeling kept away, I had to struggle against despair of ever getting anywhere. It was proving difficult to establish a therapeutic relationship with this couple. What strategies might I use? Surface reassurance to calm their paranoid ideas would not be effective. Competing for intellectual dominance was a temptation to help me not feel stupid, but I squashed that urge because it would be better to receive the projection of inferiority and work with it. True to my belief, working with my countertransference would hold the most promise. I chose to address my feeling stupid when failing to get what they were talking about. I was not acting dumb to get information, as is sometimes suggested in systemic therapy. This was not a tactic of being clueless and curious to seduce the couple into telling me what I needed to know to help them. It was a genuine expression of my experience from which I felt we all could learn and hopefully move beyond it. I spoke to them about feeling kept out by their way of creating a sense of mystery around exactly what had happened to cause conflict. I began to wonder what they are defended against. What is their shared anxiety? Perhaps like me they too feel inferior. There might be useful information from their childhood histories, but I don't want to ask directly. I prefer to hear more about their couple relationship first.

Problems in the relationship

JSS: Back to the present then, you got together again, with some trepidation having to do with that earlier break up. But again, I don't know quite how that works between you.

ROSE: Well, maybe I, from my point of view anyway, the way I see myself—the way I saw me carrying through the old relationship was a lot like how my mother carried out her relationship with my father, which is that ... (I need to be very general about it—about things in general, was that ...) there were a lot of times when I thought that Winston was being an absolute ass-hole in a lot of day-to-day ways as well as big major ways—and I reacted in a way that I saw my mother reacted when my father acted the same way, which is sort of when I sat back and said to myself, ah, you know, something along the lines of, "Men will be men" or, "It's OK", or you know, "If I just sort of grin and bear it this time, the next time he won't do it again." Or, "Maybe I just hang in and wait for him to grow up." Now, of course it's not exactly the same because my mother had an additional excuse of having to stay together for the children, which wasn't applicable in this case, in my case. Uhm, but I think when I say, when I talk about trepidation and anxiety this time around, a lot of that is because I'm afraid that, well, it's a two-part fear; A) I'm afraid that Winston is going to revert to his former ass-hole behaviour, and B) I'm afraid that if that happens, I'll react the same way that I did before, which is to grin and bear it.

JSS: Hmmm-hmm. Well, how would you describe the ass-hole behaviour? What did it consist of?

ROSE: The day-to-day?

JSS: Yeah.

ROSE: Do you want me to go into this?

WINSTON: Of course.

ROSE: Uhm, thoughtlessness, carelessness, inconsiderateness, rudeness—and those are the mild ones. Rose hesitates.

JSS: Now, you feel hesitant to say it on the tape?

ROSE: Well …

JSS: Or to hurt him or what? He knows what you're talking about.

ROSE: (To Winston) Do you?

JSS: Does he not? Have you not told him before? Maybe not?

WINSTON: (Nodding) She has, but whether I know it or not it doesn't strike me as the point. I think it's better to say it regardless. (He says this as if it is her privilege to say it, as if it does not actually apply to him and require his input).

JSS: But, we have an example right here, of being reticent, or not saying things, which is like your mother.

ROSE: Correct.

JSS: And I'm trying to understand what goes into that holding back.

ROSE: Ah, well, part of it is that it's almost as if I feel like it's something I want to talk to him about alone, without you or the cameras around.

JSS: Hmmm. Hmm.

ROSE: Ah, but another part of that is just that he's heard it all before, so in a sense I'm almost like repeating myself.

JSS: Hmmm. (Pause.) Well, you know what Rose is talking about. I, I am mystified, I mean, I'm not able to help you if I don't know what we're talking about.

ROSE: Well, the manifestations of the adjectives that I just mentioned were things like—well, the one that comes to mind actually is being late all the time. I don't know why that comes up first, but … and not just late as in ten or fifteen minutes, but late as in hours late. Uhm—consistently late. Uhm. And then, and it wasn't even a case of not having a good excuse at the end, it was being unaware that the lateness engendered the degree of worry in me, that it did. I don't know if it was forgetfulness to call, or thoughtlessness in not calling. And then sort of breezing in and expecting everything to be OK.

JSS: Well, what I'm thinking now is that as I've been talking with you, I've been aware of feeling mystified a lot, and I have to press for more and say, well what do you mean by that? What type of cause or, you know, what university were you at?

ROSE: Hmmm.

JSS: There is a feeling of not really knowing and yet feeling that there's a lot that together you share that you can take for granted, that you instantly understand and know as you're talking, but I think as a couple perhaps not realising that *I* don't already know what *you* know. I think that's the same thing you're describing with Winston not realising what your experience was, or was not.

WINSTON: No.
JSS: Do you feel she's sensitive to the effects you …?
WINSTON: Well, I suppose not always to tell you the truth. No, she's not always observant either.
JSS: In which ways have you noticed that about her?
WINSTON: Well, considering the wedding for example, which ironic though it seems, was only mentioned in the negative context, that is that, uhm, it doesn't—the idea of marriage doesn't mean a lot to me, the institution is one that I have almost zero respect for, based as I think it is in property relations, and that I would marry her in an instant if that's what she wanted, but with the knowledge that it didn't mean anything compared to the willingness to say I want to be with you, and I'm willing to make a commitment to be with you. Uhm, but in reference to the marriage in general, not in general, the specific example that I use is her desire to have me dressed up for, essentially, a wedding, which was gonna be a civil service and in a Judge's Chambers. I found myself in a position of being in a store that I hated being in, around snobbish sales people that I wouldn't give the time of day to, whose opinions I could careless about, feeling really oppressed and encumbered that I even had to—pick through clothes that I wouldn't wear. Uhm I didn't even think of, I mean, I did think of, the money—I was like, I wouldn't wear $150 pants, I mean, if somebody gave them to me, I'd take them back and get the money for them. I mean it's nothing I could feel comfortable in anyway. Then I find myself almost paralysed, like, what am I gonna do? I mean, I didn't want to say no, but neither could I accept it. So, no, I wouldn't say she's always completely observant either, though the burden rests on me.
ROSE: Well, I think in general we have the same—we started out with the same expectations that it would be, originally it was—well, it's a long story—but originally it was supposed to be a mothers' only affair because my parents are separated and I didn't want to deal with having my father there at all. I just wanted my mother to be there. Ah ….Winston was, and did I think, call home and ask just his mother to attend.
WINSTON: I didn't particularly want my father there either.
ROSE: Right, but for various reasons. The Judge that married us was a friend of his parents—it was actually a friend of his father's, and so for that reason, we had to have his father there.
WINSTON: It was what you'd call, a seriously external factor, ahh.

Winston and Rose have some paranoia about authority but they have pushed past that to seek help. Intimacy is hard for them, and so it is hard to establish an intimate therapeutic relationship. Once in session they find it hard to voice their concerns. Yet they do reveal their pain and their struggle very clearly. They deliver it into the therapeutic relationship. They reach desperately for words to describe their difficulties. They have a limited access to emotional language. Winston agrees Rose might as well state her grievances even though he has heard them before, but he seems to think it is just a list to be mentioned, not something for him to deal with, and Rose obliges to meet his terms. She gives a list of nouns rather than telling a story about how awful it must have been to sit home for hours not knowing where her husband was. Winston wants to be with his wife but he runs away to substitute objects. As a couple they are in a state of fight or flight. In telling of the snobby sales people they show their vulnerability to feeling looked down on. I felt glad that I was wearing casual clothes myself, and that cued me to realise that the couple might be worried about me seeming snobby. I could appreciate Winston's love for repairing cars, and this moment of joining his experience helped me to overcome the perception of myself as superior and unable to relate to them. I am hearing about the mothers-only wedding, and I think now the mother part of me is being allowed in to their relationship but a father part of me is still being kept at bay. The cause comes before the person as if his wife is redundant. When she said "in this case" not "in my case" I think that she herself feels redundant. I am sure there are antecedents in their family histories, and now I have a natural segue into that.

Object relations history

JSS: I'd like to know how did your families feel about the match between you?

WINSTON: Hmm. Interesting question. Well, I hadn't thought that her mother thought much of me, before. Mostly I would've put it down to my politics—being a radical is not something that a conservative Japanese family would go for, but I have since learned, and the experience in the past several months has confirmed that, that was not a—politics was not a factor for her mother, that in fact, I think she does like me—and I like her. Her father is out of the picture, and … Politics, as I said, politics may have been something that he'd held against me, but he is like, not a factor anyway. My parents are more interesting, and more difficult to fathom, because I certainly had the feeling that of all the women that I've known in my life that Rose was certainly, as far as they were concerned, the most desirable as a match for me. Harvard, first and foremost, I think, in that criterion. Their latent racism would have counted against Rose inasmuch as she's Japanese, but I don't know, I think on the balance, they liked her and they would have hoped that I would marry her or someone like her, as opposed to anyone else I've known. But, their conduct in and around the wedding, doesn't really bear that out, I'll have to say, something of a mystery for me. They came to the wedding, I mean, I never gave them one indication or another, that I was gonna come dressed like in my work uniform, or that, you know, that I was getting an expensive suit just for the occasion or something. I never gave them any indication one way or another. They showed up, frumpy you know, frumpy suburbia. My sister, who was with them, was dressed quite nicely and looked great, and I'm just like, now, why would they do that? My father showed up to go into the Chambers of this Judge friend of his, you know, looking like he could, I don't know, he would never do that under any circumstances. He would never enter that courthouse in anything less than a dark suit, as far I could ever imagine him doing, and yet, here he is with his son getting married in his

Judge friend's Chambers and he shows up in some idiot looking plaid pants and some raggedy sports jacket. I mean, I, I had to like wonder, like, are they not in favour of this? I mean, do they not like this, or, do they not like her? Quite honestly, I didn't give a damn. I don't care much about my parents. I did it out of a sense of responsibility as far as my mother went, and my father had to be there, cause we wanted this judge for other purposes. Ah, I didn't think a lot about it. I don't care a lot about him.

JSS: But you …

WINSTON: But it is something of a mystery.

JSS: Well, a lot of the anxiety about the marriage ceremony focuses on the clothing of the male—whether he's gonna meet expectations or do what he pleases, or do what he usually does, or come up with something new or whatever. I don't know what that means either. One thing I do notice is that you both have fathers you'd like to get rid of.

ROSE: Why don't you give the example of how he didn't take you to the hospital?

WINSTON: That's not really as telling at all to me as the incident where a group of my friends—this was—sophomore year of high school, junior year? Junior year, it must have been. We went—we were roaming the neighbourhood, there was a big park area, adjacent to it was the home of some friends of theirs—multimillionaire, a real shithead. The wife was nice enough and their children were my younger brother's and sister's age, so they were, they were at one time fairly close. But he had an indoor pool—this guy—and was away on vacation, ah, had in fact given my parents some kind of permission to use it, though I would not have gone under regular circumstances. Failed to lock the door to the their glass-enclosed-indoor pool, and so we hit upon it, I don't know who discovered the door was open, and we went in and were swimming around and having a time, and I remember I remarked to my friends as I left, that, that it's funny that I had permission to go and ended up sneaking in with them, right? So one of the friends stuck around and, actually he wasn't a friend, one of the people who was there, one of the group, stuck around, and when he was questioned by some gardener or something, used my name after the fact when he was seen by somebody there. And I walked home, I walked into my parents' kitchen, like so what, what's going on, what's the big deal?—and was slammed up against the wall. I was physically beaten and abused, I mean, for daring to threaten their relationship with this person. I mean, they literally—my father wrestled me to the ground, my mother was kicking me—they were so upset, and I was like, you know, these people are sick. It didn't really strike me at the time I was numb, but I realise now just how perverse their priorities are. I don't care about millionaires, you know, I mean, take them from a Doonesbury cartoon, they can chop them up and ground them into hamburgers for the homeless, I mean, I (laughs), so even at the time I had fairly rebellious ideas, though, certainly no structure to it. Yeah, I—no, I don't, I don't understand paying thousands of dollars to belong to a country club while you can't afford to finish having braces on your children's teeth, and have to have them taken off half way resulting in, you know, a lot more trouble and hassle later when *I* had to pay $2,500 to have my teeth straightened, and it would have been even less expensive and less painful if they had never done it, but instead they did it half way. And then they give me some shit that they didn't realise it would be a problem. You shouldn't have them done half way—I'm sure the dentist told them up and down don't stop now—you're half way into this (laughs), and then they just told me later, "Well, we never, they never told us that." C'mon, be real. Any dentist worth his salt would say that just so they would get the bill paid.

JSS: But you felt they didn't really have your needs as a priority.

WINSTON: No, no, I don't think they, I don't think they ever have—I mean ...

JSS: And they probably felt that you didn't understand their needs.

WINSTON: I didn't appreciate their concerns, yeah. I didn't really live to up to their expectations either. Oh well.

JSS: Now that part is like what Rose said about you, which is not being aware of the effects of your actions on her. I mean, although you can't be bothered with millionaires, you went into their pool nonetheless.

WINSTON: Mmm.

JSS: You didn't say "I'm not going to that place."

WINSTON: Oh, hell, I mean, I'd expropriate their property and put him up against the wall in a heart beat, but, I don't think that—some how, I think it's more like being a first son and being doted upon. I learned from my mother, if not, from both my parents, that I was spoiled and that created an expectation that people would do things for me and that I wouldn't be aware of their expectations of me.

JSS: Hmm.

WINSTON: I mean, that much I can buy, but as for needing to accept their life style and their social values, no. I don't equate my rejection of that with callousness towards the woman I love, no. I don't see any equivalence there if that's what you mean.

JSS: No, that's not what I meant.

WINSTON: Then I wasn't aware of (motions not understanding what JSS meant.)

JSS: Well, I think there's some carry over of your need to reject their values, and to stay immune from their feelings about you, that carries over to Rose.

WINSTON: Hmm. Their feeling about me ...

JSS: Where you kind of block off what impact you're having on her because in the past that impact has not seem to you to make sense. It seemed to be not evidence of concern for you, but evidence of having the wrong priorities.

WINSTON: Hmm.

JSS: (turning to Rose) Now, I would like to ask about your father, about having to blank him out. How did you feel treated by him?

ROSE: Well, I guess I should talk about how I was brought up because it's very different to the way that Winston was brought up and it's probably very different from how most people are brought up. Ah, my father worked for the United Nations, which meant that we lived sort of peripatetically. Ah, I was born in Turkey and then we moved to the Netherlands and then to England from there, during which time my father was working in France. And then I went to college after that. So, I was brought up without a feeling of having a home or, I mean a home as in a country, or having to deal with neighbours, or you know, growing up with the same kids, and going to the same high school and so on. Given that, it made the family the only unit that I could identify with. So, it became the centre. So it was all the roots I had, basically, was being part of a family, and essential to my feeling of belonging to a family and all that, was to keep up the myth that it was a perfect family and that it was a family that I could feel good about, and one of the myths that I was brought up with was that my father was a wonderful guy. Both he and my mother told me, and who was I to think differently, being so young. Ah, and the reasons why even as a child I had problems accepting the myth, ranged from sort of an ass-hole behaviour on my father's part, uhm, inability to show affection, sneering, hum callousness, ah sort of blaming the children, and especially me because I was a lot older than—I was the first born and also because I'm a lot older than my brother. Blaming me for his life and the inadequacies that he thought thereof, that he perceived. Blaming me for the way his marriage wasn't working out the way he wanted it to, blaming me for not being able, for his not being able to leave his job. Once he blamed me for the fact that he was unable to commit suicide—cause he had to stay alive to look after me basically, and so if it wasn't for me, life would be a lot easier for him.

JSS: Hmm. So it was a big responsibility.

ROSE: Oh yeah. Oh, yeah, but, anyway, that's one part of it. There are other things too like the way he could, he expressed anger which was very indiscriminately. I mean, he was bad at expressing anger toward something that he was angry at, that is, you know, the boss at work, or whatever. Instead he would sort of take it home and dump it all on us at home. Um, and a lot of it was directed at my mother, of course, and a lot of it just sort of spilled on to me. Uhm, there were other things too, but I think in terms of child rearing, ah, unlike Winston I guess, I sort of, don't think of my parents as together. I think of my father as being very separate from my mother. In other words, ah, when it comes to child rearing it's hard for me to say, yeah, my parents did this and this to me. It's more like, I mean my father's idea of child rearing was to tell me to be good otherwise my mother would get it. Uhm, he would tell me unless I was good my mother would leave him. Unless I was good my mother would kill herself. Uhm, so when I was applying to colleges, uhm, what I really wanted to do was to, actually what I really, really wanted to do was to go to an American Ivy League college. Uhm, even before I got accepted anywhere my father said to me, first he said, well, I would never get in, so why bother trying. And then he said, 'well you know even if you did get in and go, it's so expensive, how can you, how could you feel right sort of expropriating family funds to go to an expensive Ivy League school?'

JSS: Each of you in your own way has a great deal of anger about your family backgrounds.

WINSTON: I think that's a safe statement—yes (laughs).

JSS: Yeah. Pretty obvious, hmm? But there is a certain theme that you talk of, of things being destroyed—conventions destroyed, values being knocked, and then an

WINSTON: Hmm, Hmm.

JSS: So I think there is really a search for integrity there and for an inner value that doesn't depend on outer signs of success, conventional beauty, or that which is approved of. Would you say?

WINSTON: I'd like to think that.

JSS: Hmm, Hmm. At the same time, I mean, all of that, I mean, it contributes to the kind of energy you take into the fight for the political cause. At the same time it is tending to destroy the relationship that you have with Rose—at least it did in the past. At the moment it is not doing so, but you're both somewhat worried that this could happen again, I think. And I would say if it did, it would happen because of unmetabolised anger …

WINSTON: Mmm.

JSS: … in you (looking at Winston) about your background, and if it did, your contribution (looking at Rose) to it would be the kind of depression that you bring to this marriage from your adjustment to your family situation, which is not one of anger—I don't think, but rather one of feeling weighed down by an unfair sense of responsibility, although in an assertive move, you did secure for yourself education at Harvard.

ROSE: And have been paying for it ever since. More or less.

WINSTON: In what sense?

ROSE: Feeling guilty.

WINSTON: Oh yeah, right.

JSS: Well, you did enjoy the fruits of it in work for a while. I mean, I know you're not working at the moment, but you expect to get a job again.

WINSTON: Yeah, yeah.

JSS: But you feel you got possession of it and it's making you guilty to have that.

ROSE: Hmm, Hmm.

JSS: Well, the other thing I noticed about you as a couple is that being very bright, you have sometimes a very intellectual way of talking, so that, as I said, it's hard for me to know what you're really talking about some times. Although it appears that you know, but then again perhaps, perhaps you don't know anymore than I know, from listening to you.

WINSTON: Hmm, Hmm.

JSS: Sometimes talking about the general vs. the specific. Things of an intellectual sort like that can mask very much simpler, more basic feelings that each may be afraid of expressing to the other or sharing together. I feel that you have a, you give an impression of being in a, very deep state of communication with each other, just understanding a great deal about each other. I don't know if it's true—it seems that way. I know that what it provokes in me is an enormous sense of being

	mystified.
WINSTON:	(Chuckles).
JSS:	And often not really knowing what you're talking about at all.
WINSTON:	Hmm.
JSS:	So I have to get very concrete and ask about this and that, which maybe that's something that you shy away from because it seems so mundane or so suburban, the stuff of ordinary human life as opposed to something associated with, you know, higher purposes.
WINSTON:	What you said, you know, some of it, the current state and, I thought that was very interesting, struck me as hitting the mark, and for me the idea that Rose would bring her depression, that I'd be identified with her father, uhm.
JSS:	Well, you did fit in a number of accounts.
WINSTON:	(Laughing) Yes, certainly.
JSS:	On callousness, on saying that you had to work when maybe you're avoiding the situation at home.
WINSTON:	Well, there is some trepidation now in terms of how we're going to make it. Ah.

Winston may have felt interrupted when I stopped talking to him in order to include Rose. I do this because a consultation is a survey of the relationship and its place in the generations. In both families there is rage and violence. As a couple they both have traumatic backgrounds. Each of them knows about pain, rejection, and fury but each deals with it differently. Rose comes across as calm and thoughtful. Winston is passionate, rebellious, and vengeful. He can be soothed by her. She remains calm because she puts all the aggressive feelings in him. As a couple they have a system for moderating rage but it fails and so they split up, but they still need the system, and so then they get back together again. Rose says poignantly that she never had a home. How do they create a home for their couple when neither of them had a safe home? They are organised against hate and contempt. It is not easy to get beneath the aggression of wanting to chop up parents and people with money, smash conventions and expensive houses, but I did feel that they wanted me to get past it to understand their need for retreat. There was so much love for protecting an old car. I could appreciate the value of that, and it led me to realise that they each did appreciate aspects of each other—intellectual competence, attention to values, her appreciation for his commitment to her, his appreciation that she is the keeper of the intimate relationship. This helped me reach past the arrogance and rage to connect with their underlying need for repair, and to experience them as a couple of integrity I could work with in couple therapy.

Aspects of assessment

For those who work in private practice a paragraph will suffice to summarise impressions and recommendations, such as I have done above. For those who work in a clinic, a standard assessment form is often required. What have we learned from this couple, and have we covered enough items on the checklist? The checklist below was constructed from a summary of the assessment form in use at the Tavistock Centre for Couple Relationships.

Details of previous therapy: None to report.

Appearance, manner, differences, and emotional state: The couple is appropriately dressed and well educated. One is from an Asian family, one is American. (this was mentioned but cultural differences were not yet addressed. For instance I would explore the childhood history of the wife's parents enquiring about war trauma and attitudes toward women in earlier generations). Both speak fluently, but have difficulty finding words for emotion, and are hard to relate to. Their arrogance covers hurt and inferiority.

Presenting Problem: Ambivalence about being a couple, and conflict over work and intimacy.

Personal histories: Both experienced trauma in their families because of their parents' way of raising them. Winston's parents are together, Rose's parents are separated, her father is somewhat nomadic and her mother frequently suicidal.

History of the relationship: They have been together off and on for a couple of years dogged by long-standing conflict and ambivalence. Now that they have been married for two weeks they are now seeking help somewhat belatedly while in transition from school to work. Their employment is not steady.

Assessment of couple interaction: The couple fits around shared issues of hatred of fathers and intellectual arrogance. These are shared defences against narcissistic hurt from adolescent trauma. The couple projects rebellion and disregard into the husband and calm resignation into the wife.

How did the couple relate to the therapist?: They kept the therapist at bay. The therapist's countertransference was one of feeling excluded and stupid. They treated the therapist as a mother who could be let in eventually. They responded to interpretation, and the therapist felt able to connect with them after all.

Significant moments: A core affective exchange occurred when the wife recognised the resonance between her husband's thoughtlessness and her father's way of treating her mother. She recognised her own acquiescence as being like her mother's and thus she found herself re-creating her parents' marriage. The most affectively charged experience in the countertransference was the feeling of mystification. Interpretation coming from that countertransference led to greater collaboration and eventual understanding.

Formulation of transference and countertransference: There was an arrogant rebellious transference to the therapist as a snobby parent obsessed with appearances. The therapist's received the transference to her as a parental snob object but did not get taken over by it. Instead she connected with a marital self of integrity, thanks to the image of the restoration of old cars. She experienced a countertransference feeling of mystification (connecting to a defence against aggressive parental objects) and stupidity and inferiority (connecting to the self's anxiety of not being adequate to the task of meeting parental expectations). Feeling put off gave way to a gradual warming to the couple.

Recommendation for therapy: The partners agreed on the nature of their problem and showed interest in understanding its antecedents. They were able to use interpretive work and become reflective about their situation. So couple therapy is recommended. This could be concurrent with continuing individual therapy for the wife, but the couple has limited means and cannot afford two therapies. So the individual therapist will be involved in their decision whether or not to accept the recommendation.

Practical considerations: Since the couple has a low income, the couple therapist for them will be at the low-fee clinic where the fee can be set at the minimum level. They will begin more easily with a woman couple therapist because of the virulent paternal transferences.

Conclusion

In this single consultation, the couple had moved a long way toward communicating more directly about their feelings and their traumas, but they will need much more time in analytic couple therapy to develop emotional muscle and understanding of themselves, of each other, and of their couple relationship. The couple and the individual therapist accepted the recommendation. Rose and Winston began couple therapy at the clinic.

CHAPTER THIRTEEN

The triangular field of couple containment

Carl Bagnini

When working with couples, I search for clinical ideas that reveal the unconscious pathological matrix of couple relating and provide therapeutic guidelines for ameliorating their destructive hold on couple life. I admit to lapses in containment when I hate couples, which usually occurs when I am prevented from gaining satisfaction from therapeutic work. I have learned to accept hateful feelings when couples resist my help because I recognise their defensive function when I am feeling inadequate like a stupid object. I recognise countertransference regressions before too much of me gets wiped out by too much of a couple's projective identification—as when I enter a schizoid withdrawal and need a rescue team of ideas to pull me out. I get pulled in losing neutrality and become over identified with what the couple cannot comprehend. Becoming enmeshed in a couple's projective dance is a triangular dynamic that can lead to enactments when containment is bombarded by powerful and primitive affects.

I also seek out concepts that free up thinking when mentalising gets blocked by disturbing affects in the dyad. Containment of the couple's primitive defences and anxieties is essential to establishing a safe working alliance, but containment and its rupture reveals how we therapists get inevitably caught in the web of triangular transferences. To meet the clinical challenge of containment in couple therapy, I have expanded the dyadic approach to couple containment by re-centreing our focus. We want to learn how the couple's pathological object relations intertwine with our emotional responses in the clinical encounter. Triangular containment utilises an object relations conceptualisation of three unconscious minds interacting in time and space observed through a wider analytic lens. We want a road map for tracking the triangular field of the couple's good, bad, and split-off objects to trace interpersonal subjectivities communicated through the couple's transferences. Who we become transferentially determines the focus of the work. We identify the objects repeatedly used that keep the couple stuck and locate their part or whole object functions as they become manifest in our internal reactions. This is the process we use to provide secure holding and to test interpretations of unconscious relational processes.

In the triangular approach to containment we expand the boundaries of the transference field to include ourselves. In principle, the inclusion of the therapist within the field is based on the belief that we cannot remain on the outside or the surface of the couple relationship. In order to comprehend the couple's matrix of unconscious communications and developmental deficits we need access to the inside realm of their experience. The clinical information we need is obtained by specifying the dyadic elements of individual transferences (each partner to us) and of each partner to the other, enlarging the field to include our individual countertransferences to each partner and to the couple as a pair. The field of observation starts from the intrapsychic and extends to the interpsychic and lastly to the triangular field. We do not sacrifice individual personality issues or depth to learn about the couple-therapist system. We utilise a breadth and depth perspective through the triangular approach which helps us to recognise non-rational, distorted and intuitive components of transferences and countertransference that oscillate and reveal important relational issues in the triadic dimension of clinical experience.

We use triangular thinking as a conceptual bridge for navigating the complexity of couple projective identifications, such as persecutory anxieties and rigid defences. The gestalt of the couple unit functions as a clinical entity that overtakes our mentalising capacity. The partners can merge in a dual unity to keep us at bay, or smother our thoughts that differ from theirs. Our clinical function becomes submerged when the triadic dimension of object relations takes hold. The couple uses joint defences against becoming known even though relationship pain has brought them into treatment. By unifying defences they may ward off shameful feelings of failing in the marriage. They may avoid being "found out" and use joint defences associated with fear in the setting of being exposed to one's partner or the therapist. Being shamed as inadequate or at fault is associated with narcissistic vulnerability and so couples protect themselves from humiliation.

The therapist observes and feels the couple's obfuscated, distorted, and contrary views. Major defences are in use and we feel caught in an oceanic mess when entering a complex primordial ooze of unconscious couple dynamics while attempting to remain dry. The couple's internalised family dynamics carry the developmental histories and tragedies of each partner, and our histories can become enmeshed, for better and for worse, since we may disidentify or counter-identify with aspects of history that we repel or merge with, depending on our partially unmetabolised backgrounds. In triadic containment the clinical elements receive close scrutiny due to affectively charged interactions between the couple and us. Triadic transferences can inform our work, once we gain access to their dynamic domain.

The therapeutic work is towards object re-integration through acknowledgement of past object relational influences and mourning lost objects. We want a method that accomplishes the clinical task in a benign way when the couple lives out their conflicts and broken dreams, and we want to use the way they represent it in treatment for understanding what went wrong, in order to determine how we might make things right. Containment and informed observation lead to interpretations, and we employ triangular transference tools when reflecting on the countertransference evoked in sessions.

Containment issues with collusive couples

With particularly collusive couples I carry a notion into the session that interpersonal communication is circular, and enactments will occur, and that partners are not entirely motivated by unseen forces—while the unmetabolised unconscious plays its part in over determining behaviour that causes misery, it is not the only force at play in the system. Very disturbed couples can consciously know what they do to each other, but they prefer not to get too worked up about the effects. That leaves us to think about what the couple cannot. We think about the unconscious contribution of the couple unit to the collusive process that promotes tolerable negative object experience. After all, a bad object experience is better than having no object to relate to. Controlling the other to prevent becoming controlled occurs when helplessness is defended against through use of counter-dependent motives. We may in the triadic sense be caught between dependency and counter-dependent expressions that need containment. We try to gather up the ambivalences being expressed but must be watchful for our tendency to become persuasive that the couple give up their resistance pre-maturely, so we can feel accepted.

Instead, we have to consider that the person one is married to has become the feared other. The fear of being taken over by the other replaces the earlier attraction to the other in the courtship; this is a complicated matter that requires time and patience to unfold, but in the meantime our frustrations, including hateful feelings can parallel the couple's unmetabolised negative transferences combined with our fear of being rejected. We use our lens into the triangular field because it permits a close monitoring of syntonic couple defences. If we get caught up in what the couple cannot recognise we are likely to respond, or react with a counter-resistance to the couple's "acceptable suffering" by arguing with the couple or by insisting they not accept their suffering. "We" are suffering and we have difficulty containing it. However, to prevent a potential impasse we examine all of the transferences, especially our own—we may be struggling against intolerable suffering that the couple's internal objects require, and we have to contain it in ourselves. We may be struggling against remaining passive not wanting to accommodate the demands of the object/s that we suffer and sacrifice to no avail. In dyadic transference analysis we may be identified with one transference dimension, and our reaction may be to join with the partner who is more painfully co-opted by the other's syntonic object relations. If we take sides we may isolate the other partner by attending to the one apparently more aggrieved and lose the couple. Couples will fiercely protect their marriage against a well intentioned therapist.

We may be in touch with our developmentally healthy protest against tyranny that the couple is unable to access. In order to work with the couple, however, we would process the negative aspect of the induced countertransference in the triangular field and be aware we would be shaming one or both into submitting to our premature demand for change, thus repeating the underlying dysfunctional family dynamics.

The transference field is a three-person field and we are affected and affect the couple by our responses to what they say and do. I have made the point that triangular transference is messy because it rapidly oscillates within the mental space of the clinical setting and is therefore not easy to track or organise for interpretive comment. The chaos from emotional saturation in heated sessions yields another notion about the triangle and our use of self. We are responsible for locating and monitoring our part in the projective process, but without becoming permanently caught up in the couple's projective identificatory patterns. If we remain emotionally distant we will not have an experience-near enough vantage point to comprehend the developmental failures we need to address, and to monitor the personal feelings evoked in us in the treatment. If our feelings remain underground, or too detached we cannot access our internal object world in order to learn what to supply for remediation. We can get caught up in side-taking and need to guard against over-identifying with one spouse due to our personal object relations history.

The triangular theory I have in mind provides scaffolding for building a clinically comprehensive practice with couples. The theory involves the interactional field that Henry Dicks (1975) proposed in his work on marital tensions. We summarise the three levels he described: First, cultural values and norms—race, education, religion, and values. Second, central egos—personal norms, conscious judgments, and expectations, habits, and tastes. Third, unconscious forces—repressed or split off including object relations.

Triangular theory aids in the search for comprehension and technique by providing a dual focus when encountering couple primitive mental states, by drawing us into undisclosed primitive fantasies, or if disclosed but not modified, rendering us null and void. When discussing primitive fantasies and ways to work with them I use the concept of triangulation ordinarily associated with family systems thinking, (undifferentiated ego mass, for example) but applicable to psychoanalytic thinking about couples. Triangulation can lead to therapeutic strangulation unless we are skilled in locating our part in the enmeshment process. I think triangulation can fit between Henry Dick's second and third levels.

Triangular field of fantasy

Triangulation of unconscious fantasy in the interpsychic world of the couple deadens desires and maintains a tolerable balance that allows marriages to go on. Transferences to the therapist limit reality when used as a splitting defence, which is when we get a splitting headache. Behavioural repertoires and mature affective responses are limited. Options are condensed and shaped by infantile issues; repetitive misuse of the other dominates relating to self and other due to narcissistic aims. In severe examples the primitive use of fantasy will shape and control the couple's aliveness as in a sado-masochistic object relationship. We can become the filter for these fantasies or the recipient for their acting out.

We need to comprehend and access the underbelly of psychic fixations that strangle or pervert desires. Triangular fantasies focus on the treatment field. The couple maintains its dance of sameness. Emotional deadness accompanies volatility while the crisis of the week disguises the central issues, namely undiagnosed oscillations between spouses' developmentally stuck levels of love and hate, driven by paranoia and persecutory anxieties of earlier developmental stages from infancy to adolescence. Left untended, these anxieties undermine any movement into mature adult life.

The more regressed couples get variously diagnosed as having personality disorders, including borderline, narcissistic, and schizoid types. Unfortunately in the triangular field we fall into the trap of using technique as though these couples function within more neurotic spheres, believing that they will respond favourably to suggestion, focused interpretations, and discussion of historical precursors, with the hope that this approach will illuminate repetitive, self-defeating interactions. While there are moments in which such depressive position interventions are useful with character disordered couples, more often transference psychosis prevails. In these instances we become non-human objects, relegated to mental furniture, bits and pieces of the non-human world, and treated as eczema, sunburn, or other irritants in the couple's space. In more developed couples the transference can be interpreted as an experience once lived with Uncle Billy, who bullied the husband as a child, and now resides in the couple's negative interactions. Not so with more primitive couples. The triangular lens detects the primitive use of fantasies that co-opt the therapist's thinking process and presses him to join in the couple's merger-rejection continuum.

Triangular thinking includes both the unconscious and conscious world of fantasies. Fantasies reveal couple preoccupations or unconscious basic assumptions. Couple sexual and interpersonal relating leans towards the paranoid/schizoid realm; we need ideas that might liberate creative thinking when caught in intractable situations, such as impasse, dead space, when we feel numb or dumb, or when otherwise stuck.

The interpsychic continuum of couples is a subject that we too easily neglect when drawn into primitive relating. We can become enmeshed in the couple's struggle over which spouse is right, who is responsible for causing the troubled situation. When affect is high we become like oppressed traffic cops, trying to maintain a measure of calm in the midst of madness. Madness, the psychotic-like world, the unanalysed, consists of a mental space that is devoid of texture. The landscape is flat and endless, a deflated world, lacking dimensionality, without emotion or creative imagination.

With experience, we can develop a meaningful presence in which our countertransference ranges between antipathy, and empathy, building a necessary tension between the internal mental space of the couple and what their fantasies force upon us. We can identify with the primal, but eventually we manage a gentle unveiling of the primacy of the couple's narcissistic wounds that harbour resentments and underscore the couple's central shared views of mistrust of intimacy.

Spousal ideations can also take on deadly repetitive flatness, so that a new ego-ideal cannot be sought. Yet the couple is there, seeking some redress, an answer, a different object experience, their analytic potential is up against all that has been. We who endeavor a therapeutic relationship are bound up in the tension of the asymmetry of profound differences between them and us. Solitude accompanies us in the field, for we are alone, immediately alone, as primitive transference takes its toll.

Unconscious triangular fantasies powerfully over-determine couple options and threaten therapeutic outcome if we are not in touch with them. Therapists who mostly stay in the interpersonal space of couple interactions come to parallel the same psychological ignorance as the couple. We want to get to the underlying meanings that could cast a new perspective on current disturbances. Enactments within the therapy offer entry into the couple system. New knowledge is obtained in the therapy triangle based on access to affect and cognition that the couple's behaviour evokes. Couple attacks on reflective thinking as psychobabble interfere with the dynamic understanding of the treatment experience. Primitive shutting down on mentalising makes us lose our way. By thinking between sessions we re-examine our confusion or paralysis and work to bring new containment during sessions that promotes a shift in the enmeshment. A language may be available that recognises the shared paralysis that has us "feeling" the couple's terror of dangerous desires, such as fears of abandonment or of becoming overwhelmed by dependency needs. We can then move into the dark interior of what was beneath what they acted out in the triangular space, and address their insecurities and pain.

I will summarise three aspects of couple unconscious object usage that deaden desire. The first is triangulation in the unconscious system, the second is phantasy, as in the Kleinian (1946) and Bionian (Bion, 1957) sense of psychotic to non-psychotic manifestations of repressed infantile object relations, including basic assumption thinking. Third, desire refers to interpersonal aspects of frustrated love and unmetabolised hate manifested in couple interactions. Desire itself is dangerous to disturbed individuals, especially if there is a history of profound early persecution, such as emotional blurring of gender or intergenerational boundary violations, in sexual over-stimulation or abuse, or in family psychosis.

When we assess the role of unconscious phantasies in repressing, or displacing couple desires, we should ask if we get enmeshed with one spouse or the other in the course of splitting process? Couple treatment is a natural emotional triangle and we monitor our total response to deep pathological relating. Monitoring requires tools to reclaim a measure of clarity of what belongs to us and what is theirs. Repressed fantasies can be connected to marital fears and dreads and fuel acting out. Couples and therapists are prone to getting caught up in addressing the acting out spouse, without exploring the multi-dimensional dynamics of shared unconscious motives. Each spouse's contribution to the unconscious dance of denial can take a second, sometimes distant backseat.

In triangulation, a dyad comes under siege by an external disturbing situation that cannot be metabolised. When the external event is combined with a conflictual primary object relationship, it leads to a calamity, and one or the other spouse then seeks a third object or part object to focus on, in order to deflect intolerable anxieties—such as abandonment, rejection, or annihilation. The object can be a part-object as in an affair, an obsession with a child, other family members or neighbours, alcohol, sexual perversion, or high levels of affective discharge, or inhibition. Almost any one can be confiscated for use. Internalised individual object relationships may carry such part objects from the distant past, or a new part-object may be constructed. The therapist may become a target for displaced object projections, used to drain off anxieties or to locate the bad object in the therapist as a temporary salve to a wounded self. The unconscious phantasy, or object one chooses, is connected to its original disturbed object relationship that resurfaces under life circumstances for which the couple is ill equipped.

Clinical example of triangulation, fantasy, and containment

A wife spoke to her mother and two sisters extensively twice every day throughout her first marriage, whether at home or on vacation. Her first husband had little interest in her preoccupation, and spent much of his time drinking and working. In the second marriage her new husband took issue with her, feeling she was unavailable to him and that she was caught up in family concerns as though it were her sole emotional responsibility to look after them. After much denial and rationalising it emerged that she had a childhood based dread of losing her mind if there was space between herself and mother, and her sisters had to be included in the telephone chain to prevent them feeling jealous of her special relationship with mother. Related to this was an unconscious fantasy that her parents would break up during her childhood if the patient became independent. She unconsciously feared mother's neediness, which when observed with father resulted in the patient panicking that he would leave them. This material gradually evolved in the treatment. My impression of this couple was that her first marriage choice had implications for the intimacy problems in the second marriage.

This concise vignette is characteristic of a triangulated couple and includes: lack of differentiation as when a symbiotic/fused relationship is threatened by a newborn, (or new spouse) and produces a negative transference-triangle. Triangulation within the couple system can stand out as the external pattern that defeats dyadic intimacy. I differentiate the external influences from the triangular use of the clinical space. In a clinical triangle, the triangular transference includes the therapist as the outsider, replicating both the original triangles of the spouses' oedipal issues and potential symbiotic struggles.

With come couples, I encounter fusion as a defensive pattern, where closeness is claimed by assumption but couple language ignores self language, or "I" statements. Any differences that emerge produce high anxiety and regressive pulls. When enmeshed spouses eventually accuse each other, the result is that neither spouse is in touch with failures or losses in the other. Emerging terrifying aggression may fuel adversarial exchanges. The deepest hurts and fears may result in fragmentation, resulting in depressive, or suicidal threats. Such is the case when there is an unexpected surfacing of unconsciously held autonomous strivings that signals destruction of the wished-for marriage of fused togetherness. Under these circumstances one or the other spouse will insist on talking about a third to avoid self-revelation, thwarting efforts to discuss how individual histories or differences contribute to their difficulties. Then the spouses re-focus on the previous "crisis" or "problem" with endless accusations and counterclaims. These couples disallow space for personal relating, with hidden areas of failure and disillusionment with life courses that are not discussed.

Through all these patterns, we are looking for triangulation in the form of fantasies that help maintain spousal self-coherence at the price of intimate relating. Disturbed couples regard love with distrust because it is front-loaded with infantile motives. If you ask such a couple what brought them together, their motives seem superficial, without awareness of the implications of their choices or with any sense of which later life adjustments might require change or growth.

Internet pornography represents a couple's object usage that prevents sexual and relationship closeness. A collusive acceptance of a partner's compulsive use of Internet pornography allows an illusion of individual freedom. Claustrophobia in one spouse's childhood consisted of fears of being controlled, and enmeshed, so that it became dangerous to be in the other's hands. With pornography the husband can control the female in his selected scenarios and since he controls the selection of the images and encounters, real relationships are kept at bay.

Triadic transference and containment in supervision of a couple case

Jan, the couple therapist, is a clinical psychologist and a graduate of a psychoanalytic institute, with fifteen years of practice with individuals, but she is relatively new to couple work.

She consulted me because the wife spoke about ending the couple therapy, saying all therapy should end and the couple should make it on their own. Jan reports that no affect accompanies the statement, as the husband remains quiet. I silently consider whether Jan has been absorbed by the couple's fear of learning about dangerous desires so that Jan might represent a threat to expose the deeper meanings of their disconnection. Jan has been seeing the couple once per week for six months.

Jan reports that the couple goes on to agree about ending while valuing Jan's help. Their generous accolades keep Jan from responding to the "threat" of ending. It feels to Jan that ending is precipitous rather than a consequence of progress. The couple started treatment because of premature ejaculation and wanted more sexual satisfaction. I initially ask Jan how satisfaction would function for the couple: Is there a plumbing issue in which anatomy is limp and sexual desire needs tweaking, or are they projecting lost or feared intimacy into erectile loss. Jan's attempts to follow up as to whether the erectile issues have been resolved, produces little continuity of material or curiosity regarding what anything might mean. Jan also reports being reluctant to discuss sex in detail with the couple.

One historical fact stood out in the early phase of the consultation: Each spouse had lost a younger sibling soon after birth—a brother when the wife was age seven and a sister when the husband was age six. But neither had shown any affect about the losses which were presented matter-of-factly. Jan reported the couple often spoke at great length about their two children, a boy and a girl. When frustrated with them, they wished they could be childless. Their parents were also twice divorced and are currently nearing a third divorce each. Jan had not thought to link oedipal or sibling aggression to the lost siblings that paralleled their wish to be "childless" so as not to have children to compete with or worry about.

Other issues in the early sessions included the wife's disdain for the husband in matters of self-assertiveness, and her wish to be protected by him. He came up short in her estimation in child rearing and decision making around time with extended kin, vacations and financial matters. He sheepishly hints at her faults: She is opinionated, not allowing him room for responding, which she justifies because he comes up short. I wonder out loud if "coming up short" may symbolise premature ejaculation. Jan is focused on the couple's style of relating: They bring up an event each session that is discussed at length. Usually it has to do with their experience driving in the car, or at the airport before a flight. In each report they appear caught in a helpless dilemma. For example, they can't find their way, or they are worried how their ten-year-old will get on the plane on a solo trip to his grandma. Jan reported with considerable frustration how she engages them in what she believes is a good faith effort to ascertain what feelings are connected to produce mutual helplessness. They do not admit to helplessness, just to being emotional for a time. They fill the session with anxiety-laden concerns, but when Jan takes them seriously they back away or change the subject. They rather enjoy, Jan thinks, the experience of filling the session space with drama without the need to explore or resolve anything.

I now brought up the matter of the couple's interpsychic collusion: They merge in a joint defence against differentiation as individuals so that the therapist is pushed to the side. If Jan individualises a communication with one partner, the couple unifies to prevent a dyadic relationship with the therapist. The supervisor's perspective is that there is insufficient interpreting of the couple's interpsychic or shared defences.

Recently Jan has gotten terse reactions from the wife who rejects Jan's efforts to link their "dilemmas" to early-life experiences of loss. Jan checks with the husband as to his perceptions regarding what is reported by the wife, to find out if they are fully enmeshed. I have a sense of a Mad Hatter's tea party! Triangulated mutual helplessness in the case is transferred into the supervisor-supervisee field from the therapist-couple situation. I think about how the supervision-supervisee process parallels several features of the case. I am becoming tense and terse with Jan as I feel she is listening to me but not hearing. The wife in the case gets terse with Jan when Jan tries to open up an idea for thinking together. I feel marginalised and I am reminded of how Jan reports the couple's collusive arrangement in which they marginalise Jan, and the wife specifically cuts the husband off as "coming up short". Castration (phallically being unable to keep it up) comes to mind as Jan and I are feeling powerless in becoming a creative couple. Jan and I are triangulated with the couple, stuck in our own way because we are enacting the pathological dynamics of fusion-fission (enmeshed in feeling helpless and not thinking together due to aggression and guilt pushing us apart). Jan may be feeling guilty for not doing better therapy while I feel tense, guilty and inadequate to help her. Our supervisory relationship has joined the Mad Hatter's tea party.

The triangular transference situation

As the summer approached Jan had to cancel an appointment with the couple but asked to reschedule it. They took their time getting back to her, saying it could wait until the next regular appointment. They asked in their voicemail, "Was she anxious about something, and couldn't wait for the next time?" The cancellations occurred during the time that the spouses were dangling their tacit agreement to be terminating, though no date had been set, nor had Jan been able to get anywhere by discussing their motives, or what they thought about their progress.

I had been feeling Jan's idealisation of me all along, and had not responded consciously to it in relation to the case dynamics due to my own narcissistic satisfaction (Quinodoz, 1994). During my musing about that and the couple's rather bizarre use of Jan, she cancelled our supervision—a first, and she did not state a reason. I began to think about the parallel process, and then more unconscious triadic material emerged. Jan had been venting in our supervisory sessions. I had allowed it, saving a few minutes for comment at the end, which she appreciated. For example, I had suggested to Jan that the couple was either dissociating or sadistically projecting their paranoid mistrust onto her by getting her to work for them while annihilating any good faith effort to reach them. Later, when reflecting on the session, I realised that I had spoken with an edge of uncustomary bluntness, and now felt badly that no supportive affect accompanied my comments. On further reflection, I thought my treatment of Jan paralleled the couple's rejection of Jan. I now thought the projective matrix was embedded in the triad of supervision. Any negative feelings Jan had in supervision and in the case had been ignored by my accepting an idealised role. Jan and the couple were absorbed in a split of toxic pseudo-idealised object relationship—good therapist—good couple, while Jan was feeling less and less competent both with them and me. By allowing idealisation in supervision, I was out of touch with the core affect of our experience, like the couple, while Jan floundered; yet she believed in me as her mentor. Attending to Jan's cancelling of the two appointments with the couple and with me, freed us up, although the complex parallel process took time to unpack.

When we met again Jan was able to see her anger at the couple and the wish to terminate with them before they did with her. But now we saw much more. Jan had temporarily left supervision by cancelling. We could now recognise the enacted aspects in supervision of deadness and stupidity in the paired relationships. The couple threatened to leave therapy but had stayed, and Jan stayed in supervision while taking flight from it. Jan could express anger that I was too detached, and was allowing her to flounder. She realised she was not able to confide her disappointment in me since she put the blame on herself. We discussed at length the parallels emerging from the cancelled appointments and I encouraged her to express the undiscussed feelings about us. Once we unpacked the cut off between us, and my role in it, we were able to get back on track. Rather than worry about losing the case, we discussed how our discovery might offer a shift in her approach to the couple's dysfunctional use of her. I surmised Jan had repressed anger at the couple that was paralysing her due to the idealisation of the supervision, which paralleled the couple's patronising attitude that did not allow learning to occur in the treatment.

Jan decided to share her observations of their need for her aliveness by keeping her attention, but also how they also kept her dead, incapable, and unrelated to their deeper needs. Jan felt empowered to say they were making a big mistake by leaving therapy, although it was certainly their choice. By inserting the two sides of the couple split into conversation Jan hoped there might be a shift in their stalemate.

The situation of impasse was replaced by the couple's acceptance that Jan was willing to let them decide the future of the treatment. They decided to continue, and the treatment now focused on the contradictory dynamics in the couple relationship that had been transferred into both the treatment and the supervision field. Their unconscious shift was aided by Jan's newly acquired frankness, provided by our recognition that supervision had re-enacted couple-therapist triadic transferences.

References

Bion, W. R. (1957). Differentiation of the psychotic from the non-psychotic personalities. *International Journal of Psychoanalysis, 38*.

Brown, L. & Miller, M. (2002). The triadic intersubjective matrix in supervision. *International Journal of Psychoanalysis, 83*: 811–823.

Dicks, H. (1975). *Marital Tensions*. Karnac: London.

Fiscalini, J. (1985). On supervisory parataxis and dialogue. *Contemporary Psychoanalysis, 21*, 4: 591–608.

Klein, M. (1946). Notes on some schizoid mechanisms. *International Journal of Psychoanalysis, 27*: 99–110.

Quinodoz, J. (1994). Transference of the transferences in supervision: Transference and countertransference between the candidate-analyst and analysand when acted out in the supervision. *Journal of Clinical Psychoanalysis, 59*: 53–68.

CHAPTER FOURTEEN

Projection, introjection, intrusive identification, adhesive identification

David Hewison

This chapter addresses the nature and processes involved in the kinds of identifications formed by couples through projective and introjective mechanisms. It begins with Henry Dicks' foundational studies of marital interaction (1967). Then it will consider the defensive processes that aim to protect couple relationships but have unconscious and unintended effects. The chapter goes on to discuss projective identification, introjective identification, intrusive identification, and adhesive identification—all different ways of trying to think about the unconscious impact that partners in a couple relationship have on each other. Clinical case illustrations flesh out the theoretical framework and the chapter ends by putting forward the idea that couples are meaning-making relationships, in which meaning comes through the taking-back of projections.

Projection

The basic idea of projection comes from Freud's (1911) work on a "Case of Paranoia" in which he tried to make some sense of a particular type of relationship between the inner and outer worlds. He wrote, "The most striking characteristic of symptom formation in paranoia is the process which deserves the name of projection. An internal perception is suppressed, and, instead, its content, after undergoing a certain kind of distortion, enters consciousness in the form of an external perception" (Freud, 1911, p. 66). In other words, when something we can't quite bear for whatever reason kicks off inside us, a process gets put into play which ends up with no sense of something going on inside us but instead with the idea of something actually happening outside of us. The location of the thing that is causing our troublesome perception shifts. Freud described projection very much in terms of a fundamental defence against external and internal unpleasurable excitations.

Freud goes on to say that projection is also a part of our normal attitude to the external world: "For when we refer the causes of certain sensations to the external world, instead of looking for them (as we do in the case of others) inside ourselves, this normal proceeding, too, deserves to be called projection" (Freud, 1911, p. 66). Projection happens in all of us when something comes up that we don't want to deal with, or we perceive something that we don't want to perceive. Freud saw projection not only as a way of making a link between us and the outside world that we project into, but also a pushing away of a sense of the outer world that we've already had.

Freud says that projection is not simply about trying to get rid of something. On the contrary, it is a normal part of life, a normal attitude to the external world. Attributing sudden sensations to the external world instead of looking for them in ourselves is a normal way of proceeding. It's also about us trying to make sense of what's going on around us, but inevitably it raises questions as to how, then, do we comprehend what's happening to us? How do we make sense of what other people are doing if we push everything out from us and say it's coming at us from outside?

In his paper, "Negation", following Abraham's (1924) elaboration of the incorporative and expulsive aspects of the libidinal stages of development, Freud wrote: "Expressed in the language of the oldest—the oral—instinctual impulses, the judgement is: 'I should like to eat this', or 'I should like to spit it out'; and, put more generally: 'I should like to take this into myself and keep that out.' … the original pleasure-ego wants to introject into itself everything that is good and to eject from itself everything that is bad" (Freud, 1925, p. 237).

Abraham located processes of taking in and pushing out in the earliest stages of development, not just in the genital stages. The taking-in aspect is more beneficial for bringing good things inside and keeping them there, and the expelling part is more aggressive, good for getting rid of bad things, and sometimes even attacking them, but of course it's important to be able to do both. This is a process of discrimination based on sensations, whether pleasurable or unpleasurable, very early on in a human being's development.

We don't perceive in ourselves whatever it is that we have projected: we perceive it in someone else. We attribute to them what we can't quite bear to know about in our own self. In addition, because of this strange process of incorporating and expelling, observing something outside of ourselves and observing something different inside, we develop a sense of internal and external worlds. Projection isn't simply about one person doing something inside themselves and that something having no impact on us: it's an experience of merging, of boundaries becoming thinner, of the self as a permeable membrane through which something passes. Projection, then, is an ascribing of something personal to another, and a merging of inner and outer experience.

If we are the recipient of projection from someone who is filled up with feelings too complex to bear and therefore pushed them out onto us, it will only register with us if there's something in us for it to land upon. Some people talk about this as having a valency for it or a hook upon which a projection can be hung. Projection is not pathological unless it distorts the nature of the person onto whom the projections are being put, or unless it is so continuous that we lose our sense of what's real in the external world around us. As couple therapists we see this happening when couples get so fired up that their sense of what is real begins to shift.

The ego uses projection to manage stimulation whenever it is too pleasurable or unpleasurable, and keep it to tolerable levels. In this case, projection is just an ordinary path to coping. Beyond this, projection draws our attention to the world around us; it becomes a kind of hypothesis testing. What kind of person is there out in the world? Is the person smiling at me across the room really in love with me? I can bask in the pleasure of imagining this before I walk across the room and discover that the person is looking at the person next to me. There is a normal urge to be related to, but this internal push may be met by an external refusal, resulting in shock or dismay. Couple relationships work well when the projections are benign and meet an appreciative response. When the projections are malign and meet a negative response, a malignant cycle occurs and what we can get back is hatred and loathing.

Dicks' hypothesis 1A

Henry Dicks was an analytic psychiatrist who worked at the Tavistock Clinic in London and who spent a lot of his time during the Second World War and afterwards trying to work out what could account for Nazism. He looked for social and familial processes and types of emotional expression allowed in families in Nazi Germany to find out what produces a Nazi. After the Second World War he was involved in a study of the impact on the social structure in Great Britain of families being separated and reunited when servicemen came home from war, and children who had been farmed out for safety returned to their families in the city. Dicks used the understanding that he developed when thinking about group and social phenomena in Germany to try and understand the dynamics of married couples in the UK. He worked with married individuals, and then supervised therapists treating individual spouses of couples, and these experiences provided a psychoanalytically based treatment for spouses. He wrote up this research project in his book *Marital Tensions* published in 1967, which is an important milestone in the development of psychoanalytic work with couples in the UK. Dicks started looking at individual personalities of spouses, their relationships, and their entire world. He came up with a number of hypotheses (1a, 1b, and 2) which helped develop present understanding of projective systems in couple relationships.

Dicks' hypothesis 1a: Many tensions and misunderstandings between partners seem to result from the disappointment which one, or both of them, feel and resent, when the other fails to play the role of spouse after the manner of a preconceived model or figure in their fantasy world (Dicks, 1967, p. 66).

Dicks found that we model our behaviour and our choice of partner on what we already know about our parents, and in his classical view of development he held that we base our own role as spouse on our identification with the same-sex parent (and we choose our partner based on our identification with the opposite sex parent). We choose our partner to be like our parent (or possibly to be the opposite of aspects of our parent that we did not wish to live with any more). However, what happens is that the spouse is not quite as we imagined and misunderstandings occur because we cannot understand why our partner is behaving one way when—as far as we are concerned—they should be behaving differently. We have a projective system which expects a relationship based on the nature of our relationship with our parents;

as indeed does our spouse, based on their experience of their parents. The two systems have an effect on each other.

Dicks' hypothesis 1b: Tensions between partners can result from the disappointment that the partner, after all, plays the marital role like the frustrating parent figure, similarity to whom was denied during courtship. This often collusive discovery leads to modification of the subject's own role behaviour in the direction of regression towards more childish responses to the partner (Dicks, 1967, p. 66).

This second part of Dicks' hypothesis is that we then become like an aggressive child in response to discovering that someone to whom we just got married suddenly seems like the father or mother we can't bear. This tension between partners results when the spouse is seen as the frustrating parent figure, a possibility that was denied during courtship. Because of the nature of the projective processes going on during courting, we had not quite seen the person as they truly are. We chose them because they appear kind, lovely, and loving, quite unlike our deeply frustrating, denying, rejecting parent, only to discover, after the honeymoon is over that they have attributes we really didn't want to know about, and of course we have attributes of the parent they really didn't want to know about either. A collusive relationship that comes into play during courting and dating only becomes uncovered once the reality of the person becomes known as we begin to live with them, rub up against them, see all their sharp edges, and generally discover that they're not quite as great as we thought they were or unfortunately are much worse. The initial projective system entangles us with the heart and sets us up for potential disappointment, resentment, and a feeling of betrayal.

Dicks' hypothesis 2: Subjects may persecute in their spouses tendencies which originally caused attraction, the partner having been unconsciously perceived as a symbol of 'lost' because repressed aspects of the subject's own personality (Dicks, 1967/1993, p. 63).

Dicks' second hypothesis suggests that we can feel persecuted by having been trapped by desire into a committed relationship with an unconsciously perceived all-too-familiar parental figure. The things that we thought we wanted from them we don't actually want anymore because they no longer have the same charge. It's a strange state of mind we get into because we don't actually know who they are when we thought we did. As young adults, we haven't found out enough about who we are as people and what we're made up of. So we've gone around trying to find ourselves in the other and refuse to see our spouse clearly because we're too busy looking at parts of ourselves that come out in the choice and in the marriage. Dicks suggests that if this remains unconscious, we will inevitably fall into conflict. However, there is another element of projection in adult couple relationships that is worth understanding—Christopher Bollas' idea of the transformational object (Bollas, 1987).

The transformational object

Bollas is an American analyst now living in North Dakota. He trained with the British Psychoanalytic Society and has been influenced by Winnicott, Masud Khan, and Andre Green. His idea is that we relate to ourselves in the world around us in various ways to make sense of our world, giving out parts of ourselves and being left with an unfinished yearning to re-find them. Sometimes we find ourselves getting a kind of desire for something that is powerful but not rational. We might think, "If only I can get the next-generation iPhone everything will be perfect: I'll always know where I am. I'll never be confused again, and somehow my life will be complete." Or, "If only my partner and I could go off to the Indian Ocean, play music, and sit on the beach for two weeks our lives will be transformed."

Bollas suggests that we are gripped by the recurrence of a previous experience of a transformational object that will complete us and make everything all right. This transformational object is based on experiences of maternal care that did actually transform things when we were babies: mother turned hunger into fullness; discomfort into pleasure, and so on. The experience in later life brings with it a quality of filling in the blanks and magically changing us. We invest in it with excessive expectations because of how magical it was to us when we were too young to make sense of mother's role in this, and as a result are likely to feel betrayed that it does not have the same magical qualities we experienced as a vulnerable, dependent baby. We get our new iPhone but then find that we can't pick up a signal every time we want; or we go on holiday but get sand in our saxophone and sunburn on our backs. Unless we realise that it is ourselves we must invest in and look to for change potential, our hope in the object will turn to disappointment. Those who get into relationships with the idea that the partner will make them better are looking to love and sex as transformational objects and they are bound to hit trouble. The longed-for thing outside cannot change us in the way that we hope—after all, we are no longer babies with mother.

Coupling is, however, often seen as offering continuation of the gratifications of infancy, and as a result it can become a place where infantile conflicts happen. It can also be a place for their re-working. A healthy relationship is one in which it is not just our wishes and needs that seek gratification, but it is also a place where we work out what it means to be dependent on someone or have them depend on us. If we've had a very good experience of being contained as an infant we're more likely to be able to feel contained and to offer containment as an adult. This ability determines the degree to which the couple relationship can rework old issues and lead to healing. Without the reworking, we just repeat some aspect of ourselves projected into the partner. In a way, it gets the job done of confronting ourselves, but it offers no comfort. We end up with a confusing mix of states of mind, feelings, perceptions, and attributions, which complicates the nature of the couple relationship.

Troublesome patterns of spousal projections

I will now consider some important aspects of couple functioning: collusion, splitting, and repression, the return of the repressed, idealisation, and scapegoating.

When partners form a marriage, there is a collusion of internal object relationships—the internal worlds of each partner come together. The couple seems to have a similar approach to the world, they feel soothed and settled in their relationship, and it takes quite a big event to shift them out of this state in which everything is rosy. Some couples who've never had an argument, and who always felt that things between them have been good, suddenly experience a problem, and they can't bear it. There's an eruption of emotional pain of one kind or another, such as an extra-martial affair, a pregnancy, a birth, or losing a job. Something happens that challenges their bond and way of being.

It's important to note that spousal projection involves both splitting and repression. We can split off a part of ourselves and project it outwards or we can repress a part of ourselves and then experience it outside of ourselves. One member of a couple may have located the angry feelings in their partner because it's much easier for the partner to be the angry member of the couple (because they have a valency for it already), and then the other one can feel good about being the calm one, the nice one, the polite one, the soother, the maker-better, and so feel reassured that he or she is not the damaging or persecuting one, and yet, this is all reliant on projection.

There is a real danger that each partner won't get back what they have projected. If the projections become clear and the couple do begin to get back aspects of themselves they've got rid of (the return of the repressed), they then discover in themselves the dangerous, damaging one. This shift can cause a huge shock to their sense of self, their friendship, and their marriage. Learning more about oneself from being in the marriage is an ordinary and normal development, but it causes a crisis in some couples, especially those in which the spouses have idealised each other.

Projections can be a way of establishing an idealised marriage as a transformational object, but this is often only escapism from the reality of the nature of the self and of the other. To keep a marriage ideal, you may find someone or something to attack, a scapegoat (who may be a relative or a child), but this attack on the scapegoat is also an attack on the self. The mechanism of projection is supposed to get rid of anxiety and anger, but those who do it feel even worse because somewhere they register the fact that they're really attacking themselves as well.

Janet Mattinson (1979), who looked at the kinds of couples who caused difficulties when they presented at an inner London social services department, tried to make sense of the ways in which the members of a couple related to each other. She identified particular defensive patterns, as follows:

- Cat-and-dog couples
- Net-and-sword couples
- Babes-in-the-wood couples

To which we can add:

- Doll's House couples
- Projective-gridlock couples

In the cat-and-dog couple, in which spouses fight all the time, there's absolutely no way of getting in between them because they are excited by their fighting and it serves a purpose for them. It's very difficult to reduce conflict by getting them to see something good about their partners, because any good qualities are split off and put somewhere else in order to avoid the dangerous feelings of dependency involved in having to rely on someone else.

In net-and-sword couples, it is not clear who is the victim and who is carrying the sword, or who is the partner who's trying to envelop the other and who is the one who's trying to literally stop some true emotion.

In what might be termed a babes-in-the-wood couple, the partners locate everything good in themselves as a pair, ban everything harmful from awareness and consign it to the outside. The partners feel quite secure and have apparently wonderful children and a good life, but their very good children can become pseudo-mature. They are together only because they all split off aggression and other hot feelings and put them somewhere else. The parental couple and the children are completely terrified of change, like Hansel and Gretel lost in the forest where the witches live who would eat them up. They are not fighting. Instead they walk hand-in-hand because that's the only safety. Notably, the babes-in-the-woods couples who stick together can find it hard to have sex except under ultra-safe conditions.

The Doll's House couple, named after the play by Ibsen (Ibsen, 1996) is like the babes-in-the-wood couple, except that a child may come along who becomes invested with all the fearsome and frightful things that are to be kept outside. That child brings these things back into the family and may destroy the couple. The Doll's House couple is so wonderful but they are afraid of what you might do to them. So the babes-in-the-woods/Doll's House couples have the same destructive potential as the cat-and-dog couples, except it is covered up.

Some couples are engaged in projective gridlock (Morgan, 1995) so that they knit together so closely that their chance of development is pushed out by having to remain fixed in a very particular position. The spouses not only have the same kind of thoughts but they sit inside each other in a state of merger; otherwise they might suddenly realise that they have two different thoughts at the same time. They are of one mind: they've got a shared thinking apparatus. There's no difference between them. The projective system is such that it's virtually impossible to imagine having a contrary thought, but if you as the therapist somehow do have a contrary thought then all hell breaks loose. The projective-gridlock couple will try to get you stuck with them and their bewilderment of what to do next. What on earth do you do with this couple? It feels like there's nothing really to be done with them. In therapy with couples who do not remain stuck and can use therapy, couple relationships grow more than, and differently to, the individuals who make up the couple.

Let's try to think some more about projective identification, which is a process of expulsion, and introjective identification, which is a process of incorporation. It's not that we have a conscious idea of a surface screen on which we project something like a film projected in a movie theatre. The idea of putting something into someone else is an unconscious fantasy of projecting into another person (Klein, 1946). It feels as if something has really been taken out of one person and put into another. The projecting person seems to be looking inside the other to find the self, but this is experienced by the projector as coming out of the other and being lost from the self. We project difficult, painful, bad feelings we want rid from ourselves. When we engage in putting qualities of ourselves into other people, we run the risk of losing ourselves in them. We project envious feelings we can't abide in ourselves, and then we treat the other as the envious one. The important thing to grasp about this concept is that it's not simply a feeling that is projected: it's thought itself. We also project demanding, longing, lustful feelings that we can't bear. Projective identification is also a wish for parts of ourselves to remain safe. We put valued parts of ourselves that we're worried about inside someone who can look after them for us. The downside is that we don't entirely know what they're going to do with them, and we may then become vulnerable to how they are and how they relate to us, and so of course we need to control them even more than we do already.

Bion (1970) suggested that these processes of attributing parts of our minds to others aren't simply ways of getting rid of something dangerous or difficult. It's actually a way of trying to communicate about ourselves. Bion describes an unconscious mental state or impulse coming out of one person and being lodged in place by another but he preferred to think of the process as containment.

Donald Meltzer (1982) thought that Klein's concept of projective identification refers to a deliberate process of putting some part of ourselves into another as an intrusive, aggressive activity, and so he introduced the term intrusive identification to describe a process that tries to force intimacy but which only undermines a couple's attempts at intimacy (Ruszczynski & Fisher, 1995). Meltzer distinguished intrusive identification from another kind of identification, called adhesive identification, a process we see in a lot of couples. It's probably behind many of the defensive structures we were talking about earlier. In adhesive identification, we do not put out a part of ourselves, instead we take over someone else's qualities by engaging in a role like theirs. For instance, as therapists we may show adhesive identification if we stick to one theoretical version of what it means to be a couple, or if we adopt a role of listening and making stock interpretations to the patient rather than being there as an interested, empathic, responsive human being. As therapists we may engage in projective identification if we project bad and dangerous parts of ourselves into our patients so that our own feelings can be understood instead of working on ourselves in our own therapy. Donald Meltzer says that adhesive identification doesn't allow for true communication, which he defines as having an experience with the other. We can see what this looks like in a couple relationship in the case of Emily and Peter.

Clinical example I

Presenting problem: mismatch over expectations

Emily and Peter got together at University. They found each other quite enticing because they were engaged in exciting activities, and this made them feel more special, interesting, and brave than their capable, middle class friends who were seen as staid, comfortable, and conformist. Both of them were active in radical politics. They experimented with sex. Peter was playing around with bondage, and Emily thought this was great and good for them. She felt that it enhanced their sex life and made her different from her parents, staid country solicitors, from whom she wanted to be liberated by this guy with his clear-vision of how the world could be better, but who she refused to see was actually rather tortured and unclear. After a couple of years of dating each other, they attended a post-event party after a highly charged and confrontational demonstration. Emily became absorbed in talking to the coordinator of the protest, hanging on his every word. Another man might have reacted to this as just a particular kind of movement that happens at a party, but Peter felt dropped. It was not just that he felt suddenly abandoned or that she was not paying attention to him anymore: It was that he felt that she had actively done something cruelly, deliberately, and systematically to hurt him.

The couple broke up but Peter and Emily kept in touch, and a few years later they got back together because they had never been able to get each other out of their minds and had to know what would happen next. Peter was even more involved in bondage and had added fetishism to his repertoire, and Emily was still searching for something different. But having once felt abandoned, Peter had a running sore. He found ways of subtly introducing that feeling of being abandoned into Emily's experience of him whenever he could so that she would suffer the kinds of feeling that he suffered; he would no longer have that pain but would be the one giving it to her. In this way he was then the person who was in control and she was the one who became dependent on him. She had to make sure that she met his needs so that he wouldn't push her away all the time.

The struggle in the therapy

Peter and Emily arrived for therapy after six years of marriage because this intrusive identification of abandonment was still going on. Emily now had a responsible job much like her parents and would no longer wear thigh high leather boots and little skirts, that they had both enjoyed so much before. She wanted to dress properly and think about having a family whereas Peter had moved into a more extreme form of bondage where he would be videoing himself in whole-body rubber suits or in painful clamps and cords. She refused to share in this sexual experience and their sex life dropped off. As a result, Peter, whose sexual tastes were longer exciting to her, felt abandoned again.

So they came into therapy, Peter complaining that Emily had abandoned him and Emily complaining about his fetish of needing to be completely encased in rubber. She felt that this meant that he had no real contact with her, and in this way he was abandoning her. In their engagement period they had been utterly joined together: everything was good. After years apart they had joyfully rediscovered that the person first spotted at University would be the one to make a radical transformation in their life. Setting out on making a life together, they were in a state where everything was wonderful and the future looked rosy. By the time they sought treatment, they were in a state of vitriol and embitterment in which Emily was filled with righteous indignation about him and Peter was filled with hatred and loathing, which made the ongoing therapy difficult, and eventually impossible.

The dénouement

In line with their problem of abandonment, Peter dared Emily to leave, saying that if she made him choose between marriage and fetish, he would choose the fetish. Against the odds, she left, going off with another man and choosing a good, comfortable life as the spouse of an accountant. This final abandonment left Peter feeling utterly wretched and in touch with loss, which he had until then avoided by providing himself with a rubber bumper against the dependency that would have come with a more vulnerable physical intimacy with Emily. Too late, he realised that he really hadn't wanted her to go, that it really did matter, and now he was in extreme pain. He was left with an intrusive identification with all of her lost and abandoned feelings, and she went off feeling competent, capable, and utterly problem-free.

Paradoxically Peter had thought ultimately that bondage and fetishism would liberate Emily who was obviously turning into a variant of her mother, and he knew how much she'd hated her mother before. We could feel his aggressive insistence but he may not have been conscious of the wish to hurt and exclude her. Emily's revenge against her parents is split off so that she lodges the feeling of "being unfairly done to" in Peter as much as possible, because otherwise she would have to know about it in herself. He had to lodge it in her, or else she would force him to suffer it. As a couple they were engaged in warfare without knowing the cause was loss that they couldn't bear, and the aim of it was a search for a transformational object to make it all right. Emily will make the same projections onto her new relationship with the accountant because she was headed to be a shining star in the field that they both worked in, and he was going to help advance her career speedily, an occupational power relationship parallel to the sexual power relationship with Peter in which he was going to help her liberate her true sexual identity.

In projective process, there's always something in the other person that can be stimulated because there's always a remnant of us which is just basically infantile, which gets mobilised in at certain points. The freer we are to know about that remnant, the less we have to use projection to deal with it. Those who don't allow themselves to know those feelings inside themselves are the ones who are much more easily provoked. They always think it's got nothing to do with them. The projective system when it works well is a way of driving the process of maturation. If we stop blaming our partners for whatever outrageous thing they've just done, we can stop and look at these annoying qualities, and get to know about them. Moreover, if we can possibly bear to know that what we've been stirred up by is something that we don't like in ourselves, then we might actually know a bit more about ourselves because we have experienced those qualities in our partner.

Adhesive identification is a borrowing of another person's attributes, a latching onto someone else's surface qualities, and sticking them to ourselves. You see it in couples where one partner seems to have all the business know-how and the other partner becomes the successful business person's partner. The other one who sticks to the brilliant business woman is a shadow and has no identity of his own but the most successful, glowing, and glittering partner doesn't see herself as having an identity of her own either. In some couples one person seems to be so much thinner emotionally than the other one and the other partner seems to be too full, too thick, too engorged emotionally. Neither partner is able to stand alone, and so they need to lean-up against someone else.

Clinical example II

I saw a couple for an assessment recently where the man was absolutely larger than life. He bounded into the room, talking ten to the dozen, took over, cackled with laughter whenever anyone said anything including himself and dominated the session. His partner by comparison was almost not there. She was absolutely quiet and timid, deferred to him, and constantly looked to him for approval. She had found a variant of a powerful, determining, defining father to run up quite close against and live in his shadow so that she didn't have to live her own life. He got someone who constantly reinforced his larger-than-life potential, mirroring him as the one who could do it, the brilliant one, the one who would make good, and whose jokes were always funny. Significantly, for the therapist, however, it was rather tedious being in the room with him, and with them. It had no life or contact, despite all the excitement and awe. Communication is not just simply about projecting into, or finding lost parts of the self, or talking at each other: It's about having a full emotional experience in the presence of the partner of whatever kind it may be at any moment—furious, angry, hateful, loving, kind, and gentle.

In conclusion: the couple as a meaning-making relationship

We can summarise all of this by thinking of the couple's psychological system as a kind of meaning-making relationship. Couples are constantly making meaning of their experience. Some couples can survive only if their relationship means that everyone else is bad, if there are no children, if dependency needs are met absolutely immediately, if each spouse has the same point of view, or if there is so much space they don't impinge on each other at all. For two partners to really make meaning and have a marriage worthy of the name, they have to really understand who and what they are, to consider each other, and to deal with loss and emotional pain. This recalls Klein's emphasis on both the paranoid-schizoid position characterised by part object relating due to splitting and repression and the depressive position characterised by whole object relating due to a capacity for ambivalence and mourning. Emotional maturity in a couple relationship isn't about avoiding pain and loss (paranoid-schizoid position) it's about being able to face painful experiences without resorting to projecting blame and guilt onto the partner (depressive position). It's about being able to move between paranoid-schizoid and depressive positions as appropriate to the circumstances the couple will face at any point.

Each partner in a couple relationship tends to have islands of maturity, and each of them can use the other's maturity. They can make use of their spouse's ability to deal with something on their behalf. Couples that are identical brew trouble. The ideal is to have a relationship between spouses of complementary strengths. Carl Jung (1928) described a contained relationship (not the same as Bion's idea of containment as a process of turning emotional experience into thinkable experience. Jung's idea is a relationship in which one partner carries the problem for the other one). In this type of couple, we'll find pushing and pulling about who is the understanding one, the mature one who "contains" the other one, and eventually they find themselves becoming irritable, grouchy, grumpy, and annoying. It then becomes clear that, hidden under the container's capacity for problem management, is a failure of containing. If the couple can bear staying in a therapy relationship in which the partners experience these hidden dynamics, they begin to discover a kind of new depth inside themselves, as the partner who was apparently immature suddenly has the ability to deal in ways neither of the spouses would ever have expected.

Couples' maturity isn't fixed. We can regress as well. Islands of maturity and immaturity can become more or less submerged depending on what's going on with the emotional global warming or freezing in a couple. So people who are mature at one point will be much less mature at another, depending on what's happening. The aim in therapy is to develop the couple's ability to access maturity and accept immaturity, move between paranoid-schizoid and depressive positions as indicated by life circumstances, and relate to whole emotional states of mind.

References

Abraham, K. (1924). A short study of the development of the libido, viewed in the light of mental disorders. *Selected Papers on Psycho-Analysis*. London: Hogarth.

Bion, W. R. (1970). Container contained. In: *Attention and Interpretation* (pp. 72–82). London: Tavistock.

Bollas, C. (1987). The transformational object. In: *The Shadow of the Object: Psychoanalysis of the Unthought Known* (pp. 13–29). London: Free Association Books.

Dicks, H. V. (1967). *Marital Tensions. Clinical studies towards a psychological theory of interaction*. London: Routledge.

Freud, S. (1911). *Psycho-Analytic Notes on an Autobiographical Account of a Case of Paranoia (Dementia Paranoides)*. S. E., 12. London: Hogarth.

Freud, S. (1925). *Negation*. S. E., 19. London: Hogarth.

Ibsen, H. (1996). *A Doll's House*. London: Faber & Faber.

Jung, C. G. (1928). Marriage as a psychological relationship. In: *Contributions to Analytical Psychology* (pp. 189–203). London: Kegan Paul, Trench, Trubner.

Klein, M. (1946). Notes on some schizoid mechanisms. In: *Love, Guilt and Reparation*, (pp. 1–24). London: Hogarth.

Mattinson, J. & Sinclair, I. (1979). *Mate and Stalemate. Working with Marital Problems in a Social Services Department*. Oxford: Blackwell.

Meltzer, D. (1982). *Studies in Extended Metapsychology: Clinical Applications of Bion's Ideas*. Perthshire: Clunie Press.

Morgan, M. (1995). The projective gridlock: a form of projective identification in couple relationship. In: S. Ruszczynski & J. Fisher (Ed.), *Intrusiveness and Intimacy in the Couple* (pp. 33–48). London: Karnac.

Ruszczynski, S. & Fisher, J. (1995). *Intrusiveness and Intimacy in the Couple*. London: Karnac.

Usher, S. F. (2008). *What is this thing called Love? A guide to psychoanalytic psychotherapy with couples*. London: Routledge.

CHAPTER FIFTEEN

Negotiating individual and joint transferences in couple therapy

James L. Poulton

I had been working with an unmarried couple I will call Jessica and Karl for over a year, so I was familiar with the scene in front of me. Jessica was in tears, frustrated and confused by Karl's persistence in laying the blame for the couple's conflicts on her. Karl, in contrast, appeared calm, caring, and encouraging, but he was also effectively disengaged from Jessica's struggles and from the therapeutic process. The couple had been talking about Jessica's decision in the prior week to have lunch with her ex-husband—a decision that had followed an argument she'd had with Karl about his distant relationship with his daughter. Karl had begun today's session by reporting that the "same old stuff" had happened again: instead of talking to him directly about her anger, Jessica had acted it out and had "threatened our relationship." Jessica had responded by claiming that her decision to see her ex-husband was not done in anger. Besides, she said, she had told Karl her opinions about his interactions with his daughter, so as far as she was concerned that was where the argument had ended. She added that if anyone was "threatening our relationship" it was Karl because he was so critical of her. As I listened to them, I felt a familiar bind: each partner wanted me to believe the other was the chief source of their problems, and did not want me to focus on their own contributions. Knowing I would encounter resistance from both, I began to explore the emotional foundations of the impasse they had once again constructed, both between themselves and within the treatment.

The multiple transferences in couple therapy

In the practice of couple therapy, the therapist faces a wider variety of transferences than is typical of an individual therapeutic relationship. Not only must couple therapists understand and work with the individual transferences each partner develops toward them, but also with the individual and joint transferences that swirl between the two partners, as well as the transferences the couple, as a whole, establishes toward the therapist and the treatment in general. The tasks of understanding, confronting, and working through this kaleidoscopic array of transferences can overwhelm therapists, leaving them uncertain which way to proceed. In this chapter, I will discuss two dimensions—individual *vs.* joint and focused *vs.* contextual—which are helpful in conceptualising the many transferences that appear in couple therapy. Because projective and introjective identification are integral to the formation of these transferences, I'll also discuss these mechanisms in detail. Finally, I'll suggest a clinical method whereby the therapist's capacity to move flexibly between the couple's multiple transferences deepens the treatment and substantially enhances the effectiveness of therapeutic interventions. I'll use the case of Jessica and Karl to illustrate the conceptual and technical points I wish to make.

The origins of transference

In object relations theory, transference is the result of the activation and projection of aspects of an individual's internal object relationships into a current relationship (Heimann, 1956; Joseph, 1985; Klein, 1952). Internal object relationships are the internalised legacies of past relationships with primary figures, such as parents and early caregivers, and comprise representations of the self, the object and of the specific emotional interactions that occurred between them. Once internal object relationships are formed, they function as implicit models for understanding, predicting, and responding to subsequent experiences with others. When a husband, for example, with an angry-mother/frightened-self internal object relationship experiences marital conflict, his internal structure will not only define the nature of the conflict (e.g., that he is the victim of his wife's intimidating anger), but it will also provide him with a limited range of options for how to feel and what to do next. This tendency of internal object relationships to mould current experience according to their own parameters is the foundational mechanism underlying transference. The most common means by which this moulding occurs is projective identification, which in couples occurs in both "one-person" and "two-person" forms.

"One-person" projective identification and individual transferences

Although there is some controversy about whether projective identification should be regarded as exclusively a "one-person" or "two-person" event (Grotstein, 1981; Scharff, 1992), both perspectives are helpful in deciphering the varying transferential phenomena couples present. In one-person projective identification, one partner attempts to eliminate unacceptable and disowned parts of self by projecting them into the other partner and then perceiving that partner "as having acquired the characteristics of the projected part of self" (Segal, 1964, p. 126). This form of projective identification implies that the target of the projection (i.e., the other partner) is perceived in terms of the projected material regardless of his or her actual characteristics. Under extreme conditions, one-person projective identifications may generate psychotic phenomena (Searles, 1963). In less extreme conditions, they are one of the primary mechanisms responsible for the formation of individual transferences (Bollas, 1987; Malin, 1966).

The individual transferences Jessica and Karl exhibited toward each other were indicative of the influence one-person projective identifications exert over couple interactions. Jessica had been raised by a depressed and detached mother and a critical, aggressive, and controlling father who allowed no one to disagree with him. As a result, she had internalised a frightening and demanding internal father from whom she could find no safety and to whom she felt required to deny any disagreement or dissatisfaction. When she projectively identified this internal configuration into her relationship with Karl, she saw him as more demanding and intimidating than he already was, and she then felt that the only way to be safe was to deny she had ever acted in opposition to him. These were the transferential dynamics underlying her refusal to consider that her phone call to her ex-husband had been done in retaliation.

Karl, on the other hand, had been raised by a neglectful and self-absorbed single mother who had been unavailable to him at key points in his development. From these experiences, he developed an internal object relationship in which he felt in danger of being abandoned by the female on whom he depended, perhaps because of failings of his own. His projection of this configuration into his relationship with Jessica created an individual transference in which he saw her as perpetually on the verge of leaving him. He defended against these expectations by detaching from her emotionally, criticising her for actual or imagined mistakes, and refusing to acknowledge his own role in creating the couple's conflicts.

Jessica and Karl's individual transferences toward each other were intimately related to the individual transferences they exhibited toward me, in large measure because both sets of transferences were rooted in projective identifications of similar intrapsychic material. Karl's individual transference toward me, for example, consisted first of a wish that I would function as a father (viz., as his absent father returned) who would repair the woman on whom he depended so he wouldn't have to face his fears of loss, and second of a two-pronged injunction that I should work only with Jessica (since in his mind she was the sole problem) and that I should treat any reference she made to his faults as her attempt to avoid responsibility for compromising their relationship. Similarly, in Jessica's transference toward me she saw me as a critical father whom she had to appease by proclaiming her innocence and denying her anger or dissatisfaction with me. On the basis of this transference, she persistently directed me toward Karl's mistakes, under a fantasy that this would mean she was blameless, and she also avoided any appearance of even the mildest disagreement with me. Each partner's individual transference toward me helped to construct the bind I described above, in which I knew I would encounter resistance no matter which way the session proceeded.

"Two-person" projective identification and joint transferences

The two-person form of projective identification adds two essential features to the one-person version. First, the projecting partner, rather than leaving his or her projection in one-person space, unconsciously attempts to induce or coerce the receiving partner into identifying with the projected material and enacting it (Ogden, 1986; Scharff, 1992). Second, the receiving partner, having experienced the induction, cooperates with it, introjectively identifies with the projected material, and proceeds with its enactment (Jacobs, 1986). This process of induction is only successful if the receiving partner already possesses characteristics that resonate with the other partner's projections. That is, the content of the projection must meet with aspects of the receiving partner's personality that are already accepted within his or her psychic repertoire and that are not overly defended against (Zavattini, 1988). When these conditions are met, the receiving partner is primed to introjectively identify with the other partner's projections, and to participate in enacting them.

Because introjective identifications activate emotions already present in the receiving partner, that partner infuses those emotions into interactions in such a way that they blend with the other partner's projected content. This additive process, which is characteristic of couple interactions that have been coordinated by the match between the projective needs of one partner and the receptive capacities (based in introjective identifications) of the other, typically results in an intensified emotional experience for each, since the shared psychic space between them is now filled with thematically similar emotions derived from two personal histories rather than one (Cleavely, 1993).

The process of projective and introjective identification does not, of course, travel only in one direction. Rather, each partner enters the relationship with a unique configuration of aspects of self that are either slated for projection or are available to resonate with material the other partner projects. When both partners' configurations "fit" each other—that is, when each partner uses projective identification to a similar degree, and when each is similarly prone to identify with the other's projections—the partners tend to establish, unconsciously, patterns of mutual projective and introjective identification in which the roles of "projector" and "introjector" are either traded back and forth (sometimes rapidly) or are held simultaneously by both partners.

One of the primary consequences of these mutual processes of projective and introjective identification is that the couple's interactions become constricted around the themes of each partner's most compelling projections. These themes tend to dominate the relationship the more each partner feels internal pressure to disown or eliminate parts of self. When such pressure is high, the resulting projective-introjective processes become repetitive, inflexible, and limited in scope, depleting the partners' internal resources and leaving them little room for creative or spontaneous problem solving (Dicks, 1967; Klein, 1963).

These constricted but mutually coordinated interactions, in turn, give rise to their own particular kinds of transferences in which both partners participate in equal measure. In these transferences, each partner essentially occupies transferential and countertransferential positions at the same time. For example, when partner A initiates a transferential sequence by projecting disavowed aspects of self into partner B, partner B's identification with and enactment of that projected material constitutes a countertransference response to partner A's original transference. Because this countertransference response, however, is comprised of both a reaction to partner A and a projection of aspects of partner B's own psyche, partner A experiences it, at least in part, as a transference originating in partner B, to which partner A then adds more of his or her own psychic material as he or she identifies with and enacts it. As the cycle of projective and introjective identification (and of transference and countertransference) continues, each partner embodies both cause and effect of a mutually constructed transference-countertransference process. Because this mutual process is organised by projected material from both partners, and because it tends to function as a quality of the couple as a whole (rather than of the individual members of the couple), it has been called a joint or mutual transference, even though countertransference responses are equally essential to its construction (Ehrlich, Zilbach & Solomon, 1996; Stewart, Peters, Marsh & Peters, 1975).

Joint transferences fall into one of two categories, depending on what target, or object, they take. I'll use the term transference-countertransference entanglements to describe joint transferences in which the object, for each partner, is the other partner. In this kind of joint transference each partner's individual transference and countertransference responses are aimed at the other and remain entwined within the confines of the dyadic relationship. On the other hand, shared transferences (as I'll use the term) arise when both partners have similar transferences about a person or event outside the couple. In this case, the mutual processes of projective and introjective identification blend the two partners' internal worlds so that they hold similar emotions or fantasies about that person or event, and each is reinforced in those attitudes by the other's contributions. Joint transferences, whether entangled or shared, influence each partner's behaviour as though they are something like a third entity, similar to Ogden's analytic third (1994), which is at least partially independent of, or superordinate to, each partner's subjective experience.

Because Jessica and Karl's individual transferences complemented each other in terms of theme, affect, and content, together they created enduring, repetitive patterns of interaction that were indicative of mutually constructed joint transferences. One such joint transference was a transference-countertransference entanglement in which Jessica's declarations of innocence and passive-aggressive expressions of anger, based in the projection of her devaluing father into Karl, both reinforced and were reinforced by Karl's fear of her abandonment and his subsequent criticisms of her, which were based in his projections of his neglectful mother into her. As each partner internalised the projections and reacted to the defensive behaviour of the other, the transferential expectations and emotions of both partners became increasingly intertwined, intensified and entrenched. The net result was a coordinated, unconscious, and superordinate system in which each partner's behaviour was defined and determined by the mutual transactions operating between them.

Another joint transference constructed by Jessica and Karl's complementary individual transferences and countertransferences was a shared transference toward me. The fundamental motivation for the formation of this transference was Jessica's and Karl's need to find refuge from their frightening internal objects. In order to find such refuge, both partners regarded me as a source of not only safety and repair, but also of judgment—of their own goodness and of the other's failures. As each partner interacted with me according to these assumptions, his or her actions reinforced the other partner's similar actions, so that both became immured in regarding me as an almost identical object, for whose judgment and approbation they persistently competed. The collusion between their unconscious needs created an almost irresistible shared transference in which I was invested with superego-like powers: in their eyes, I could legislate who was correct or at fault, and I could use my power of judgment to force either partner to rehabilitate him or herself.

Contextual and focused transferences

Individual and joint transferences may also be classified as either contextual or focused, depending on whether the transference focuses on a specific object or on the surrounding environment. The distinction between contextual and focused transferences was first described by the Scharffs (D. Scharff & J. Scharff, 1987; 1991), who noted that infants have two very different kinds of experiences with their caregivers, corresponding to what Winnicott called the "environment-mother" and "object-mother" modes of relating (Winnicott, 1963; while Winnicott used the word "mother" in each of these terms, his concepts apply more generally to the infant's primary objects, whichever gender they may be). The environment-mother mode of relating refers to that aspect of the caregiver that manages the infant's environment, provides the context in which it explores and develops, and is responsive in times of crisis. In this mode, the caregiver is diffuse and more an element of the background than the foreground. The object-mother mode, in contrast, refers to the caregiver's tendency to offer him or herself to be used as the specific object of the infant's desires, emotions and impulses, which places the caregiver in a direct one-to-one relationship with the infant. In this mode, the caregiver is discrete and reasonably well-defined as an object (or, at least, as a part-object).

As infants grow, they internalise experiences in both the environment-mother and the object-mother modes of relating, resulting in internal object relationships that can be roughly differentiated in terms of whether they contain discrete objects that are held in the foreground, as the centre of focus, or objects that float less visibly in the background, blended into the environment itself. In adulthood, these two kinds of internal object relationships form the foundation for focused and contextual transferences. In focused transferences, aspects of internalised object-mother modes of relating are projected into the relationship, in which case the other becomes the direct focus of the projecting individual's emotions, desires and expectations that are linked to the one-to-one experiences with early objects. All of the individual and joint transferences described above may be categorised as focused transferences.

Contextual transferences, on the other hand, derive from projections of internalised material from environment-mother modes of relating, which in turn influence the partner's attitudes toward the physical and emotional environment in which the relationship takes place. For example, if in childhood one partner's caregiver failed to protect the child from anxiety-provoking intrusions (e.g., violence from other family members, or the mother's bouts of anger or depression), that partner will be likely to experience both the couple and the therapeutic relationship as insufficiently powerful to ensure safety from anxiety. This is not a focused transference because it is not specifically about either the other partner or the therapist. Instead, it targets the relational environment as a whole and treats it as a source of diffuse and amorphous danger.

Throughout my work with them, Jessica and Karl exhibited both individual and joint contextual transferences that arose from both partners' often-unconscious expectations that they either were or could be exposed to danger from the interpersonal environment. Although this danger was linked to the possibility that they would each encounter their frightening internal objects, their contextual transferences centred on the environment itself and its inability to protect them from the appearance of those objects. Thus, their contextual transferences occurred in an amorphous affective background, and because of this they were often more visible in retrospect than in the moment. It was typically after a session was over, for example, that I would realise how tense each partner had been and how they had approached me, and the therapy in general, with a sense of urgency.

The tension and urgency each partner exhibited came from slightly different sources. Jessica's history with her detached mother led her to expect that she would find no protection from her father's devaluations. Consequently, even as I was the subject of her focused individual transference (in which she saw me as judgmental and attempted to coax me into being on her side), the treatment environment was also the subject of a contextual transference in which she anticipated she would find no aid or safety—either from me or from Karl. Karl's contextual transference was anchored in his experiences of his absent father who was unable to protect him from his abandoning mother. At the same time he exhibited a focused transference toward me (in which he hoped I would cure Jessica of her tendency to leave him), he also expected, on the basis of a contextual transference, that he would only find absence in the treatment environment, which would once again expose him to anxieties about loss. The tension both partners brought to therapy was thus rooted both in their urgent need for relief, and in their unconscious expectations that no relief would be found.

Although each partner's individual contextual transference arose from differing psychic content, the anxieties both felt about imminent environmental failures were quite similar. Because of this similarity, the partners developed shared contextual transferences toward both the treatment and the couple relationship itself. On the basis of these transferences, they experienced the treatment and the relational environments as sources of anxiety in themselves, since in each they felt that their hopes would not be actualised, and that in the end they would still be left without rescue. Just as in other joint transferences, each partner's emotional experience, when infused into the couple's interactions, had a tendency to kindle similar emotions in the other partner, and to augment the emotions the other partner was already feeling.

Working between the individual and the couple

In the object relations approach to couple therapy, the therapist strives to help both partners to: First, recognise the individual and the interactive sources of their conflicts; Second, develop within themselves the capacity to explore and understand their own and the other's needs to project unacceptable parts of themselves; Third, re-integrate those parts of themselves they had heretofore projected into the other; Fourth, become more tolerant of their partner's projections, and the regressive needs that may give rise to them, when they occur; and Fifth, utilise the synthesising capacities of their interactions to introduce creativity and liveliness into the relationship.

In essence, this implies that the therapist helps the couple establish what Dicks called a "complete marriage," in which the partners achieve an "undisturbed flow of two-way communication between [their] conscious and unconscious parts" (Dicks, 1967, p. 117), and in which the mutual processes of projective and introjective identification become decreasingly relied upon as methods of managing internal and interpersonal conflicts. The most central technique available to the therapist to help the couple achieve these goals is the analysis and containment of their multiple transferences.

In containment, the therapist takes in the couple's projected material and reflects upon, mentalizes, and reformulates it so that, when it is re-described to the couple, it is in a more tolerable and comprehensible form. This process not only allows the partners to reclaim and acknowledge the projected material as their own, but it also provides them with the psychic resources necessary to develop their own tools for working through difficult emotions, thereby making those emotions less likely to be enacted or split-off and projected.

Because couples in treatment exhibit the wide variety of transferences described above, the couple therapist must be prepared to provide containing interpretations for each form of transference. That is, in any session, the therapist must understand the individual and interpersonal aspects of the couple's dynamics sufficiently to be able to shift, sometimes often, between offering containing interpretations for individual transferences on the one hand, and joint transferences on the other, depending on the material the couple presents in the moment and on the therapist's determination of which transference would be of most benefit, for the couple, to illuminate. Such a comprehensive approach has numerous advantages.

First, it counters both partners' tendency, common in dysfunctional couples, to assume that what they have projected into the other constitutes the other's "true" nature, and that they need not investigate, re-internalise or re-acknowledge the projections that have created their distorted perceptions. The therapist's equal focus on individual and joint transferences emphasises that both partners together have contributed to the couple's difficulties, but that each partner individually is also capable of resolving those difficulties by re-internalising the parts of themselves they have projected.

Second, a comprehensive focus on individual and joint transferences underscores that individualities and mutualities make up the couple and that holding the two in equal balance is essential to maintaining the relationship's equilibrium. Denying either individualities or mutualities leads to distortions in the couple's self-conception, and to misperceptions and misattributions of significant emotional events. As Clulow has stated: "An assumption that everything is shared denies individual differences just as much as the assumption of individuality disregards the essential relatedness of experience" (Clulow, 2001, p. 92).

Third, a comprehensive approach to the couple's transferences facilitates the two-pronged development of both individual responsibility and an empathic connection between partners, since each partner, in being asked to recognise, accept and work with their own and their partner's contributions to conflicts, is required to, if they are to be successful, reach a state of empathy and compassion for the vulnerabilities and fears both partners have brought to the relationship.

Finally, the comprehensive approach helps the couple develop their own capacities for containment. A couple that undergoes object relations treatment gradually accumulates the skills necessary to function as their own "marital container" (Cleavely, 1993), in which each partner becomes capable of exploring, understanding, and containing the psychic material embedded in both partners' projections. When both partners have the confidence to function with each other in these ways, both in individual and shared dimensions, they are able to remain relatively free of repetitive conflicts, and enjoy instead the fruits of a lively and benevolent relationship, "each holding the other's interests at heart without outraging his own" (Cleavely, 1993, p. 66).

An example of the comprehensive approach to Jessica's and Karl's multiple transferences occurred later in the session I described at the beginning of this chapter. Due to space limitation, I will only sketch this session, but the reader should keep in mind that more often than not, in the object relations approach to couple therapy, the therapist's illumination of the couple's various transferences occupies most if not all of each session.

After the couple's initial skirmish, I began to focus on Jessica's individual, focused transferences toward Karl and me, in which she needed me to see her not only as reasonable and innocent, but also as the victim of Karl's unfair treatment. In my attempt to offer a containing interpretation, I suggested that perhaps she was angry at Karl, but was afraid of my reaction if she admitted to it. She said no at first, but then associated to her father, which allowed me to make a link between her current behaviour and her past. I suggested that she might be frightened of offending me in the same way she was afraid of offending her father. She said, thoughtfully, that this might be the case.

As she was saying this, Karl was nodding his head. When we reached a resting point, he said, with apparent compassion, that this was what he had been talking about—Jessica was bringing to the relationship issues from her past that needed to be worked through. Taking this as an opportunity to illuminate Karl's individual transferences, I said that I thought he was attempting to convince both Jessica and me that he was fault-free in creating the couple's conflicts, and that this may be his way of protecting himself from a feared realisation that he might be responsible for pushing Jessica away. Karl had difficulty with this interpretation, and wanted to argue against it. I said that it was only a tentative view of what might be happening, and I asked that he consider it. He said he would.

At this point, Jessica said that she was glad I said this to Karl, because it was so difficult for him to accept his role in their arguments. As she said this, I had an image of her as a child tattling to a parent about the misbehaviour of her sibling. When Karl then joined in to say that the reason he found this difficult was that he didn't really believe he played any role in their conflicts, the two launched into a brief, but familiar, argument. Shifting the focus now to their transference-countertransference entanglement and their shared transference toward me, I suggested that because both were frightened of being the trigger for the other's anger, they were now caught up in a collusive interaction in which each was trying to blame the other and each was using me as the parent who would decide who was to blame and who wasn't. I added that although this was an indication of their individual fears that they would find no safety with me (a brief reference to their contextual transferences), it had also become a shared fear that had mobilised their competitive attempts to make me their ally. My interpretation of their shared fears had many more layers, and we discussed it, the ways it had developed, and its influence over their interactions for the rest of the session.

Working with the multiple transferences that appear in couple therapy requires the therapist to track the complexities of not one relationship, but three (one between the partners and one between each partner and the therapist) and perhaps even four (if the relationship between the therapist and the couple as a whole is included). In order to accomplish this, couple therapists must be aware of and appreciate the many possible dynamics—individual and joint, focused and contextual—that may underlie the couple's transferences. By doing so, however, couple therapists not only expand their capacity to conceptualise couple interactions and formulate more effective interventions, but also create a field of investigation in which analyses of individual and shared psychic states inform and enrich each other, allowing therapists and couples to develop a more penetrating view of the entire range of the experience of being in a couple relationship.

References

Bollas, C. (1987). *The Shadow of the Object: Psychoanalysis of the Unthought Known*. New York: Columbia University Press.

Cleavely, E. (1993). Relationships: Interaction, defences, and transformation. In: S. Ruszczynski (Ed.), *Psychotherapy with Couples: Theory and Practice at the Tavistock Institute of Marital Studies* (pp. 55–69). London: Karnac.

Clulow, C. (2001). Attachment theory and the therapeutic frame. In: C. Clulow (Ed.), *Adult Attachment and Couple Psychotherapy: The 'Secure Base' in Practice and Research* (pp. 85–104). London: Brunner-Routledge.

Dicks, H. (1967). *Marital Tensions: Clinical Studies Towards a Psychological Theory of Interaction*. New York: Basic Books.

Ehrlich, F. M., Zilbach, J. J., & Solomon, L. (1996). The transference field and communication among therapists. *Journal of the American Academy of Psychoanalysis, 24*: 675–690.

Grotstein, J. (1981). *Splitting and Projective Identification*. New York: Jason Aronson.

Heimann, P. (1956). Dynamics of transference interpretations. *International Journal of Psychoanalysis, 37*: 303–310.

Jacobs, T. J. (1986). On countertransference enactments. *Journal of the American Psychoanalytic Association, 34*: 289–307.

Joseph, B. (1985). Transference: the total situation. *International Journal of Psychoanalysis, 66*: 447–454.

Klein, M. (1952). The origins of transference. *International Journal of Psychoanalysis, 33*: 433–438.

Klein, M. (1963). On the sense of loneliness. In: R. Money-Kyrle (Ed.), *The Writings of Melanie Klein, Vol. III: Envy and Gratitude and Other Works 1946–1963* (pp. 300–313). New York: The Free Press, 1975.

Malin, A. (1966). Projective identification in the therapeutic process. *International Journal of Psychoanalysis, 47*: 26–31.

Ogden, T. H. (1986). *Matrix of the Mind: Object Relations and the Psychoanalytic Dialogue*. Northvale, NJ: Jason Aronson.

Ogden, T. H. (1994). The analytic third: Working with intersubjective clinical facts. *International Journal of Psychoanalysis, 75*: 3–19.

Scharff, D. E. & Scharff, J. S. (1987). *Object Relations Family Therapy*. Northvale, NJ: Jason Aronson.

Scharff, D. E. & Scharff, J. S. (1991). *Object Relations Couple Therapy*. Northvale, NJ: Jason Aronson.

Scharff, J. S. (1992). *Projective and Introjective Identification and the Use of the Therapist's Self*. Northvale, NJ: Jason Aronson.

Searles, H. F. (1963). Transference psychosis in the psychotherapy of chronic schizophrenia. *International Journal of Psychoanalysis, 44*: 249–281.

Segal, H. (1964). *Introduction to the Work of Melanie Klein*. London: Heinemann.

Stewart, R. H., Peters, T. C., Marsh, S., & Peters, M. J. (1975). An object-relations approach to psychotherapy with marital couples, families, and children. *Family Process, 14*: 161–178.

Winnicott, D. W. (1963). The development of the capacity for concern. In: *The Maturational Processes and the Facilitating Environment: Studies in the Theory of Emotional Development* (pp. 73–82). Madison, WI: International Universities Press, 1965.

Zavattini, G. C. (1988). The other one of me, that is my other half: Reflections on projective identification. *Rivista di Psicoanalisi, 34*: 348–374.

CHAPTER SIXTEEN

Narcissism in a couple with a cocaine-addicted partner

Carl Bagnini

Brief theory of personality disordered couples with sado-masochistic features

Contemporary psychoanalytic theory of personality disorders combines an appreciation of the particular difficulties of these patients in tolerating self—other differences, and most importantly, the lack of integration of life's pleasures and pains. Narcissism is ubiquitous but in extreme pathological forms we observe the dialectic between an individual and a social persona; we use Winnicott's characterisation of how a false self arises in understanding the social persona of narcissistic personalities (Winnicott, 1965).

In developmental terms, we assume a parenting situation occurred where little opportunity was present for safely separating and differentiating. An intolerance of reflection is assumed in the parent, leading to failures in empathic attunement, with the result of identity diffusion in the child. The child's basic curiosity may have been misinterpreted as arrogance, and deep shame may have been felt in areas of childhood sexuality and interpersonal striving. The child pulls into itself to protect the true self. She will construct inordinate defences, such as a paranoid sensitivity to the dangerous and exploitive human environment. False self defences are the child's bargain for survival of the true self ensuring its future potential under favourable conditions. In adult partner selection there is both a hope for a favourable human environment that fosters self esteem and trust, and dread of repetition of childhood exploitation and degradation (Rosenfeld, 1971). Affectively charged configurations are typical with narcissistic patients and their mates due to sharp personality distinctions in their relationships. Narcissistic partners are usually extraverted. They defensively split self—other relationships into idealised and denigrated parts, and project them into others. With marital partners the split is between libidinal and anti-libidinal motives that lack integration (Fairbairn, 1952). Primitive affects and anxieties flood reality testing keeping the marital relationship rigidly defined as: "you are with me or against me". The introjected maternal object is rejecting and demanding and it presses into the couple's expectations and saturates marital expectations. The less narcissistic partner may carry the requirement of providing complete satisfaction to the other to make up for developmental deprivations, in contrast to the narcissistic partner who is unable to empathise with the all-giving other due to feelings of deprivation. This situation is one of narcissistic entitlement. The receiving partner cannot realise the full debt of his obligation to the giving other due to primary dependency conflicts. The narcissistic partner may have gained temporary specialness in childhood that was exploited by the parent who turned suddenly away, perhaps in favour of a new baby, while expecting continued adoration from the child. Both partners carry underlying and common features of shame and envy. The entitled partner envies and fears his partner's desire to please, while the other partner envies the apparent independence, ambition, and self preoccupation of the narcissist.

Early environmental failures shaped psychic structure and identifications with bad objects intermingle with predispositions that impede ordinary marital pleasures. Narcissistic patients fear aggression and mistrust love. The typical unconscious relational paradox of the more borderline form of the narcissistic partner is to be terrified of high levels of affective expression, and to dread quiescence and calm. In the borderline individual affect is charged with extreme anxiety. There is a lack of depth, preoccupation with minutia, repetitive references to victimisation, intolerance for reflective thought, and severe narcissistic vulnerability. I would characterise a driven quality in more malignant forms as sadistic flows of consciousness—the attempt to colonise and dominate the partner whose separate identity must be denied. I add these attributes to the well-established clinical view of narcissistic patients as self-serving, self aggrandising, and rejecting of criticism. The schizoid narcissist tends towards preoccupation with fantasies of independence, ambition as saviour, and counter-dependence as a psychic refuge from being taken over by the needs of others. A schizoid individual may marry a borderline to ensure object distribution. At an unconscious level the schizoid needs a partner who is exciting and stimulating, which brings some aliveness to the schizoid's life; the schizoid provides evenness, stability and consistency missing in the fluctuating borderline. The projective couple matrix combines the schizoid partner's obsessional traits needed to maintain stability while fearing dependency, and the borderline partner who fears abandonment, and requires dependency, and admires the partner's seeming self confidence. We encounter the paradox of unintegrated self-reification presented as narcissistic epiphanies while offering the couple self and other evolution. Cocaine abuse in one or both partners overrides external possibilities for reality checking and self-reflection. The challenge is more formidable in working with malignant narcissism because cocaine addiction fuels omnipotent "madness" (Rosenfeld, 1964) and it conflicts with a saner part of the self and reality.

Movement toward taking responsibility for affecting others is a problem for narcissistic patients, and addiction muddies the waters further by altering self-states which the non-addicted partner attempts to regulate. A masochistic motive to save the addict takes the form of superego dominated rule setting, or in psychological "mouth to mouth" dialysis; such as by replacing the cocaine high with a transfusion of love or moral virtues. Unfortunately, as long as there is active use of an abusive substance the despairing and clingy partner must fail, although they continue to cling to the illusion that the addicted partner can change.

Aggression and narcissism in couples with cocaine addiction

Character disordered couples without a history of drug abuse have trouble managing aggression. Aggression consists of negative emotions that threaten internal objects. In ordinary development there is a hierarchy of aggressive affects that have to do with organising experiences, particularly related to interactive solicitation between infant and mother to obtain nurturing supplies under favourable conditions in which the infant aggressively communicates its needs. The display of aggression under these conditions is easily modified when anticipated by an attuned parent. An attuned parent usually recognises infant distress, and reduces it by timing the delivery of nurturing supplies before distress accumulates frustration to a point of acute psycho-physiological breakdown. The ideal pairing is of an infant that is capable of being comforted with a parent who is attuned.

Character disordered couples with cocaine addiction (Kantzian, Halliday, & McAuliffe, 1990; Morgenstern & Leeds, 1993) frequently exhibit breakdown in attunement because of hypersensitivity to affects, emotional lability, and sensation-seeking behaviour. Euphoria and unmitigated aggression are associated with deficits in self-care. The drug numbs aggression. Interruptions in self-medication usually bring back aggression, which can trigger a bipolar or cyclothymic overlay. Constitutional and environmental (superego) conflicts are associated with an absence of a sense of danger or fear of deterioration. A depressive aspect is usually out of awareness. Needs and need meeting responses in couples with a cocaine abuser are infused by phantasies of rejection that may be defended against by entitled phantasies for a loving, accommodating, and devoted mate. An addicted partner does not readily anticipate individual needs in the other partner due to preoccupation with personal gratification or as a result of trivialising the other's needs. When infantile needs rapidly surge, they are expressed as demands that intimidate or push the other away. The couple rapidly descends into aggressive, hostile-dependent patterns of relating. A "me-versus-you" antagonism results. This may be the catalyst for turning to therapy when the aggression surfaces, either in the addicted partner trying to give up the substance, or in the other who has reached the breaking point in accommodating the addict's self absorbed behaviour.

Fears of aggression are mingled with disappointments and a sense of failure. While angry exchanges are plentiful at the outset of couple treatment and appear impossible to clinically penetrate, there are underlying abandonment anxieties and rejection worries that need to be addressed. Although this list is incomplete, many of the characteristics I have touched upon are observed in treatment and call for attunement and titrated technique, use of consistent holding, empathic interpretations and a gradual comfort with confrontations when dealing with "negative therapeutic reactions" (treatment rejection) (Spillius, 1990).

Technique

Dealing with narcissistic disorders requires a therapist who can breach the narcissistic cocoon by using himself as a therapeutic instrument (J. Scharff & D. Scharff, 2000). When working with the unconscious of regressed couples, premature clarity of understanding must be replaced by uncertainty until co-created meanings emerge. This approach is in contrast to current training in which a simplistic resolution is sought for complex subjective unconscious process. A central aim involves getting the narcissistic partner's attention. Cocaine abuse adds to the wide array of discharge-withdrawal tendencies. The non-addicted partner may try to reason with or go along with the infantile, grandiose, and self serving demands of the abusing one, or join in as will be evident in the upcoming case.

In treatment, we offer interpretive observations in unsaturated forms due to these patient's sensitivities to being scrutinised. We respond to couple conflicts by collecting examples of the differences between their stated aims and the consequential troubled results of couple relating, but without insisting we are certain. We wonder out loud asking the couple to examine means and ends, mostly from the here and now interpersonal perspective. Our technique focuses on marital communications, testing the couple's capacity for depressive position ambivalence because the splitting of paranoid/schizoid relating typifies disturbed interactions and the polarised state the couple is in when treatment begins. We take this approach because it is gentler and more immediate than historical linking of couple projections to individual childhood events. Historicising the couple's conflicted interactions requires imagining and linking current troubles with their origins, which is not possible early on due to the massive defences against helplessness that re-evoke childhood dependency. While the approach to the narcissistic component is sound, the major determinant for succeeding in couple work with an active addiction depends on the influence of drugs on the couple's capacity to work on a psychological level. Here and now reality testing has to be utilised to ascertain how the couple can do any work while drugs predominate the couple's day-to-day lives. No good result is possible unless adjunctive drug related treatment is introduced in the course of getting to know the couple. Individual sessions can sometimes persuade the addicted partner who experiences humiliation in the presence of the partner to consider one to one adjunctive drug treatment before the couple work can proceed.

Childhood events may be too toxic and impossible to think about for couples that were traumatised, and whose minds are currently colonised by powerful parental introjects of unquestioned loyalty to oppressive persecutory objects. Family histories frequently reveal addictions of many types, in parents, siblings, or grandparents that resulted in broken families, illness, or eventual death. If addiction is treated, the couple approach may allow the couple to tolerate emotional moments with the therapist as potentially different and less toxic from experiences in which presumptive, hard wired thoughts ruled. The opportunity to think about one's thoughts anew is a therapeutic aim, at first employed by the therapist's countertransference reflections. If we are successful in making a safer holding, later the patient may become aware there are two or more minds in the room capable of allowing differences in experience. Then new truths may emerge. Early exposures to interpretation are often rejected, though the therapist maintains an interest and curiosity about what the narcissistic patient is holding, since the patient's worldview is loaded with primitive reactions that disturb functioning, prevent faith in relationships and stymie hope for a better future.

Treatment therefore consists of gradually increasing the patient's ability to tolerate split off parts of the self and object world. Tolerating some abstinence is likely to cause regression and potential rehabilitative placement. Patients' unconscious anxieties, feared impulses, or persecutory object representations are often associated with affective or cognitive splits. We view these as defensive manoeuvres against the surfacing of unbearable anxieties, and appreciate their function as self-preservative necessities. Cocaine as self-medication functions to block unbearable anxieties but at a high price in the marriage. Projective identifications operate in moment-to-moment session interactions, and the therapist's experience of his countertransference resonates possible meanings for use. As couples enact transferences that communicate about interpersonal conflicts, the therapist gradually identifies them by a surface to depth commentary, including the possible basis for addictive choices, so as to illuminate their unconscious purposes. There is no need to immediately return to the childhood precursors of these transference encounters. It is sufficient to work on moment-to-moment affect tolerance, with the therapist taking the lead in tolerating the affect disturbances that involve primal dependency conflicts. We need time to build trust so that analytic depth can come later.

One technical aid for improved affect tolerance is the use of language that accepts the best level of functioning available to the narcissistic patient or their spouse, while generating the couple's potential for imagining a more desirable outcome. Ambivalence, the ability to recognise self and other limitations, or to consider two sides of an issue, is underdeveloped, or at worst non-existent.

In sessions, non-verbal and verbal communications, heavily loaded by projective and persecutory identifications are scrutinised through the lens of countertransference. Pathological communications to the therapist may carry an expectation of taking sides. Instead of taking sides we allow space for reflection in an atmosphere of acceptance that promotes a new opportunity for the previously unassimilated object relationships to be newly experienced. The therapist that can tolerate contradictory couple expressions increases patient awareness of splitting, leading to an increased consciousness of defensive strategies and their origins. The template of this process consists of titrating interventions in the here and now, and holding firmly to the process of enquiry into all aspects of what is said and done by the patient/couple. Frank discussion of patient concerns includes pointing out contradictory forces (love *vs.* hate) as they emerge.

While we empathise with all narcissistic wounds, it is most important to interpret split-off idealised or persecutory objects projected into the treatment, whether they occur between the couple or the couple and the therapist. Covert unconscious aggression is the stock and trade of masochistic narcissists, and somatic complaints are used to convey suffering, but with an edge that evokes a feeling that the therapist is responsible for causing the breakdown by pursuing unconscious buried treasure. The masochistic patient fears overt aggression, within the self or others. A shaky marital stability may depend on its repression, in that the aggressive borderline spouse carries the feared aggression. Aggression can be discussed in the context of how the treatment frustrates the couple. While its expression is most feared by the masochistic partner, we must recognise the pleasure it can eventually bring to the partner unconsciously seeking individuation. For more expressive and angry partners, the feeling that they are never understood can be modified when we recognise the suffering and loneliness beneath the defensive anger. When each partner bears witness to hidden worries about abandonment, rejection, or colonisation, a potential space provides new experiences that soften the anger and reduce isolation.

At the same time when encountering an actively sadistic and derogatory narcissist, the therapist must set ground rules that limit unbridled attacks on the therapist, or continued devaluation of the treatment process.

Case vignette: narcissistic motives, addiction, and strains on containment

I want to illustrate some features of the treatment situation emphasising the containment of narcissistic couple object relating under traumatic-addictive circumstances.

Eva, aged thirty-nine and Dave forty-one, married sixteen years, have three children from this marriage (Diandra, seventeen, Blanca, fourteen, and Helen, nine). Dave's daughter Celia, twenty, from his prior marriage, is at a state college and lives with the family when at home. The couple has been separated for one year, demanded by Eva who caught Dave in an extra-marital affair with her best friend and confidant. The couple history included an early decision to allow sex with others for Dave as long as he told Eva who it was with and when. In fact Eva reported she preferred to choose Dave's sexual partners so that she would not have any surprises. The rationalised agreement seemed to be the couple's method of establishing honesty and loyalty, although fidelity did not seem to matter to Dave. Eva was accommodating, at first.

Over a recent four year period the couple's "house of cards" tumbled. Dave's sexual appetite for multiple partners was increasing and the prior cooperation from Eva began to dissolve. Eva went along with joining in a four-way sexual liaison set up on a gambling trip to Las Vegas with their local couple friends who enticed them into group sex. Eva enjoyed the attention and the sex from the other husband, which sent Dave into a jealous fit. Dave's insistence that Eva was not supposed to experience anything but sex with another man went unheeded. Eva's passivity gave way and she became angry at Dave for his selfishness. Eva reported she was shocked but pleased that Dave was upset, and her displeasure emerged that she had always resented accommodating Dave's excessive needs.

To compound the couple instability during the past five years the police have been called over violent outbursts in which each spouse accused the other of trying to injure or "kill" them. The local police recommended an order of protection for Eva against Dave which was granted and obeyed, although visitation has occasionally caused flare-ups since Eva's new boyfriend stays over, and Dave has seen him with the children. Dave is living with a new girlfriend and the parallel lives of the spouses are another trigger for arguments about broken loyalties. Then the disclosure of Dave's ongoing cocaine addiction placed some of the impulsive, confusing, and destructive couple behaviours in perspective.

The couple gave a history of Dave's cocaine addiction which accompanied the sexual arrangements. Eva participated once or twice in cocaine snorting but tired of it. Dave reports giving up cocaine in the past year, but Eva does not trust that he has. She is in individual therapy as are Diandra and Blanca, and Eva actively attends an ACOA (Adult Children of Alcoholics) group. Dave is not in any support group or therapy.

The first two sessions revealed the information I have given, in fits and starts with contentious disagreements over whose story was credible. I began to notice signs of addictive influences including Dave's unreported alcohol use. However, Eva's behaviour was as also erratic, which reminded me of a folie à deux.

Sitting with the couple I was aware of the "object usages" employed by each spouse to avoid loneliness, and fears of being taken over by a powerful, destructive other.

The couple was in a paranoid-schizoid state—polarised, angry, and using language to expel and deny culpability, while insisting their reactions to each other were justified.

I wondered silently how I would survive their raging insistences that sucked the oxygen out of the room. I was compelled to listen, feeling an empathic disequilibrium, as the venting and accusing took over. While I felt considerable tension, I also got a sense of their survival skills. After a while I voiced an interest in what brought them to me. Had they considered why they came to me?

They paused and Dave lowered his head, sadly, saying he still loved Eva and wanted to find a way to reconcile. Eva became teary and lowered her head, as if defeated, or at least exhausted, sharing that she did not want the constant fighting. She went on to discuss the children briefly and their suffering. I did not yet observe an interest from her to reconciling; it was more an expression of exhaustion and worry about the children's suffering.

My aim in the initial intervention was to contain their destructive and "known" chaotic edginess characteristic of the paranoid-schizoid position by gauging the couple's capacity for receiving an idea, an offer of hope, through exploring the basis for coming to see me (depressive position). I thought their internal representations were of the dyad's destructive elements and deficits: neglect, narcissistic preoccupations with exciting objects, exploitation, and paranoid fears of being controlled that repressed sadness over loves lost. The couple discussed past failed attempts at therapy, couple and individual (each with a different therapist). Both were employed in Eva's family business. She reported that her father was a tyrant, and she had always wanted Dave to keep her father out of their marital and family life. He had done the opposite, becoming more involved in meeting her father's insatiable need for intimate knowledge of their home life, which Eva abhorred. Eva had not been able to individuate but was seeking a strong partner in Dave who would save her from the intrusive father. What emerged were the "rescue" fantasy and the failure in the couple to secure its boundaries.

The couple-father triangle discussion triggered a verbal brawl, in which Dave and Eva returned to previous tirades about sexual exploitation and broken trust. At first this return to the polarised couple state forced me into the role of traffic manager. The couple detonated the discussion of family dynamics and their negative effects on marital trust. I paid attention to the regression, but salvaged the links that suggested the intergenerational transmission of psychotic intrusiveness that might explain the couple's break down. A split had occurred because of traumatising parental-child (couple and Eva's father) boundary violations and had promoted the couple's sexual disloyalties. The split was wreaking havoc—too much couple aggression and denial of the intergenerational part, and preoccupations with the marital breakdown caused by disillusionment on Eva's part, and Dave's joining symbiotically with his father-in-law (likely Dave's father hunger as a poor solution to denial and hatred of maternal dependency).

In my second attempt at containment, I made firm eye contact with each partner, held up my hands, signalling them to pay attention. They needed several reminders to look at me. I presented the sequence of what had just occurred. At the same time I told them I was not taking sides, and that I wanted to be of some use to them. With narcissistic patients pointing to thwarted dependency requires a language of curiosity rather than certainty. I wanted to preserve both partner's selves while offering a language of conflicted means ends. I slowly repeated the sequence: The problem was failed dependencies. Dave and Eva relied on her father for financial security and Eva did not trust her father's motives in inserting himself in their marriage and family. Dave appreciated his father-in-law for bringing Dave into the business, and felt obligated. The couple's extra-marital arrangement broke down just like the daughter-father-husband's business arrangement. These co-existing conflicts were hidden by their so-called workable solution to Dave's sexual appetite that Eva accommodated to because she did not want to be controlling like her father. I waited.

The couple took in very little from me and argued further about who had let whom down, but with less steam. I noticed they were triangulating their affect by focusing on the father's intrusiveness in their marriage, diffusing a bit of the dyadic polarity of the first and most of the current session—a softening of the "you versus me" impasse. The session ended with a request from Eva to have more marital sessions. As we said goodbye I recalled my previous doubt that Eva was interested in working on the marriage. I still doubted the couple's capacity for change, but her request for more sessions was a sign that the containment was sufficient for motivating the couple's return.

Therapist perspective

The couple's omnipotent "highs" and grandiosity privileged victimhood over all else. The witch's brew of inseparability and fusion brimmed with fits of exploitation and rage at being unfulfilled but stuck together. Dave's intolerable feelings were about being on his own, as he needed her more when they were apart then when together, unless she shared his entitlements for extra-marital sex and addictive excitement. In his magical thinking it was unnecessary to consider negative consequences of self-indulgence. For Eva abandoning Dave was keeping her hostage to Dave's pleas he would change; although she was shifting I thought about giving up on him. I was faced with an impossible task due to the regressed state of the couple, the ongoing addiction that prevented authentic participation, and the prominent way narcissistic object relations took over attempts to find a thinking space. The couple as a unit could not foster a dialectic to organise experience (Autistic-contiguous position) beyond a primitive discharge of sensory data. They were so engorged at an asymbolic level that therapy could not provide a transitional experience for development of observing egos (Ogden, 1989).

I have presented characteristics of narcissistic patients in marital relations along with a basic technical understanding of containment. I illustrated the difficulty in containment with a case of malignant narcissism, collusive extra-marital sexual exploitation, and cocaine addiction, and addressed the suffering in these patients as the therapist tried to make a difference. Therapists working with this population pursue a therapeutic alliance that often evades them. Tolerating identity diffusion, primitive defensiveness, and anxiety driven attacks on linking (Bion, 1963) make treatment difficult, long, and challenging. Hidden affects are the bedrock for understanding the dynamics of these patients. They reveal the developmental failures that form the substrate of individual and couple cognitive, behavioural, social, and psychosomatic organisation of the two personalities by acting them out. Therapists often complain that there is too much affect with these troubled couples and that managing it is the primary requirement for treatment to occur. Why look for more affect? In terms of one's timing and early pacing of therapeutic options we must reduce chaotic affect. The object relations of self and other interconnect with the couple unconscious substrate and it takes time for the layering of deeper woundedness to emerge. In the meantime the therapist accepts and works with opportunities to develop potential for working with a fuller narrative, and to think about controversies and conflicts in terms of personal tragedies. The material we need to access is derived from developmental dramas and anxieties lurking in the unshared couple past, and brought to us as secret potentials intuited by the myriad of transference enactments. We are well served when we appreciate the richness of this clinical fact. In some cases we may not be able to gain access to a nameable dread for therapeutic purposes. Mourning and retrieving lost objects may not be possible due to the sadistic-masochistic disordered partners' collusive bond. We ultimately get hooked into a language stripped of discernible meaning. When we are driven by destructive motives, we are often left holding onto our frame without the company of the couple. In this couple the wife instituted divorce. They continued destructive relating during and after the divorce, and a year later were back together. Their children had all moved in with other relatives or were in out of state colleges.

Therapists may complain there is already too much affect to manage. I reply: We are not entitled to a better functioning couple, and we suffer for their limitations. What we have to offer is an understanding that hidden affects about thwarted dependency are the buried treasure that fuses the couple to their disturbing dance. When we offer empathic curiosity about woundedness, and unmet needs, we may expect a range reactions, from a breakdown to a break up, and at times a breakthrough.

References

Bion, W. R. (1963). *Elements of Psycho-Analysis*. London: Heinemann.
Bromberg, P. (1995). Psychoanalysis, dissociation, and personality organization reflections. *Psychoanalytic Dialogues*, 5: 511–528.
Fairbairn, W. R. D. (1952). *Psychoanalytic Studies of the Personality*. London: Routledge.
Freud, S. (1914). On narcissism. *S. E.*, 14: p. 90. London: Hogarth.
Kantzian, E. J., Halliday, K. S., & McAuliffe, W. E. (1990). *Addiction and the Vulnerable Self*. New York: Guilford.
Klein, M. (1946). Notes on some schizoid mechanisms. *International Journal of Psychoanalysis*, 27: 99–110.
Lachkar, J. (1992). *The Narcissistic/Borderline Couple: A Psychoanalytic Perspective on Marital Treatment*. New York: Brunner Mazel.
Morgenstern, J. & Leeds, J. (1993). Contemporary psychoanalytic theories of substance abuse: A disorder in search of a paradigm. *Psychotherapy*, 30(2): 194–206.
Ogden, T. H. (1982). *Projective Identification and Psychotherapeutic Technique*. New York: Jason Aronson.
Ogden, T. H. (1989). On the concept of the autistic-contiguous position. *International Journal of Psychoanalysis*, 70: 127–140.
Rosenfeld, H. (1964). On the psychopathology of narcissism: A clinical approach. *International Journal of Psychoanalysis*, 45: 332–337.

Rosenfeld, H. (1971). A clinical approach to the psychoanalytic theory of the life and death instincts: An investigation into the aggressive aspects of narcissism. *International Journal of Psychoanalysis,* 52: 169–178.

Segal, H. & Bell, D. (1991). The theory of narcissism in the work of Freud and Klein. In: J. Sandler, E. S. Person & P. Fonagy: *Freud's, On Narcissism: An Introduction* (pp. 149–174). New Haven: Yale University Press.

Scharff, J. S. & Bagnini, C. (2001). Object relations couple therapy. In: A. S. Gurman & N. S. Jacobson (Eds.), *Clinical Handbook of Marital Therapy,* 3rd Edition (pp. 59–85). New York: Guilford Press.

Scharff, J. S. & Bagnini, C. (2004). Narcissistic disorder. In: D. Snyder & M. Wisman (Eds.), *Treating Difficult Couples.* (pp. 285–307). New York: Guilford Press.

Scharff, J. S. & Scharff, D. E. (2000). *Tuning the Therapeutic Instrument. Affective Learning in Psychotherapy.* Northvale, NJ: Jason Aronson.

Spillius E. B. (1990) (Ed.). Introduction to Part 2. In *Melanie Klein Today; Developments in Theory and Practice, Volume 1: Mainly Theory.* New York and London: Routledge.

Stern, D. N. (1985). *The Interpersonal World of the Infant: A View from Psychoanalysis and Developmental Psychology.* New York: Basic Books.

Winnicott, D. W. (1960). Ego distortion in terms of true and false self. In: *The Maturational Processes and the Facilitating Environment,* 1965. Madison, WI: International Universities Press.

CHAPTER SEVENTEEN

The dream space in analytic couple therapy

Tamar Kichli Borochovsky

The realm of dream is a relatively unexplored space in analytic couple therapy yet one that is full of potential. Exploring a couple's dreams opens a new space that lets us work at a profound level. The dream sphere opens a door to understanding the projective identifications occurring in the couple and in the transference and counter-transference processes. Each dream gives access to an element of the couple unconscious

In this chapter, I (TKB) describe my view of the unconscious, the function of dreaming, and how to understand dream language. I show how dreams when combined give meaning to the inner couple link of a couple in analytic couple therapy with me. I present clinical vignettes from their treatment, showing work with three dreams: the husband's dream, the wife's dream, and my own dream. Dreams and vignettes from the context of couple therapy illustrate the emergence of the couple's unconscious fantasy, needs, and desires in the therapy.

I think of the unconscious as an invisible organ of the body, small but vital, like the heart pumping blood to the entire body, the stomach taking in nourishment, and the kidney clearing it of toxins night and day. I also think of the unconscious as an inner sense like the one that tells birds to migrate and newborn giraffes to stand up. Contemplating the invisible bodily organs and the unconscious from an individual stance like that, I do not readily see their social function as clearly as that of the hands, which in addition to having allowed us to hang from a tree and gather fruit, give us a way to reach out and touch others with a pat, a handshake, or a punch. Nevertheless the bodily organs and the unconscious do respond to social situations with increased or decreased activity, and shifts in their functioning send signals to others who respond even though they are not conscious of having seen any evidence of upset or arousal. The unconscious sends signals to the conscious part of the individual's mind in images, actions, symptoms, and dreams.

Studies show that an average person has five to seven dreams a night (Friedman, 2012). Of these fifteen hundred dreams a year, only a few are remembered and even fewer are told. Children dream less frequently when they have no one to whom they can tell their dreams (Friedman, 2012). If there is no potential listening space, no dream will appear. Yet without being elaborated, dreaming is silently steadily doing the work of the unconscious. The dream is a ventilator that clears the system and lets the soul breathe. It allows body and mind to rest. It converts the unconscious wish to a socially accepted purpose. It alerts the conscious mind to pain so that it knows to ask for help. According to Freud (1900) experiences that are too conflicted or overwhelming for the conscious mind appear in an individual's dreams. Freud (1907) sees dreams as a nightly emotional coping mechanism. Dreams protect sleep from intrusion by overwhelming content. They allow the dreamer to be in an intermediate space—awake enough to be aware and sometimes to remember, and asleep enough for the body to remain rested. Dreams give a route for expressing unconscious conflict instead of suppressing it and converting it into a symptom.

The unconscious sends signals not only to the conscious part of the individual's mind but also to the social sphere, as other people respond to images, react to actions, and listen to dreams (Neri, Pines & Friedman, 2002). The unconscious has an inter-subjective dimension. Unconscious material that causes mental distress, but cannot be expressed in remembered dreams or in words, lies at the basis of individual symptoms. When therapists open a space for dreaming, the unconscious has an alternative route for revealing its conflict.

Dreaming clearly serves to protect the individual mind and body from disruption by conflict, overstimulation, and threat, but does it also have an inter-subjective function? In olden times, dreams were understood to have a prophetic function. They reflected a political reality and warned of a potential social catastrophe. They were claimed as collective cultural icons. Each element of the dream was thought to have a specific meaning and so the dream could be interpreted by an outsider using a system of symbols, as Joseph interpreted the Pharaoh's dreams—to their mutual advantage. It was Freud who found that the elements of each dream are multiply determined, each one loaded with many possible meanings, all expressions of the dynamic unconscious.

This knowledge from individual psychoanalysis applies to analytic therapy with couples. When one member of a couple reports a dream, it reflects the couple link at the same time as it carries personal meaning for the individual (D. Scharff, 2012). The couple's relationship is the meeting point of two unconscious worlds and their link to the interpersonal unconscious of past and future generations (D. Scharff & J. Scharff, 2005; D. Scharff, 2012). States of intense emotional conflict raise many feelings that threaten the couple's security and prove difficult to contain. The sexual relationship adds a physical element to the multi-layered and multi-dimensional link (Caruso, 2012) and intensifies the conflict. Intimate partners use their hands to explore each other's bodies. Their eyes meet, their scents mingle, and their pheromones mix. Tongue meets tongue, fluids are exchanged, bodies align, and two organs join in intercourse. The individual dream of an intimate sexual partner is dreamt in a shared bed, in the presence of the person in relation to whom the sex drive is fulfilled or frustrated. In the couple space, having a dream has meaning in terms of the couple context. Telling it to the partner may be a request for guidance, reassurance, and containment of conflict too difficult to contain in the realm of sleep and dream (Friedman, 2000). It may be a vehicle for intimacy or for hostile attack.

In analytic couple therapy, a spouse or partner may tell a dream. Even though the partner has heard it previously, re-telling it in the therapeutic session will give the therapist an opportunity for extended exploration and interpretive work. Dreams shed light on the couple's intimate relationship and on their internal space. If the couple therapist is not oriented to working with dreams, the couple will not bring in a dream. When couples do bring dreams to couple therapy, their dreams disguise threatening and intolerable conflicts that have been suppressed and distorted and are now looking to be revealed and contained, as can be seen in the following example in which the husband, the wife, and I, the couple therapist, work on our dreams to arrive at understanding of the couple's relationship.

Clinical vignette

A couple I will call Theresa and Ridge started analytic couple therapy with me four years ago. Ridge is a vice-president of a hi-tech company and Theresa is a secretary. They had been married for twenty years and have two children, a five-year-old son and an eleven-year-old daughter. Seven years ago, Ridge had met up with Monique, a computer consultant he had known as a girl from his high school and whom he had found again on Facebook. Ridge fell in love with her, and carried on an affair with her for the next three years. During this time, Ridge brought Monique and her family with him and Theresa and their children on long trips abroad. Theresa did not like Monique and felt suspicious that she was more than a friend to Ridge. During these two family vacations, Ridge and Monique were indeed having sex, but when Theresa confronted Ridge, he denied the accusation and shouted at her for being so suspicious. Monique and Ridge's sexual affair remained unproven. While engaged in the affair, Monique introduced Ridge to her scheme for hacking computers in order to steal credit. Unlike their affair, their credit card theft was discovered. They were accused as a pair, remanded, and held at jail to await trial.

Theresa found out about the reality of the affair only when she came to post bail for Ridge at the jail, and saw that Monique had been arrested with him. Paying the lawyers and returning the stolen money took all their savings, cost them their house, and made Ridge and Theresa bankrupt. The betrayal was immense. Theresa lost faith in her husband and she lost her financial security. Ridge lost his good name, was at risk of losing his marriage, and was suicidal. In this state of impending devastation, they started therapy with me shortly after the case was featured in the media, and continued during the two years prior to trial. Our therapy was interrupted by Ridge's conviction and sentencing. While he was in prison, I stayed in contact with the family. Immediately after his release, the couple returned to therapy.

In therapy, Theresa wanted Ridge to understand how upset she was by his outbursts, his criticising her, humiliating her in public, and controlling her by limiting the amount of money she could spend. She was furious that Ridge had lost all their money and that an injustice had been done to her. She was angry that he had fallen in love with a teenage fantasy with which she could never compete. She felt he stayed with her only as a default position. Ridge on the other hand, asked Theresa to understand his need to run from home: since the children were born he had felt neglected by her taking care of them and obsessively cleaning the house, his needs for intimate and sexual connectedness no longer important to her.

The couple tended to think and express their reactions to each other in concrete rather than symbolic terms, a characteristic that was probably intensified in reaction to the trauma. Their conversation was limited, with many silences and a palpable fear of connecting. They did not bring in dreams. They found it difficult to think about themselves as individuals or as a couple, and they could not relate their couple relationship to the things that were happening to them. The first time I saw Ridge and Theresa together, I thought of them as two people in parallel. It felt as if they could not reach each other. Yet although they could not communicate with each other, each of them was able to create intimacy with me in individual sessions.

Eventually Ridge and Theresa became able to express their emotions more freely to each other. Theresa said to Ridge, "Your mother always spoiled you. She preferred you to her husband. She was like a maid and took care of you like a king. So you don't realise that you can't scream like a baby when you don't get everything you want." Ridge said to Theresa, "You were like a mother to your brothers, and so you know how to be a mother, but you don't know how to give a man what he needs." They responded to these comments with silence and outrage. As time went by, they gradually became able to think in metaphors that allowed them to express their feelings.

After Ridge was released from prison, tensions in the couple relationship escalated. He was sent to sleep in the guest bedroom, and divorce was on the horizon. When he and Theresa resumed therapy, they entered my office in silence. Ridge said nothing. Finally Theresa brought up her feelings of distrust and betrayal. She said, "I don't know who he is seeing. I'm afraid to be a sucker again. Before Ridge went to prison, we separated as if we were going to die. Now we are here alive and together, but I'm not what I used to be. After ten minutes of work, I'm finished. Once I could run like hell. I'll die if something like this happens to me again. Once a cheater, always a cheater. If you want to cheat again, leave me first and don't lie to me." Ridge, as if he were unconsciously fulfilling Theresa's expressed need for honesty, told a dream.

Ridge's dream

"Theresa, I had a dream I just have to tell you. We sat there in the room, me and Monique. She annoyed me, and I pounded the computer with my fists. I got so angry that I'm hitting the computer really hard. And somehow this was happening in prison. And someone told the warden who came and yelled at us."

Theresa responded saying, "I can't believe you're dreaming about her." Ridge blamed me for it. He said, angrily, "Now it turns out that I dream of her. See what you did! Digging too deep will drive us crazy." He added, "What's done is done. That's why I didn't tell her the dream before." Theresa responded, "If you told me at home that you dreamt of her, I would have thrown a vase at your head."

At home, and before the appearance of the dreams, both had avoided discussion of anything that was connected to the betrayal. By recounting the dream, Ridge brought the topic up, and showed himself getting mad at his lover. Identifying his emotion did not change the behaviour and the aggression intensified instead. I noted the repetition of angry words in Ridge's dream—annoyed, pounded, angry, hitting, yells—and I noticed that it evoked in Theresa a violent image of her helpless frustration. Ridge's dream did not mention the response of his lover, and he was left alone with his rage. Telling the dream was a way of attempting to satisfy the partner's demand for honesty, thereby protecting the dreamer and the relationship. But Theresa found it hard to bear the existence of Ridge's former lover in his dreams, and Ridge could not contain Theresa's anger. By not reacting to Ridge's anger, I contained it and allowed it to be expressed in the link that joined the three of us.

The dream described an out-of-control emotion like a child's tantrum. This led me to think that Ridge might be describing an experience that relates to his relationship with his parents. His father was an introverted person who tended to have frequent tantrums. His mother, who was a victim of incest, needed Ridge close by for protection, and so she did not allow him to separate from her. So he had a symbiotic relationship with his mother and felt distant from his irascible father. At the surface level, the warden seems like Theresa finding out what Ridge was up to and yelling at him, but it may also represent the third person entering the symbiotic relationship of the mother and child—the voice of the father, and in the transference the intervention of the inquiring therapist who is experienced as causing trouble. In the dream, the warden (representing the father) is supposed to be protective, but instead he yells and leaves the child with anger and loneliness.

What we see here is an intergenerational transmission of attachment style and temperament. As a husband and father himself, Ridge was withdrawn and angry, unable to be intimate in his relationship with his wife or calm and affectionate with his children. Ridge used the word "hitting" to describe his angry actions displaced onto the computer. In Hebrew "hitting" has a double meaning. It refers to having sex without intimacy. Perhaps Ridge is using the dream to process his conflated aggressive and sexual drives. In addition to representing Theresa's anger after the betrayal, the angry warden may be seen as representing Ridge's anger towards himself that was earlier expressed in having been suicidal. Lastly the figure of the warden refers to me in the transference as a therapist whom they expect to protect their couple relationship but whose facilitation of discussion reveals their anger and frustration about the betrayal of their hopes for love.

The telling of the dream in the couple therapy space creates the possibility of listening differently. It expands the potential space for treatment and builds a new space for symbolic thinking and creative partnering, different from the domestic space, but a model for a new way of being. In the domestic space, Ridge would have hidden his dream because if he had told it there, Theresa would have thrown something at him. But in the analytic couple therapy space, Ridge dares to tell his dream and Theresa is helped to listen, knowing that her responses will be worked with. The unconscious link between them and me has expanded and now carries the potential for transformation.

In the next session, despite her dreading the future with Ridge, Theresa was trying to move on. Repeating Ridge's words from the last session, she said, "If I dig deeply it will drive me crazy. Better to keep it in the past and move on." But then she went back to expressing her pain. She said, "Yesterday I lost it when he told me to iron. I was ironing for him, and I felt that he was going to meet her looking good in that ironed shirt." Looking detached, Ridge said hopelessly, "So, what can I do? Not tell her to iron?" It was then that Theresa brought up her dream.

Theresa's dream

Since Ridge went to prison, I often dream I am flying from one place to another. This week I dreamt I was flying, and there were zombies there. They looked alive but they were dead. One of them sat on the grass. I didn't know him. His head was bent over. "He walked towards me. It scared me, and so I flew out of there".

Talking about the dream Theresa said that Ridge was the zombie. Her dream was possibly connected to the last session in which she had referred to separation as a death. She continued, "I don't know this person who cheated on me, stole, and went to prison. This is the husband I used to worship? No one else would have stayed with someone who had done that to her." I was thinking she wants to let him know how difficult it is for her to bear the current version of Ridge—alive and returned from the dead of prison, but also dead to her but alive to Monique. In *The Interpretation of Dreams* Freud (1900) explains that one symbol can signify many emotional processes. The zombie might symbolise a development in their relationship as it contains elements of feeling both dead and alive. Perhaps it heralds a move towards the depressive position (Klein, 1968) which is more integrated than the splitting that had been going on. I heard her threat of flying away when scared as a request for empathy for her defence mechanisms of avoidance and repression. Perhaps the dream was warning me that she needed me to slow down.

Returning to the dream some months later, Theresa said, "A part of me is dead. Some part of me and my past doesn't exist anymore." Maybe the zombie represents Theresa herself. She continued, "I guess it is easier to run away from what is happening than to stay on the ground and face it." Theresa was warning me that if I prematurely forced her to meet her parts that look alive but are actually dead, she would fly away. Perhaps she was afraid that Ridge and I would not be able to hold on when faced with her half-dead, half-alive organs. The zombie also represents the couple relationship now containing both dead and alive bits, positive and negative attributes that were denied previously by splitting Ridge into a hero to worship and a cheater to excoriate.

The therapist's dream

During the course of this therapy, I was pregnant with my child who is now two-years-old. I gave birth the very week that Ridge received the court decision that he would go to prison, and Theresa was concerned about how she would manage. I stayed in touch with them and didn't "fly away" as Ridge felt Theresa had done after she gave birth. I had become a mother, and yet I stayed in the relationship with them. By doing so, I was still there, containing the couple and making reparation for betraying them with my husband. Encountering a dream about a couple is like running into a patient when you least expect it. Dreaming about specific elements from patients' dreams is even more overwhelming. My dream is long and detailed, and I choose to present only some of the particularly relevant parts:

In my dream I am five weeks pregnant. As Ridge and Theresa arrive at my clinic, Theresa looks at my abdomen and makes a point of my being pregnant. She says that my belly is still small, but she can see it is pregnant. Then I am driving with both of them in a car towards some new buildings where they now live in the city near the prison. I am thinking to myself, "What am I doing with them in the car?" and wondering, "How can she see I am pregnant?" This makes me feel ashamed.

I was reminded of a dream Theresa had while Ridge was in prison. Theresa's dream from that time:

In my dream Ridge had a child from Monique. In the dream, I went there and asked him to come home with me to their children, but he refused.

Later in my dream:

I am sitting with Ridge in their home. Ridge tells me that he told Theresa that he is leaving her. I ask him, "Did she do something?" and he says, "No". I answer, "So you can't leave her." His son enters the room and Ridge tells him they are not getting divorced. Then I ask Ridge to remove a tree that is lying dangerously over his bed. Ridge doesn't see it as dangerous, but when I give him a stern look, he removes it. Ridge puts a hat over his head. I notice that he is now wearing two hats. I go outside.

Ridge tells me in my dream that he is leaving Theresa, words that his lover Monique would like to hear. Ridge projects onto me his sexual and emotional feeling for his lover. Theresa might have been suspicious in the beginning of the dream that my fetus was Ridge's, like the child Monique was carrying in Theresa's dream, a child that threatened to take Ridge away from her. She might fear that the fetus in my womb could also entice Ridge to leave her. By the end of the dream it turns out that Ridge makes the decision to stay home. The new other woman, I, the therapist, tries to prevent damage. My advice is rebuffed at first and then accepted. The dream raised my awareness that while trying to offer a remedial experience I might be caught in a rescue fantasy.

Therapists' dreams may be viewed as countertransference reflecting unanalysed infantile conflict or as reflecting the therapy process. In my view, the focus of the therapist's dreams is not only on the therapist as a person in her own right but as a receptacle for projective identification processes within the therapeutic relationship (Bernstein & Katz, 1987; Kron & Avni, 2003; Wilner, 1996). It is difficult for therapists to analyse their own dreams as clues to their patients' unconscious. One technique I use is to focus on the dream as if it were a literary text. Dream and text both use symbols. A dream is a sublimation of repressed drives that, through the dream, can be represented in symbols and so reach the surface. A story is an aesthetic representation of drives and emotions lurking behind the words. Displacement and condensation abound in dreams and in literature. Reading a text or listening carefully to a dream, we view it in its context, and we also dismember the dream and inspect it piece by piece, each element differing significantly from the concrete story the dream appears to tell, and in this way we try to unravel the hidden meaning to reach the deeper message of the dream. Since a dream shares characteristics with a literary text, it can be approached using literary analytic instruments.

For instance, applying Lacan's ideas on phonetic similarity of words, one can look at the image of the "tree" as a disguise of the word "three" referring to the dangerous third for the spouses who go along in life not as a pair but as parallel individuals. I am afraid of that dangerous tree and also of Ridge's lack of fear. My request to him to take down the tree (the three) can be seen as an attempt to reduce his sexuality drive or even threaten castration. A repeating word or affective charge is also significant. For instance the repetition of words hit, pound, and angry in Ridge's dream indicate the persistence of aggressive affect. The word sit appeared in all three dreams, referring to a property that patients and therapist shared as we sat together to do our therapy work. The fragmented quality of the dreams matched the silences and gaps in their verbal communication in sessions and speaks to the broken-ness of the couple.

The three dreams reflect imagination, biography, need for containment, and wish to communicate. They give voice to emotions and tell us what we need to know about the couple, the therapist, and the therapy process at each stage when a dream appears. In Theresa's dream there is fear of death and no-response (she is afraid of the zombie and she runs away); in Ridge's dream, there is anger (he is fighting and yelling); in my dream there is fear, anger, and shame (I am afraid of a dangerous tree and of Ridge's failing to see the danger, embarrassed about being seen to be pregnant, a sign of my sexuality and freedom). Ridge is angry and fighting and Theresa is afraid and in flight. My dream adds the shame in reverberation with their shame, but in my case it is the shame of being married and being able to be intimate whereas in their case the shame pertains to absent sexuality and subsequent deprivation and betrayal (D. Scharff, 2012).

The dream reveals the main emotion and the threat as the story introduces its theme and central conflict. Telling the dream to the spouse or partner, and needing to tell the story of that particular dream, reveals the individual's narrative and conflict in the couple relationship, and it shows the partner's way of listening and responding, and so sheds light on the relationship. The therapist's dream is not merely a manifestation of infantile neurosis but a countertransference response that contains the couple's anxiety and moves the exploration forward. As dream, story, and reaction flow together, couple and therapist engage in the therapeutic space to deepen their understanding of the couple relationship.

Discussing the sequence of dreams with a group of colleagues widens understanding of the therapeutic process further (Bernstein & Katz, 1987). Kron and Avni (2003) consider the therapist's dreams about patients an opportunity for dialogue, with the focus not on the therapist as an individual but as a participant in the couple's projective identificatory processes. Kron & Avni (2003) claim that, in addition to reflecting the mental state of the therapist and the patients, therapists' dreams indicate the status of the therapeutic relationship, while Abramovich and Lange (1994) mention the dreams' diagnostic function. Wilner (1996) focuses on the unraveling of clues to the patient's unconscious. Whitman, Kramer, and Baldridge (1969), Bernstein & Katz (1987), Blechner (1995), and Wilner (1996) study the function of therapists' dreams about patients as servants of the transference and countertransference, which when properly used shed light on the therapeutic process.

Writing up the story of Ridge and Theresa led to more dreaming and more insight when I prepared it for presentation to a large group of colleagues and students in a videoconference course where I could share a long-term complex analytic couple therapy (Kichli, 2012). I wanted the group to help me see parts of our interaction I had not seen in the therapy and develop new angles of approach of benefit to the patient-couple, to me as the therapist, and to the therapy itself. Reading my paper, receiving comments, and engaging in discussion was a hidden request for containment buried in an offer to contribute to a teaching and learning process. I received containment for Theresa and Ridge's individual and shared dreams and for my dream and its inherent rescue fantasy, in a parallel process to the couple's request for containment and rescue.

The couple's space presents a creative and refreshing opportunity to meet difficult and indigestible emotions. In a relationship, through projective identification, either of the spouses can split from intolerable emotions and convey them to the other. The committed setting of the marriage allows the projector to expose and contend with these emotions in a somewhat protected manner, but when they become too toxic, the more protected space of therapy is required. A dream constitutes a text full of encrypted emotions and symbolised projective mechanisms. Analysing the dream in couple therapy opens a space for direct speech between the projector and his projections and the emotions and memories driving them. In the potential space of the treatment room, the emotions are reflected on retrospectively in a space in which it feels safe enough to observe them and take responsibility for them. The feelings become quite heated at times but with help they can be thought about. Analysing the dream reveals the spouses' projective identificatory system so that they can become more aware of projections and detoxify them as they occur.

Some therapists find it hard to imagine that dreams, which are so useful to the analyst in reaching the troubling unknown of the individual, can be analysed in couple therapy. Provided we adapt our techniques of dream interpretation, the individual dream becomes a shared experience for learning for the couple. A dream that is told in couple therapy opens a web of experiences, emotions, thoughts, and associations for the dream teller, his spouse, and their couple therapist. The couple in treatment has a place to bring their dreams. Knowing of the potential space for contemplating dreams may even encourage them to create these dreams in order to bring them to treatment. The dreamer expresses not only emotional content in his dream, but also fantasies about the way he thinks his dream will be reacted to, for instance, hoping to be admired, or fearing being laughed at. Hearing the dream, the spouse may also have fantasies about, and emotional reactions to, her partner's dream. For instance Theresa, disappointed and angry at her husband's dream content, fantasised throwing a vase on his head. Once told to the partner, the individual dream becomes a shared dream that sets the relationship in forward motion again through confrontation with its intolerable contents.

I took the dreams of both spouses and searched for shared motifs. I also looked for a discourse between the emotions that were conveyed in each of the individual dreams. I tried to find whether there was something in common with, or different from, each other's manner of telling the dream, responding to it, and remembering it. I connected the dream to the literary story, and applied the techniques of literary text analysis to the dreams in order to understand the therapy, the patients' relationship and internal worlds, and the unconscious connection between couple and therapist. I reflected on my own dream as providing information about the couple. Unlike the thought of the horrifying child of the other woman that will take Ridge away from Theresa, the discovery of the fetus in my womb is followed by Ridge's decision to stay home. Theresa says that the relationship that was once dead only exists in the past. On top of its ruins a new relationship has grown in which Ridge is no longer adored but is recognised for all his weaknesses and strengths, and in which Theresa no longer perceives femininity as fragile and subservient. She has found strength in her heart to live with the zombie. In other words, the split between the strong and the weak, between the voice of the guiding father and the creative surviving woman, is reflected in and contained by the countertransference and transference shown in the therapist's dream.

Follow-up

The couple continues to attend therapy. I am amazed to hear them acknowledge and talk about their difficulty to be close without falling back on destructive actions that communicate their distress. When Ridge is temporarily stuck in anger, Theresa does not fly away as she used to. She can stay connected, respond supportively, and help Ridge calm down. In a meeting with them as I was writing this piece, they defined their marriage as "a second chapter, a second chance, a second marriage." Previously dealing in action and the concrete realm, they can now talk in metaphors and use symbols to help them think about each other and about their relationship without blame. Theresa says, "My dreams helped me see Ridge for his weaknesses and strengths. I no longer adore him and I no longer let him control me." Ridge says, "I need to work on my ability to be intimate with my wife." Hearing him say this made me proud of his gains. They are proud too at what they have overcome and what they have accomplished against huge odds.

When I told Ridge and Theresa that I would like to write up my work with them as a chapter, they gave permission gladly, happy that others might be able to learn from their story. It would obviously be simplistic to attribute their insight and their improvement only to dream analysis, but I hope to have shown that the process of working with dreams was instrumental in helping this husband and wife take responsibility for themselves, develop insight, and move from a parallel stance to one of togetherness. The dreams of husband, wife, and therapist brought the problems of the moment, created change, and at the same time showed the process of change.

References

Abramovitch, H. & Lange, T. (1994). Dreaming about my patient: a case illustration of therapist's initial dream. *Journal of the Israeli Association for Analytical Psychology, 1*, 1: 21–32. (in Hebrew).

Bernstein, A. E. & Katz, S. C. (1987). When supervisor and therapist dream: The use of unusual countertransference phenomenon. *Journal of the American Academy of Psychoanalysis, 15*, 2: 261–271.

Blechner, M. J. (1995). The patient's dreams and the countertransference. *Psychoanalytic Dialogues, 5*, 1: 1–25.

Caruso, N. J. (2012). *Sexual Desire Disorder—A Case Study*. Couple Therapy Videoconference Course. International Psychotherapy Institute, Chevy Chase, MD, Wednesday 4 April, 2012.

Freud, S. (1900). *The Interpretation of Dreams. S. E., 4 & 5*: 1–627. London: Hogarth.

Freud, S. (1905). *Three Essays on the Theory of Sexuality. S. E., 7*: 125–243. London: Hogarth.

Freud, S. (1907). Delusions and dreams in Jensen's Gradiva. *S. E., 9*: 1–95. London: Hogarth.

Friedman, R. (2000). The interpersonal containment of dreams in group psychotherapy: A contribution to the work with dreams in a group. *Group Analysis, 33*, 2: 221–233.

Friedman, R. (2012). How to work with dreams? Three uses of the dream story in group therapy. Workshop.

Kichli, T. (2012). Case presentation to Richard M. Zeitner. Analytic Couple Therapy Training Program on videoconference, the International Psychotherapy Institute, Chevy Chase, MD, USA, 28 March, 2012.

Klein, M. (1968). *Envy and Gratitude and Other Works (1946–1963)*. London: Hogarth, 1975.

Kron, T. & Avni, N. (2003). Psychotherapists' dreams about their patients. *Journal of Analytical Psychology. 48*, 3: 317–339.

Lacan, J. (1968). *The Language of the Self: The Function of Language in Psychoanalysis*. Baltimore: Johns Hopkins University Press.
Lacan, J. (1998). *On Feminine Sexuality, the Limits of Love and Knowledge, The Seminar of Jacques Lacan Book XX, Encore*: Jacques-Alain Miller (Ed.), B. Fink (Trans.). New York: W. W. Norton.
Neri, C., Pines, M., & Friedman, R. (2002). *Dreams in Group Psychotherapy: Theory and Technique*. London: Jessica Kingsley.
Scharff, D. E. (2012). The concept of the link in psychoanalytic therapy. *Couple and Family Psychoanalysis, 1*, 1: 34–48.
Scharff, D. E., & Scharff, J. S. (2004). Using dreams in treating couples' sexual issues. *Psychoanalytic Inquiry, 24*, 3: 468–482.
Scharff, D., & Scharff, J. S. (2005). The interpersonal unconscious. *Funzione Gamma*, 21 (Online journal in English and Italian) at *www.funzionegamma.it*.
Whitman, R. M., Kramer, M., & Baldridge, B. J. (1969). Dreams about the patient. *Journal of the American Psychoanalytic Association, 17*, 3: 702–727.
Wilner, W. (1996). Dreams and the holistic nature of interpersonal psychoanalytic experience. *Psychoanalytic Dialogues, 6*, 6: 813–829.

CHAPTER EIGHTEEN

Clinical narrative and discussion: a couple who lost joy

Pierre Cachia and Jill Savege Scharff

Two-career couples in their early thirties experience conflict and stress over finding the right balance between work and family life, and between family time and couple time. The joy of finding each other and falling in love may become eroded by the pressures of marriage, work, and family life. Attending to babies and needy children, the mother and father may all too easily lose sight of themselves as husband and wife. When they come to the marriage with a shared sense of neglect and hunger for a good object, they find it all the more difficult to meet each other's needs and cope with the demands of family life. This is what happened to the couple whose problem we will study. The couple therapist will describe the couple's presentation and history gathered during the consultation and early phase of treatment. He then recounts in detail a session from the sixteenth month of treatment. As the narrative unfolds, we will interrupt from time to time for discussion of the couple dynamics, transgenerational influences, the therapist's countertransference experience, and the power of therapeutic action. Without reference to standard texts, we will simply focus on the clinical narrative to provide an experience-near illustration of analytic sensibility in couple therapy.

A joyless couple

We will call the couple Edmund and Catherine. They are married, with three school-age children. They have come to the realisation that their shared life is both fun-less and plagued with conflict. Edmund, a sales executive, and Catherine, a professional singer, are very busy throughout the week, and in the weekend family commitments fill their day. They share a general sense of unhappiness about their way of life as a family. Frustration leads to anger and fighting over the children. They are aware that their family discord stems from problems in the couple relationship: Catherine pursues and attacks Edmund; Edmund retreats; and that intensifies Catherine's pursuit. Their sex life is compromised by their discord and is therefore limited to times when they feel in a better place. They have tried to instill life into their relationship but they have not succeeded. They are clear that they do not need simple instruction on how to get along but require in depth work because they believe it is very much the sum of their characters that creates the state of affairs they now live with, and this they want to understand and change.

The couple therapist describes the consultation

In the initial consultation with me (Pierre Cachia), prior to the commencement of the couple therapy, Edmund and Catherine's relationship had a flat and rather dead feel about it, conveyed to me, at least in part, by their initially expressionless faces. Edmund seemed stressed and de-energised although he came alive as he spoke. Catherine was rather stony faced but, again, as she spoke her face softened and lit up. Both of them communicated in a caring and sensitive manner while betraying a sense of caution. The wife's face had some pigmentation of the skin on the upper part of her left cheek. For a minute, I had a fleeting thought that this might have been a bruise but quickly erased that thought in favour of supposing it to be a facial hyper-pigmentation, not an injury. At this stage I chose not to inquire about its nature, partly to avoid the discomfort involved in pointing to a facial feature and partly because there was nothing in their story or manner to indicate risk of violence. Indeed, it seemed that for the most part all passion was suppressed. Later in the therapy the significance of this aspect of the couple's presentation would be understood to be rather more significant.

Edmund and Catherine's relationship started some fourteen years ago and they have been married for twelve years. A mutual friend had invited Edmund to a festival Catherine was taking part in while touring London with her band. Although she resented the fact that her friend seemed to be setting her up with Edmund, she was pleasantly surprised by his "really sweet" protective attitude. In particular, she recalled how he rescued her by defusing a situation with a drunken individual. When asked what he liked about Catherine, Edmund simply said "everything" but the laughter and light-heartedness of his comment suggested that he was very much excited to be with her, and yet somewhat embarrassed about the implied sexual desire for her.

Edmund and Catherine said that their relationship changed significantly with the arrival of their first son. Catherine was somewhat depressed after the birth (but with no diagnosis of postpartum depression), and the quality of their being together as husband and wife deteriorated. Edmund and Catherine believed that they never recovered after that birth. Edmund, however, insisted that they had always had difficulty enjoying life and relaxing, and the responsibility of caring for their kids simply made this more difficult. His reaction to her distress and difficulty with coping was to withdraw. He was present and tried to help but felt uninvited. His efforts were not really good enough, and nothing he did seemed to elevate her mood and physical distress. Catherine experienced him as silent and resentful, and found his lack of presence unbearable. In many ways their relationship remained in this frozen detached state. She longs for more engagement and finds his retreat unbearable: He claims to be as present as he can, considering how unwelcoming she is. Together at home the tension between them is palpable. They have stopped doing the things they enjoyed most, and their relationship has become increasingly joyless. They now find being together unbearable, particularly after Edmund returns home from work, silent and withdrawn. She experiences him as angry: He experiences her as angrily disappointed in him.

Furthermore, Catherine's father, to whom Catherine and Edmund are both very attached, has been diagnosed with a life threatening heart condition which has deteriorated significantly in recent months. Having learned that his prognosis is not hopeful, Catherine and Edmund had re-doubled their efforts in making their relationship work. In recent months they had organised a number of nights out as a couple but this offered no relief or joy.

Family histories

At first, Catherine painted a rather serene picture of her childhood and family life. Her father, of whom she is particularly fond, worked as a solicitor during the early years of her childhood. When she was about eighteen, he left work as a result of some form of personal crisis. He engaged in counselling around what seems to have been a depressive episode and subsequently re-launched himself with a career in a local charity. Catherine's knowledge around this important change was partial, and she gave the impression that that there was more upset within her and her family about this event than she wanted anyone to know. Catherine's mother initially worked as a teacher but when her husband abandoned his lucrative career, she furthered her training so as to secure more income for the family. In spite of this, financial problems remained a source of conflict between her parents. Catherine felt close to her father after his career change as he was around more, but through her childhood he was unable to respond any more than her mother did. She described her mother as cold and somewhat insensitive as is evidenced by her apparent lack of concern for her husband's current vulnerability, this time due to his illness. Catherine is terrified he might die. She is sad that unfortunately she lives too far away to be able to give him the attention she believes her mother fails to provide.

Edmund's family history is more colourful. His parents had a very difficult relationship. Edmund described his father as self-centred, entitled and generally difficult to be around. He rarely saw him while growing up, and never met his father's daughters from the previous marriage. Edmund's parents lost their first baby, born shortly after they married, and after this loss they broke up. A couple of years later, they reunited and Edmund was born. They stayed together until Edmund was twelve-years-old even though their relationship was "absolutely bleak and empty." His mother subsequently remarried and now seems happy. His father is still fond of the hedonistic philosophy which he professes guided him throughout his life. He is currently very unwell, and this is the only reason Edmund bothers to meet him a few times a year. Indeed Edmund's father audaciously boasts that he is now ready to tolerate the ailments of old age because he has had the fullness of pleasure in his younger days. Edmund sees this as further evidence of how impervious the man is to the pain he causes those around him.

Edmund and Catherine each reported experiencing guilt about taking time as a couple on their own or with friends, as this seemed to them to be self-indulgent and damaging to their children. They agreed that Edmund especially resists the intrusion of friends into their limited time together as a couple or family, and he recalled having similar feelings of resistance around the birth of their first son. Edmund linked his guilt and self-imposed deprivation to the intense repulsion he felt—and still feels—towards his father's hedonistic outlook on life. Catherine connected her current sense of guilt to a belief that she had damaged their children by becoming depressed and depleted following their births.

During the consultation, Edmund and Catherine struck me as highly driven, conscientious individuals. When told that the clinic offered fees on a sliding scale, they decided without question or pretence that they, being financially secure, "should be paying the top fee," and said so in a matter-of-fact manner. Despite the security of steady incomes and their committed relationship, they had lost a sense of joy in being together, and paying for the therapy was their least concern. The impact of the reality of their joyless relationship on their personal wellbeing and that of their children was far more important.

Discussion: dynamic formulation and assessment of suitability for couple therapy

Edmund and Catherine work hard and function well but they have lost joy. Their marriage serves as a defensive structure to keep things going but without bringing them pleasure in being together. What anxiety or hidden affect might they be defending against? We look at their childhood experiences and current perceptions of their families of origin. In Edmund's case, the parental couple was a bleak place in which the father's hedonistic pursuits reigned supreme. Edmund cannot understand why his mother tolerated his father's manner and perhaps blames her for what he went through. In any case, he experienced her as not able to be mindful of her son's distress. Catherine has little sense of why her father changed careers. It comes across as if she experienced what he did, and the subsequent financial difficulties he caused his family, as rather capricious. They both admit to having very little sense of what good parenting looks like. It seems that their capacity to manage each other's anxieties and their children's developmental difficulties is not to be trusted. They feel that they cannot offer a good wholesome experience to each other or to others. They want to be better people and better parents than their own parents were. Catherine's father's prognosis has faced them with the fact that life is time-limited and this has forced them to connect with, and try to do something about, the resentment they hold about their compromised quality of life. We can now develop a hypothesis that the resentment that they level against one another is linked to unconscious as well as conscious anger at their parents for being neglectful.

To arrive at a recommendation, we review our assessment of the couple's suitability for analytically oriented couple therapy. Edmund and Catherine showed an enquiring attitude, were able to link various aspects of their experience and use interpretation to further their understanding. They seemed to have the capacity to think in depth and use symbolic language. Clearly, both wished to understand their experience, as opposed to simply seeking behavioural change. These features, we thought, would make them good candidates for analytic couple therapy with a reasonable chance of constructing a suitably containing marriage and re-finding in each other a desirable object to relate to. At the end of the assessment session, Edmund wanted to know how long the therapy was likely to last, a reflection of his concern about how much time and energy he could afford to invest in himself and his awareness that the span of life is finite.

The couple therapist describes the intial stage of therapy

Edmund and Catherine agreed to my recommendation of weekly analytic couple therapy. It was five months into couple therapy before the couple revealed two traumatic childhood events. The first concerned Catherine. She had been sent to a specialist boarding school for the arts where she felt devastated by being away from home, and was even more upset when her parents failed to respond to her need for attachment to them. The school actively bullied and ridiculed her by exposing her longing in front of the whole student assembly. The second involved Edmund. He had been sexually abused at the age of ten and had never spoken about it to anyone, not even to Catherine. Now, five months into the couple therapy, he told what had happened but only as an explanation of his state of emotional shut-down, not as a topic for deep exploration. He felt that the abuse happened because he was so unseen and unattended to by his parents. For instance, he recounted how he would regularly leave the family home for extended periods of time and, finding an open space, he would lie down, covered with his father's greatcoat as protection from the rain. Hours later he would return home. No one ever noticed his absences.

Fourteen months into treatment, Edmund visited his father and returned with a detailed account of his father's psychological condition which seemed to indicate a post-traumatic state. At lunch, his father had recounted details of his exploits as a soldier in the British military, including details of war atrocities he had experienced or committed in service in Asia. Edmund was literally nauseated, a sensation he had often experienced as a child in his father's silent, enraged presence. Edmund linked his experience to what he had heard regarding the traumatising effect that proximity to battle-scarred soldiers returning from Afghanistan had on their families. Edmund himself was not a violent man, but on one occasion he had lost control, angrily slamming a door with such force that it came away from its frame and hit Catherine in the face. Here was the explanation for the facial discoloration that I had felt unable to inquire about during the consultation. It was a bruise. When I later acknowledged that I had seen it, Catherine was taken aback and commented that she needed better make-up skills as she had actively tried to hide it.

One month after the revelations, Edmund and Catherine took their children on a vacation and for the first time had an excellent family holiday. This happened even though, as they later recounted, the resort they had booked had not been completed by the time they arrived and building works were still in progress throughout their stay there.

Discussion

The vicarious trauma that Edmund suffered in childhood in relation to his father (such an ambivalently held object) and his neglectful mother (a non-responsive object) left Edmund vulnerable as a target for sexual abuse. His mind developed in association with a father who, though never violent was often seething and, as Edmund now knew, had a mind filled with memories of unbearable rage. As for Catherine's bruise, perhaps the therapist's reluctance to explore the possibility of violence (in spite of having worked closely with domestic violence services in the past) resulted from identification with the couple's hiding of shame. The unacknowledged bruise certainly served as an apt metaphor for their shared hidden shame, for Edmund's wish to escape the feeling of violence, and for Catherine's difficulty in acknowledging surface phenomena and what they represent of her conflict over unmet desire.

The emergence of their stories requires an elaboration of the original formulation. Edmund and Catherine share an experience of neglectful unavailable, unreliable, hurtful and traumatogenic objects. Even though they also share a dread of repeatedly being dropped, they are functioning better than either of their parent couples, including that they can confront their marriage as joyless and in need of attention. Working over time, the couple therapist joins them as a witness to the emergence of relational trauma, and serves as a container for their pain—that is, a facilitator of thinking about unbearable past experience and its re-enactment in their life and in their therapy sessions. They slowly started to feel able to face together experiences that they had wanted to hide from.

This improvement stemmed not only from opening up shameful topics but also from their finding and creating in their therapy sessions a container for their shame. This helped them to move forward to a position from which they could enjoy a family vacation. In the sixteenth month of treatment, however, the couple slips back into a defensive state of retreat and accusation, but as the session progresses we see them reach a new level of understanding.

The couple therapist's process note on a session from the sixteenth month of treatment

Edmund and Catherine walked in on time and went through the normal routine of taking off their jackets and hats before seating themselves. However, this time Edmund made his way to the inner chair, away from the door, the one that had always been occupied by Catherine. I noticed that Edmund had a bag from one of the fast food chains located in the vicinity of my consulting room. He placed it on the side table which perhaps accounted for the change in seating arrangements. We sat in silence for a few moments, and then to my surprise Edmund proceeded to take a tub of Japanese noodles out of his food bag and a pair of jointed wooden chopsticks, which he split. He looked at me for a moment, and asked if he could eat, adding that he was starving. For a moment, I was confused by the unusual demand and presentation. I became curious what this was all about and did not wish to rush into replying. I think I enquired whether he had come to his session straight from work. He said that he had not been mindful of the time and just about managed to get some food for himself on the way to the session. "Better eat something than not be present at all because of my hunger," he said. I was sympathetic but I did not really feel it was appropriate. For a minute I toyed with the idea of asking him to make his way back to reception, and then come back when he was ready.

Before I could utter a word, Catherine reacted to Edmund's intention to eat. She seemed rather irritated and suggested that he had found the perfect way of not participating in the session. She predicted that he would stuff his mouth with noodles, and simply opt out. He was clearly taken aback, and defended himself by repeating that this was a better option than him being mentally absent for the whole of the session. Catherine questioned why he had happened to forget having a snack. He became silent, very silent. She seemed to become a bit concerned, and asked in a more interested, caring, less accusatory voice whether he had eaten at all. He added rather sheepishly that he does not stare at the clock when in his office—time simply flew by. Just as he made it into the clinic's reception downstairs, I had called them up, and so he was forced to have something now. Putting down the food he had not started eating as yet, he said he would not eat. It felt like he was having a bit of a tantrum. Catherine then asked whether he had really thought it was okay. He said rather forcefully that it was not a problem and he would not eat. He seemed silently furious. "Do you really think it is okay that people enter the room and smell Japanese food in the clinic? And what about the impact on Pierre?" she asked him. I thought she had a point: This was the last session of the evening and the blissful smell of the food and the flavours I imagined were already proving to be a serious distraction. My hunger was stirred up. Again the thought came back that I should ask Edmund to move out to the reception area to eat, and then return to our session when he was finished. Perhaps he would get a more reasonable reception there than he was getting from his wife!

Discussion continued

Catherine and Edmund shared a feeling that their efforts and needs were not fully appreciated: Edmund hoped that Catherine would be mindful of his needs and Catherine wished he would be concerned about hers. They have disappointed each other, and yet they cannot usefully confront their disappointment and work through it. Their default solution is to retreat from each other without engaging in any real attempt to find a mutually satisfying solution, such as that they could have agreed to shorten the session while Edmund recovered from his hunger.

Bringing in food is felt as a striking challenge to the frame of therapy. The therapist's fantasy of removing Edmund from the session is his attempt to repair the frame. On a deeper level it also represents a complementary countertransference reaction of identification with Edmund's maternal object. It reflects Edmund's experience with a mother who also may have found his demands overwhelmingly stimulating of her own sense of need, and so pushed him away. Edmund was saying in essence that he was starving for supplies that he could not expect to find with Catherine and the therapist. He would have to take care of himself or suffer. Since he was seated in what had always been Catherine's chair, we can imagine he might be speaking for both members of the couple in feeling that ravenous hunger was an unbearable state that could not be expressed and contained in the therapy session, but had to be satisfied, literally, by eating noodles. The splitting of the chopsticks brings to mind the image of the couple coming apart or, more hopefully, differentiating in order to work together.

The couple therapist continues his account of the session

Edmund again said in a tone of frustrated resignation that he accepted the fact that he should not eat in the therapy room. Just then, Catherine seemed to have decided to turn up the heat. She told him that, considering the conversation they had the previous night, she thought that he was going to start today's session. He looked blank. She reminded him that he had said that he thought that they needed to talk about ending therapy and agree on time frames and end goals. She added that he had said that he thought of therapy as an expensive hobby. Apparently the conversation had taken this turn after he had asked her about the session she had with me when he had been away. Now he seemed absolutely taken aback, even embarrassed by what

Catherine was saying. He did not think therapy was a waste of time, he said emphatically. She was wrong. He knew they had really benefited but he did not want this to last forever. He just wanted to know, what was the endgame?

Discussion continued

Edmund had missed a session, and had missed any reaction from the couple therapist to his absence, and now was thinking of terminating. Perhaps Edmund felt that in failing to mention the session that Catherine attended alone when he was away, the therapist had not noted his absence, just as his parents had not missed him when he was gone for hours in the field. But the therapist had indeed sensed how much Edmund missed having been present for that session. He remembered that Edmund had really wanted to use a recent couple therapy session to present his own issues and think about his experience on a personal/historical level as well as on the couple level. So this is why he was starving! The therapist also sensed his envy of Catherine having the session all to herself, but he did not offer any interpretation of his envy here because he thought it would have been grossly premature. He felt Edmund's envy and his loss, but he sensed that he had to be careful how he approached him or Edmund could dismiss him. Edmund, in particular, was not quick on picking up aspects of his experience, and he needed time.

The couple therapist describes the session drawing to a close

I picked up on Edmund's use of the term "endgame," a term that was very much splashed across the headlines in reference to the war in Libya. I validated how difficult therapy had been through the past month, and said that indeed, they needed to have a sense when they had had enough—in either of the two possible meanings of the phrase. They both smiled. Edmund added that he did not want therapy to last for ten years, or something. Turning to his wife, he gave the example of married friends they had known for many years and who were perpetually in treatment. Catherine refuted this as a relevant example. She said that in any case, she and Edmund were in couple therapy while these friends were in individual treatments. I sought to offer some reassurance that couple treatment hardly ever runs that long and that if things became stagnant this would really need to thought about.

Turning to Edmund, I asked what he thought the exit point should be. He said he had no idea and simply longed to know. He said that there will always be room for improvement and that he was just objecting to the method and the emphasis on the negative, on what does not work, when most of the time things had been running smoothly. Characteristically, he then proceeded to dismantle completely the argument he had just presented concerning the need to focus on the positive by complaining that Catherine had had her friend coming over to live with them. Catherine was quick to state that her friend had left their home yesterday. Edmund added that a difficult atmosphere had developed between them on account of this but said it in an all encompassing way that obliterated the impression I had had from the previous session in which they had described getting along well when on holiday and when planning the make-over of their home. I noted that he spoke as if they had not had a better time around their holiday and home-decorating planning. I said that it was as if all good experience had been wiped out.

Catherine suggested, or rather stated, that they needed to come to a point where they can have a disagreement and recover from it without the matter becoming catastrophic. A silence followed. On a positive note, at least they had been able to disagree. I picked up what Catherine had said and noted how they had, for the first time, allowed themselves to have a real live row in my presence. They allowed me to witness the emergence of upset "in vivo" whereas normally they recounted events that had developed over the previous weeks. Catherine seemed absorbed and preoccupied with herself and simply looked on while Edmund seemed visibly touched by what I was saying. I sometimes feel that Edmund draws great relief from my offer of a reflective space in spite of his desire to run off. More silence followed. I waited, thinking that I had done enough talking and now they had to do the work of getting themselves out of the silence and dread created in the room. My task was to let them to re-establish themselves as a couple in relation to me.

Catherine again attempted to reach out to Edmund and show a willingness to accommodate his demand, suggesting that he should eat if he really thought it was okay. She only spoke out, she said, because she did not wish the session to be wasted and she was concerned for the impact on others using the room. Edmund replied with the proverbial "It's okay", meaning that he could wait but in a tone of voice that betrayed an angry, resentful resignation to the demand for delay placed on him. I waited a bit more but he remained silent and unresponsive. I waited to see if he again would assume the embryonic position I had seen in the earliest sessions and which reminded me of his parents' dead baby for which he had been the replacement. But Edmund simply sat looking downwards and occasionally daring a blank look at me.

I described what I was observing to them. I said that they had come in and had a disagreement as the session began, and that before I could really discuss with them the manner in which hunger and eating might have been managed, Catherine had objected to Edmund having a snack in the therapy room. Catherine immediately suggested that her speaking out had made my life easier. Rather unsure what to make of her comment, I simply nodded, and added that he had very, very quickly responded to her request and put the food away so that no dialogue, process, or conflict took place between them. What developed then was a silent, hostile and angry standoff which left him feeling resentful and Catherine feeling she was being punished for spoiling his fun or not responding to his needs. Edmund immediately reacted to my underlining of this dynamic by saying as usual, "It is okay", but he was again really unable to disguise his upset and anger. Catherine reacted, saying that that is what Edmund always does: He retreats and disengages, leaving her feeling utterly miserable and alone. This loneliness resonated for me with her depression around the birth of her first son, an allusion that was made conscious when she said angrily that she could not even taste the noodles Edmund had bought for himself because of allergies she had developed around the time she had given birth to their son.

I then posed a direct question quite consciously pushing Edmund to respond and react: "Why did you feel you had to do what Catherine asked of you when you clearly had other plans?" Before Edmund could again say it was no big deal, I pointed out that he did seem upset and that his cold silence was experienced as punitive. He now looked relieved and simultaneously confused. "What could I have done?" he asked. I suggested that he disengaged and conformed in order to avoid an escalation of conflict, fearing that if he pushed and she resisted he might become visibly upset. He believed that he was relatively better off trying to keep his upset to himself, as covert as he could manage, a feeling I, myself, had had earlier when I avoided the topic of the bruise. He did not speak but he nodded, and I felt that clearly we were together in this. The dread in the room seemed to start lifting as if the unmentionable had been named.

Edmund said something to Catherine which I think was an attempt to connect with her. I think he asked her a question but I am not sure. Catherine then spoke of feeling perplexed about him bringing food into the session because she had prepared food at home and they would be eating within thirty minutes of the session being over. I enquired whether she was irritated that the food she prepared might not be eaten. He joined in, this time in a more upbeat manner and insisted that he would eat both meals, as if he recognised that his hunger went beyond what one would expect.

The tension receded for them, but I felt exhausted. I had been balancing my insight and dosing my interpretations, struggling to avoid being drawn into a concrete place. I had felt frozen in my ability to work with symbolic meanings. I called time, commenting that perhaps, within the space of today's session they had outlined the task ahead. They said their farewells and agreed that they would be coming the following week. When they returned for their next session, Catherine reported her relief that Edmund had not stayed angry at her. The upset had been contained in the session because hunger and anger had been expressed and acknowledged. The session proved to be a pivotal one after which the couple could enter into conflict and recover from upset more quickly and reliably.

Final discussion

The therapist's account allows us to see how he attempted to hold in mind both the extent of Edmund and Catherine's hunger, the threat of their object loss, and enormous death anxiety, not just about the end of their treatment, but about the death of the couple. He shared a sense of relief at the outcome of the session, but he felt exhausted. He must have been exhausted by their hunger for him and by his effort to protect them from moving too fast which would have amounted to feeding them more than they were able to stomach. He did not want the therapeutic relationship to split up before the birth of a sturdier couple relationship.

Like split chopsticks, Edmund's parental couple had separated before his birth, and had never come back together securely, and so Edmund was born starving into a field that was starved of affection. How uncontained Catherine and Edmund must have felt in childhood. They share an emptied out, absent maternal object, in reaction to which Edmund carries intense desire. He finds in Catherine a desirable object to be longed for but she feels empty because she has the same lack and cannot respond. His desire has a further deadening effect on Catherine. The attack on desire is one source of their shared sense of shame in having so much and yet feeling such little joy. They both want to hide shame: Catherine's humiliation of carrying a bruise as the evidence of a violent moment of breakdown of her marriage, Edmund's experience of abuse as evidence of his parents' neglect and failure to respond, and shared difficulty in absorbing the war trauma which his father defended against by hedonism and silent rage. By this time in the treatment process, the actual bruise as a physical manifestation of upset has given way to the psychological expression of bruised feelings, a progression that speaks of improvement for the couple. Earlier, the couple would have split, Catherine expressing the anger and Edmund becoming infuriatingly numb, unable to respond to her, she becoming the abusive one, he the non-responsive other.

Edmund and Catherine started thinking of the prematurely proposed endgame of their treatment in order to flee from loss, longing, shame, and a shared fear of unconscious catastrophe potentially coming into the session once more. Therapy itself must have been perceived as a death. That would explain why food must be brought in to the session. With the hunger abated, they could start to fight, experience aggression safely and constructively, and then they could start to eat the figurative meat of the session, and later enjoy literal food together. Following the manifestation of death anxiety, libido could come into the session in a preliminary way. At this point in the treatment process, it is still difficult for Edmund and Catherine to discuss their sexual relationship. When they are in a state of dread and disconnection, they avoid sex and cannot use it as refuge or reparation after upset.

In the session, Edmund and Catherine erased their good experience of being on holiday. Perhaps it was dangerous to become a better couple than either of their parents. They found something good and then spoiled it, as they did in treatment. Perhaps the couple had felt attacked and split when the therapist had agreed to see the wife alone. Progress was attacked by Edmund's upset about missing a session and feeling that he had not been missed, after which he threatened to eliminate any further growth by thoughts of terminating and Catherine introduced the spectre of leaving treatment into the session. This is a function of envy, the fighting, hopeless couple in the session making an envious attack in response to the agreeable, hopeful couple of the vacation. This envious attack is a function of their death anxiety.

Few Englishmen would be comfortable eating noodles with chopsticks while participating in a meeting. Edmund must have been used to them, his father having been in Asia. We can imagine that his use of the chopsticks might be pointing to his conflicted attachment to his father and to the problem of dealing with him. Could he use his chopsticks and eat his noodles with the same lack of regard for his effect on others that was so characteristic of his father? The chopsticks could be a way of introducing the problem of dealing with his father. Given the discussion concerning the "endgame," the chopsticks could have been pointing unconsciously to war trauma transmitted from the previous generation. Edmund's father's silent rage and self-absorption seems to be connected with trauma witnessed and experienced as a soldier fighting wars in Asia.

An issue mentioned but not dealt with in this session is the impact of the baby on their relationship. The couple's first baby is associated with the threat of death to the mother, an issue introduced by the presence of noodles to which she is allergic, and the accompanying anger to which both she and Edmund are allergic. Edmund's own birth followed the death of a baby and its impact on his parents' marriage. Edmund and Catherine each have an internal damaged baby, an image of a vulnerable self that was not seen, not held, and not contained. They will need to experience that internal baby being seen and understood in couple therapy, and then they will be able to hold each other fully in mind, contain anxiety for each other, and establish a couple relationship that is felt as a nourishing, detoxifying container for their growth as individuals and as a couple, and for the development of their children.

Subsequent developments

Over the course of the following months, the couple acknowledged and resolved various issues. They could express and contain their upset within the therapy hour, and transferred this ability for containing conflict to the at-home situation. Catherine and Edmund became more able to manage anxiety, which meant that their children became less anxious. In order to proceed with their home renovation they cleared out piles of accumulated clutter and made space within the home for them to relax in. Edmund fertilised the garden and created an outside play area for their children. They reclaimed their love for food, which Edmund likened to sex in that it allowed for the satisfaction of need which, in his mind, made it a very intimate and private matter. Edmund and Catherine were now becoming a robust enough couple to invite their therapist into their home symbolically, allowing him to see their newly found capacity for good experience without feeling too threatened that he might destroy their good feeling. He could confront them directly, and they could voice disappointment in him when an interpretation failed to grasp their experience. As the therapy relationship was becoming more resilient and the couple less fragile, we could imagine a day when termination would be arrived at, not prematurely as before, but at an agreed time when Edmund and Catherine could have confidence in their recovery of joy.

Conclusion

We have provided an experience-near account of many months of analytic couple therapy with Edmund and Catherine, and detailed process of one pivotal session in the mid-phase of treatment. In our discussion we show various ways of making sense of this experience at that point in time: we develop hypotheses and formulate interpretations to be tried out as therapy proceeds, not necessarily in the subsequent session, but rather at an appropriate time when the therapist might find it possible to offer an interpretation in a meaningful way and work with the couple's reaction. The session described shows the demand that analytic couple therapy makes on the therapist and makes the point that, even when a session feels frustrating and the therapist feels blocked, the emotional work of joining with the couple and seeing them through establishes the basis for further analytic work and greater resilience in preparation for working autonomously on their relationship.

PART III

UNDERSTANDING AND TREATING SEXUAL ISSUES

CHAPTER NINETEEN

How development structures sexual relationships

David E. Scharff

It is a commonplace of analytic theory that early development structures the individual mind, and that the earliest relationships such as the mother–infant and oedipal period matter to later life. However, development does not stop after childhood, adolescence, getting married, or ever until death. Periods of transition are the ordinary stuff of life, shifts that mark life's inconspicuous continual growth. These periods draw upon a reservoir of creativity that enables us take what we are up to at a certain point and reinvent ourselves. We retain this creative developmental potential to change how we live all of our lives (Scarf, 1987; Viorst, 1986). Occurrences of discontinuous development from birth to old age are critical to a full understanding of couples and their families. Family members' overt difficulties always intertwine with their development. My attention has long been drawn to the idea of a late life crisis when older people need to find new organisations that fit with their new capacities, incapacities, relationships, and opportunities. In general, individuals, couples, and families seek help at vulnerable points in their lives; these are typically at transition points. Even though couples who present with sexual difficulties may act as though their sexual life is unrelated to other aspects of their lives and their current development, therapists know that is far from the truth.

Maturational reorganisation

Freud and his early followers thought that oedipal reorganisation, not only of sexual aims but more importantly of the mind, began about age three and lasted until about six years of age. For Freud, this was the first time that awareness of relationships moved to the centre of consciousness for children. He believed that this oedipal period formed the foundation for the structuring organisation of mind, setting the stage for all that followed. Freud did not emphasise the continual reorganisations of mental and emotional process throughout life; he and his early followers were preoccupied with the ones that took place relatively rapidly from childhood through the end of adolescence.

All periods of maturational reorganisation are times of discontinuity. They show great variance and are not precisely predictable ahead of time because they are determined both by individual differences and the crucial influence of external events. Nevertheless, they form a rough map of development that serves to orient assessment and treatment planning for individuals and couples, including those with sexual difficulty. I will be thinking especially about sexual development within the life cycle in this chapter, highlighting life events that influence and structure relationships within the family. Developmental discontinuities present vulnerabilities that may be expressed in sexual symptoms at various stages. Such developmental shifts have been ignored by many couple therapists and specialists in sexual health. But when therapists create a map of each patient's or couple's life course, we need to locate the meaning of a difficulty or symptom within the narrative of their life course. Seeing sexual symptoms as the product of development and personal narrative helps individual patients and couples (D. Scharff, 1982; D. Scharff & J. Scharff, 1991).

Early-life parental attachment

Recent work on development has helped us to understand with more precision how the earliest relationships between children and parents form a developmental foundation for all that follows. Building on Bowlby's (1969, 1973, 1980) work on attachment, Fonagy, Target, and their colleagues (2002) argued that the earliest attachment to parents promotes children's mental development, especially their capacity to understand the workings of other people's minds. Our minds are formed in the crucible of relationships, and minds free from excessive anxiety and fear develop to create healthier relationships. Trauma and marked neglect, on the other hand, constrict both brain growth and the richness of interpersonal understanding. Someone growing up with unreliable or abusive parental relationships will later interpret many aspects of the couple relationship and most sexual signals as dangerous rather than as safe and inviting. So the quality of the early attachment relationship has direct relevance both to general emotional maturity and to the sense of safety in relating that is needed for intimacy and sexual expression (Clulow, 2001).

Each of us carries a template for attachments throughout life. Recent work has shown that an adult's attachment style can be classified in ways comparable to those of children. An adult's attachment style and security is also predictive of the attachment bond they will establish with their children. On the other hand, despite the lasting quality of early parental attachment, having new healthy relationships as might occur in a good marriage or psychotherapy can help people achieve an "earned secure attachment" to replace their previously insecure or disorganised styles.

Sexuality

These attachment issues from children's early development affect the current attachments and sexual interactions of the sexually active adolescent or adult. Sexual interactions are expressed in intimate relationships and embedded in internal object relationships. Even solo masturbation is centred on internal aspects of relating. The template for attachment patterns formed in the early years is the model each person carries when forming primary emotional relationships in later years. If a woman is capable of secure relating, she is off to a good start, even if she has some specific difficulty with sexual functioning. Ideally, she enjoys relationships, picks partners who are securely attached, and enjoys sex without feeling that she is unreasonably obligated to provide it for her partner. On the other hand, if a woman has an anxious or wary attachment pattern going into a sexual relationship, that longstanding pattern tends to undermine her capacity for sexual relating. She may feel that she cannot rely on the relationship, so she is likely to feel she had better be sexually available to hang on to a partner. This way of using sex may then leave her feeling exploited, resentful that she has to be sexual with her partners in violation of her own wishes. People with a severely dismissive attachment style may only be able to have sex with a partner to whom they have no emotional attachment. Those who carry the template of a disorganised, fearful attachment need to constantly check on the other person for safety. They may feel particularly vulnerable during sex with a partner, and their behaviour may be quite unpredictable to themselves. Their partners may experience them as suspicious, frightened, untrusting and unpredictably rejecting, never suspecting how much they fear for their own existence. This fear tends to attack the capacity for sexual feeling.

Adolescents often develop sexual interest slowly, at first using masturbation to try out their sexual feelings, and later talking with same-sex peers with less sense of threat than when confronting possible sexual partners. They often move with peers in groups of several teens, protected against premature intimacy. But some young adolescents, or even pre-teens, rush headlong into sexual relationships, and then feel trapped by the resulting physical arousal and heightened feeling. If they feel that sex is the only intense feeling they are capable of, they may substitute sex for intimacy.

> Fifteen-year-old Susan was interested in boys, but also frightened. Coming from a disorganised family, she looked to peers for a stability she lacked. She recklessly threw herself at boys without thinking. When two boys used her roughly sexually and then spurned her, she turned to an older girl for comfort. When Susan was seventeen, this motherly girl persuaded Susan that boys were all like that, and that Susan would be safer as a lesbian. Susan surrendered to an active homosexual pattern. Only later did she question the basis for her decision to become lesbian, and began to notice that not all boys were exploitative.

When does sexual symptomatology develop?

Sexual symptoms are signs that a person has internalised relationships in a way that presents sexual behaviours as a solution to problems in relating. A number of factors predispose children, adolescents, and adults to develop sexual symptoms (D. Scharff, 1982).

First, disruptions to safety or health during periods in which sex is a major way of handling things: the period of infantile masturbation, the oedipal period, or the normal period of adolescent sexualisation of development.

Second, families that overly sexualise developmental processes. For some families, everything is sexual, beginning with the first identification of the genitals at birth. These parents talk about sex and flaunt sexual life, predisposing their child to later sexual symptomatic patterns.

Third, families that strongly suppress sexuality. In these families, nothing is recognised as sexual: oedipal sexualisation is unrecognised and denied, for instance. Families that suppress sexuality tend to produce young adult children for whom sex is denied, feared and avoided.

Fourth, in some love-starved families, parents look to their children for love. A parent may say openly that the child gives what the spouse denies. The ensuing excitement can sexualise children's growth and, at the extreme, lead to incest. Even without incest, this pattern may contribute to premature sexualisation of adolescent relationships.

Fifth, sexual abuse carries this tendency to a disastrous extreme. The invasion of a child's body by a parent is fundamentally a sexual invasion of mind. The result skews development, to varying degrees depending on how closely related the abuser is and the amount of support the child gets in dealing with the abuse. The sequelae vary, from serious disruptions of total personality like multiple personality, to sexualisation of all development, or to phobic avoidance of genital sex or all personal intimacy (J. Scharff & D. Scharff, 2008).

Sixth, trauma to a child's parents, even when not directly communicated to the child, can still influence development through unconscious communication. Projective identification refers to the way a part of the parent's mind is unconsciously communicated to the child when parents cannot tolerate or contain their own anxieties. This is done through their overt and covert expressions of anxiety and fear, and their over-protectiveness (J. Scharff & D. Scharff, 1991). When parents have suffered physical or emotional trauma, such as the overwhelming trauma of a parent's own sexual abuse or the horrors of the Holocaust, they often communicate the anxieties of their horror to their children who then build their mind around the expectation of trauma.

> Freda came to see me because of persistent pelvic pain. Her gynecologist could find no organic cause. She knew that her parents had been negligent, but only in therapy did she discover that she had been invited into their bed from the age of three to watch intercourse. Later she remembered her father had forced fellatio and intercourse on her at least as early as the age of eight. At fourteen he stopped when she threatened to kill herself. When she married, she "wasn't there" during sex with her husband just as she had psychologically removed herself from her body through dissociation when her father forced himself on her. Her childhood dissociation led to her adult dissociative mechanism and her sexual symptom.
>
> Freda's children grew up avoiding their maternal grandfather whom they thought was "a lecher." They were without symptoms themselves until Freda's fifteen-year-old son, Tom, hooked up with a disturbed, traumatised girl, who began to threaten him with suicide unless he agreed to have a baby with her. The whole family got involved in caring for this desperate girl, until a family session uncovered the way that Tom was unconsciously trying to repair the damage done to Freda through taking care of his girlfriend. That realisation set the family free of the spell cast by the girl, whom they persuaded instead to get personal individual psychotherapy.

Freda had communicated her anxiety about sexuality as a traumatic factor to her husband through her growing sexual reluctance despite her love for him, and to her children through her inability to discuss her father's seductiveness despite her obvious distress whenever he was around. Her wordless state of tension communicated her heightened anxiety through unconscious projective identification that put them on guard, but without the words that would have enabled them to understand why she was constantly on guard against her father. Then Tom undertook to guard another female against sexual trauma, but in a roundabout way that would have exposed him to another trauma. Verbalising the trauma that had happened to Freda freed the family for appropriate action.

Adult developmental transitions

Development continues into adulthood, and includes decisions about marriage, attitudes towards sex, having children, marital separation, marital affairs, and divorce. The ticking of the clock is always a part of these developments. Marriage or pairing with a mate of the opposite or same sex either happens, or life is channelled to a significant degree by the fact that it does not happen, so that an individual either chooses to live outside a committed partnership or does so by the default of being unable or unwilling to marry. Having or not having children introduces the same dilemma: either you do it, or your life is partly defined by the fact that you did not.

Mate selection

The choice to get married (or partnered) shapes each person's life in significant ways, although the patterns of married and partnered life now vary widely. Each of us carries within our psyche an "internal couple"—a composite image of loving couples, warring couples, the couple-as-parents, sexual couples, divorced couples,—an internal organisation that is first formed in childhood. The internal couple plays a significant role in orienting each person during mate selection and the trying-out period of courtship or living together that tests compatibility for relationships.

> Michelle and Lenny came to see Jill Scharff and me with a strange complaint. Michelle said, "He wants to get married and I want to break up. So we should do something about that. Can you give us something? A pill maybe?" "Would it be to break up or to stay together?" Jill Scharff asked. "To break up," said Michelle. "I don't want to stay with him, even though he did ask me to marry him and gave me a diamond ring. I had to try it on. It was so beautiful! But I had to give it back."
>
> Michelle and Lenny had a teasing, emotionally perverse relationship in which he clung to her like an infant with a cruel mother while she taunted him mercilessly. Yet they did offer something positive to each other.
>
> Lenny said, "I'm the rock in the river for Michelle, there for her while she runs up and down stream." Michelle said, "He's immovable. I have to light a fire under his tush or he won't move."
>
> For Lenny, being the rock meant providing the stability and durability Michelle did not have, while she provided the liveliness and vitality he feared that he lacked. Although Michelle hated Lenny's immovability, she secretly leaned on him for the stability that shored up her shaky self-esteem.

People unconsciously seek mates to make up for deficiencies in their selves and to repair bad things that have happened. When their lives have been good, they seek a mate with whom to continue what has been good and loving. In seeking partners, everyone wants someone to support them, through whom they can find meaning by giving. At the same time everyone wants someone to give to them, to help find goodness in themself by accepting what is offered. At another level, people look for partners, partly like their self, those who share values and interests at the conscious level and a sense of fit between internal object relationships at the unconscious level so as to provide aspects of themselves that have been lost or about which they feel deficient. Then through projective identification, they hope to find in mates and partners help for the parts of themselves that feel bad or weak.

> Michelle could not bring herself to break up with Lenny because he was a convenient receptacle for the badness she unconsciously felt in herself and because when he offered to suffer her recriminations and insults, he unconsciously knew that he was doing her a service. He said, "I grew up learning that men could be terrible to women, and I vowed that I would make up for that." When he offered to be the rock in the river, he felt good about the way he made her feel better, and while he found a vitality in her that he felt he lacked, he also felt an increase in his self esteem by standing by her.

Commitment and marriage

Sexuality plays a central role in adult partnering, carrying the physical aspect of emotional intimacy and playing a continuing role in renewal of that intimacy over the long haul (Scharff, 1982). But among couples that seek help, a strange thing has often happened at the altar or at the moment of commitment—which is no longer necessarily simultaneous with the wedding in Western culture. During courtship, as the intimate partners woo each other into a long-term relationship, the forces of romance, yearning, and mutual idealisation cover over each partner's darker fears, anxiety, anger, and distrust. If this were not so, many people could not ever get married. Indeed, some couples now choose to live together for seemingly endless periods, shunning actual marriage for fear of what will be brought on by the formal seal of commitment.

Sex is often caught up in this reordering of personality. Under the exciting, come-hither organisation of courtship, sex often goes well, only to fall victim to the emergence of disappointment and aggression following marriage or commitment. This may parallel a general deterioration in the relationship, but it may happen for other reasons. Often one partner unconsciously locates the frightening or frightened feelings in the genitals and breasts. That is to say, the person acts as though these parts of the body contain a threat to the self and the partner. This conversion reaction occurs when a bodily problem comes to stand for an emotional problem. A couple may appear to have a generally loving relationship, but closer examination reveals that sexual incapacity contains a mutual sense of dread. When this happens, an ongoing loving relationship may help them move past the difficulty, but often couples are unable to overcome the sexual dread without psychotherapy or sex therapy.

> Gabbi is twenty-nine. His mother died when he was fifteen. His father, who had immigrated from Israel, never felt fully at home in the United States and had always been self absorbed,

spending long periods back in Israel and leaving Gabbi and his sister alone. The parents had married when Gabbi's father was forty-one and his mother twenty-five. His mother died after a yearlong painful illness when Gabbi's sister was four. Gabbi had a series of girlfriends he felt passionately about and had good sex with at first, only to pull away from them sexually after several months. Now he was in my office because he had found Indira, a beautiful loving Indian-American woman. He was pulling away from her too, but this time he felt that the relationship was too good to sacrifice to this pattern. The threat of having to make a commitment to a woman he loved had repeatedly attacked Gabbi's sexual desire. In therapy, we were able to understand that the loss of his mother together with the repeated abandonments by his father formed an important part of his anger and distrust of women. The model of his father as someone who had only made a marital commitment late in life also contributed to Gabbi's unconscious distrust of women at the same time that he longed for a mother to care for his lonely and needy self. The fact that his mother's protracted death came when he was a newly sexual, but still needy adolescent had folded the sense of combined need and distrust into his sexual interest. The idea of making a commitment to a woman then aroused his deep but unconscious anger and distrust, and in the ensuing unconscious battle, he lost sexual interest.

In ordinary courtship, excitement about the other person and sexual excitement supports the couple's path towards each other. But at the moment of commitment, each person cries out to be fully known by the partner, and this is often a time of trouble. It is important to ask if anything changed at the moment a couple first felt really committed, decided to get married, or met on their actual wedding day. In primary relationships, the unlikable parts of each person also cry out for recognition—the parts they are afraid others will not tolerate, much less love. Some partnerships are able to tolerate and soothe these aspects of partners, but many are torn by previously repressed forces that now come out from hiding. A man who felt neglected as a child wants his wife to understand and compensate for the deprivation he suffered. A woman who was victim to her father's rage carries unconscious resentment that now, for the first time, is unleashed on her lesbian partner as though that partner were the angry father.

Often one partner is surprised by this previously hidden part of the other, although there may have been hints that were, however, overlooked before marriage or commitment. But it also often seems that the partner was unconsciously chosen precisely because of the traits that were consciously ignored. For instance, a man had chosen to marry a woman with low self-esteem who was constantly self-defeating. Picking a needy partner like this provided him with endless opportunity to heal her, and this filled an unconscious fantasy that he could repair his depressed mother.

Infertility

For most couples, pregnancy and the birth of children are joyful despite the troubles children inevitably bring their parents. For many couples nowadays, fertility has been a concern as the average age of marriage and conception have risen remarkably for middle class couples. Infertility and struggles to conceive often become formidable obstacles to ordinary and satisfying sex. Feelings of inadequacy and pressures to perform on a limited and precise schedule impinge on spontaneity and a sense of sexual adequacy. Many couples that have had good sex for years experience a decline in satisfaction, frequency and pleasure as they try to comply with the rules of fertility treatment or deal with disappointment at their inability to conceive. The drugs used to promote pregnancy take a physical and emotional toll on women, expose them to risk and create a climate of anxiety. While most couples survive these hazards, they also report that the going has not been easy and often, afterwards, that there is a toll on their ongoing sexual life. One such couple was on the verge of divorce after many failures to conceive, when a pregnancy they no longer expected almost miraculously revived their relationship, which later succumbed to the forces of hostility that had dogged the relationship before the surprise pregnancy.

Here is a story with a different wrinkle on infertility.

> Dr and Mrs T came because sex had always been infrequent, but more or less satisfying to them. Their individual stories made sense of the rather low levels of sexual desire they each had before meeting. Mrs T was a runner who lost her periods during adolescence as she tried to keep up with her four brothers. She remained unsure of her femininity. Dr T's divorced parents had sent him to boarding school where he had occasional homosexual experiences with teachers that became mixed with a distrust of his self-absorbed mother, leading to worries about himself and distrust of women. This couple loved each other, but sex was infrequent, and when they did not conceive, they adopted a baby boy. But when they went to the adoption agency again, the vigilant caseworker realised that their infertility might reflect their sexual inactivity rather than a medical problem. With sex therapy, Dr And Mrs T discovered these dynamic issues rather quickly, began a more active sexual life and were able to have three children over the next few years.

Pregnancy

Pregnancy brings bodily and hormonal changes to the mother, but it also brings psychological change to the father who experiences his wife's changes physically and emotionally. A woman's preoccupation with her body and her own wellbeing, or concern whether continued sex will harm the pregnancy may constitute barriers to sex. When pregnancy goes well for a couple, both partners relate to the pregnancy as the culmination of their love and hopes. The fantasies of the baby present a future that expresses each of them in creative ways. Hope triumphs over anxiety. But there are many unavoidable anxieties that may overpower the hopes for couples with a shaky start.

> Tammy came to see me because she thought her husband of two years was having an affair. She was six months pregnant with their first child, and he had been getting suspicious mobile phone calls that she had traced to a work colleague. In a joint session, Don quickly but shamefully admitted to the affair, the first he had had, and said he loved Tammy. He did not know why he had begun an affair with a woman he did not respect. We were able to trace the panic that led to his affair to his intense neediness for Tammy. He grew up with an anxious needy mother. As Tammy's anxiety about her pregnancy increased, Don's unconscious fear of losing

Tammy increased. Work on their shared neediness enabled this couple to pull together and slowly put the affair behind them.

Parenthood

Children are a significant challenge to the intimacy and sexual life of couples. All couples experience a challenge to intimacy and sexual expression at one or more phases of their children's growth, but for some it is worse than usual. One couple, pregnant immediately after marriage, suffered during and immediately after the pregnancy. Each partner felt that the other no longer had eyes for them. The husband also felt threatened at work, while the wife was increasingly depressed as she had gone off anti-depressant medication during pregnancy. When their baby girl was born, they each loved her, but she came between them as a barrier rather than a bridge. They came to therapy after the husband began to scream and threaten his wife, echoing for the first time the volatile anger of his own parents.

As a child grows older, a mother may be angered by her four-year-old daughter's oedipal love affair with her husband because she feels shut out by both of them. For some parents, having a boy may be threatening because it triggers memories of some painful event in the past, while for others, a girl baby symbolises something painful. Or the accumulation of several children may overwhelm parents who did well with a smaller family. Or a child's burgeoning sexuality in adolescence may challenge one or both parents who have not mourned the passing of their own youth, or for whom their youthful and newly sexual children contrast painfully with their own aging bodies.

For any given couple, it is not that any one event will automatically introduce strain, but that the meaning of any event may be toxic when it would not have been in different circumstances or for other couples. It is the specific meaning of the event to the couple that matters. Almost any couple, even in the heartiest and most loving marriages, can be strained to the breaking point by the serious chronic illness or death of a child.

Illness

The same considerations that apply to developmental strains in early or middle adulthood continue to exert influence throughout the life cycle. Middle aged couples continue to experience developmental crises. Menopause in women and early sexual aging processes in men may cause physical wear and tear, with or without loss of desire as they lose hormonal support: A man may experience erectile difficulty, while a woman may experience diminished lubrication, vaginal dryness and dyspareunia . All these events introduce individual changes that affect the couple's relationship. Some couples handle these better than others, but as they grow older, all couples have to face challenges, including those of physical illness. Whether the illness is acute or chronic, the challenge to a couple to continue their intimacy and maintain support for each other can be severe. The more serious the illness and the longer it goes on, the more difficult the challenge as a couple struggles to maintain equilibrium. Losses, guilt, anger, or the resurgence of previous marital strain may come into play. It is important for the clinician to know the obstacles particular illnesses present to sexual function—cancer, heart disease, rheumatoid arthritis, gynecological difficulty—but it is also incumbent on us to look for the psychological causes that result in anxiety and fear in couples who have done well together but who now pull away sexually and emotionally. Of course, aging and increasing illness and disability go together, so we have to look at the complexity of reaction to both of these factors when they co-exist. Illness can have profound impact on sexual and emotional life whenever it occurs within the life cycle. Here's an example of gynecological difficulty in a relatively young couple.

> Robert and Irene, in their mid-thirties, grew up in physically abusive families and vowed not to express anger or raise their hands against each other or their children. "If it came to that," Robert said to me, "I'd leave first." So Irene's complete hysterectomy, done to stop hemorrhagic periods from uterine fibroids, came as a challenge to them. Having difficulty mourning the loss of her fertility, she became depressed, and developed pain on intercourse for the first time. No physical cause could be found, but with vaginal pain she became reluctant to have intercourse, and began to feel moody, tired, and irritable. Robert felt her withdrawal, exacerbated by her moodiness and her new angry irritability. He too became resentful, and motivated by his determination not to express the anger, he withdrew. Now Irene felt depressed and abandoned. She told me, "I knew that Robert missed sex, but I got to resenting him for wanting it, even though he never insisted." Over time, their distant and resentful relationship came to bear little resemblance to the loving and cooperative one they had for the first several years of their marriage.

Infidelity

Therapists are often too anxious to ask about extramarital affairs. Most do not know what to think if a patient or couple has had affairs. Even so, direct questions about infidelity often do not yield a straight answer, but at least it puts the therapist on record as wanting to know and as believing that this information is important. With familiarity, a therapist can learn to think about affairs with the same clarity as about other marital issues. For most marriages, affairs express disappointment and deprivation that has developed in the years leading up to the affair. One or both partners seek out—or are susceptible to—invitations from someone who offers what the partner does not. Affairs are a living extension of the fantasies discussed a moment ago, but when affairs actually take physical sexual form, they dramatically restructure a couple's relationship. Now the partner reacts to the secrecy that almost inevitably accompanies affairs, to the exporting of love and interest that goes with it, and to the sense of violation that comes with discovery. The discovery of an affair can catalyse a new opportunity for growth and rediscovery; or, at worst, it can deliver a deathblow to a marriage. Affairs are considered more thoroughly in Chapter Twenty-Three, but they also need to be considered here in the context of development of couples throughout the life cycle.

> Zachary, a successful money manager, idealised his wife Sarah and felt emptiness about his own life and career. He saw Sarah as a beautiful, successful doctor, himself as underachieved and worthless. He could not explain the affair he began a year ago with his office manager, whom he felt had seduced him and then flaunted the affair in front of his friends. Sarah hired

a detective who got her the evidence, but still Zachary denied the affair until one day the light dawned. He broke off the affair and begged Sarah's forgiveness. He could see the origins of his actions in his own depression and in a critical mother he carried within, but he felt his wife had done nothing to deserve what he had done to her. When I saw them, I felt that Zachary's affair had come about in reaction to Sarah's aggressive control. He had no awareness of her domineering style, but underneath the surface, I thought, he was reacting to it. She demanded complete submission and repentance, and that he "submit to therapy." Zachary accepted her terms and admitted to all the blame, and because I agreed that he did need individual therapy as well as couple work, I referred him to a colleague. Sarah, having no insight into her own role in the marital tension, soon ended the couple therapy, continuing the pattern of placing blame on Zachary and, I thought, dramatically limiting the chances for growth in the marriage.

Divorce and other losses

Divorce is the end point for a marriage that failed, regardless of the reason for the failure. But there is the rest of life to be lived. Frequently people have difficulty investing in what is next. But being single again, or being a single parent, forces a new perspective on life, brings on new challenges and calls on new resources. A man who makes a positive decision to leave an unhappy marriage may nevertheless founder at the prospect of being on his own, or a woman who is bereft when her husband of twenty-five years leaves or dies, may find that the new structure of her life holds opportunities she had never dreamed of. The key to successfully negotiating these adult restructurings is the capacity to mourn, to give up on lost loved ones, and go through a variable sequence of angry protest, sadness or despair, and the generation of new hope.

> Thomas came to see me because his second wife complained about his lack of sexual interest in her. He had married her after having an affair with her during his first marriage. Unable to give her up although more interested in his first wife, he had driven that first wife to distraction until she finally demanded a divorce. Now, eight years later, he was still preoccupied with the first wife and unable to invest in the second marriage. The divorce should have led to a reconfiguration of his life and, through mourning, to a capacity to invest in someone new. His inability to commit to either woman, and his incessant dwelling on his lost first wife—despite the fact that she was happily remarried—was now costing him a second chance.

The incapacity to mourn a lost marriage, regardless of whose fault the divorce was—usually both significantly contribute!—can make it impossible to move on. But when the lost marriage can be mourned, sadness gives way to openness for reconnection to the next phase of life, whether single or partnered. This is true of all life transitional stages: The progress of mourning determines whether such losses will become a developmental dead end or will offer a new beginning.

Old age and death

Losing a mate through death and living with a mate with a chronically debilitating illness impinge on the phases of late adult development. These conditions restructure life, and their successful negotiation requires active restructuring in turn. In elderly couples, one spouse often lives for several years with a debilitating physical illness or dementia from Alzheimer's or stroke. Then the relatively healthy spouse has to decide whether to limit her own life in order to care for and stay with the debilitated one, or whether to carve out time and space for herself.

> A woman in her seventies, married to a man a few years her junior, was able to care for him as he grew weaker from diffuse vascular disease that affected his mobility and strength, although not his mind. For ten years she was restricted by his disability punctuated by medical crises requiring hospitalisation. In the last two years of his life, she could not leave the city to see her children and grandchildren, because each time she did, he went into a life-threatening crisis. He died when she was over eighty. She mourned him deeply, saying she had lost her best friend and sexual partner. But she also took the new freedom to travel and to visit children and friends. She said she felt she didn't have much time with good health, and she was going to enjoy herself while she could.

Losing a partner through death is a challenge to everyone who survives a spouse, whether in a young marriage or at the end of a long partnership. Sometimes the surviving spouse feels she doesn't have the energy to reshape life, but that feeling is not limited to the elderly. Depression is more frequent in old age, but can immobilise those who suffer loss at any age.

A summary: when things do not go well

We all have unconscious fantasies that guide us through life at every stage, maintaining deep hopes to repair the damage of our childhoods and imagining a better future. These fantasies are embedded from past experience and former relationships. The conscious derivatives of these deep-structure fantasies include daydreams and night dreams, the hopes and fears present from the time a child dreams of becoming a hero or movie star, the fantasies of being a pop star or having a love affair with one, and the fantasies about sexual partners that are fed by erotic magazines and movies. Some people imagine a secret life of sexual passion or mundane extra-marital affairs even from the beginning of their marriage, so as to gratify their longings and calm their fears that they unconsciously feel will contaminate marriage. This may be a minor theme that can be contained by the marriage, but in people who later turn to therapists for help, it often happens that the vitality needed by the marriage has been depleted as so much is funneled into fantasy life.

> Ian, a mild mannered man in his thirties, loved his wife, but had no sexual interest in her. He thought he never had, although he knew she was beautiful. His lack of interest seemed inexplicable. She grew increasingly angry that they had no sex and no children. He masturbated, but felt upset when she suggested sex. In therapy, he told me about a secret fantasy life that excited him greatly. He was held in a sultan's prison. The sultan's beautiful wife would seek him out. They had passionate sex, but in the end, fearing betrayal, and with great regret, he felt he had no alternative but to kill the sultan's wife. The cycle of passion, regret, and violence excited him greatly as he masturbated.

The fantasy contained the split-off versions of his experience of his mother. An alluring and unavailable woman, she was also a frightening ball-breaker. His wife had no chance of being seen as warmly accepting. His sexual fantasies were deeply entwined with hate, and so he had to protect his wife from his sexual fantasy life in order to protect her from his hateful internal object relations. Out of fear and concern that she would become the victim of his unconscious fury at his mother, he had suppressed his sexual interest in her. Therapy helped him to become conscious of the paralysing effects of his fantasies, and move slowly to an active sexual life with his wife.

Final thoughts

The more therapists have a developmental framework in mind, the easier it is to form a life map for their patients. Therapists all have life experience to draw on, and so in a way, the older they get, the broader their personal map. Fortunately, everyone draws on more than their own individual experience. All they have read, the movies they have seen, the study of development, and everything patients teach them goes into their data bank. As careers go on, the bank gets richer. This is one of the elements of the profession that is most satisfying: Life, in its infinite complexity, gets more understandable as it goes. Understanding the developmental processes throughout life is an important aid in helping couples keep growing and changing in response to the forces that restructure their lives.

References

Bowlby, J. (1969, 1973, 1980). *Attachment and Loss, 3 Volumes.* New York: Basic Books.
Clulow, C. (Ed.) (2001). *Adult Attachment and Couple Psychotherapy: The "Secure Base" in Practice and Research.* London: Brunner-Routledge.
Fonagy, P., Gergely. G., Jurist, E. L., & Target, M. (2002). *Affect Regulation, Mentalization and the Development of the Self.* New York: Other Press. Reprinted Karnac, 2004.
Jacques, E. (1965). Death and the mid-life crisis. *International Journal of Psychoanalysis,* 46: 502–514.
Scarf, M. (1987). *Intimate Partners: Patterns in Love and Marriage.* New York: Random House.
Scharff, D. E. (1982).) *The Sexual Relationship: An Object Relations View of Sex and the Family.* London: Routledge. Reissued in paperback with a new introduction 1998. Northvale, NJ: Jason Aronson.
Scharff, D. E. & Scharff, J. S. (1991). *Object Relations Couple Therapy.* Northvale, NJ: Jason Aronson.
Scharff, J. S. & Scharff, D. E. (2006). *New Paradigms for Treating Relationships.* Lanham, MD: Jason Aronson.
Scharff, J. S. & Scharff, D. E. (2008). *Object Relations Therapy of Physical and Sexual Trauma.* Lanham, MD: Jason Aronson.
Viorst, J. (1986). *Necessary Losses.* New York: Simon and Schuster.

CHAPTER TWENTY

Assessing the sexual relationship

Jane Seymour

This chapter will serve as a guide when seeing couples (and individuals) who present with sexual problems. A basic assessment model is outlined together with some thoughts on the more common presentations. In a chapter of this length it is not possible to cover the more complex cases and further reading is recommended. Brief clinical examples will give a flavour of the likely presentations. The chapter will also highlight cases which need referring for medical investigation or psychosexual therapy.

A thorough assessment is the first requirement of any responsible therapy since it provides the initial hypothesis on which any therapeutic intervention is based. Information on couple dynamics and general assessment are to be found in other chapters of this book and should be taken into consideration. This chapter contains details of the further issues to be kept in mind when focusing on the sexual aspect of the couple relationship.

While it is true to say that a sexual difficulty can have a corrosive effect on the entire relationship it is also a notoriously difficult topic to discuss for both patient and therapist. Some couples will be able to name the sexual difficulty right away. For others, who find this too difficult, a variety of issues may be cited as the "presenting problem" which, on further enquiry, are found to be rooted in the sexual relationship. Therefore a gentle exploration of the sexual relationship is an important part of any assessment process even if only to rule it out as a part of the problem.

Once it is clear that the problem lies, at least in part, in the sexual relationship the therapist can proceed to a more focused assessment. This will lead to a provisional diagnosis and treatment plan. Psychological, biological, medical, educational, and cultural factors all have an important part to play in sexual functioning and need consideration at every stage of assessment. There is no rush—the assessment should be conducted at a pace the clients feel comfortable with and may take several sessions. This is almost certainly the first time the couple have told their story in such detail and a gradual unfolding will be far more helpful than a series of quick-fire questions. Having a therapist who is prepared to listen to the story and make sense of it, can lead to a huge sense of relief for the couple. Hence the assessment process itself offers a powerful therapeutic experience.

An assessment will include an exploration of the following elements: the presenting problem, the shared history of the presenting problem, the individual sexual and medical histories along with the predisposing precipitating and maintaining factors of the presenting problem. The therapist will probably need details of a typical sexual encounter before making a provisional diagnosis. If the work continues this diagnosis may require further refinement and modification. For the purposes of this chapter the above elements are presented in a particular order. However as the assessment progresses, factors usually overlap and appear in more than one category—the important point is to gain an understanding of the aetiology of the problem.

Throughout the process it is vital to bear in mind the possibility that the sexual symptom is being caused wholly or in part by an undiagnosed medical condition. This can be the case even where there is ample evidence of psychological and relational distress. In such cases a medical referral will be necessary since, clearly, therapy alone will not resolve the problem. Where there is a permanent underlying organic condition therapy can enable the couple come to terms with this and devise new ways of managing their sexual contact.

The presenting problem

People describe their sexual interaction in different ways and, as a therapist, it is important to be sure you really understand what is being said and resist the temptation to make assumptions in order to save embarrassment on both sides. For example "I am impotent" can mean "I am unable to get an erection", "I am unable to sustain an erection", "I am unable to ejaculate", "I ejaculate before I can penetrate", "I feel unable to challenge my partner" or "I feel I have no control over my life". The therapist will also need to know how the sexual symptom has impacted on the rest of the relationship. There may be a lot of anger and resentment between the couple or, on the other hand, they may get on well apart from this problem. Major difficulties in other areas of the relationship will usually need attending to in therapy before the sexual relationship can be worked on. When exploring the presenting problem bear in mind there may be co-morbidity—for example if he presents with difficulty sustaining an erection it may also be the case that she finds penetration painful. It should also be noted that partners will often differ in their view of the situation.

When discussing the presenting problem the therapist needs to understand who is the "symptom" a problem for? For instance, some women do not orgasm on penetration but are quite happy to orgasm in other ways and so do not see it as a problem. However, the partner may feel he is not a good lover if she does not orgasm when he is inside her.

The symptom will also have a particular meaning for the couple. So, in a case where there has been a long period of fertility treatment, it is common for one or both partners to experience a loss of sexual desire. This makes sense in as much as sex has become about failing to make babies so any attempt to make love is simply a reminder that the intercourse will be "uncreative".

Typically, couples will have attempted various solutions prior to deciding to undertake therapy. An exploration of these will give the therapist a good idea of how well the couple can cooperate together and what information they have been able to access. At this stage it is sufficient to get a clear understanding of how the couple view the problem in the context of their relationship and lifestyle. Later, as the therapeutic alliance develops, there will be time to explore the sexual encounter in more detail.

The history of the presenting problem

How did the problem start, gradually or all of a sudden? Sex might have been a problem right from the start. On the other hand if sex has been good in the past at least there are positive memories to draw on. In this case they know (and so do you) that they have been able to function well. If the difficulty had a sudden onset some kind of traumatic event might be indicated. An exploration of what else was going on for the couple at the time the problem began will often prove to be fruitful in these cases. Where onset has been gradual some developing medical condition or creeping relational problem might be present. A long slow decline in the quality of the sexual relationship is not unusual. This can happen as over-familiarity sets in and the relationship slips down the list of priorities. The demands of work, children, and friends take over and it seems as if a chasm has opened between the couple. In this way they become physically estranged from each other although there is no particular dysfunction present. Therapy can be very useful in facilitating a gradual reconnection for these couples.

Individual histories

History taking is best conducted separately in order that each partner can speak freely about past experiences. Information may be disclosed of which the partner is unaware. This can pose a dilemma for the therapist who may hold information from which the other partner is excluded. However, it is important to know if there is some pathological behaviour, undisclosed illness or an ongoing affair since this will have important implications for the ongoing therapy. An exploration of childhood experiences will give a good understanding of individual psychosexual development. An investigation of the way sex was handled in the family—as a good thing or as something dirty or possibly even sinful will give some indication of the conscious and unconscious conflicts at work.

These days, especially since the advent of the internet, there is a wealth of information available on sexual functioning. Yet some clients still have very limited knowledge of sexual matters. This leads to unrealistic and inaccurate expectations. One might wonder with the client how he or she has managed to avoid accessing this information. However, at some point, it will be useful to correct some of the mistaken beliefs and suggest appropriate reading material. Psychosexual therapy frequently contains an educational component for such clients.

A medical history can be taken at this point which would include any psychiatric issues, major illnesses, and operations. Recreational drug use, prescribed medications, and excessive use of alcohol can all impact on sexual functioning. Some detail of previous sexual relationships will indicate if the problem predates the current relationship—where this is the case some individual work could be indicated. An exploration of sexual fantasies, if possible, may reveal cases where the fantasy is pathological or incompatible with the current partner. This meeting also offers a chance to explore the true level of desire in each partner along with some detail about the current masturbatory style. Although it may feel intrusive to ask about this it can be helpful when making a diagnosis for the following reason: If there is no difficulty when self-stimulating a psychological or relational cause is indicated. Where a problem such as erectile dysfunction occurs during masturbation as well as when with a partner a medical referral will need to be made.

The predisposing factors

These are the factors in the individual's past which make this person or this couple more likely to experience difficulty in their intimate adult relationships in general and the sexual relationship in particular. An exploration of early childhood and family life will be necessary as with any assessment in order to clarify and conscious and unconscious influences which might be at work in the current situation. We also know, for instance, that child sexual abuse is a predisposing factor for subsequent sexual difficulties. A disturbed attachment history, poor body image and insufficient or inaccurate sexual information all play their part. In some cases, a strict religious background can make it difficult to engage sexually especially before marriage.

The precipitating factors

These are the life events which trigger the sexual problem. It is important to discuss how the symptoms first appeared and what else was happening in the couple's life at that time. General relationship dissatisfaction may be the precipitant. On the other hand a physical trigger such as an unwanted pregnancy, traumatic birth, or the symptoms of a serious illness in one or other partner could be responsible. Other possibilities might include the death of a family member, redundancy, or an ongoing affair. In the case of an affair it is worth exploring the state of the sexual relationship prior to this. It may be that the affair developed as way of drawing attention to a deficit within the relationship.

Some couples are unaware that the natural ageing process can change sexual functioning. Men will tend to need more direct stimulation than they used to and may not be able to perform as frequently as before. Some women have lubrication and arousal difficulties post menopause.

There are cases where it is not possible to identify a particular event which marked the start of the problem. Couples will talk about a gradual almost imperceptible decline in frequency. As a result of this they become a bit unfamiliar and awkward. Anxiety impacts negatively on the arousal process and makes a random failure likely. Once this has happened a vicious circle sets in as the next time the couple attempt to make love their anxiety is even greater and so on.

The maintaining factors

These are the issues which keep the difficulty in place and so will need consideration when formulating any treatment plan. Some popular magazines would have us believe everyone is having highly satisfying sex on a frequent basis. This myth causes great distress to those who are in relationships where there is no sex or where sex is difficult. Couples often feel their sexual problems are a shameful secret from friends and family. They can end up feeling excluded or "not normal". In some cases they begin to wonder if they are no longer a "proper couple". A discussion about the kind of relationship this couple want for themselves can often be very constructive. As can normalising the problem. For example, how many young couples with three children under five and where both parents have full time jobs really have the time and energy for frequent lovemaking?

A typical sexual encounter

In many cases it will be necessary to discuss the specific details of a sexual encounter in order to identify the precise difficulty. Since this can be difficult for both therapist and patient it is sometimes avoided and important information may be missed. For instance, in a case of premature ejaculation, it might become clear that the woman is ambivalent about the sexual act and is trying to "get it over with as quickly as possible". An absence of foreplay is common as the focus of the sexual encounter narrows down to genital functioning at the expense of any sensuality or eroticism. This can make it difficult for the partners to achieve full arousal. By taking a couple through the stages of their lovemaking the therapist can ensure that any contributory factors are fully understood. This exploration would include what the couple are thinking and feeling at each stage as well as what is going on physically. From this it is possible to see if performance anxiety and spectating are inhibiting the arousal. When spectating, rather than focusing on the experience one or other partner will begin to observe and assess their performance. They then lose contact with their own bodily arousal process. An idea of how they talk about sex together and if they have agreed an acceptable vocabulary will indicate if there is work to be done in this area. Being able to state what they want or do not want is important too along with some idea of how the other likes to be touched.

Diagnosis and further treatment

By this stage the therapist will be in a position to answer the "chicken and egg" question. That is to say: is there a difficulty with the sex which will, over time if not already, have a negative impact on the rest of the relationship? Or is there a problem with the general relationship which is having a negative impact on the sex? In the latter case the couple are likely to be suitable for ongoing couple therapy. In the former they may need to be referred for medical treatment and/or psychosexual therapy.

The DSM-IV-TR (1994) contains diagnostic criteria for sexual dysfunction. However, in recent years research has moved on, especially in the field of female sexuality, so these criteria are not always as helpful as they might be. The most common dysfunctions are listed below, as they appear in DSM1V, under three headings following Kaplan's "tri-phasic concept of human sexuality" (1979). That is to say the desire, arousal, and orgasmic phases along with the addition of a fourth category for the sexual pain disorders.

1. **Sexual desire disorders**
   a. Hypoactive sexual desire disorder—often referred to as HSDD or as loss of desire. Can apply to both male and female patients
   b. Sexual aversion disorder—can apply to both male and female patients.
2. **Sexual arousal disorders**
   a. Female sexual arousal disorder—referred to as FSAD—an inability to become physically aroused. This results in lack of lubrication and swelling response
   b. Male erectile disorder—often referred to as ED.
3. **Orgasmic disorders**
   a. Female orgasmic disorder—can also be referred to as anorgasmia
   b. Male orgasmic disorder—frequently called delayed ejaculation
   c. Premature ejaculation—commonly called PE.
4. **Sexual pain disorders**
   a. Dyspareunia—is pain on penetration for either sex
   b. Vaginismus—this occurs when a spasm in the vaginal muscles render penetration impossible. This condition must not be confused with an unruptured hymen.
   (DSM-5 now lists dyspareunia and vaginismus under the umbrella of genito-pelvic pain/penetration disorder. I tend to think that while pain penetration disorder diagnosis could be indicated in some cases, the differentiation between vaginismus and dyspareunia is still useful. Suggestions for further reading follow at the end of the chapter.)

Once the disorder has been identified there are two further details to clarify:

1. **Is the disorder lifelong or acquired?**
   A lifelong disorder has been in place since the start of adult sexual functioning and so indicates an individual problem whereas an acquired disorder has somehow developed along the way with the current or a previous partner.
2. **Is the disorder generalised or situational?**
   With a generalised disorder the problem occurs all the time every time and with a situational disorder it only occurs in certain situations.
   The next stage in the assessment process is to share your understanding of the problem, its aetiology and meaning with the couple in as straightforward a way as possible. This formulation will give the couple some insight into their situation along with a rationale for any further proposed work.

Medical referral

At this point you might suggest a referral for a medical assessment. This might apply to any dysfunction but it is particularly so for erectile dysfunction, dyspareunia, and vaginismus.

This chapter is not intended to give an exhaustive guide on the details of the various dysfunctions but some comments are made for the reader to bear in mind.

1. **Hypoactive sexual desire disorder**
   This is the most common (and potentially the most complex) presenting problem. It could be the result of some hormonal imbalance, depression or other medical condition. On the other hand, desire is also affected by general relationship satisfaction levels. It is not surprising therefore that a significant proportion of couples presenting for therapy will report low levels of desire. A typical example might be where the woman presents with loss of desire but on exploration reveals that she is very angry with her partner. His perceived lack of support with childcare and household chores makes it difficult for her to experience loving sexual feelings. In these cases, when the relationship improves, the sexual problem may well resolve itself. In other cases the loss of desire might be masking an underlying sexual dysfunction. For example, a man presenting loss of desire might also be unable to ejaculate during intercourse. His loss of desire (either conscious or unconscious), protects him and his partner from the distress caused by his failure to ejaculate. Addressing the ejaculatory problem in this case may well also resolve the loss of desire.

   Rosemary Basson's research is important when thinking about assessing sexual desire (Basson, 2003; Basson, Leiblum, Brotto, et al. 2004). Basson proposes that some women do not experience spontaneous desire. Rather, a woman might be either unavailable or in a more receptive state. When in a receptive state she will be able to respond to her partner if he initiates although she is not aware of any desire at this point. She can begin to engage in the arousal process but the desire only appears at a much later stage in response to the physical arousal she experiences. Orgasm may bring satisfaction but it may be the emotional intimacy that is more important for her. This model dispels the myth that "normal women should have desire". It also encourages the couple to work together to identify what helps her achieve a more receptive state. This in turn leads the man to have more confidence when initiating and means he avoids the risk of rejection. Although this model was developed with women in mind it is sometimes relevant to male loss of desire.

2. **Erectile dysfunction**
   This may be psychological but can be the first symptom of type 2 diabetes or coronary heart disease and may appear as much as eighteen months before any other symptoms.

3. **Male orgasmic disorder**
   Typically the couple will have intercourse for a prolonged period of time as the man attempts to ejaculate. This can cause dyspareunia in the woman.

4. **Dyspareunia**
   This can be psychological but can also be caused in women by damage or deformity of the vagina. In the man damage to the foreskin or a too tight foreskin can cause dyspareunia. An undiagnosed infection could also be responsible. In cases of dyspareunia a medical referral is indicated.

5. Vaginismus
Frequently has psychological genesis but could be mistaken for an unruptured hymen or some other physical problem.

Psychosexual therapy

A referral for psychosexual therapy should be considered where there is a dysfunction present and where the couple might benefit from paying particular attention to the sexual interaction with the possible inclusion of some cognitive behavioural exercises. However, it is quite usual for there to be some general relationship work needed prior to focusing on the sexual relationship. Ideally the couple need to be in a "good enough" state before they can begin to explore their loving sexual feelings for each other. A referral might also be indicated if the couple have unrealistic expectations and poor information about sexual functioning where the current therapist feels unable to provide this.

Conclusion

The sexual relationship is important for the majority of the couples (and individuals) we see. It is also, as a rule, a very private matter. Therapists are in an ideal position to conduct a thorough assessment of the sexual relationship since they can take the time needed to get to know the couple and gain their trust. This chapter has covered the most important aspects of assessment and will be of use to the therapist who is beginning to work with couples. Hopefully, some readers will be sufficiently interested in this fascinating aspect of couple relationships to continue with further reading and training.

References

American Psychiatric Association (1994). *Diagnostic and Statistical Manual of Mental Disorders* (DSM-1V-TR). Washington, DC: American Psychiatric Association.

American Psychiatric Association (2013). *Diagnostic and Statistical Manual of Mental Disorders* (DSM-5). Washington, DC: American Psychiatric Association.

Basson, R. (2003). Biopsychosocial models of women's sexual response: applications to managements of "desire disorders". *Sexual and Relationship Therapy*, 18, 1: 107–115.

Basson, R., Leiblum, S., Brotto, L., Derogatis, L., Fourcroy, J. Fugl-Meyer, K. et al. (2004). Revised definition of women's sexual dysfunction. *Journal of Sexual Medicine*, 1, 1.

Kaplan, H. S. (1979). *Disorders of Sexual Desire*. New York: Brunner/Mazel.

Further reading

Clulow, C. (Ed.) (2009). *Sex, Attachment and Couple Psychotherapy*. London: Karnac.

Daines, B. & Perrett, A. (2000). *Psychodynamic Approaches to Sexual Problems*. London: Open University Press.

Davies, D. & Neal, C. (Ed.) (1996). *Pink Therapy*. Maidenhead: Open University Press.

Hiller, J., Wood, H., & Bolton, W. (2006). *Sex, Mind and Emotion*. London: Karnac.
Levine, S., Risen, C., & Althof, S. (2010). *Handbook of Clinical Sexuality for Mental Health Professionals*, (2nd Edition). New York: Routledge.
Scharff, D. E. (1982). *The Sexual Relationship*. London: Routledge. Reprinted Lanham, Maryland: Jason Aronson, 1998.
Schnarch, D. (1991). *Constructing the Sexual Crucible*. New York: W. W. Norton.

These books are full of useful information and also suitable for clients to read

Heiman, J. & Lo Piccolo, J. (2009). *Becoming Orgasmic*. London: Judy Piaktus.
Zilbergeld, B. (1999). *The New Male Sexuality*. USA: Bantam Doubleday Dell Publishing Group.

CHAPTER TWENTY-ONE

Addressing sexual issues in couple therapy

Norma Caruso

Introduction

Sexuality is a fundamental aspect of a couple's relationship. It is intricately woven with a couple's emotional life, vital to their functioning, and a source of considerable distress when dysfunction arises. Despite its importance, therapists often feel ill-prepared to address sexual difficulties in the marital relationship. There is a dearth of literature that provides therapists with guidelines for treating sexual dysfunction, particularly from a psychodynamic perspective. This chapter attempts to fill the gap by presenting theory of couple dynamics, sexual symptom formation, and therapeutic action in couple therapy. I will discuss the sexual dysfunction of a marital pair. I will present an object relations model for conceptualising sexual difficulties that centres on understanding internal objects, with reference to the return of the repressed (Fairbairn, 1943), hysterical states (Fairbairn, 1954), unconscious marital dynamics (Dicks, 1967) and the application of object relations theory to families and couple therapy (D. Scharff & J. Scharff, 1987). Additionally, I will discuss the evaluation and treatment of the couple's sexual dysfunction; and describe a treatment approach that integrates psychoanalytic and behavioural sex therapy techniques (Kaplan, 1974; D. Scharff & J. Scharff, 1991) with an emphasis on the use of transference and countertransference as therapeutic tools.

Model of sex and marital therapy

Dicks (1967) combined Fairbairn's (1944) model of endopsychic structure and his description of the return of the repressed bad object (1943), with Klein's (1946) concept of project identification to create a framework that explains marital and sexual functioning in couples. By forming a "joint personality" each spouse locates split-off and repressed aspects of the self in their partner through projective identification and either treasures or attacks those aspects, depending on how those parts were treated. The "joint personality" also allows each member of the marital dyad to re-experience aspects of their primary object relations in their partner through projective identification. Dicks' conceptualisation of marital dynamics is applicable to the sexual functioning of a couple.

Sexual difficulties illustrate the process of mutual projective identification infiltrating a couple's physical and emotional intimate life, the genitals serving as the body screen for the projection of split-off conflicts with attachment figures and intimate partners through the mechanism of conversion (Fairbairn, 1954; D. Scharff, 1982).

Case illustration

The couple

Lourdes and Singh, a couple in their early twenties, sought treatment because of the absence of sexual intercourse due to Lourdes' aversion to sex. The couple met in college and dated several years before marrying. Early on, Lourdes thought Singh misread her friendly interest as a sexual invitation, when he attempted to kiss her and open her blouse. Initially, she decided to terminate contact, but eventually their common interests led them to an exclusive relationship supported by Lourdes' appreciation of Singh's sense of fun, and Singh's love of Lourdes' caring, gentle nature. Several months into their relationship, they began to have intercourse which they describe as pleasurable. As they made plans to marry, Lourdes began to feel guilty and to experience sex as "boring." Singh reluctantly agreed to suspend intercourse until after the wedding.

During their one-year marriage, Lourdes and Singh have not had sexual intercourse. Lourdes attributes the absence of sex to problems with their emotional connection. She describes Singh as "rough and greedy" and believes that his behaviour reflects his lack of sensitivity to her. She also claims that Singh is more dedicated to his mother than to her, an accusation that he denies. Singh perceives the problem as purely sexual and views their sexual difficulties as adversely impacting their emotional relationship, leaving him rejected, sad, and angry.

Background information

Lourdes was born in Colombia and moved to the United States to attend college. In keeping with their repressive culture and Catholic traditions, her family prohibited dating and closely monitored her clothing choices. Lourdes complied with these sanctions which mostly came from her father. Lourdes' mother who gave up a promising career to become a wife and mother became profoundly depressed when Lourdes was in her early teens.

Singh is of Indian descent and comes from a family that did not discuss sexuality or openly express affection. He adopted the norms of his culture which favour dominant men and subservient women. Singh is responsible for a dependent mother whose needs intensified after his father's death when Singh was twelve.

Lourdes' shy, smiley persona, which creates a girlish appearance, is in striking contrast to Singh's reserved and confident presentation. Neither partner had prior dating or sexual experiences.

Evaluation

I used Dicks' model to formulate Lourdes' and Singh's marital and sexual dynamics after I gathered their family, marital, relationship, and sexual history in multiple sessions. To promote comfort and openness, I obtained each partner's sexual history in an individual interview. I also used a sex survey (LoPicollo & Steger, 1974) to understand the couple's sexual attitudes, practices, desires, and sexual interactions, as well as each partner's perceptions about the other's desires and experiences. Prior to the evaluation, Lourdes' gynecologist had determined that there was no medical basis for her sexual problem. Additionally, no medications or psychopathology accounted for her difficulties.

After I explain Lourdes' and Singh's marital and sexual functioning, based on Dicks' model, I will outline my plan of treatment and provide segments that illustrate the integration of psychoanalytic and behavioral treatment techniques.

Dynamic formulation: from an object relations framework

According to Dicks' model (1967), the genitals can serve as the medium for expressing unresolved intrapsychic conflicts, thereby compromising the expression of libidinal energy. Based on this formulation, it is my impression that together Lourdes and Singh project a split between desire and dread onto their genital interaction.

Lourdes' vagina embodies dread. She deposits her denied sexual longing in Singh and then attacks him for being "too greedy" sexually. Unconsciously, she was drawn to him because of his open expression of sexuality, a denied, split off part of herself. Her refusal to yield to Singh's sexual demands allows her to identify with her repressive religious and cultural dictates and to view herself as chaste and gentle. At the same time, Lourdes' attacks of Singh promote the illusion that she has shed the subservient role of women in her culture. Singh's genitals represent the exciting and dangerous aspect of desire. Although he presents as comfortable with his sexuality, he actually represses and inhibits it, as suggested by his lack of prior dating or sexual experiences. Singh denies his inhibitions, projects them into Lourdes, and then blames her for the absence of sex. Unconsciously, he was attracted to Lourdes because of her valence to accept these projections based on her history. Singh's acceptance of Lourdes' projections that he is oversexed bolsters his self confidence, while the lack of sex in the marriage allows him to maintain his unconscious primary allegiance to his mother whom he idealises and resents. He is unaware how he colludes to avoid sex.

Feedback and recommendations

Following the evaluation, I provided Lourdes and Singh with feedback and recommendations in a joint session. I told them that their sexual problems reflect larger difficulties within the marriage that are captured in the way they mutually attack each other. At the same time, their sexual problems intensify their marital struggles. I also identified each partner as struggling with family of origin conflicts that predate their marital union and form the basis of their sexual dysfunction.

I recommended that prior to couple sex therapy, Lourdes and Singh have a course of marital treatment to address their general pattern of relating that leaves each of them feeling victimised, rejected, and in turn, justified in hurting each other. Additionally, marital therapy could improve their skills to address conflicts, increase their understanding of the other's point of view, learn how their sexual difficulties embody the conflicts within their marriage, and enhance their ability to blend their two cultures. I also suggested that individual treatment for Lourdes might be incorporated into the treatment at a later point. At the time of the evaluation, Singh had been in individual treatment for one year with another therapist.

Treatment

This paper presents an approach for treating sexual difficulties that combines psychoanalytic work with behavioural sex therapy techniques. The psychoanalytic techniques are particularly useful in addressing unresolved conflicts. Because it takes time to link sexual difficulties to early attachment histories, the early phase of treatment tends to focus on the details of the couple's sexual activities and their responses to each other. During this period the therapist prescribes a series of behavioural exercises in a particular order. Commonly referred to as sensate focus exercises (Masters & Johnson, 1970), they are designed to increase a person's awareness of their own and their partner's needs and to encourage them to focus on sensual experiences.

Helen Singer Kaplan (1974) added a psychoanalytic component to the behavioral exercises that included making psychodynamic interpretations. David Scharff (1982; D. & J. Scharff, 1991) modified Kaplan's model. His approach requires the couple to complete the exercises twice weekly in the privacy of their home. The therapist reviews their experiences in the subsequent session, adds an exercise as the couple masters each level, and asks the couple to repeat the exercise if they encounter difficulty. When the couple relates their experience of doing the exercises, the therapist works to understand the material from a psychoanalytic perspective, using psychoanalytic techniques. Specifically, the therapist asks the clients to make associations, report their dreams, and identify their emotions, fantasies, anxieties that are triggered by their physical experiences. The therapist also analyses resistances and makes use of transference and countertransference to understand the couple's experience. By focusing on changing behavioural components of the couple's sexual activity and their thoughts and reactions to the exercises, unconscious material emerges. This material arises as a function of the psychoanalytic approach and because of the intimate interactions of the exercises. The successes and failures in carrying out the exercises exert psychic pressure on the couple which, in turn, triggers the emergence of unconscious material. A treatment approach that combines psychoanalytic and behavioural techniques tends to take longer than one that relies solely on behavioral techniques because it focuses on the totality of the couple's relationship.

The exercises begin with non-threatening, non-genital pleasuring of each other and end with intercourse. They are a form of in-vivo desensitisation in that a feared situation is gradually mastered by breaking it into discrete steps that are experienced under safe conditions. The exercises create new learning experiences in which pleasurable responses are reinforced and anxiety is diminished as the pressure to succeed decreases. Attached to each exercise are object relations issues (J. Scharff & D. Scharff, 1991) related to experiences within one self and in relation to others. Each exercise provides an opportunity to work through the issues that are a source of conflict.

In the remainder of this chapter I present segments from the sex therapy work with Lourdes and Singh. The first few segments are from the beginning phase of treatment when the couple worked on the first two exercises; the last two segments illustrate the exercises from the mid phase of treatment. The clinical material demonstrates the issues that emerged as the couple performed the exercises, the use of psychoanalytic techniques to address these issues, and how the body and genitalia served as a vehicle for the expression of internal object relations. The full sequence of exercises and the associated object relations issues are described in the Scharffs' book on couple therapy (D. & J. Scharff, 1991).

Couple therapy

Lourdes and Singh spent ten months in marital treatment before beginning the sex therapy portion of the work. During this time, they became aware of their discomfort with emotional, as well as physical intimacy. They also developed an understanding of how their mutual attacking wards off feelings of longing and how this dynamic manifests in their sexual difficulties. Segments from the beginning phase of sex therapy follow:

Lourdes reports: "Doing the exercise was great. I could relax knowing it was not going anywhere." She compares this scenario to what usually transpires, when she tenses as she anticipates intercourse. However, Singh had not complied with the instructions. He had attempted to fondle Lourdes' breasts. Singh laughed and said, "I knew it wasn't right, but I thought I'd give it a shot." He admits feeling frustrated by the limitations of the exercise.

Because the first exercise serves as a foundation for the success of subsequent exercises, it is particularly important that the couple correctly complete it. This exercise also helps clarify what couples can expect from sex therapy. In the above segment, Singh violates the instructions, therefore, the exercise is reassigned. When the couple returns the following week, they report that Singh again tried to touch Lourdes' breasts. His behaviour left her feeling tense and she wondered when Singh would violate the instructions again. He dismissed her anxiety. But this time, Lourdes set limits, although in a playful, rather than forceful way.

I confront Singh about the damaging impact of his behaviour and Lourdes looks delighted. When I assign the exercise a third time, I emphasise the importance of lowering Lourdes' anxiety and establishing safety by adhering to the limits, a prerequisite for moving on to the next stage. Singh is annoyed, though Lourdes laughs and says she had told Singh that his behaviour would have this outcome.

In the first two sessions the couple demonstrates considerable resistance. Singh dismisses my instructions. His behaviour is aggressive and demeaning; he ignores Lourdes' need for safety and compromises her experience. Although I suspect that behind Singh's behaviour is his fear of sensuality, nevertheless, I feel countertransference anger. He covers his difficulty tolerating his tenderness with aggression which he projects into me. In turn, I take a controlling stance and confront him about the damaging impact of his behaviour. Additionally, Singh's annoyance at being reassigned the exercise engenders in me the feeling that I am depriving him of sex. I feel angry and withholding and my reactions help me to connect with Lourdes' experiences in relating to Singh. In short, I make use of Singh's transference to me and my countertransference to better understand the working of the couple's relationship.

At this point, I am feeling more sympathetic to Lourdes, but I believe that Singh's spoiling of the exercise reflects the couple's shared fears. Lourdes' resistance subtly manifests in her failure to deal forcefully with Singh. Her patience covers her underlying anger. I hold her anger and assume the role of confronting Singh which seems to delight Lourdes.

In the transference Singh reveals his use of aggression as a defence against tenderness, and Lourdes demonstrates her use of patience and tolerance to avoid her fury. In turn, I get a clearer understanding of how they relate, that is, they deny dreaded aspects in themselves and deposit them in the other.

Over the next few weeks the couple's resistance increases. Lourdes complains of fatigue and difficulty maintaining the stamina needed to massage Singh. Physical intimacy seems to deplete, rather than revitalise, her. They report difficulty finding time to do the exercises. As a solution, Lourdes suggests that they shorten the exercises and that Singh watch TV while doing the massage. The absence of vitality and passion is striking.

Lourdes and Singh display the same difficulties within the sessions. They often come late, and once in the session, seem worn out. I feel like the teacher who makes her students do their homework. Their resistance is interfering with learning from what I offer them. Within the contextual transference the couple has difficulty being psychologically held by me. This difficulty that plays out with me is mirrored in their difficulty receiving pleasure from each other.

Faced with the couple's lack of vitality, countertransferentially, I feel a need to supply energy and hope. Also, because of their frequent lateness, I share their feeling of having little time to complete my work. In turn, Lourdes' recommendation to perform two activities feels applicable to my experience, as well.

During the next few weeks I reassign the same exercise and continue to explore the couple's difficulty carrying it out. They admit feeling that they are in the "remedial" class at school and struggle to comply with my instructions and to experience pleasure. Lourdes and Singh respond to my confrontations about their resistance by explaining that they have busy schedules. Nevertheless, because they begin to adhere to boundaries and to enjoy the massage, I assign the second exercise. I tell them to continue massaging each other's whole body, but now to include genitals and breasts in passing, but not beyond the point of mild arousal. In reporting on this second exercise Lourdes says she crossed her arms over her breasts, closed her legs, and worn underwear. When I suggest we try to understand her need to protect herself, she says:

"I don't understand. I've never been traumatised and it's not that I don't trust Singh. I'm not thinking that he'll rape me, when he is passing over my vagina. Maybe, it just has to do with progressing on to the next exercise." I make a mental note of Lourdes' reference to her transference about the therapy but only comment on her relationship with Singh. I say, "I have the impression that you feel violated by Singh and so you feel unsafe." She concedes, "You're right. It's the way he grabs my breasts." Singh adds, "Not just when it comes to sex, but in our relationship in general." Lourdes says, "I create unsafe situations around driving or spending." I say, "You often feel assaulted by Lourdes' criticisms. The way she finds fault violates your sense of yourself as a responsible man." Singh says, "It does feel like Lourdes has a rifle and is shooting at me." I say, "You also feel that I'm shooting at you, too, when I challenge your way of relating. Lourdes, you also feel that I am pushing you into unsafe territory, so you need to take cover from me, too."

In the early phase of treatment, Lourdes and Singh make slow progress in learning to give and receive from each other. They have a slow rhythm in relation to each other that is mirrored in the slow pace in which they take in what I offer. When Lourdes connects her need to cover herself with her fears of progressing in treatment, she reveals her transference to me on behalf of the couple. That is, she expresses the couple's perception of me as a threat, and in the face of it, they retreat from the work. In turn, the work slows down and I feel disconnected from them. Similarly, this dynamic of becoming disconnected occurs in their relationship.

In sum, by making use of the transference and countertransference, I gain an inside appreciation that the unconscious meaning of the couple's slow movement is a shared unconscious fear of being violated. Whereas Lourdes fears being violated physically, Singh fears emotional violation. I use this understanding to interpret how this dynamic manifests, in the transference to me and in each partner's transference to each other. The couple then has the opportunity to respond to my interpretation by exploring their internal world and its impact on their relationship within the safety of the therapy.

Couple therapy: middle phase of sex therapy

Months later, Lourdes and Singh perform an exercise that requires Lourdes to insert the glans of Singh's penis into her vagina, while she sits astride him. Soon after beginning this exercise, Lourdes develops a urinary tract infection which she attributes to penetration. She reveals that she typically lacks any awareness of the urge to urinate, until it is very strong. She also says that when she was having intercourse, she discovered that urinating afterwards allowed her to "get rid of the semen and clear out (her) system." I say, "I have a sense you equate penetration with being dirty and think urinating can rid the toxins from your system." She associates to my comment and says, "Semen is sticky" and Singh adds, "It is like acid if it touches her skin."

At Singh's suggestion Lourdes relates her childhood history of stress incontinence. Due to her family's prohibitions about genital contact for unmarried women, Lourdes reports that her parents largely ignored her problem. During her teen years, however, they took her to a doctor who catheterised her, but did not support follow up visits. Her father's suppressed rage regarding her catheterisation emerged later when he found tampons in her car. Lourdes says:

"My father was preoccupied with the idea of something entering me before marriage. He said if I wasn't a virgin when I married, he would be so ashamed that he would have to leave the country. His words were harsh." Lourdes begins to cry and admits having felt terribly ashamed. I say, "I think you are still carrying that shame and the belief that sex and anything associated with it is damaging. It's not just Singh's body that you find dirty; it's your own as well. I suspect you have cut off all sensations in the genital and urinary systems. As a result, you have not only lost awareness of your sexual urges, but your urinary urges, as well. Your father intruded on your space and you are reluctant to reclaim what is yours." She says, "He had no reason to be ashamed of me" and admits feeling angry.

In the subsequent session, Lourdes reports that my interpretation regarding the psychosomatic component of her urinary tract infection left her feeling "foolish" and she wants to provide me with scientific evidence that emptying the bladder after intercourse prevents urinary tract infections. Her resistance to my interpretation illustrates her difficulty being entered psychically and captures the psychosomatic component of her sexual dysfunction. I then interpret her anger at me and suggest that she felt invaded by me in much the same way that she felt intruded upon by her father's beliefs and by Singh's attempts to penetrate her. She agrees. In suggesting that Lourdes bring up her childhood history of incontinence, Singh has set in motion the process that lets us understand that Lourdes equates mental penetration with physical penetration and recoils when confronted with either aspect. He puts Lourdes forward as the one to receive my penetrating interpretation. Seeing her survive the process should help him now confront his fear of emotional penetration.

Conclusion

We will leave the couple there, mid-way through their treatment. Their clinical material illustrates the use of object relations theory to explain unconscious, intrapsychic factors that formed one couple's partnership and compromised their sexual functioning. It considers the couple's sexual problems as rooted in unresolved conflicts with internalised primary objects, with the genitals serving as a vehicle for their expression. In negotiating their sexual relationship, each member of the dyad re-experienced in the other aspects of their split-off and repressed conflicts through projective identification. Additionally, it captures the psychosomatic component of sexual dysfunction. Lourdes' and Singh's inability to tolerate these dreaded aspects within themselves and within each other challenged the resiliency of the couple's relationship. The clinical process described illustrates the integration of behavioural and psychoanalytic techniques. Particularly, it makes extensive use of transference and countertransference as therapeutic tools to work with the complex issues that emerge as the couple completes the prescribed sex therapy exercises. This chapter aims to provide a way to conceptualise, evaluate, and treat sexual difficulties.

References

Caruso, N. (2003). Object relations theory and technique applied to sex and marital therapy. *Journal of Applied Psychoanalytic Studies, 5, 3*: 297–308.

Dicks, H. V. (1967). *Marital Tensions*. London: Karnac.

Fairbairn, W. R. D. (1943). The repression and the return of bad objects (with special references to the 'War Neurosis'). In: *Psychoanalytic Studies of the Personality* (pp. 59–81). London: Routledge & Kegan Paul, 1952.

Fairbairn, W. R. D. (1944). Endopsychic structure considered in terms of object relationships. In: *Psychoanalytic Studies of the Personality* (pp. 82–135). London: Routledge & Kegan Paul, 1952.

Fairbairn, W. R. D. (1954). Observations on the nature of hysterical states. *British Journal of Medical Psychology, 27*: 105–125.

Kaplan, H. S. (1974). *The New Sex Therapy*. New York: Brunner/Mazel.

Klein, M. (1946). Notes on some schizoid mechanisms. *International Journal of Psychoanalysis, 27*: 99–100.

LoPiccolo, J. & Steger, J. (1974). The sexual interaction inventory: a new instrument for assessment of sexual dysfunction. *Archives of Sexual Behavior, 3*: 585–595.

Masters, W. & Johnson, V. (1970). *Human Sexual Inadequacy*. Boston: Little Brown.

Scharff, D. E. (1982). *The Sexual Relationship: An Object Relations View of Sex and the Family*. Northvale, NJ: Jason Aronson.

Scharff, D. E. & Scharff, J. S. (1987). *Object Relations Family Therapy*. Northvale, NJ: Jason Aronson.

Scharff, D. E. & Scharff, J. S. (1991). *Object Relations Couple Therapy*. Northvale, NJ: Jason Aronson.

CHAPTER TWENTY-TWO

Unconscious meanings and consequences of abortion in the life of couples

Yolanda de Varela

Introduction

When treating individuals and couples who have had abortions themselves, or have known of their parents' having an abortion, or have been informed that the option was merely considered, we often find that they take these acts as a rejection. They often repeat abortion as a way of getting rid of a split off part of the self that encapsulates affects of a needy kind. Part of the self is turned against another part of self, suffocating any expression of need, vulnerability, dependency, or suffering for the lost object. Usually the partner in the couple or their live child is a perfect recipient for such projections.

I have seen this need to abort a part of the self in many cases. In the first case, a man who had been rejected by his mother since childhood, and who knew of her later aborted pregnancies, felt afraid of her violence and wondered if she might wish to kill him too. He tried to get rid of a part of himself concretely through attempting suicide by jumping from a cliff, but was stopped by a friend. Psychologically, he constantly expressed his wish to unburden himself of his internally bad self, the part that could feel the emotional pain of rejection. In another case, when a woman heard of her mother's three abortions the day her mother told her friends, "I got rid of it three times!" she reported an impulse to jump off a balcony, but her more adaptive defence system prevented her from acting it out and she brought it to treatment instead.

The theme of the abortion of a part of the self has been acted out in many forms. Because of the difficulty in mourning losses and accepting reality, these patients show a way of dealing with reality through symbolic equation (Segal, 1957). When separateness from the object cannot be established, it cannot be represented by a symbol. The symbol is equivalent to the object. Aborting means not going through with a pregnancy. By symbolic equation, it also appears as an equivalent, for instance, as feeling the urge to defecate during a therapy session; dropping the treatment in a sudden way; cancelling sessions repeatedly; and rejecting their own needy selves by projection into their children who then try to commit suicide.

In *Mourning and Melancholia*, Freud (1917) describes a process in which the loss of the external object brings on the loss of a part of the ego. This dissociative aspect of unresolved mourning is alluded to by Freud (1920) when briefly talking about abortion, pointing out the gap between the conscious and unconscious information about our erotic life that leads to abortion without remorse. These people, said Freud, love without knowing that they love, or they do not know if they love or not, or they think they hate when in reality they love.

Abortion might be the result of a symbolic equation, as the foetus is equated with and stands in for this dissociated and lost part of the ego that the person needs to get rid off. But it might also stand for a part of the self that was "never psychologically born" as a result of maternal deprivation. A child knows if he has been unwanted, and strives to survive in a relationship where he must forget and repress that part of the self that was experienced as an additional burden for the caregiver. The external dynamic is replicated in the internal world and then again projected outside into a couple relationship, with one person expressing the rejected part and another controlling and rejecting its expression. In a compulsive repetition of the trauma, these individuals perpetuate the process of abortion in their minds by relentlessly attacking and expelling the suffering part of their selves. Any effort of the analyst to get close to this disowned part is received as if the patients' own survival is in peril.

I have come to think of a constellation of symptoms along a trans-generational continuum that goes from maternal deprivation, overwhelming longings for maternal love, dissociation of affects especially of a needy kind, abortion of this part of the mind, concrete abortion of the unborn child, and suicide or suicidal ideation in the live children. My main interest relates to the impact of abortion on the children of these couples, and the dynamics behind the abortion as a joint unconscious phantasy of its members. Trans-generational issues serve as a background for many of these cases. The case of Mr and Mrs A will illustrate my ideas.

Mrs A

Mrs A is a tall attractive woman, highly intelligent and a successful professional. Her colouring, black hair, and green eyes would make her stand out in any crowd. She is the second child in her family. Mrs A describes her mother as cold and emotionally distant. In moments of frustration she could be verbally abusive, making Mrs A feel unwanted and unloved. She remembers as a child going to visit her friends' houses and witnessing the love and affection between her friends and their mothers. At night she would go to bed longing for the closeness and tenderness of a mother that she did not have, and for a love that never came. She was attached to her five-years-older sister, who was similar in looks and character to her mother, but who was less defensive than her mother. When her sister married, she was devastated and could not stop crying; it was her father who consoled her on that occasion. She remembers being punished at any sign of conceit about her intelligence or looks, to a point when she started to doubt her own intuition and perception of reality. When she herself married, a family secret was revealed to her; that of her mother having been divorced and having left behind a daughter in order to marry her father. As an adult she also found out that her mother's older brother had sexually abused her mother.

Mr A

Mr A is a chubby man whose looks are more cute than attractive. With only one older sister, he had been the target of adoration from both mother and sister within a highly eroticised and exciting family environment. The father, more properly affectionate but very distant, was treated as unimportant, like a "zero at the left of a number". In the environment of his father's neglect, Mr A became a pleasure toy for his sister and cousins. Before puberty they masturbated him frequently to see his erect penis. The father was not available to rescue his son from the abuse of both mother and sister. During puberty, perhaps as a concrete act with the unconscious hope of recovering the lost phallus of his father and his own, he seduced the houseboy into fellatio many times. Mr A met his wife early in their adolescent years. Soon they started an active sexual life interrupted by periods of doubts about his gender identification. He liked women but felt highly attracted to men. Within a repressed society of the early fifties, in a womanising environment, Mr A did not have a chance to freely explore gender issues. He is an intelligent and highly successful banker, well respected and appreciated by colleagues and clients, but he is emotionally distant with trouble reading cues and understanding emotional states. He is still attached to his family of origin, and the incestuous relationship with his sister continues now in the form of boundary issues expressed in his way of managing her financial situation during her divorce and allowing her to place him in the middle of her couple's issues.

The couple

Mr and Mrs A came for couple therapy because of sexual issues. They got married due to her pregnancy when she was seventeen and he was twenty. She described her childhood and adolescent years as lonely in spite of many friends. The relationships in her family of origin were highly intellectual and she found something very different in Mr A. He came from a passionate family, very caring but also, as she found out later on, very dysfunctional. She felt well received in his family from the start. Her relation with Mr A was complicated. He had periods when he withdrew from her, and she, feeling rejected, used to get depressed, wanting to die because of the unbearable pain breaking up with him would bring. Slowly she would force herself to move on and start life again, and would be fine for a time until she would reach out again for him and start pursuing him. Every time they got back together Mr A, realising that he had almost lost her, became more attentive and committed. She had tender feelings toward Mr A, and felt that she needed to be close to him.

At fifteen Mrs A got pregnant for the first time and had her first abortion, the first of two according to her. Mr A remembers six abortions, and after the last one he felt pressured to marry her. She is not sure but remembers two at most. There is a lack of affect towards the foetal losses in both of them, as they recount the experiences of abortion. At the time of the last pregnancy, he was still in college, and they decided to have another abortion. This time Mr A, feeling guilty for the previous abortions, talked to her parents and they offered to support them until they could be on their own so they could get married and have the baby. They were happy and relieved by this support. Things went on without her being aware of how lonely she was as she was busy raising her children.

Mr A continued to withdraw emotionally. Although he was polite and tender with her, he was not emotionally available when she needed him. They had two sons. Crisis erupted when their second son reached adolescence. As Mr A was busy at work, Mrs A assumed the father role in trying to give some structure to their son's education, but she ended up acting as a persecutory and rejecting mother. The relationship with her youngest son deteriorated, and he became more attached to his father. He started using drugs and his life was in peril many times due to drug overdose. He came home drunk and late every night from parties, and was failing at school. As soon as he graduated from high school, they sent him abroad for college.

The couple was in their late thirties when they first consulted me. Mrs A faced an empty nest with dread, realising how little there was between them. Sex was infrequent and they did not have much to talk about. Mrs A confronted Mr A with this and began to complain. After some sessions he confessed that the reason he withdrew from her was due to some confusion about his sexual identity. His confusion went back as far as adolescence, when he would distance himself from her because he did not want to hurt her. He also confessed to homosexual acting out during their marriage. He could not live without her, so he tried to put his bisexual impulses behind him, promising himself not to do it ever again and to try to have a good marriage with her.

Devastated, she said there were clues that she had ignored. Now she could understand the withdrawal and the lack of frequency of their sexual encounters. She felt her own sexuality had finally awakened, and she was becoming more aggressive in bed, but he would reject her. Without consciously knowing about her husband's situation, she had begun an affair with a neighbour who was also married but with whom she found the emotional fit that she could not find with her husband. With this "human being" she could be professionally successful, intelligent, emotional, affective, spiritual—and sexual. They had some brief sexual encounters but the relationship was mainly platonic. Mrs A felt very guilty, but now she understood that she was looking for something that was missing in her life. She suggested Mr A should start individual therapy and he complied, but soon he "aborted" treatment feeling that the therapist downplayed his homosexual issues.

History of treatment

During individual evaluations both confessed to me about their infidelities. Mrs A felt her lover had helped her stand the heart-breaking pain of her husband's confession. Mr A felt he was pushed into his homosexual affairs by her rejection of him as a sexual partner. They refused to open up to each other and they each kept the secrets of their current extramarital affairs from each other. However, they decided to give the marriage another chance and each of them ended their affair.

Problems started again when he was unable to have an erection with her even though he was taking Viagra. He blamed her for his sexual difficulties saying that he could feel her rejection for the things he had done. She said she never again wanted to perform oral sex on him.

Then things started to get even more complicated. Their youngest son started to fail in college. It turned out that he was using drugs again. They sent him to a different country to continue his studies. Again, he failed and was suspended from college for delinquent behaviour. The parents refused to support him anymore, and he moved in with friends on whom he became emotionally and financially dependent. He became more depressed and again tried to kill himself several times with overdoses.

In sessions, I was appalled at the disengaged way Mr and Mrs A would talk about their son, and at their apparent inability to understand his emotional problems. Instead, Mrs A turned into a controlling mother, reprimanding him for his behavioural misconduct. The more problems they had with their son, the more withdrawn Mr A became. She was furious with him for leaving her alone to deal with their son. Eventually they realised that having him living with these friends was not the best solution for him, and they offered some financial help if he agreed to work, which he did. They terminated couple's therapy but Mrs A continued to see me in individual sessions.

The couple now took a trip together to Mexico City, and while they where visiting the Virgin of Guadalupe Cathedral Mrs A broke down, and could not stop crying while thinking of her son and of the possibility of losing him. This led to a breakthrough in the treatment, as she was able to get beyond her anger and for the first time to be in touch with her sadness and fear.

Mrs A now resumed her affair with the neighbour. She suspected Mr A was doing the same. I interpreted to her that most of the time her lover was offering parental advice on how to deal with her children, something that her husband was failing to do. He helped her ward off the destructive maternal identification she carried in her internal world.

By then the oldest son, who until that moment was the successful one, also got depressed and attempted suicide on three occasions. The husband came back for a few sessions. After Mrs A complained to him about his emotional detachment that left her burdened with the emotional horror of their children's attempted suicides, she became so furious that she threatened to kill him if something happened to one of their children.

A few months after this incident, now frightened of Mrs A, Mr A decided to leave her to sort out his confusion. He moved in with a younger man with whom he had no sexual difficulty. A month after his leaving she also attempted suicide, at which point he returned home. But things were not well between them as he continued to refuse treatment. Now she was the one having reckless affairs in a way that left me full of dread for her safety. I realised that I had internalised her fears in the desperation of an unloving environment.

Finally, after a period of her agreeing to more intense individual therapy, they both calmed down, and made a commitment to try living together in marriage again. They were able to help their sons by offering more structure and emotional support. At this time Mrs A told a dream that I regarded as the couple's dream conveyed to me by her. The dream helped me understand the internal dynamics that were projected into the relationship, and then to speak to them about their aggression against scared and vulnerable parts of themselves and external objects that represented their vulnerability. In the dream she was scared and hid inside a dark closet. Suddenly she found a light bulb. She turned it on and was relieved that she had some light. But she was still scared of being found out by someone outside. This dream depicts the fragile attempts of the couple to give light to their internal fears and needs, and shows the overwhelming power of the aggressive and persecutory part of themselves, projected outside into each other, into their children, and into me, and then returning against them so as to leave them no space to come out of their defensive system.

Discussion

This couple could not stay together when the relationship needed to include a third such as dead babies, their separating adolescent children, and their own, split off, vulnerable selves. They got rid of their babies as easily as putting out the trash. They were unable to mourn those babies or to think about the impact on the way their relationship started and how it has since unfolded. Mrs A's fragile ego needed a symbiotic relationship that did not allow any difference between her and her husband. After her children were born she shifted her dependency from Mr A to her second son, but once he started to separate from her she could not stand it, and in reaction to the threat of losing her son, she got rid of him by sending him far away to college.

In the mysterious way in which unconscious communication is transmitted, their children tried over and over to unburden their parents by suicide attempts. Attractive, intelligent and economically well off, they destroyed any opportunity of success, leaving professional success solely to their parents.

Paradoxically, the ambivalence of this couple in relation to their children was due in part to a shared defence system of omnipotent power over life and death, thinking that only by keeping them close by could their children stay alive, as if to say: "We created them; we can choose to destroy them or keep them alive." The couple tried to rid themselves of bad projections into each other until they could not stand it any more, and then they had to separate. Then, in order to stay alive, they found new untainted partners with whom they attempted to project life, concretely, into their sexual reproductive organs, and hoped it would flourish there (D. Scharff, 1998). Failing to confirm life and potency through his penis—the masculine part of himself—by intercourse with his wife's vagina, Mr A turned his attention to another, younger man to do so. A man offered Mr A the opportunity to feel more potent, magically helping his penis to enlarge in a way that he could not allow a woman to do, most probably because of the guilt he felt because of his early incestuous situation.

Mrs A laboriously worked at getting phallic power from Mr A in order to "become" her own phallic mother, so that she could avoid needing her mother herself. In a split-off way she also expressed the masculine aspect of the couple, and he the feminine part. At the same time, she tried to find a man who could provide the maternal care and warmth that she had not received from her own mother. She looked for the lost warmth of the mother in a sexual relationship, looking toward being penetrated by a penis (acting symbolically as a nipple), a compensation in which it was not important whether she found sexual pleasure as long as she got the maternal care only possible from a man.

Mrs A wanted a man like her father, who would prevent her mother from getting rid of her as she got rid of her first daughter by abortion in the previous marriage. In this way, the abortions represented her mother's rejection of her. Then she felt the incestuous guilt of the unconscious aspects in the relationship. Being a mother also put her in conflict with her desire "for the mother herself." When she experienced her son's "rejection" as he left for university, a part of her identified with her rejecting mother's coolness. This recalled the fact that it was her mother who had taken her to the abortion clinic each time, repeating a history in which both mother and daughter disposed of repudiated aspects of themselves through an aborted baby. The difficulty in mourning those losses derived from the way they aborted these parts of themselves repeatedly through unborn babies who disappeared from their lives not even leaving graves as reminders. These unborn, rejected babies simply disappeared into a void. The trans-generational issue of mothers abandoning children was repeated in Mrs A's life, first through the concreteness of the abortions, and later in the rejection of her husband and in the children whose suicidal attempts were, in part, a way of fulfilling the introjected death wish of the parents.

Mr A spent his life in a struggle trying to control the expression of a masculine strong part of himself that would force him to separate from his mother and becoming a sexual plaything in his sister's hands. At the same time it left him longing for a protective father who could support his masculinity by allowing identification with him. His own vulnerability overwhelmed him, so he had to look for protection from a male sexual partner. Impregnating his wife threatened a repetition of his own catastrophe, sending a part of him to prison inside her body. His recognition that his wife carried an unwanted part of himself was the link to a shared joint phantasy of unborn babies representing parts of themselves that they could dispose of through abortion.

The aim of both individual and couple therapy was the re-introjection of needy and rejected parts of their selves. Treatment confronted them with the many aborted parts of themselves. The process was slow and painful, following closely the theme of the repeated abortions in their relationship and in their minds. The force of the abortion theme as a repetition compulsion was often expressed in the sessions as a symbolic equivalent, for instance when Mrs A experienced cramps and a need to defecate. She never did, but the impulse was a way of aborting the feelings stirred up in the session by my understanding of her needy part. The abortion theme recurred in Mr A's dropping in and out of therapy and in the couple's repeated cancellations for frequent vacations. My own countertransference was also a clue to their dilemma, as many times I found myself wishing I could get rid of them. In that sense, there was also a part of me trying to "abort" the unbearable feelings of loss, pain and violence they infused in me.

In this case there was a conjunction of many things. We can see how unresolved mourning of maternal losses and incest was transmitted to the next generation in the form of melancholia that prevented working through subsequent losses, fortifying a split of the self in which a part stays deeply buried. This part, kept outside their observing egos, is the affective rejection that can only be expressed in an "as if" or hysterical form. Because this part cannot be contained or metabolised, it needs to be expelled through mental defecation from mind and body, all within the mode of symbolic equation.

The shared unconscious phantasy of this couple took the form of a belief that only through their sexual reproductive organs could they attain the love and acceptance of another person. But in this unconscious belief was also a trap, because when they got in touch with any kind of need, sexual or otherwise, the urgency to get rid of that part was acted on again. Eventually the couple managed to return to a life together but without much sex. Only in this way could they stay together and guard against the violence and frustration that internal identification with a persecutory object provoked in them.

There is a need to broaden our understanding of the concrete act of abortion, interpret the various symbolic equations that refer to it, and understand the multiple meanings and consequences it has for individuals, couples and families. The only way we can offer help to these couples is by slowly helping them re-introject these rejected and aborted parts of themselves that have been projected outside. We do so by closely following our own countertransference feeling that is inevitably stirred up by exposing ourselves to the violence of their shared inner life.

References

Freud, S. (1917). *Mourning and Melancholia. S. E., 14*: 237–258. London: Hogarth.
Freud, S. (1920). The psychogenesis of a case of homosexuality in a woman. *S. E., 18*: 145–172.
Scharff, D. (1998). *The Sexual Relationship. The International Library of Group and Group Process*. London: Routledge.
Segal, H. (1957). Notes on symbol formation. *International Journal of Psycho-Analysis, 38*: 391–397.

CHAPTER TWENTY-THREE

Working with affairs

David E. Scharff

A common precipitating event that brings couples to our attention is an extra-marital affair, from impulsive one-time flings in an otherwise faithful marriage, to long-term arrangements that go on for years. In some cases one affair or many affairs co-exist throughout a long-term marriage.

The morality of affairs has been debated for many years and in many different cultures. Some cultures implicitly support a man's right to have affairs, or even several wives, while others have a moral stance against infidelity. Since this book's focus is on therapy, I take the view that from the standpoint of the clinician, an affair is a symptom of marital breakdown. It signals that the strain that led to breakdown has not stayed within the bounds of the marriage. Our job is to understand the meaning of the affair, the marital weaknesses it points to, and whether there is a likelihood of being able to help repair the marriage. We also do well to think of the impact and meaning of affairs on the whole family.

As therapists with a couple state of mind ourselves, we try to understand events presented to us from the standpoint of the couple, even though we include individual meanings as well. Frequently one partner will come in blaming the other in a moralistic state of mind. Then we want to understand what leads that partner to be so caught up in blaming her spouse. We try to make all roads lead to an understanding of the couple itself, because that is the overarching organisation that guides us.

We also see marriages that have come about because of affairs. Second marriages commonly arise after the partners had an affair while married to others, and many of these couples later get into trouble themselves. Frequently, the guilt one or both has about the way their marriage began, the animosity of the children of the first marriages, or the difficulty with attachment that led to the original meeting, may haunt this second or third marriage.

Types of affairs

There is an infinite variety in types of affair. For example, the man who goes for regular genital massage from the beginning of his young marriage; the woman who had liaisons while travelling for business but was faithful at home; the woman who had an affair with her husband's best friend; the man who then had an affair in reaction to the spouse's affair; the affair by a woman whose husband became senile. There is an infinite variety in the meaning and consequences of an affair from the one-time opportunistic sexual liaison to the affair of many years duration. In a marriage that is already moribund, an affair may signal its death. It is not always best for a couple to stay together, so the question of whether the couple, or each partner, wants to stay married is important. In each case, it is learning the unconscious meaning of the affair that offers the crucial help to couples, regardless of outcome for the marriage itself.

When we begin to assess the meaning of an affair, we need to understand the context in which it has occurred. Does either the culture or the "contract" between the couple sanction affairs? Some cultures, such as the Latin or French cultures, seem to sanction affairs. Or it may be, as in the United States in the 1970s and 1980s, that the marital agreement included permission for an open or "swinging" marriage. These permissive attitudes do not, however, safeguard a particular couple from the hurt of these arrangements. Even permissive cultures or contracts are only factors. In our culture, with its agreement about monogamy and marital commitment, open marriages increase vulnerability to breakdown, loaded already with the introduction of third party allegiances. This vulnerability is further tested whenever the marriage or partnership comes under strain from life developments, or from vulnerable individual character structure.

Psychodynamically, affairs represent a splitting of issues in the interactions between the couple and the partners to include a third participant. Internally, affairs actualise splits in internal object relations in each of the spouses and in their shared unconscious organisation or link. What had been lived out unconsciously between them is now lived out with a third participant who becomes an object, consciously or unconsciously, for both of them, and who receives their projections. Marital difficulty between them is now spread into a wider field. When that couple comes to therapy, our role offers an opportunity to be a very different kind of third that offers healing in the place of divisiveness.

The internal split the affair presents has poignancy because it concretises the psychological issues in psychosomatic intimacy. The body's role in intimacy resonates with the intimacy of mother–infant exchanges. Because of this resonance, bodily intimacy always has a special impact. (Scharff, 1982) When the affair is triggered by sexual failure, sexual intimacy may be vicariously expressed for both spouses.

A couple in their thirties had thought of themselves as good parents and friends, but sex had been on the back burner for years, from the birth of their second child, and had disappeared completely two years before they sought treatment. At first they had argued about the lack of sex, the wife complaining about the husband's loss of interest, but finally she tried to resign herself. When she began a series of work trips, intimacy with a colleague led to sex. Her husband, now shaken by the disruption of a marriage he had been satisfied with, begged for another chance, and felt the return of sexual desire for his wife. She gave up the affair in favour of re-establishing their marriage. The affair made him realise that he had ignored her needs and alienated her, and that he had done so because he felt inadequate in many ways and had been afraid she would reject him. His withdrawal had then precipitated the rejection that he feared.

Factors leading to affairs

Table 1

Conscious factors precipitating affairs

Marital decline, including growing resentment
Sexual inadequacy
Lack of intimacy
Lack of mutual understanding
Illness or disability
Opportunism
Cultural sanction

It is more useful to think of predisposing factors than of single causes for affairs. (Table 1). These reasons may be readily understandable when the couple presents, but it is likely that unconscious organisations either cause the affair or make it part of a larger picture. Some unconscious motives are shared by the couple, some are individual (Table 2).

Table 2

Unconscious factors in affairs

Injecting love into a loveless marriage
Getting the partner's attention
Inability to relate to whole object
Fear of engulfment and intimacy
Control of the object of desire
Splitting object of desire into exciting *vs.* dependent object parts (Madonna/Whore split)
Oedipal issues projected into the third person
Fear of physical sex (e.g., fear of penetration; location of bad object in sexual organs)
Fear of aging
Children's development challenging sexual adequacy and desirability
Fear of death
Issues of sexual identity

Some affairs are unconscious attempts to inject love into a loveless marriage, an unconscious motive that we might consider on the benign side (Dicks, 1967). In these cases, if the betrayed spouse also comes to see that the deficit between her and her husband essentially pushed him into the arms of another, and that he was also expressing her own longing for love through projective identification, there is hope for repair. In some cases, such realisation may come too late. Other unconscious motivations have to do with protecting the spouse, for instance the Madonna/Whore split in which a man feels that his sexual object is dirtied by his desire, so he exports the unconscious sense of damage onto a third person while keeping his wife unsullied.

Or a man's aging and that of his wife arouse fears of death, impelling him to seek a younger woman. In still other cases, one person's uncertain sexual identity leads to a heterosexual affair that might be an attempt to shore up an unsure heterosexual identity, or it might be a homosexual affair that expresses the internal split in identity. What matters are the specific and particular unconscious reasons in the couple before us, the balance between individual factors and shared unconscious issues. Some individual personality issues make fidelity unlikely or unvalued by a partner. In each case, the betrayed partner has to decide if she wants to live with the situation.

The role of secrets

Secrecy itself has a dynamic function. Sharing secrets develops intimacy. Children delight in secrecy to exclude others and build closeness. In marriage, partners share things that bring them closer and exclude those outside their relationship. Conversely, secrecy that excludes a marital partner supports a gap between them, whether it is a sexual secret or not. In this way, fantasy affairs or overly close work relationships may be as divisive as sexual ones.

> Throughout her marriage, Mrs Thomas nursed a fantasy of love for a high school teacher she felt would always have been her ideal mate, never sharing this fantasy with her husband. Then, in community theatre, she met a man who fit the same mould. In her unspoken fantasy love affair, he unconsciously represented the exciting but dangerous man of her dreams who would never look at her in real life. These secret fantasies formed a wall against a close relationship with her unexciting, reliable husband whom she had chosen precisely because he did not present the danger inherent in sexual excitement. She had been the apple of her father's eye, a man who had many affairs that denigrated her mother. In her fantasy affair, she triumphed over her defeated mother through being desirable. At the same time, by not living out an affair, she protected herself from the internally dangerous, sexual man. The secret distance from her husband had much the same effect as an actual affair.

Secrecy from a spouse divides the two of them, while secrecy with the other man or woman unites them. The dynamic life of secrets occurs on several levels developmentally: splitting in the paranoid/schizoid mode, manically uniting in the mode of a depressive position triumph over a feared object; attachment to the new object and a distancing attachment to the marital object; control of the object at what might be considered the anal level; and increasing intimacy at the oedipal level. All of these considerations need to be worked with in treating the secrecy in affairs.

Non-sexual, emotional affairs

Affairs that are intensely emotional but unconsummated may have much the same effect as affairs that are lived out, because of the degree of preoccupation and the distancing that leads to and results from them. It is not actual sexual infidelity but the emotional gap in the couple relationship accompanied by an emotional investment in another person that needs to be confronted. Sometimes the work is easier because an affair has not been concretised with physical sexuality, but other platonic affairs represent an emotional gulf that is just as difficult to bridge.

Internet affairs and secret use of pornography

Since the development of the internet, secretive use of pornography and internet affairs have become frequent reasons for referral. The two patterns are different, but often intertwined. A man or woman using the internet for sexual interest may be spending time on internet sites and finding heterosexual or homosexual internet partners for emotional exchange and/or for internet sex. Frequently these affairs are discovered because the partner sees clues left on the computer, but excessive time away, secretive behaviour and a growing distance from the spouse are much the same. The investigation of this area involves the questions and techniques we are discussing throughout this chapter, but if a more addictive, attitude emerges, that has to be confronted before dynamic exploration becomes possible.

Unconscious collusion

There is always the question of how much the betrayed partner supports the affair, either directly or unconsciously. A spouse uninterested in sex, for instance, may openly authorise her husband to seek sex elsewhere. Frequently, a spouse who keeps emotional distance will unconsciously support affairs, either by sending non-verbal signals or by standing by while knowing about them unconsciously. Diagnostically, we want to assess the degree to which the infidelity has been known but not acknowledged, and the degree to which it stems from other things known but unaddressed.

> Mr and Mrs Brown, married thirty years, came with a history of marital and sexual unhappiness. Mrs Brown said she had known almost from the outset that her husband had multiple affairs. He said her sexual inadequacy forced him into them. She felt he always blamed her. Her resentment, a chip-on-her-shoulder attitude, was evident in every session and included an edge of resentment to me because she felt I took his side, although I actually felt that his behaviour was abusive, and I worried about her continuing to suffer it. His condescension towards her and me was equally evident. He said he would stop the affairs and try to reconstitute the marriage, but when she found that he had again betrayed her during a trip, she told him not to return home. He agreed the marriage was over. Now she panicked, begging him to return, becoming so depressed she had to be hospitalised. In individual therapy after the hospitalisation, Mrs Brown gradually came to terms with her collusion based on her fear that no one would love her. Therefore she was powerless to confront her husband for humiliating her throughout the marriage. The sources went back to rejection by her father that was never validated by her mother, and a well of feeling unlovable. I surmised that Mr Brown had stayed in a marriage of such mutual resentment and mistrust because he was narcissistically wounded by his own parents, and had identified deeply with his father who had numerous affairs, thereby denigrating his mother. To my mind, divorce in this case represented a good outcome, for the marriage was deeply unsatisfying to both parties. In individual treatment,

Mrs Brown's resentment entered the transference when she felt that I, like her mother, failed to confirm her humiliation. Working in the transference we confronted the life-long feeling of being unlovable that made her hostage to her husband.

Developmental causes of affairs

Assessing affairs is a matter of uncovering meanings in all possible dimensions.

Individual developmental causes

Developmental causes run the gamut from psychopathy in the erring partner to individual splitting of good objects from bad in which the exciting object has to be protected from the bad and rejecting object by being projected into two entirely different people. When the good, clean object has to be a different person from the exciting, dirty one as in the "Madonna/Whore split," a wife idealised as a saint needs to be protected from the fantasy of damage that sex unconsciously brings. Some patients carry a fear that attachment brings engulfment. For others, strains in sexual identity propel them into heterosexual affairs to shore up shaky sexual identity, or into same-sex affairs that express ambivalence about their sexuality.

Mr Levine felt his wife's relationship with her woman friend was squeezing their marriage. Her interest in her friend had the hallmarks of an affair, which she denied. After some weeks of evaluation, Mrs Levine said she was ending the marriage. She proceeded to construct a lesbian partnership. She had been ambivalent about the marriage and sexual object choice for years, and now moved to consolidate a homosexual identity.

Individuals who previously suppressed homosexual or bisexual inclinations in heterosexual marriages no longer feel the need to do so. We may see these affairs as the emergence of suppressed identifications, but on the other hand, some of these affairs represent strain in marriages expressed in this way. For many of these latter marriages, therapy to repair the marriage is enough for this alternate identity to fade.

Marital strain

Severe marital strain may precipitate extra-marital liaisons or affairs. Frequent travel, overwork, sexual difficulty, or accumulating chronic anger all pose different risk factors from those stemming from individual developmental vulnerability. There are also issues in adult and marital life that increase risk, such as the birth of a child that unconsciously threatens a parent, whether a boy or a girl, or a child's specific stage of development. For one couple, having a normal but oedipally sexualised child will feel like an attack on the same-sex parent, while for another couple the developmental sexualisation of a teenager threatens. Losses of virility or femininity inherent in aging, menopause, the death of a parent, or decline in career threatens others. Long-standing sexual difficulty or inactivity pose risks. These surface factors then trigger unconscious issues.

Affairs in homosexual marriages and partnerships

I have had only a few cases of homosexual partnerships in treatment over the years, presumably because I am identified as a straight therapist. There has been a perception that many homosexual patients have less secure attachments with fleeting sexual connections. That may hold for a subset of individual homosexual patients but for those who are in a gay or lesbian couple, we find the same sense of loyalty, the same feeling of disaster on break up, the same need to mourn lost committed relationships. If a member of a gay or lesbian couple has a heterosexual affair, there is a feeling of betrayal similar to the feeling when a member of a heterosexual couple has a homosexual affair. The same principles apply for gay and lesbian couples as for heterosexual couples.

The effect of affairs on the family

Often we see individual or couple patients, or children, whose parents have had affairs. Almost invariably, the children are deeply injured. They identify with the hurt of the betrayed parent or feel betrayed themselves. Or they may unconsciously identify with the parent having the affair, feeling that it was justified because of anger or misbehaviour in the marriage.

> A woman's father had many affairs throughout the parents' marriage, including one that was still going on. Her devastated mother had stood waiting with the children outside the woman's apartment building. The mother wailed at her plight, oblivious to the children. This picture became part of my patient's adult suicidal depression. She married a completely faithful man, but the family denigrated him as not successful or attractive. Meanwhile, her brothers had flagrant affairs in identification with the father, and her sister-in-laws complained to my patient in much the same way as her mother continued to do.

The other man or woman

This summary cannot be complete without considering the affair's other man or woman. From the standpoint of the marriage, we see this person as the recipient of projections, a repository of split-off unconscious issues of the marriage. But as individual therapists, we see "other women" as patients. Many are drawn to unavailable partners for unconscious reasons that come from all developmental levels—issues of insecurity, needing to avoid feeling trapped or engulfed in a fully available relationship, and oedipal attraction to a parental object. Some of these relationships eventuate in marriages, many of which are successful, so we cannot say that all the relationships in which such a person engages are pathological or faulty. But for many, the relationships result in a developmental dead end for which they seek our help. While this perspective is not our principal focus in this chapter, it is one to keep in mind (Tuch, 2002). There is another point that brings us back to the couples with affairs: As we help them toward an empathic yet dispassionate stance in relation to the third party, we also help them develop a capacity for concern and reparation towards each other.

Assessment and treatment of affairs

Table 3

Areas to assess concerning affairs

Overall state of the marriage
Degree of trust, love, and commitment to a future together
Marital strains, degree of anger and resentment
Financial strains
Interest in a future together
Developmental issues of each partner
Developmental issues in history of the marriage
Secrecy and sharing
Sexual history
Unconscious fit
Quality of couple state of mind
Precipitants of affair
Sexual quality of the affair
Interest in continuing affair(s)
Willingness to re-commit, even with existing doubts

When we evaluate marriages with an affair, we need to look more at the meaning of the affair itself (Table 3). We explore the strength of the marriage, the degree of love and desire for the marriage that still exists, and the hurt that either led to the affair or that resulted from it. We explore the strengths of the marriage and the family as a whole, the meaning of the affair, and fault lines that existed before the affair. We ask about the strains over the years and immediately preceding the affair. We explore the role of the secrecy, but also the degree of trust and mistrust that surrounded it and that characterise their relationship now. Early on, we address the hurt in the betrayed spouse, because without recognising that, nothing else is possible. This includes the hurt of being denied information from the secrecy.

Revelation of secrets

At times in evaluating a marriage, say for sexual difficulty, we discover unrevealed affairs in individual interviews. My policy in these cases is to have a careful individual discussion with the one having the affair about revealing it. An affair usually poses a crisis that threatens the destruction of the marriage. We hope to turn the crisis into one with positive possibilities. If the betraying husband tells his wife, she may decide to leave now that she has full information. If he does not, they will be attempting to reconstruct their flawed marriage on a flawed foundation. While the decision whether to reveal has to remain with the individual, it may not be possible to offer effective treatment without revelation. On the other hand, revelation may make the facts of her situation clear to the spouse who has been in the dark, and may catalyse treatment. In any event, I do not think it is possible to work effectively in marital therapy while there is an ongoing affair. If one partner refuses to end an affair, I would generally withdraw from that treatment. Revelation of the full facts is the best basis for work with trust, and more often than not, it sets a firmer floor on which to begin to rebuild (D. Scharff & J. Scharff, 1991).

Once we have looked into hurt intrinsic to the affair, I try to move to dealing with the strain leading to it, including the role of secrets. Rebuilding of trust by exploring issues that have sapped it always takes time. Such work increases the strain of the moment as painful issues resurface. The therapist's capacity for holding can be severely tried while helping the couple build stronger holding for themselves.

The role of transference

As in all couple therapy, transference to the therapist is an important factor. The therapist takes on projections similar to ones previously put onto the third person in the affair. This offers a principal opportunity for the couple to relive issues that had previously been exported into the affair. Anger at the therapist for seeming to take sides, feelings of being misunderstood or not being cared for, or feeling hurt by the therapist all come into this category. (See the case of Mrs Brown above.) The therapist's countertransference offers further first-hand information about the couple's unconscious life. Work with these transference and countertransference issues is the everyday work of the marital therapist.

The course of treatment

Once we have begun work on the issues I have been discussing, treatment moves to become like any other—which is to say it is unique for each couple in ways we are used to. I think of myself as a marital therapist, not a divorce therapist. Most couples that come to me with affairs have been able to reconstruct a better marriage. Nevertheless, some marriages are best ended, as with two examples above. While we must be open to that outcome, we usually find that in most marital therapy the healing forces intrinsic to marriage will help couples overcome their difficulties.

I close with an example of analytic work with a couple, in which both partners had affairs, but who were eventually able to reconstruct their marriage.

Shared fear of intimacy after infidelity

Robert and Diane, in their mid-forties, were referred to me on the brink of divorce. (D. Scharff & J. Scharff, 2011) Robert travelled constantly with a multinational corporation, while Diane cared for their children at home. Diane broke off their college romance, met another man, got engaged, and became pregnant by him. When she realised that she did not respect her fiancé, she terminated the engagement and the pregnancy. She returned to Robert who still adored her. They soon married, but he remained hurt over the earlier break up and her pregnancy with another man. Their sex was always more perfunctory than passionate. Diane seemed physically and emotionally uninvolved, and Robert had periodic difficulty with his erection. She doubted Robert's love; he doubted her love and his potency. Nevertheless they wanted to renew the marriage.

In individual meetings, each told me about undisclosed affairs. Early in the marriage, Diane had had an affair in which she enjoyed sex more than with Robert. Two years ago she had another affair in which she enjoyed terrific sex including her first orgasm in intercourse. Robert had used prostitutes on frequent business trips. Six months before the consultation, he had a brief passionate affair with a friend of Diane's, feeling loved as never before. Robert and Diane warily revealed their affairs to each other, and began to explore their meaning, realising that emptiness in their marriage was connected to the fullness in the affairs. Each felt more sinned against than sinning. Expressing hurt and outrage, they then opened up to each other emotionally and sexually with newfound passion, until, as usually happens, passion gradually faded in the ordinary light of day. The couple continued slowly to rebuild their relationship in couple therapy.

A month later, Robert reported a dream. "I'm in a restaurant with Diane and her ex-fiancé. Diane ate part of my roast beef sandwich, and he started to eat it, too. Our housekeeper, who brought the sandwich, was there but with horrible black spots on her face. We wound up in my old Mercedes, the ex-fiancé driving and Diane rubbing his arm. I threw punches at him from the back seat, but I couldn't hit him hard. I also hit out at Diane but without power. He said, 'Hit me if you can. Perhaps I deserve it, but you're not strong enough to hurt me.' I felt that it was really my penis that didn't have enough power."

Robert said that when Diane had angrily threatened divorce the previous week, he remembered how devastated he was when she had left him thirty years earlier for that fiancé. He remembered how humiliated he felt during a time of extended impotence when she had no sympathy. Associating to the spots on the housekeeper's face, he said that the marriage seemed poisoned. Associating to Diane and the fiancé sharing his sandwich, he remembered how he had cringed last week when she yelled at him that he could eat his lover's vagina if that was what he wanted.

Diane associated to the restaurant as the place where she saw Robert's lover occasionally. The spots on the housekeeper's face made her think that Robert thought she, Diane, was ugly.

Robert had two more brief dreams:

"A big guy wanted to beat me up. I told another man I would give him $2,500 to defend me, and he did." And, "I was at a motel where people go with lovers. I was in the bathroom there with Diane and an Indian man. We were naked, measuring our penises. I had a strong erection. His was stronger with a better angle." He associated to a woman who had an affair with an Indian man. Afterwards her husband forgave her. Perhaps he could forgive Diane, too.

The dreams reminded Diane that Robert had told her that his lover had once caressed his penis as they drove to a motel. Perhaps he wondered if she, Diane, had done this to another man. She thought Robert, being the youngest in his family, felt inferior to other men, and so had to make his affair less bad than hers. Robert thought that Diane's affair was worse because she is a woman. She said that he could not forgive her for being with a sexually effective man because it meant accepting his weakness and inferiority.

Robert began to cry, "We had so much to look forward to. We both did something terrible. I've failed in the most important task in my life." I said, "I noticed today, that you, Diane, were initially fairly silent, leaving Robert exposed while you hid behind him. Then you stressed his weakness and humiliation—which you may also feel." Robert said, "I feel humiliated and angry." "What occurs to you about paying someone $2,500 to defend you?" I asked. Diane said, "$2,500 is a lot to pay for defence." Robert said, "It's to buy my way out of inadequacy. I paid prostitutes to make me feel better."

"How do you feel about paying me to defend your marriage?" I said. In response Robert said, "I want my marriage to work. So, I buy your help. You protect us from having more affairs." Diane then said to Robert, "Or maybe he'd protect you from disclosing an affair if you went back to that woman."

I said, "You each disclosed affairs with my encouragement. You felt threatened and beaten, yet also protected and helped. Is there a fantasy I penetrate the depths of your marriage at a more effective angle than you can do yourselves? Do I humiliate you?"

Robert replied, "You made me reveal the affair when I didn't want to, but you did it to turn our relationship onto a positive track, instead of a race about who could humiliate the other more."

I said, "Diane, you felt I beat you up too?"

Diane said, "I feel both, you beat me up but also that you're helping me."

Diane's dream

Two weeks later, Diane reported a dream that began in a swimming pool—a link to the pool near my office as well as to a previous discussion of being in a pool.

"I was swimming with other people in a gorgeous pool below a waterfall, wearing a white bikini that looked great. It was time to go home. A guy got out of the water with me. As we walked up a hill, over some rough spots, he placed his hand on my shoulder. I said he was abusing me, and he reacted like, 'You're a stupid woman to think I did something wrong!' We got in the car. Another guy sat next to me. It was crowded, and his legs touching mine felt awful. Now the white bikini seemed more like underwear. I felt naked, exposed, but not vulgar. I had to tip the driver, so I looked for a dollar bill. In my purse, there was money from all over the world in various denominations of 500, 800, 1,000, but no dollars. I said, 'These other currencies are worthless.' I didn't feel good. These men were taking advantage of me."

Diane said that she felt uncomfortable wearing clothes like underwear in the company of these men, reminding her of the discomfort of her affairs. The money reminded her of her husband's use of prostitutes all over the world. Robert countered that the dream suggested she felt like a prostitute.

"I hate to think I feel like a prostitute," Diane said. "I never had sex for money. I looked better in the dream than I feel, but I felt vulnerable."

I said Diane felt undressed by therapy. She agreed. I asked about the threatening man who put his hand on her shoulder. She remembered a time when a man had called her repeatedly, and then denied sexual intentions. She said, "There's a sense of fear as I walked to the car, fear about the way the floor has fallen out from under my life."

Robert said, "The two guys stand for her two affairs. The money is cheap currency."

Diane said, "I feel cheap. I wound up acting like a prostitute. I'm so sorry."

Robert added in an unempathic, self-serving way, "I feel like a good part of me has gone out of the window. I was bad to her by having my own affair, but I spent twenty-five years being good, begging her for love. Look what my love got me!"

I said, "The sexual woman alive in the affairs and in the pool feels uncomfortable in underwear with the men in the dream just as Diane feels reluctant to bare herself at home with Robert and to expose her feelings in therapy." (I also had the thought that, unlike a prostitute who takes money from a man for sex, Diane takes money from Robert while not having sex.) I asked, "What might it mean that you were searching for a dollar bill for the driver?"

Diane said, "The car is therapy, which feels too close for comfort. You touch me uncomfortably when you remind me of unpleasant things. In the dream, I couldn't pay the driver. If we couldn't pay you, we couldn't see you. You only see us for money."

I began to see that I was also the prostitute, working intimately only for money. In this way I was linked to their degradation. I said, "Robert, you feel inappropriate when you approach Diane, and Diane, you feel accosted by Robert's sexual advances. Perhaps you feel that about my comments. Do you think using money to 'tip' me demeans me like you demean each other to lessen the pain of needing my help, just as you try to lessen the pain of needing each other?"

Diane said, "Robert can't reach out to me, he's so busy flying around the world, making money that won't buy what we need most. That's why we need you. Partly I don't like needing your help, but I also do feel good about coming here."

In this session, the couple worked analytically to explore the stresses that had led to the affairs, the individual issues that made them vulnerable, their unconscious dynamics, and the way the transference to me recreated feelings that had been part of the affairs. These matters stemmed both from their own individual histories and from strains in their marriage. The secrecy about affairs became part of the problem that they now dealt with as they explored their unconscious worlds, thereby reconstructing in the transference—and in my countertransference reception of their shared situation—the unconscious origins and meanings of the affairs. In working through these matters over and over again, we work to integrate all these forces towards reconstructing trust and building new marital bonds. Eventually, this couple achieved repair and have continued to have a better sexual life and mutually satisfying marriage.

Affairs constitute an important presenting problem for any couple therapist. When they do, our work to understand their role in marital dysfunction is intrinsic to everything else we do. Affairs do not represent a single symptom, but a complex condensation of forces from individual, couple, and social dynamics that require all our skills to decode and work with.

References and further reading

Dicks, H. V. (1967). *Marital Tensions*. London: Routledge and Kegan Paul.
Fisher, H. (1992). Why Adultery? In: *Anatomy of Love: The Natural History of Monogamy, Adultery and Divorce* (pp. 75–97). New York: Norton.
Levine, S. (2010). Infidelity. In: S. Levine., C. Risen., & S. Althof (Ed.), *Handbook of Clinical Sexuality for Mental Health Professionals* (pp. 57–74). New York: Routledge.
Scharff, D. E. (1982). *The Sexual Relationship: An Object Relations View of Sex and the Family*. London: Routledge. Reissued in paperback with new introduction, 1998. Lanham, MD: Jason Aronson.
Scharff, D. E. & Scharff, J. S. (1991). *Object Relations Couple Therapy*. Northvale, NJ: Jason Aronson.
Scharff, D. E. & Scharff, J. S. (2011). *The Interpersonal Unconscious*. Lanham MD: Jason Aronson.
Tuch, R. (2002). *The Single Woman-Married Man Syndrome*. Northvale, NJ: Jason Aronson.

PART IV

SPECIAL TOPICS

CHAPTER TWENTY-FOUR

The couple as parents: the role of children in couple treatment

Janine Wanlass

The parenting dimensions of the couple relationship enter treatment through different avenues. In my role as a child therapist, I routinely receive calls from distressed parents requesting help for their child. In these instances, the child holds the position of identified patient, and my work with the parents begins in this context. For example, a parent may call about a pre-school child's paralysing separation anxiety, a year five's oppositional attitude toward homework, or the discovery of an adolescent daughter's self-mutilation. The parent views the primary focus of treatment as the child, with couple and parenting issues placed in the distant background. Alternately, I may receive a referral for couple treatment, where parenting issues appear in the couple's initial list of difficulties or slip into the treatment through a side door. For instance, the wife may complain that the husband is preoccupied with work, leaving her as the sole functioning parent and ignoring the needs of his children. In these instances, the couple relationship is the primary focus of treatment, and parenting is discussed as a problematic aspect of that relationship. Although these different entry points to treatment convey important aspects of the couple and family dynamics, each brings the issue of parenting to the centre of treatment. In this chapter, I will discuss the differences between parent work and couple treatment, common issues and mechanisms for change that occur in the parenting aspect of couple therapy, two clinical illustrations of these concepts, and challenges for the therapist in this arena of couple work.

Parent work vs. couple work

I began treating couples somewhat reluctantly, believing I needed training and experience in couple work to benefit my child patients. Like most child therapists, I quickly surmised that the potential progress of my child patients was either helped or hindered by the actions and mindset of their parents. Additionally, the easiest way to lose a child patient is to forget that parents are part of the mix. Unless their needs are met and a therapeutic relationship forged, the child's stay in treatment may be short-lived and any therapeutic gain sabotaged.

Rustin (1998) contends that child therapists are ideally suited to work with parents, because we understand the regressed aspects of the parent personalities. We easily view parents as the adults they are now and the little children they must have been. She states, "Our attunement to the infantile in our patients allows us access to the disturbance in adult and parental functioning that needs to be addressed," (Rustin, 1998, p. 244). Child therapists are accustomed to therapeutic multi-tasking during sessions, playing the role of the witch in a puppet drama while monitoring one's countertransference and formulating the next interpretation. This translates well to the complexity of couple and family work, where the therapist simultaneously considers the multiple roles (e.g., father, husband, man, child), developmental levels, interrelationships, and dynamic conflicts of the participants. Additionally, child therapists routinely observe the concrete projection and representation of self in an "other", dramatically conveyed in child play where animals, dolls, and mythical creatures become the voice for the child's internal conflicts. Perhaps this facilitates an attunement toward the ways each member of a couple displaces unwanted aspects of the self in a partner or child. Furthermore, child therapists engage in many parental functions, providing containment for overwhelming primitive affect, facilitating the development of a thinking capacity, surviving attacks of aggression, and working through trauma. Every parent and every child therapist has felt like the ragged, old blanket the toddler drags around—loved, hated, and used in whatever capacity needed.

As child therapists, we routinely deal with parenting issues. But what are the similarities and differences between what might be considered parent work and couple treatment? How does a parent consultation session differ from a couple psychotherapy session? Both Rustin (1998) and Ludlam (2006) suggest aspects of parent work that overlap with common goals of couple treatment. Rustin (1998) contends that parent work facilitates improved parental functioning during times of developmental crisis, may address individual problems of a parent, and should shift overall family functioning in a healthy direction. Couple work may accomplish these same treatment goals, as creating a positive shift in couple relating changes the family dynamics. Ludlam (2006) suggests that both parent and couple work explore what the child represents for the couple and highlight the couples' childhood experiences, including the parenting practices, conflict resolution strategies, and marital relationship of the couple's parents.

Despite these similarities, parent work and couple work do differ. In the former, the child retains the focal point of both interpretations and guidance. The therapist keeps the child in mind and relates to the parental couple rather than the marital dyad. Aspects of the couple relationship other than parenting such as sexual functioning, shared unconscious phantasies, individual and shared styles of responding to couple conflict, and projective identifications within the couple system usually receive little or no focus. Couple treatment contains all these elements, with child and parenting issues typically considered as extensions of couple relating. Thus, the individual needs of a child or the specifics of a child-parent interaction may receive less attention in couple work than they might in parent work. While these distinctions in emphasis and scope do matter, both approaches can benefit the child and the couple. In each approach, the therapist often feels like the child, a third excluded from the couple dyad and intruding on a history that started before her arrival.

Parents in couple treatment

How do parenting issues and concerns about the couple's children appear in couple treatment? In this chapter, I will discuss two cases where parenting becomes a focal point of the couple work. In each case, the child carries the couple conflict and disowned or desired aspects of the parent. For instance, a father's own neediness is denied, projected, and harshly reprimanded in his son. Secondly, the child-parent relationship provides a venue for the intergenerational transmission of unresolved trauma (Faimberg, 1986; Fraiberg, Adelson, & Shapiro, 2003), both as direct repetition and as potential for repair. For example, Andre Green's (1986) concept of the dead mother moves eerily from one generation to the next, without parental awareness and leaving the child with a frozen sense of longing that directly replicates his mother's childhood. Thirdly, each child serves as a developmental reminder, pulling their parents into their own childhoods with emotional potency and force. These children surface issues of oedipal competition, highlight fractures in the couple relationship, become objects for deposit and evacuation of couple affect, create potential for multiple identifications in both couple and therapist, and carry the couple's secrets. They provide a lens and means for couples to see and work through existing issues. Additionally, in responding to their children, the couple find themselves in a parent role, illuminating identifications with their own parents. Thus, the children provide motivation and a potential space for the couple to work through prior points of couple impasse.

Clinical vignette one: Jack and Sally

Jack and Sally re-entered couple treatment three months ago, following Jack's relapse into alcoholism. Sally called to make the appointment, asking if I still treated couples and had available space. Five years previously, they ended couple treatment abruptly after I insisted that Jack needed more intensive treatment for his alcohol abuse. Although he begrudgingly complied with my recommendation, he did not return to treatment once his inpatient stay ended. He quit drinking for five years, but his own individual issues and the couple difficulties remained. At our first meeting after re-entry, Sally voiced her concern about Jack's drinking, his lying, their struggles with intimacy, and her sense that some core part of Jack remained unreachable and unknown. Jack worried that Sally would give up on him, expressed frustration with his addiction, and commented on his struggles parenting their children (eleven-year-old Elizabeth, seven-year-old Sam, and four-year-old Kevin). He thought Sally gave low priority to him and their marital relationship, focusing much of her attention on the children. Both identified trust and communication as significant problems in their relationship.

Jack is a forty-three-year-old, highly successful president of a technology company. He grew up as the second child and only son in a sibling set of four. His mother was always "sick," making her unavailable to the children. He describes her as absent, passive, and vacant. His father was a driven man, a career focused functioning alcoholic. He held high expectations for his children, particularly Jack, who always felt like a disappointment. Jack's father was emotionally detached much of the time, but he would erupt into rages over small infractions by his children. Although his drinking affected the family, it was never discussed. Between the ages of four and seven, Jack was diagnosed with leukemia, necessitating extended hospital stays where he recalls being left alone. In retrospect, he believes his parents were overwhelmed by the potential loss, but at the time felt only abandonment. Outwardly compliant, Jack rebelled during adolescence, sneaking alcohol and cigarettes. Jack met Sally in senior year of high school, and the couple married when he turned twenty-two. His parents intensely disliked Sally, blaming her for Jack's limited investment in the family. Jack is a charming, funny, intelligent man, but all interpersonal interactions remain on the surface. He has few real friends and is very isolated.

Sally is a forty-one-year-old graphic artist, who spends most of her time at home with her children. In her family of origin, Sally is the third of five children. From ages six to eight, a gymnastics coach and close family friend sexually molested her. After the molestation was exposed, the convicted coach committed suicide. Sally's parents were supportive, but her needs got lost when her father suffered a business reversal and her older teenage brothers began acting out. Her mother became entirely focused on the boys, and the overly compliant Sally was forgotten. Sally has limited contact with her brothers, but she describes feeling emotionally connected to her two younger sisters. Her husband Jack is the favoured in-law, a fact she reports laughingly but with an edge of envy. Sally's children and role her as a mother are important to her. Although she always wanted children, she was fearful of bringing them into a world where bad things might happen.

As a couple, Jack and Sally seem an odd fit. He comes to the session dressed to perfection in expensive suits. Sally appears neat, casual, and understated in her attire, rarely wearing anything flashy. Her outward calm hides a struggle with panic attacks, which sometimes erupt during the sessions. Jack is loquacious, indirect, entertaining, and charmingly narcissistic. If allowed, he takes up most of the session time. He has this habit of repeating phrases rather dramatically, but his words convey an inner emptiness. Sally communicates in clear, direct words, speaking sparingly yet effectively. Jack adopts a victim stance within the couple, blaming everyone else for his drinking. Sally displays greater capacity to think about them as a couple, considering the interplay of their shared vulnerabilities. As I listen and interact, they seem more like a mother-son dyad than a married couple.

Their children, Elizabeth, Sam, and Kevin, are frequent topics in the couple sessions. Although he expresses love for the children, Jack is an absent father, leaving the discipline and childcare to Sally. He appears surprised when the children do not follow orders, as though expecting his presidential work role to carry over at home. He struggles to set any limit with the children, fearing their hate and rejection. When he eventually asserts his parental authority, he does so in an angry, coercive manner. In essence, he becomes the angry father he hated and the absent, detached mother he despised. His relationship with Sam, who replicates Jack's position in his family of origin, is particularly strained. Sally tends to fill the void of Jack's parenting, much like her mother did with her father. She agrees that the marital relationship gets dropped in her prioritising of her children. Sally expresses upset about the way Jack lies to the children about his drinking, resenting her collusion in a family secret, known but not discussed. Although the two support each other in parenting interventions, they do not appear united as a parental couple.

So what of the couple's individual and joint struggles are located in the children and the couple's parenting functions? For Jack and Sally, the children represent both the repetition of their childhood issues and the chance for repair. Sally becomes the overinvested, controlling mother of her childhood, sacrificing her marital relationship for her mothering function. Jack is the absent, "dead" mother of his childhood, alternating with the raging father he feared. Jack engages in secretive behaviour covered by lies, a replication of his father's family secret. He displays both a concordant and a complementary identification (Racker, 1957) with Sam, aligning with the defiant bad boy and the disapproving father. He both envies and hates Sam's open defiance, a son who is able to stand up to his father in a way Jack cannot. Kevin is viewed as the "happy-go-lucky" child, overtly entertaining and pleasant. He holds the intergenerational family cover-up, the pretense that everything is fine. Elizabeth carries the over-functioning qualities of her mother, viewed as the strong child less affected by family difficulties. Elizabeth and Sam mirror their parental couple, where Jack is viewed as damaged and Sally as resilient. Sally puts the victimised, damaged parts of herself into Jack, who carries the neediness and vulnerability. She notes that part of him is inaccessible, much like the victim parts of herself, partially worked through but managed through a kind of omnipotence.

Through examining their parenting functions, the couple identifies ways they assume roles once held by their parents. Jack is chagrined by his harsh words toward Sam. "I never wanted to be like my dad, and I am." They have considerable difficulty, however, observing how they use their children to carry less obvious intergenerational issues or to be repositories for the unwanted aspects of themselves. At this early stage of the work, these identifications remain unconscious along with Jack's jealousy and oedipal competition with Sam for Sally's affections. Jack seems to resent his children for forcing him to grow up. He makes a slip saying, "Sally is always off with the other kids," unconsciously conveying his regressed state and the sense of abandonment he felt during his childhood leukemia. Sally struggles to see her need to remain the idealised, long-suffering parent, represented in the way she gets the children to express her frustration and resentment toward Jack. They make comments about how "Daddy doesn't care" or mock his attempts to set limits. Kevin noted, "Mommy, Daddy is starting to be all strict and bossing us around. Doesn't he know that's your job? He can't do it."

As treatment progresses, it is the children who provide the means and motivation for change. Sally's unexpressed rage and hurt emerge when Jack's near-fatal traffic accident illuminates her failure to protect her children from loss, placing them in danger just as her parents did with her. When Sam voices hatred toward Jack, Jack's wish to hurt Sam floods him with his own bad objects. For the first time, Jack decides he needs to stop drinking. When I suggest that the couple's intense conflict over Sam may be connected to their own traumas at Sam's age, the couple begins to grieve their shared experiences of absent, ineffective parents. We begin to understand the unconscious fit that drew this outwardly mismatched couple together. Although the children never present for treatment, their "presence" in the sessions becomes a vehicle for their parents to change.

Clinical vignette two: Kate and Travis

Kate and Travis entered my consulting room as the parents of seven-year-old Henry, an anxious, fearful boy with emotional regulation difficulties. Following a family vacation where Henry's explosive behaviour "ruined the trip," Kate called requesting treatment for her son. As is typical in my assessment of children, I met with Henry's parents to gather a developmental history, understand their view of the problem, and form the beginning of a working relationship. While the parents were cooperative, responsive, and articulate, something felt amiss. Guarded and cautious, their answers to basic developmental questions were overly contained. Travis knew very little of his son's developmental history, as if he had been away during Henry's early years. United in their experience of him as a persecutory object, Henry's parents seemed unaware of Henry's terrifying fears, something I sensed in my countertransference.

What Henry held and represented for his parents became clearer when I asked a routine question about his conception. The room became oppressively silent, and I felt as though I could not breathe. I had the impression I had made an unforgiveable social blunder, so I commented on the discomfort in the room. Travis and Kate looked at each other for a few minutes. Finally, Travis commented, "I just don't see why it's necessary for you to know that kind of information." Eventually, Travis and Kate began to tell me of their affair, made public by Kate's unwanted pregnancy with Henry. Uncertain whether they would stay together, Kate clung to baby Henry for emotional comfort, while Travis avoided contact. During this discussion, I sensed this couple remained frozen in this stormy time period, unable to resolve feelings of guilt and loss to become a loving couple with a new blended family.

Henry existed as a constant reminder of his parents' mistakes and mess, portrayed concretely in his explosive outbursts at home and his alternately over-contained and chaotic play in my office. In his initial session, he drew a picture of a beautiful, pristine meadow. He handed the picture to me, but quickly grabbed it back, adding dark thunderclouds and lightning bolts. He spoke about how storms scatter things about, noting the way the fall wind tosses about families of leaves that want to stay together. Although consciously denied, he seemed worried about his family's fragility. Once Henry's individual sessions began, his parents nearly disappeared from treatment, repeatedly cancelling our scheduled parent consultation sessions. I felt as though I was given this child to "fix," yet I became convinced that any improvement in Henry would be temporary without some corresponding shift in his parents. When I encountered his siblings in the waiting room, I was overcome with profound grief, hopelessness, and desperation. I looked at Kate, who presented as a haunting replica of Andre Green's (1986) dead mother, intensely depressed and sleep walking through her life. Jolted out of my own dead sleep, I insisted on a parent session.

Arriving late, Kate and Travis spent the first twenty minutes complaining about Henry. I felt my irritation rise when they reported telling Henry's siblings that the family's summer trip would be cancelled as a result of Henry's problems. In that moment, I felt impatient as I struggled to understand Henry's parents, particularly Kate who seemed unmoved by her son's struggle. I was struck by their lack of empathy for Henry, whom I experienced as an anxious, engaging child, painfully suffering as he tried to hold his fragmented family together. The parents' view of Henry held an angry, judgmental quality, which I struggled to metabolise and suspected was a central feature of their couple relating. Trying to help the parents develop some reflective functioning, I described how I thought Henry experienced his world. Gradually, Kate began to soften, hearing a resonance in her own childhood where difficult things could not be voiced. Later, I would hear of her sister's debilitating car accident, Kate's guilt, and a mother emotionally numbed and deadened by the trauma. As Kate spoke of her identification with Henry, Travis became overwhelmed with sadness. In this affectively charged moment, he began to realise the ways their couple issues were carried by Henry.

TRAVIS: I'm just so sad. What have we done to him? I've been blaming him all this time, frustrated with him for something I've helped to create. This is really a family problem isn't it? Our stuff is leaking onto the kids, Kate, it is.

KATE: Not that much.

TRAVIS: No, we have to face it. What's unresolved between us, that's part of what Henry's carrying, isn't it? We've left him to hold what belongs to us. That's part of why he isn't getting better. We've been so impatient with him. I never wanted this to happen, for my kids to suffer because of me, because of us.

As Travis explores his strained relationship with Henry, Kate speaks of how Travis pushes Henry away. I describe the ways this family is frozen in the past, unable to move toward a more cohesive whole, blocked by guilt, resentment, and un-mourned losses.

THERAPIST: Perhaps you two have carried forward your earlier relationship, the way you described it to me the first time we met. Travis, you kept your distance from Kate and Henry, because you didn't know if you would be able to raise Henry or be with Kate. And Kate, you mentioned clinging to Henry, yet resenting him in a way. It's like the relationship between you three has never shifted from that time.

Some understanding is unlocked, and the couple works together with me to help Henry. Over the next few months, Kate and Travis regularly attend their parent consultation sessions. Each enters their own individual treatment, and Henry's symptoms improve. As Kate becomes less depressed, I see a playfulness emerge in her interactions with Henry, but her distress over her marriage only intensifies. Kate is wary of couple therapy, detailing past experiences that were harmful and unproductive. Feeling comfortable now in the parent consultation sessions, the couple asks if they can pursue couple therapy with me. I struggle with the decision and consult with a colleague. I wonder how I am getting pulled in, as my waiting room is beginning to feel like this family's living space. Am I playing out Henry's omnipotent wish to make everything better? Would Henry be losing or gaining something if I work more intensely with his parents? Leaning toward seeing them, I talk with Henry about the possibility of helping his parents talk together. He seems relieved and comments, "Maybe my mom won't be so sad."

Couple therapy with Kate and Travis is difficult. They are defensive and accusatory, frequently escalating into the stormy battles Henry fears and enacts. Hate and deadness alternate within the couple. Most painfully, they battle through their children. Travis criticises Kate relentlessly for her frustration with his biological son Brad. Travis retaliates by ignoring Kate's daughter Hannah, who desperately wants a father. Travis locates their couple difficulties in Kate, characterising her as angry, depressed, and unloving despite his best efforts as a husband. In the face of his criticism, Kate either blows up or collapses, which seems to validate Travis's perceptions. When Travis seems workable, Kate attacks the treatment. Any good between them is quickly destroyed. Now that the difficulties are located in the couple, the children improve, but I worry that their progress is short-lived.

Over and over, I interpret the couple's need to destroy any good between them and point out how the unwanted parts of themselves are placed in the children. Travis begins to acknowledge that his dislike of his stepdaughter's neediness reflects his own wish for love and reassurance. Kate admits that her criticism of her stepson's emotional distancing is both a commentary on her own withdrawal and a retaliatory attack against her husband. The two begin to recognise how they have paired with their oldest children rather than each other. Two years pass with limited improvement in the couple, and I wonder if they will stay together. Is this a bond of hate, an entrenched yet hostile entanglement? Very slowly, almost imperceptibly, the couple work shifts. The children are mentioned less, as the couple grapples with their own struggle.

Talking about why he provokes Kate, Travis discloses his desperate longing and projected self-hatred.

TRAVIS: Well, I just want attention. I just want you to notice me, even if it's negative attention. (Turns to therapist) Negative attention is better than nothing, right? (To Kate) I think I just want to be loved or know you love me.

KATE: But you do it in a way that assures I'm going to be irritated, meaning I'll probably either just ignore you or make some sarcastic comment back. I know sometimes I just look at you like you're crazy, but that's how it feels to me.

TRAVIS: I know. It is kind of crazy. I don't really understand it myself. Maybe this is a better topic for my individual therapy. Maybe I should sort it out there.

THERAPIST: But it's coming up here, which makes me think it has some connection to you as a couple.

TRAVIS: She hates me.

KATE: See, this is what I mean. I don't hate you Travis. Of course, I do sometimes when I'm frustrated, but not now.

TRAVIS: I'm sure Kate would agree with me that she finds me irritating about eighty-five to ninety-five per cent of the time. Isn't that right? Wouldn't you say about ninety per cent of the time?

KATE: I wouldn't say that.

TRAVIS: Ninety-two per cent of the time then. Just admit it. You hate me, and I consistently irritate you. You want me to just go away.

He continues unrelenting until Kate says,

KATE: Really Travis, I don't hate you, but I'm starting to.

I point out that while he wants Kate's love, he puts her in a kind of chokehold until she finally agrees that she hates him. Kate talks about feeling suffocated, having no space for her own feelings and experience. She tells Travis that he holds a rigid, rejecting view of her that she cannot change. Travis carries a parallel view of Henry, insisting he hates him as well. Kate responds,

"He's just a little boy who wants a dad. Maybe I deserve your criticism, because our relationship is really messed up, but he doesn't. We have to stop putting our crap on him. Besides, he really loves you and so do I, but it's like it doesn't matter." Kate begins to sob.

Round and round we go. I comfort myself with the fact that the couple is developing a more empathetic stance toward their children. Henry leaves treatment doing well, despite the uncertainty of his parents' marriage. He has a better relationship with his father, who finally believes Henry loves him. The children are calmer, yet more playful, less overtly distressed over their parents' conflict. Kate and Travis begin talking with each other about their own growing up, which pulls them from their deadlocked, repetitive stance of destroying anything good. Each describes their guilt over being unable to save their sibling or curb their mothers' unhappiness. As Kate understands her own neglect and deprivation, she finds more liveliness in affects other than anger. Travis begins to see people in less polarised ways, finding kindness for and in Kate. Gradually, the family continues to shift. Occasionally, Kate and Travis laugh at each other in session, finding a humor and playfulness long missing.

About a year later, the couple ends treatment. Although I view the termination as premature, I hope the progress they have made will help sustain them. In my estimation, they could not have reached this place without their children, who led their parents to treatment. I think my knowing their children helped. Certainly, we used the children to move the couple out of deadlock, to find the good in their creative coupling. Still, much internal work remains.

Challenges for couple therapists

Dealing with couples as parents introduces both a heightened complexity and an increased opportunity into the therapeutic space. It moves the intergenerational perspective (Faimberg, 1986; Fraiberg, Adelson, & Shapiro, 2003; Siegel, 2004) into the room, allowing the couple to see their intergenerational patterns in concrete form. Through Henry's experience of her, Kate found her own dead mother buried deep inside. Sally discovered her repetition of her mother's overinvestment in her children, allowing her to reclaim her marriage before losing Jack. Children provide their parents with multiple opportunities for identifications. They serve as repositories for disowned aspects of the couple relationship and as reminders of the parents' own childhood. Elizabeth and Sam expressed in open aggression toward each other what their parents hid with alcohol and emotional withdrawal. Sam's age and temperament brought his parents' unresolved childhood traumas to the surface. The child's representation of the internal couple, like Henry's pile of leaves easily scattered by the wind, provides the couple with another view of themselves—close, yet distant enough to examine. Children also represent the creative coupling of their parents, serving as motivation for growth and movement. Ultimately, it was the children who helped these couples find each other.

For the couple therapist, however, dealing with parenting issues can be difficult. Any child therapist knows that talking with parents about their children can be a minefield. The powerful fear of being deemed "a bad parent" leaves parents feeling vulnerable, defensive, and attacked. The couple therapist can feel pressured to act too quickly, prompted by their identifications with the children negatively affected by the couple's difficulties. Developmental needs and stages do not wait for parents to heal. A sense of helplessness can prevail, as the therapist sees damaging intergenerational patterns re-enacted in the present moment. In the therapist's own counter transference, it can be difficult to track the multiple identifications and transferences with the various characters in the field (Ferro, 2005). The therapy room can feel crowded and suffocating, loaded with powerful primitive affects that are difficult to contain. It is easy to become polarised, as I did frequently with Henry's parents, losing track of the couple in my mind and aligning with a partner or a child. Thus, the complexity is both the gift, allowing for multiple points of access, and the challenge. As always, dealing with parenting issues brings to the surface our own issues as children and parents, adding yet another layer of countertransference complexity.

The parenting dimension of the couple relationship finds limited discussion in the couple literature. Given its clinical relevance and importance, both to the couples we treat and the generations of children that follow, this topic merits further attention, thought, and discussion.

References

Faimberg, H. (1986). The telescoping of generations—genealogy of certain identifications. *Contemporary Psychoanalysis, 24*: 99–117.

Ferro, A. (2005). *Seeds of Illness, Seeds of Recovery: The Genesis of Suffering and the Role of Psychoanalysis.* New York: Routledge.

Fraiberg, S., Adelson, E., & Shapiro, V. (2003). Ghosts in the nursery: a psychoanalytic approach to the problems of impaired infant–mother relationships. In: J. Rapheal-Leff (Ed.), *Parent Infant Psychodynamics: Wild Things, Mirrors and Ghosts* (pp. 87–117). London: Whurr.

Green, A. (1986). *On Private Madness.* London: Hogarth.

Ludlam, M. (2006). Psychotherapy for the parents as a couple. In: J. S. Scharff & D. E. Scharff (Eds.), *New Paradigms in Treating Relationship* (pp. 87–97). Lanham, MD: Jason Aronson.

Racker, H. (1957). The meanings and uses of countertransference. *Psychoanalytic Quarterly, 26*: 303–357.

Rustin, M. (1998). Dialogues with parents. *Journal of Child Psychotherapy, 24*: 233–242.

Seigel, J. (2004). Identification as a focal point in couple therapy. *Psychoanalytic Inquiry, 24,* 3: 406–419.

CHAPTER TWENTY-FIVE

Divorce and parenting wars

Kate Scharff

In order to work with any couple or family in crisis, clinicians must sort through a web of transferences, countertransferences, projections, and projective identifications while attending to the needs of family members as a group and as individuals at varying cognitive and developmental levels. Before any struggling couple can make changes in ineffective patterns of relating, they must recognise the painful aspects of themselves projected into the other. They must realise that it is futile to expect new outcomes while continuing to treat each other in the same ways. They must accept that they will never metamorphose into versions of each other's ideal fantasies or compensate each other for pain suffered at the hands of primary objects. When they admit the hopelessness of their illusions, couples can—sometimes, when things go well—be helped to recognise and reclaim disavowed parts of themselves and establish new paradigms of relating.

Clinicians working with separating and divorcing families see couples who are either unable to get themselves to treatment, experience unsuccessful treatment, or experience successful treatments that bring them to a realisation of fundamental incompatibility. Divorce, with its wrenching losses and separations, narcissistic assaults, financial devastation, and destabilisation of life on every level is not only traumatising, it is re-traumatising. No one who has experienced divorce is unfamiliar with its powerful capacity to reawaken sleeping demons and call forth defensive strategies we thought long abandoned, even to amplify them—old ways of being and feeling now intensified as we wrestle with this new assault on our ego's capacity to cope. Passing homicidal and suicidal thoughts are not unusual in the first two years following a separation—particularly for those who do not initiate the break.

For some couples the possibility of divorce is introduced into their marriage gradually, a slow growing toxicity made manifest in a crystallising moment. For others it feels sudden, precipitated by a life-changing event. For most, the concept of divorce has been a spectre in the marriage for many years, a central spot from which they have moved closer and further in an asymmetrical dance over time. But once it has been named, a marital fault line is formed that often cannot be fully repaired.

Having made their way into our offices, some of these couples tell us that they are tottering on the brink of divorce. Others come in with the explicit intent to work on the marriage, but you will soon come to learn that one or both members of the couple are actually seeking a way out. Most problematic are the couples in deep trouble who nevertheless tell you that divorce is not an option under any circumstance. Unless a couple can contemplate the painful loss of the marriage, they will be unable to tolerate the psychic pain associated with the exploration of trauma that is essential in reclaiming lost aspects of themselves and developing new relational paradigms.

This chapter describes analytically informed work with couples in three types of specific moments. First, I will explore the challenges of working with couples who either come to the decision to divorce through their psychotherapeutic work with us, or who come to us grappling with the decision but ultimately do decide to separate. Second, I will explore work with couples preparing to separate, either at the onset of their work with us or as an outcome of it. Third, I will address techniques needed when consulting with already divorced couples wanting to work on their co-parenting relationship. Finally, I will conclude with some reflections on the critical impact of the interaction between divorcing couples and the legal system in the United States, which may be slightly different from the legal technicalities of the UK system. I will not deal here with those couples who pull back from the brink and go on to a psychotherapy of marital repair, since that is the topic of many of the other contributions to this book.

In working with separating and separated couples we are reliant on our capacity to assess, in an ongoing way, the nature of the couple's projective identificatory system. Are they functioning from the paranoid-schizoid or depressive positions? As individuals? As a couple? As in couple therapy we rely heavily on an examination of our countertransferences and make heavy use of both focused and contextual holding. While the work with separating couples is crisis work focusing primarily on containment, work with already separated clients may allow for some interpretive work since, while we are not working to rebuild intimacy, we are attempting to shift relational paradigms when necessary and possible. In both cases, however, our work is more narrowly focused than in other psychotherapy. We are not emphasising the exploration of transference. Rather we work with it only when necessary. Post-divorce counselling, even when analytically informed, is directive and makes heavy use of parent coaching and education.

Couples in treatment contemplating divorce

The experience of working with couples who are in distress, perhaps even acute distress, but in a "live" marriage with or without the potential for the creation of a psychological space for exploration is quite different from that of working with a couple in a marriage in the process of dissolution. In our work with marital dissolution, none of our therapeutic tools penetrate the couples' maladaptive defensive strategies. Conversations loop endlessly in cycles of mutual accusation and defensiveness, often characterised by a strongly sadomasochistic flavour. These are typically couples who have had several previously failed treatments, often reporting that they have fired or been fired by other therapists, who they report have told them that they are "unhelpable." In the countertransference we may move between fantasies of omnipotence, impotence, boredom, rage, anxiety, and role confusion. One couple induced in me a recurrent fantasy that I was standing by the bedside of a loved-one who had been intubated and was on life-support, and that I had been tasked with the job of deciding when to "pull the plug." In working with another couple I often found my mind floating into a daydream in which I was coaching a football game, watching the sky grow ominously dark and wondering if I should "call the game" before the storm was upon us. In the end, all we can do is reflect to the couple what we see; they are not making progress, one or both are becoming more angry or depressed, their children are in increasing distress, or (as is commonly true), one member of the couple seems already to have given up.

The decision to divorce is rarely mutual. Rather, it normally comes about as a pronouncement from one member of the couple to the other. Often the marriage has been troubled either from the start or for many years; characterised by miserable fighting, or by a lack of intimacy (what I often describe to clients as either the "hot war" or the "cold war"). Sometimes the reluctant spouse (bafflingly) hears the news as a shocking bolt from the blue, even when the suggestion (or threat) of divorce has been made many times (sometimes even by them!), when they themselves have been vocally angry with and even disdainful of their spouse for years, or when there has been an affair. In fact, the "leav-ee" is surprisingly often the spouse who has been unfaithful. There are an infinite number of "fact patterns," but the nearly universal presentation is one where one member of the couple feels blindsided, then panicked, bereft, humiliated, and desperate and another who may or may not be empathic but who is already emotionally checked out of the marriage, but may still be deeply frightened of the implications of his or her decision—in the emotional, financial, parenting, and community arenas.

If you are the therapist for a couple for whom separation becomes inevitable, you have come to the end of your analytic work. They have now moved into profound crisis. Ordinary cognitive and reflective processes are overwhelmed by the enormity of looming losses. The therapist is tasked with the momentary stabilisation of the family through a containment offered from the position of an understanding of the fundamental implications of the early stages of marital breakdown. Let's take a look at those.

Disbelief, begging, and the initiator's response

Being in the presence of a couple in which one partner or spouse has announced that he or she wants a divorce when the other does not, is often almost unbearably painful. For the bereft spouse, in the matter of a moment, life has taken on an unreal, nightmarish quality. For that man or woman the central contract of their life has been broken, and the very person to whom they would normally turn for solace is suddenly not only unavailable but the perpetrator of their torture. In the same way that couples idealise each other in order to manage the anxieties attendant with marriage, the member of the couple choosing to divorce must de-idealise the other in order to manage the pain of the attendant losses. The result is that the reluctant spouse feels unimaginably betrayed.

The intra- and inter-psychic responses of spouses to the decision to separate and to the reactions of the other will be highly informed by the extent to which the current trauma echoes past traumas. But whether the couple has a history of significant trauma or not, when the promises made in the context of their central somatic and intimate adult relationship are broken, the result is the inevitable awakening of a combination of memories of earlier painful experiences and frightening babyhood/childhood fantasies associated with their earliest, somatically intimate relationships. Because these memories and fantasies are in part pre-verbal and are always primitive and fundamental, the emotional power they wield is overwhelming. A wife who has just learned for the first time that her husband is planning to leave her becomes a daughter abandoned. A father who suddenly faces the horrifying reality that he will have to spend at least half of his time without his children is suddenly a boy for whom primary objects have evaporated like ghosts.

The unconscious defensive responses of the initiator, and therefore their manifest responses, vary widely. Some experience the pleading of their spouse as irritating and become dismissive or disdainful. This response is often reified as their spouse becomes increasingly desperate, pleading, bargaining, self-blaming, and masochistic. Others seem to have made the decision to split only nominally, and become caught in an endless loop of guilty explanations and attempts to comfort, and an agonising inability to move into a stance of emotional distance that reflects the reality of the situation.

The job of the clinician in these moments is to remain evenly in the psychic space of both spouses, each of which exerts enormous psychological pressure for us to ally with them. The partner who has made the decision to leave will be exquisitely sensitive to the ideas that we are either coddling or vilifying their spouse. The spouse who feels he or she is being left will have antennae out for any evidence that we support the idea of the split or empathise with the spouse who has made the decision to leave.

The moment of breakdown of a couple's emotional homeostasis (of the stability created by their unconscious fit) presents us with technical challenges. In that moment we are called upon to adapt our container such that it can provide holding no longer to the "third" represented by the couple but to two, new, split apart and highly fragile "singletons" with competing needs for sustenance and space. We are faced with the difficult task of tending simultaneously to both, in a moment when each is regressed so that their object permanence is likely at low ebb or not in evidence at all.

Clinicians new to the work often find themselves literally at a loss of words, and, in fact, silence that comes out of close somatic attendance (leaning in, eye contact, focused attention) is quite often the most powerful and appropriate response.

Robert and Ellen

Robert and Ellen, a couple in their mid sixties, had been married for ten years—a second marriage for both. The catalyst for their seeking treatment was that Robert had, during a recent argument, confessed that he had been having an affair with a college girlfriend. Ellen was furious and devastated. Robert said that he felt guilty and culpable. Both said that they loved each other and wanted to save the marriage.

In sessions the couple bickered impenetrably in a relentless "tit for tat." Each kept score of the other's transgressions, which prompted me on several occasions to remark that they seemed to want me to serve as judge and proclaim one of them guilty and the other innocent.

Robert admitted that he had been ambivalent about the marriage from the outset, as Ellen had a "ferocious and uncontrolled temper." Ellen admitted that she did have a tendency toward yelling and lashing out "below the belt" when she felt let down by Robert, even over seemingly trivial offenses. She linked the origin of this behaviour to her adolescence, and to her burning sense of indignation and outrage at her parents' inability to see her subjectively and respond to her emotional needs.

For his part, Robert acknowledged that he had "intimacy issues." He sheepishly admitted that on many occasions in which he and Ellen argued he had either threatened to leave (always vague about whether he was threatening to leave the marriage or simply to leave the house for some period of time). On several occasions, usually around family holiday celebrations or other events in which attending with Ellen would constitute (in his mind) a public declaration of commitment to her, Robert had in fact disappeared for several days without explanation. After such incidents Robert always returned, tail between his legs. Ellen took him back, but her anger was reified and, over time, so was his sense of himself as a beleaguered martyr.

After only a short time in couple treatment, Ellen accepted a referral for an individual therapist and began to progress in the management of her temper and angry outbursts. Robert acknowledged that things between them were better. But one day, Ellen discovered evidence that, despite promises to the contrary, Robert was continuing to have telephone and email contact with the woman with whom he had had the affair.

At this point Ellen became furious and desperate. She gave Robert an ultimatum; either he sought treatment or she would seek a divorce. Robert was resistant. In couple sessions he spoke for the first time about his narcissistic mother and his father, a psychoanalyst—an emotionally wispy figure who had forced Robert from a young age to serve as the receptionist for his practice and who employed what Robert called "Skinnerian" parenting techniques (i.e., using sleep deprivation as punishment for bad behaviour). After some couple work, Robert did agree to seek treatment but, in the end, picked a psychoanalyst who lived and worked in another city and with whom Robert could only meet on the phone or sporadically in person. For some months the couple reported improvements in their marriage. They planned a trip to Scotland for a reunion of Robert's extended family. On the eve of the trip, Robert told Ellen that he could not take her. He left for the trip even over her vociferous protestations.

Immediately after he boarded the plane, Robert was consumed with remorse. He tried unsuccessfully and with mounting panic to reach Ellen by phone. These attempts continued during the weeklong trip. When he returned home, he found that Ellen had moved out of their home. After desperate pleading, he was able to convince Ellen to come to see me for what she called "one final session."

Robert sobbed for the duration of the session. He claimed that he had had an "epiphany" during his time away, and that he knew now that he desperately wanted to save his marriage, was responsible for most of the difficulties in the marriage, and would do "whatever it took" to convince Ellen of his commitment to her. But Ellen was, in her words, "done." During the time that Robert had been in denial about the impact of his early trauma on his capacity to maintain intimacy, Ellen had been in a phase of anticipatory grief. She had emotionally de-cathected from Robert. Robert, on the other hand, was now left alone with the full impact of his self-sabotaging behaviour. The experience of being with him was of being in the presence of a child who had wished for the death of a parent who was the object of both longing and rage and, magically, had effected that death. The overwhelming affects associated with his experience of existential injustice (how could he be held responsible for behaviour that was out of his control?), panic, and grief seemed to simply glance off of his wife. Where she became his persecutory parents, he now became to her more like an early agonised version of herself and she was now her own disaffected parents. Ellen suggested that I take Robert on as an individual patient; he begged her to continue the couple work. In the countertransference I wanted to flee—both from her desire that I take him off her hands, and from his wish that I force her into offering absolution. All I could do was name those forces, offer empathy for his pain, suggest that they continue their individual treatments, and let them know that I was there for them as a couple in the future should the need arise. As they left, there was no escaping the painful juxtaposition of her relief and his feeling of being thrown out onto the street desperate and alone.

Couples who have decided to separate

Once the decision to separate and/or divorce has been reached, the clinician's job becomes a kind of psychological triage. What are the primary emotional and practical needs of the spouses? Of the children? How long should we remain in the case? What is our role to be? What are the next steps for the couple? Are we in a position to make referrals to new professionals?

The period of time between the couple's decision to divorce and their physical separation is one of the most challenging. This is the limbo phase. Regardless of how clients behave, it is now that clinicians begin to feel internal pressure to encourage a speedy physical separation. Occasionally one member of the couple will move out poste haste, but more typically there are financial and legal issues to be ironed out before they can do so.

For "reluctant" spouses, co-habitation keeps alive fantasies of saving the marriage. They typically swing between periods of ineffective and humiliating begging and periods of lashing out—which leave them feeling complicit and devastated. The spouse who is more anxious for separation often moves into the guest room. He or she feels trapped and begins to exert pressure on the other to move into a legal process toward divorce—often making terrifying threats about finances or custody, most of which are not supported by legal realities, but all of which induce panic in the other and serve to raise the level of acrimony to critical levels. Some couples begin to live parallel, separate lives under the same roof. Others function on the surface as though nothing has changed. A third category seem to get along "better than ever." While this is typically due to the fact that the initiating spouse now sees the light at the end of the tunnel, it is a confusing and torturous dynamic for the reluctant spouse, who may now develop fantasies of reunification or wonder "why it couldn't always be like this?"

The children

Some parents will have a clear sense of how their discord and impending separation (even if it has not been openly discussed) is affecting their children. Others will stubbornly cling to the notion that "the children have never seen us fight and have no idea," or "are oblivious." Other couples with an uneven amount of psychological awareness will disagree strongly on this point (often arguing about how and when to "tell the children," or whether psychotherapy for the child/ren is indicated.) Sometimes, the spouse who has initiated the divorce views the parental concerns of the other as an attempt to inflict guilt or psychological punishment. Paranoid clients may see one parent's suggestion that the children are suffering and should be seen by a psychotherapist as early attempts to lay down a trail to be used in later custody litigation—which it sometimes is. Whatever the situation of the children, it is important for the couple therapist to understand the process of separation and divorce from the child's point of view (Johnston, Roseby & Kuehnle, 2009).

In the trajectory of a divorce, this is often the most difficult time for children who, regardless of the parents' level of awareness, are always at least unconsciously highly attuned to their parents discord and have been living (often for years) in a state of anticipatory anxiety. Most children have repressed their fears, while some have asked questions about the possibility of divorce that have been minimised or rebuffed by their parents. These children are often highly symptomatic. Their difficulties run the gamut, but are typically in the areas of school failure, social difficulty, disturbances of conduct, regressive or clingy behaviours (such as an unwillingness to sleep alone, wetting the bed, etc.), anxiety, and depression.

An affair or new relationship for one member of the couple creates dynamics with potentially devastating impact on the other spouse and on the children. Naturally, it is painfully challenging to the spouse who feels cuckolded. He or she is in pain while the other is in the throes of new love. But for a child, this may mean being enlisted in an alliance with the bereft spouse against the villainous future "ex," or being emotionally called-upon as a replacement love object. Perhaps most problematic is the situation in which the emotional reality of the child ("This is a sad, frightening thing that is happening to my family!") does not synch with the emotional reality of the parent who is emotionally distracted and in the psychological haze of a new romantic love.

Affairs, too, often present challenges to the development of what I call the "shared narrative," the story that we help our clients to develop together as parents (containing aspects of each of their realities but emotionally authentic to both) that is aimed at the child's developmental capacities to take in and process information but that explains what is happening in their lives. Healthier parents have no difficulty understanding that children are best served when neither parent is vilified in the narrative. They have done their research, and they know that the two factors most important in determining a child's successful adjustment to divorce are the parents' ability to shield their child from parental conflict, and each parent's willingness and ability to support the child in having a full, rich relationship with the other parent. But when there is an affair, even the healthiest clients who understand that affairs are most often painful symptoms of a mutually constructed maladaptive pattern of relating, are hard pressed to mask their sense of the unfairness of their circumstance.

William and Melanie

After fifteen years of an acrimonious and sexless marriage, William engaged in an affair with a much younger woman and announced to Melanie that he was leaving the marriage in order to marry her. During the marriage, William had worked long hours as an attorney, and Melanie had stayed home caring for their now eight-year-old son, Sam. William admitted that he had done very little of the "nuts and bolts" of parenting, but expressed concern that Melanie was "over-involved" with their son and had no life-interests outside of him.

Despite her conscious wish that Sam have an ongoing relationship with his father during and after their divorce and that in order for Sam to do so he would need her emotional permission, Melanie shared details of William's "bad behaviour" with her son. When William moved out of the marital home necessitating that he spend time with his son away from Melanie, she found ways to heighten Sam's anxiety at the moments of transition. She said such things as, "If you miss Mummy I'm just a phone call away," or "I know you're mad at Daddy, but he loves you and needs to see you." Sam gratified her by telling her that he did not want to spend time with his father, and by beginning to sleep in her bed at night. For his part, William was unreliable in sticking to the arranged time-sharing schedule, blaming lateness and last-minute changes on work obligations. He continued to rely heavily on Melanie for making plans for Sam on William's custodial time.

Cohabitation before the split

Many patients describe the period after they have decided to end the marriage and before they have achieved a physical separation as a tortured "limbo" period. Since most couples cannot afford to quickly set up two homes, and so must wait for the legal process to catch up to their need to settle on a financial mechanism for doing so, they are forced to find some way to navigate living together for an indeterminate period of time. Some describe this as living under a death sentence.

In an effort to lesson tensions that often become intolerable, some therapists work with the couple to develop some version of an "in-home" separation—where the parents divide time with the children and either rotate in and out of the house (either for periods of time during the day or for overnights). While these schedules can serve to relieve some pressure on the family by decreasing the amount of the time that the couple is together and driving home the reality of the impending separation for a spouse in denial, they rarely work well, and generally result in petty fights ("you left me a sink full of dirty dishes"), a sense of intrusion ("if you don't leave the house on my time I feel you are hovering!"), a feeling of being homeless ("where am I supposed to go on your time? I can't stay at the gym for eight hours and I don't want to be in some impersonal furnished apartment!"), and confusion for the children ("Does this mean I can't ask Daddy for help with my homework if he is upstairs in his office on Mummy's night?").

Most problematic, though, is that cohabitation delays the moment in which the couple must face the reality of the restructured family. During this phase the toxic aspects of the marital dynamic operate in full, even exaggerated force. In general I recommend that therapists encourage their clients to work with their attorneys to effect a physical separation as quickly as possible, even if one parent has to procure temporary housing. I discourage in-home separations as well as "nesting" (where the parents rotate in and out of the marital home while the children stay put) except as a very short-term arrangement.

Sometimes there is a jockeying over which parent will ultimately leave the marital home. Despite the fact that woman are three times more likely to initiate a divorce than are men, they are still more likely to remain in the marital home. This trend is changing, however, along with the legal presumption of maternal primary custody. Most parents see it as a parental advantage to stay in the marital home. For parents who anticipate continuing in demanding jobs that will make it difficult for them to spend time with their children during the week, remaining in the house to which the children are already cathected often feels like a short-cut to creating a space in which the children will want to spend time in the absence of the other parent. It is helpful for therapists to explain that while keeping the marital house in the family has the advantage of minimising the number of changes in the children's lives, doing so gives the parent who remains in the house if anything only a minor advantage, since home is essentially a psychological construct. I often say that what we are aiming for is a configuration in which there are two home bases, rather than a home base and a satellite.

Brian and Jim

Brian and Jim had lived together for twenty-five years and had three adopted sons under the age of fourteen. When gay marriage became legal in the jurisdiction in which the couple lived, Jim denied Brian's wish to get married. The couple stayed together. Brian's career as an attorney soared. Jim worked part-time, ran the household, and took primary care of the children. Both had brief and repeated sexual affairs. Brian decided to end the partnership when Jim refused to end a close friendship with a man with whom Brian insisted Jim was having romantic relationship (though Jim denied this, and insisted that the other man was straight). Both men wanted to remain in the marital home. They were working on their rather complicated financial settlement with attorneys, but sought my help on dealing with the interim period of cohabitation.

Although both men reported that they fought constantly and viciously, they refused to consider any mechanism for a temporary separation fearing that to do so would put one or the other at a potential legal disadvantage, in terms of both finances and custody (a fear not corroborated by either attorney). While Brian had historically been the primary family breadwinner while Jim had done most of the hands-on parenting, Brian now denied that he had been any less involved with the children and demanded equal time with them. At the same time, he felt a greater entitlement to the couple's money and other assets. He unilaterally cut off all joint credit cards and closed joint bank accounts. He "kicked" Jim out of their shared bedroom (relegating him to a small guest room). Jim, terrified of being cut off financially, felt he had no choice but to comply. He doubled-down on his time with the children (which meant he had to cut back even further on his part-time job thus further reducing his income). This intensified Brian's sense of being exploited, and heightened his own anxiety about being cut out of the children's lives.

Despite the fact that the men received calls from their sons' teachers reporting that the boys appeared depressed and withdrawn, neither parent supported the idea of psychotherapy for the children. They did say, however, that they recognised the negative impact that their ongoing fighting was having on their the boys. We did our best to design a time-sharing schedule in which the two had minimal contact with each other; one parent was responsible for mornings, the other evenings, and the weekends were split. The "off duty" parent agreed to vacate the family home during the other's "on duty" time.

Tensions increased. Jim complained that he had no access to money and that Brian was hypocritical in his sudden insistence on spending equal time with the children. Brian insisted that he had always been an equal parent, and that he would no longer allow Jim to rely on him financially—especially in the light of Jim's alleged infidelity. Their interactions, even around the children, ranged from silent hostility to fights in which one or both would scream and become violent, throwing glassware against the wall or, in one case, dumping a plate of food on the other.

Both men complained that the other was non-compliant with the time-sharing schedule. Neither could tolerate being excluded from any aspect of the children's lives. While each found ways to delay the legal process that would ostensibly lead to the eventual physical separation (and each blamed the other for unreasonable delay), they flaunted the plan at every turn. Sessions became virtual parodies. In one moment they would hurl invectives, in the next, they would discuss the importance to the children of doing things "as a family." They planned weekly "Sunday dinners" with the children which they would both attend and during which they would argue over everything from who would plan to meal to whether either had the "right" to discipline the children on the other's "time". Brian planned a ski trip with the children, invited Jim, and then refused to pay for Jim's portion of the trip. It was only when I said that I was going to withdraw from their case that they agreed to rent a temporary apartment and re-design their temporary time-sharing schedule so that each parent spent separate time with the children while the other lived elsewhere.

Exploring next steps

It can be difficult to ascertain the right moment to refer the couple on for new services and thereby to terminate the therapeutic relationship. Some couples flee treatment at the moment that they make the decision to separate. Sometimes one member of the couple will want to remain with the therapist for individual work, often with the full support of the other spouse (whose guilt may be alleviated by leaving their spouse in your good hands, or who may feel you can serve as a buffer between them and their spouse's ongoing angry or pain-filled communication). Some therapists are comfortable to keep one member of the couple on; others are not. I prefer not to for three related reasons: First. the couple may choose to attempt reconciliation and may want to return in the future. Second, the couple may want to return later to work on co-parenting issues or may want the couple therapist to treat one of their children in the future. Third, if they have children, the couple is now entering a period of restructuring their relationship. If the therapist that treated the couple continues to treat one member of the couple, not only is the transference in that work highly tainted in potentially problematic ways, but the therapist is likely to be quoted in strategic and distorted ways during moments of disagreement between the couple. This can feel like a confusing and painful attack on the internal object that the treatment experience represents in the mind of the spouse who is not part of the ongoing treatment and can leave the therapist feeling complicit in—or in fact being drawn into—splitting behaviour.

Some couples ask for help in navigating their separation. Here we can be helpful in making needed referrals to individual therapists and, if we are knowledgeable in the area of child development and divorce, we can be helpful to the couple in thinking through such issues as when and how to tell the children. Therapists who have particular expertise in separation and divorce may be effective in helping the couple develop interim time-sharing schedules and shared narratives for family and friends. If the couple therapist has particular expertise in separation and divorce he or she may be tempted to remain involved with the couple essentially as a mediator/consultant to help them develop a parenting plan, a.k.a. a Custody Agreement. I discourage this "morphing" from a therapeutic to consultant role, as the two are mutually incompatible (the former being non-neutral, based in transference, and primarily non-educative, and the second being neutral, not based in working in the transference, and highly educative). At the point at which the couple requires the services of a family mediator, I recommend that the therapist refer the couple on to a colleague who is well trained in mediation.

Referring children to a child therapist

The question of whether a child or children of a couple who has recently decided to divorce should see a child therapist is not simple. Sometimes angry or bereft parents will project their own experiences into a child. They may insist that the therapist "listen to what [the child] has to say," about the other parent, or report that the child is symptomatic. Other times one or both parents will defensively refuse even to consider the possibility of psychotherapy for a child, either insisting that the child is fine, or saying are concerned that therapy will make "the whole situation into a big deal" or stigmatise the child.

I generally recommend against getting treatment for children in the days, weeks, or early months following the announcement of the divorce, in order to give the children space for the ordinary range of emotional responses. This also gives helping professionals the opportunity to observe the way in which the new parental dynamic will form, and to note any toxic projections from the parents into the children. Putting children into treatment carries the risk of reinforcing the children's fantasy of culpability, but it also puts them at risk if they are the target of the toxic projections of one or both parents in the context of a custody fight.

On the other hand, any child who asks for treatment, whose parents are too anxious or depressed to offer emotional support, or who is having difficulty processing feelings associated with the divorce, needs and deserves treatment. We should offer referrals to any parent of such a child.

Referring the couple to an attorney or mediator

Most often members of the couple will find their own attorney or family mediator, and I generally recommend that therapists stay out of it. The decision to seek legal counsel is an important passage. Some spouses do it without consulting the other, which may be viewed as "going on the attack," or a sign of giving up. Others will resist, perhaps in order to delay the inevitable, or play for time in the hope that the other will change his or her mind. Many couples will fight over access to money to retain an attorney, or will accuse the other of choosing an attorney who is too expensive. Sometimes, though, they will ask for your help, and this makes sense; we are helping professionals on whom they have come to rely. However, I would tread carefully here, making a referral only when you are clear that you have buy-in from both members of the couple. I would also encourage a therapist who is not knowledgeable in this area to do enough research to make an informed recommendation (see conclusion).

Post-separation co-parenting "counselling"

Divorced couples with children, even when they have difficulty co-parenting effectively, rarely seek therapeutic intervention. One reason is that low-conflict couples don't usually require outside intervention, while medium to high-conflict couples usually cannot agree that they need help (since each blames the other for any difficulty) and cannot agree on a specific therapist (since each distrusts any recommendation from the other). For these reasons therapists who are approached for post-divorce co-parenting counselling would be well advised to be thoughtful before taking on a new parenting couple. Some questions to ask:

Is one or both members of the couple being court mandated to seek counselling or have they agreed as part of a court order? If so, why?

Sometimes conflictual couples (those who settle custody by the skin of their teeth or who actually litigate) will be ordered by a judge or will voluntarily choose to write dispute resolution language into their custody agreements that includes the use of a mental health professional. This is typically a role that includes a blend of mediation and arbitration functions. It is not normally a protected role (therapists who take on this role are often subpoenaed to testify in court). In some jurisdictions this role is referred to as that of parenting coordinator, but in others it does not carry a separate designation and is therefore easy to mistake as psychotherapeutic. Be sure to ask if there are any documents suggesting or mandating the use of such a professional, and how they describe the scope of the authority and confidentiality of the professional. Unless you have special training, steer clear of any case in which you are at risk of ongoing legal involvement.

Has either parent ever sued an attorney or mental health professional in the past, or filed a complaint with any licensing board?

A high percentage of law suits and complaints against mental health professionals come from disgruntled divorced parents.

Are there now or have there ever been any reports to child protective services levied by one parent against the other or orders of protection filed by one parent against the other?

Therapists are often surprised by how often allegations of abuse and molestation (frequently false) play a part in divorce narratives. Their existence may not be a reason to turn down a case, but they may be a reason to turn down a case if you do not have expertise in the relevant areas or are inexperienced in working with high conflict couples, and you will not know if these documents exist if you do not ask. The issue of false accusations of abuse is a large topic beyond the scope of this chapter.

Is one or both of the parents hoping to modify an existing custody agreement or child-sharing schedule?

If so, find out before you begin your work with the parents. If they are both willing to consider the possibility of a change, and you have experience facilitating such conversations, you may be on safe ground. But be very clear with yourself and with them about what, if any, specific recommendations you will be qualified or willing to make. If this is not an area of expertise for you, suggest they go elsewhere.

Does one or both parent have questions about the fundamental "fitness" of the other or are they alleging untreated substance abuse?
If the answer is "yes" to either of the above, suggest to the couple that they seek a referral from their attorneys for a professional who can offer them the necessary evaluative process.

Once you have ruled out legal involvement and other high risk factors, you'll be left with a parental couple motivated by such factors as:
1. The desire to enhance their capacity to co-parent effectively
2. The desire to communicate less acrimoniously
3. The desire for information about child development and how to address parenting challenges (i.e., how to introduce new significant others or manage questions of disciplinary consistency across households)
4. The desire to consider mutually agreeable changes to the parenting plan to accommodate logistical changes in their lives (i.e., a parental relocation) or their children's changing developing needs

These and other goals represent good reasons for a co-parenting couple to seek help, and ones in which a well-trained therapist with knowledge of child and family development might offer effective help.

Managing the re-emergence of the marital dynamic

The work with divorced parents will go best if the working triad is clear at the outset about the parameters of the work. Most parental couples will be relieved if you are explicit about the fact that you are not attempting to repair the marriage, or even to make the two better friends. It is helpful to explore with them whether either or both is anxious that the other will pull for an unproductive rehashing of past difficulties, and come to an agreement about the forward-looking nature of the process. It makes sense to acknowledge that old disagreements, hurt feelings, and patterns of behaviour will inevitably emerge, but that you will follow the affects associated with them only to the extent that to do so will move you forward toward resolution on whatever issues they bring to the table.

Mark and Linda

Mark and Linda, parents of a thirteen year-old boy, had been divorced for five years. Mark had initiated the split. Initially Linda had been devastated. Over time, however, she came to see that theirs had been a marriage based largely on their shared desire to create the sense of "home" that both had missed growing up, and that otherwise they were fundamentally incompatible. Her resentment of the ways he did not meet her expectations during the marriage had made her angry and disdainful of her husband (ways her mother had felt about her), which had left

Mark feeling emotionally abandoned and looked down on (much as he had by his own father). Once Linda was able to recognise her own contributions to the dissolution of their marriage and to see it as an opportunity for her to find happiness elsewhere, her anger at Mark largely evaporated. Over time he was able to acknowledge that he had withdrawn emotionally from Linda and had relied on her to be the responsible party—managing the children, the household finances, and their social life, while experiencing her as patronising and controlling (again, like his father). The two never had an explicit conversation about their expanded understanding of what had transpired between them. Instead, they managed to co-parent more effectively as a divorced pair then they had as a married couple—less polarised in their disciplinary styles and more able to provide a united front to their children.

But things began to unravel when their son Jessie entered puberty. Suddenly, the boy began to talk about hating his father. He started refusing visits, claiming his father was unreasonably strict and punitive. Linda, who did not want to be drawn into the fray, nevertheless felt unable to force Jessie to comply with the timesharing schedule. Mark accused Linda of forming an alliance with their child against him by being too "soft" with their son, thus making Mark out to be the bad guy. The two sought a consultation with me with the shared desire of getting things between Mark and Jessie back on track.

I saw the parents for one session. While Mark was initially angry and critical of Linda, he soon was able to get in touch with the pain of feeling rejected by his son. When he saw that she took no overt pleasure in the growing distance between them, he did not reject the link that she made between the fact that Jessie was now a teenager and the fact that Mark's own father had rejected him when he was thirteen and began to "have opinions of his own." Mark acknowledged that he was terrified that he would behave like his own father, or that his son would experience him as though he did. He admitted that it was easier to see his ex-wife as the villain (in the same way that he had when they were married), than to experience the terrifying feelings that were being stirred up by his son reaching the age that he had been when the trouble with his own father had begun.

For her part, Linda explored the ways that she had leaned emotionally on her son both during and after the marriage. He had, she admitted, provided her with the unconditional love that she had not received from her own mother, as well as a sense of competence that her mother lacked and that she had internalised as a sense of herself as damaged and damaging. She acknowledged that she, too, was having difficulty as their son moved into adolescence and away from her. She allowed that she had felt unconsciously gratified by Jessie's rejection of his father, in that it brought Jessie closer to her—as well as the fact that she might have unconsciously encouraged the rift by disparaging Mark in subtle ways.

The couple had no interest in, nor was there need for, further exploratory work. They had accomplished a "reset." They left the office having decided that Mark (now much less anxious) would have a frank but simple discussion with Jessie about his insights about his own contribution to their new difficulty getting along. Linda agreed that she would make a renewed effort not to engage with Jessie in discussions about his father, that she would enforce their time sharing schedule in a crisp and matter of fact way, and that she would work in her individual therapy on doing a better job allowing for Jessie's healthy individuation from her.

Conclusion

Divorce and the legal system

The amount of mutual psychological awareness (what led to what), volition in the process to divorce, and relative psychological health should be predictive of a divorcing person's capacity to navigate grief, reclaim projections, and move through the divorce process in a relatively healthy way and with a relatively low refractory period (one to three years). But it turns out that it's hard to know at the beginning which couples are going to navigate the process with only ordinary difficulty, and which are going to crash and burn. Separating couples are people for whom the homeostasis provided by their marital system of mutual projective identifications has broken down, leaving each member of the couple emotionally unstable, and the legal system is a perfectly designed magnifier for people for whom splitting and projection are in full swing.

Divorce is now statistically normal. It is no longer an affliction of the few, but rather a life passage in many families that affects all members of our society, but we still live in a world which mythologises marriage and demonises divorce. Courtrooms are battlegrounds, and you cannot have a battle without an enemy. While "no fault" divorce is now available in all parts of the U.S., it's a misleading phrase. It's true you no longer need to convince a judge that your spouse abandoned you or committed adultery or mental cruelty in order to qualify for a divorce. But courts are ill equipped to deal even with the concept of lack of fault, because the system is based on an opposition and conflict scenario in which a wrongdoer is identified and consequences are meted out. Not all lawyers are bloodthirsty gladiators, but all lawyers are trained to root out their "opponents'" vulnerabilities and make hay of them. They are taught to strategise, to low ball, to thrust and parry, and to win. A world in which one should never ask a question to which one does not know the answer and in which a third position—one in which compromise in the service of resolutions that can meet the needs of all parties—is unimaginable, is the very definition of the paranoid schizoid position.

In recent years movements away from the traditional litigation model toward a concept of so-called "therapeutic jurisprudence," such as mediation and Collaborative Law (Scharff & Herrick, 2010) have begun to take hold. But there is significant resistance from many members of the traditional litigation system. A large part of the problem is that there is no training for attorneys or allied professionals in the interpsychic and intrapsychic interface between the inner worlds of the professionals and their clients. Even enlightened attorneys who understand the potentially devastating impact of a win/lose mentality are powerless when they run up against an opposing counsel who is operating from a paranoid stance. Countertransferences are powerful in these cases. It is impossible to work with a divorcing family without feeling the stirrings of our own internal couples, our own exciting and rejecting objects. It is also impossible not to experience the activation of defences against the affects associated with these stirrings. While there are now law school classes on alternate dispute resolution models, there are none on the dynamics of divorce. Attorneys are not trained to understand the ways in which divorce affects their clients' object relations and their own states of mind, how to sort out the interplay, and how to use understanding in order to avoid massive enactments.

Attorneys are not alone. There are not, to my knowledge any graduate school classes for mental health professionals on working with divorcing couples, let alone working with divorcing couples in the context of the legal system.

While there is little literature on working dynamically with divorcing couples, there is significant literature on working with high conflict couples. Supposedly this is ten to twenty per cent of the divorcing population. But conflict exists on continuum that depends not only on the pathology of the members of the couple, but most importantly on the level of pathology and self awareness of the professionals in the case. This all affects the type of process that clients choose in order to effect their divorce. In my experience nearly every case that is embedded in the legal system becomes some version of a high conflict case.

When couples choose a divorce lawyer, they are getting on a train, and the conductor is their attorney. Whether the process will be adversarial and toxic or collaborative and humane is completely dependent on this choice. Divorce rears its head in every clinical practice, and therapists are often in a position to offer advice. I end with a plea: Educate yourself as to the range of legal divorce options available to clients in your geographical region, consider availing yourself of a training in multidisciplinary divorce work, and, finally, whenever possible, steer your clients toward a non-adversarial, out-of-court process that attends not only to the family's financial and legal needs but that also focuses primarily to the emotional needs of the family now and in the future.

References

Johnston, J., Roseby, V., & Kuehnle, K., (2009). *In the Name of the Child*, 2nd Edition. New York: Springer.

Scharff, K. & Herrick, L. (2010). *Navigating Emotional Currents in Collaborative Divorce*. Chicago: American Bar Association Press.

CHAPTER TWENTY-SIX

Trauma in the couple

Jill Savege Scharff

I will discuss trauma within the couple in the light of attachment patterns, object relations, and dissociation (Ainsworth, Blehar, Waters & Wall, 1978; Fairbairn, 1952; D. Scharff & J. Scharff, 1991, J. Scharff and D. Scharff 1994). I will consider the impact of trauma as an organising or disorganising couple dynamic on each of the partners and on the couple in various ways. I will think of the effect of one member of the couple bringing a trauma history to the couple relationship, and lastly I will give an example of one situation in which the couple itself was traumatised.

Trauma may be brought to the marriage by one partner who has a trauma history, by both partners who each have trauma histories in their own generation or in their parents' generation, or the couple may become traumatised by some event that occurs during their relationship. Whatever the cause of the trauma (see Table 1) it may be of the single shock variety, or it may be cumulative over time. Either way, trauma may become an organising principle for the couple. In that case, partners are drawn together as a couple to resonate with and perpetuate a trauma, or to fight it. The couple's relationship develops in ways to contain the trauma or to disavow and avoid it. When it is disavowed or avoided, it has a tendency to be repeated in the couple relationship or is projected into the next generation. Equally likely, trauma may be impossible to contain or avoid, in which case it becomes a disorganising principle that eventually breaks up the couple.

Table 1. Types of trauma.

• Attachment trauma:	Ill-health, unreliability, and the death of a parent, nanny or grandparent
• Family trauma:	Death of a child, fetal loss, death of a parent's parent, loss of income, loss of home, relocation, infidelity or divorce
• Physical trauma:	Beating, spanking, accidental injury, domestic violence or murder
• Sexual trauma:	Sexual abuse, most pathological when done by a family member, rape, incest or social phobia
• Medical trauma:	Congenital deformity, medical hospitalisation, invasive procedures, surgery and loss of any body part, especially sexual organs: mastectomy, hysterectomy, vasectomy,
• Disaster trauma:	Earthquake, fire, tsunami, loss of home
• Societal trauma:	Racial and religious prejudice, genital mutilation, persecution, bullying, genocide, economic depression
• War trauma:	Post traumatic stress disorder, loss of country, child soldier, father or mother absent and in harm's way on deployment

Individual effects of trauma

First let's think about the effect of trauma on the individual as a child. The child, having an immature ego, is overwhelmed by trauma, from which it cannot escape, being dependent. Trauma disrupts the safe environment for growth and development and disorganses the primary attachment. It is helpful to visualise this fundamental requirement for a safe environment in reference to Winnicott's concept of the mothering person as the environment mother and the object mother. The environment mother provides a zone of good contextual holding—what we have called the "arms around" relationship—which encompasses the secure home, the comfortable crib and stroller, the loving embrace (D. Scharff & J. Scharff, 1987). The object mother provides the eye-to-eye, I-to-I relationship through sensitive interactions via gaze, voice, and touch (see Figure 1). When the environment and object aspects of the mother—the contextual holding that she provides and the direct object relating—are satisfactory, a secure attachment relationship develops. When this safe environment collapses at the hands of trauma, the boundary around the individual is broken, and his thought and verbal expression are invaded and disrupted, sometimes permanently (see Figure 2). His overall brain is smaller, less flexible and less well modulated than the non-traumatised brain. The impoverishment of his right brain constrains its capacity for connectedness among elements of the neural pathway and for responsiveness to emotional stimuli. Without modulation from well-integrated higher centres, the amygdala fire off reflexively in response to stress and create aggressive responses that do not aid navigation through emotional territory. This makes for difficult communication in marriage, and robs the couple of the simplest mechanism for building the secure context that they need for building a new, sustaining attachment.

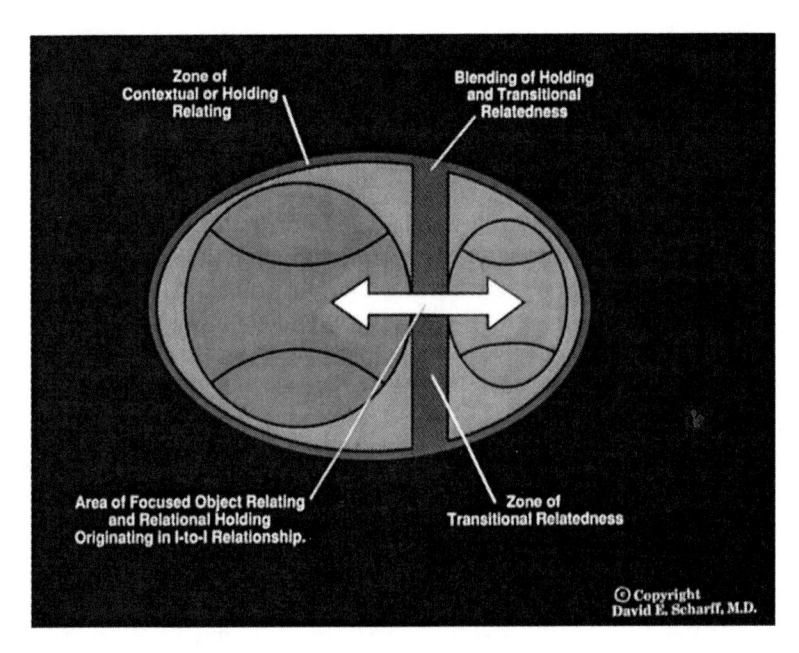

Figure 1. Winnicott's holding environment.

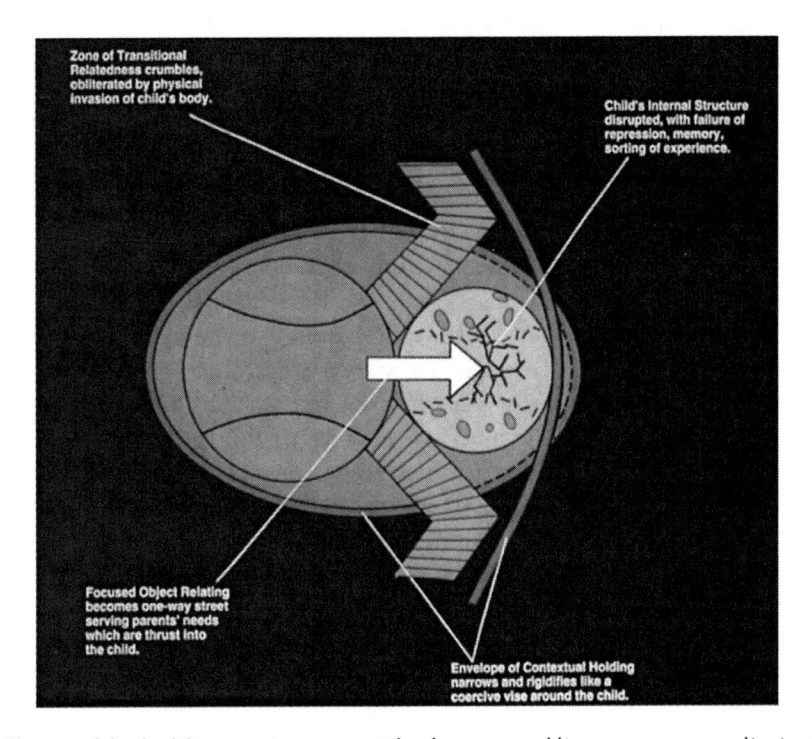

Figure 2. Collapse of the holding environment. The fragmented lines represent splits in the endopsychic structure; the small circles represent connected and disconnected bits of self and object in a state of disorganisation. The transitional zone gets collapsed.

Table 2: Effects of childhood trauma on development.

---
1. Normal parental holding and handling has been replaced by intrusion, control, and imposition on the child.
2. This force collapses the transitional zone of relatedness, squashes any interplay, and thereby stunts growth.
3. The adult breaks through the child's physical and emotional defensive barriers.
4. The adult shatters mental structure sometimes so severely that the split up parts cannot grow together, leaving the child's mind fragmented and afraid.
5. The greater the trauma and the weaker the ego, the more likely the child will defend by encapsulation as if the trauma could be sealed, buried, and forgotten.
6. This leaves a mind with gaps where traumatic internal object relationships have been secreted.

Trauma to a child is mediated by the parent. When the parent has been traumatised by some event near the time of the birth (including the death of a parent, relocation, loss of home or spouse), or carries trauma from the past, that parent is not able to provide a consistently safe environment or be present reliably as an object for relating directly and intimately, and therefore cannot detoxify the child's trauma. Sometimes the parent actually is the person perpetrating the trauma (which is the worst possible scenario) or is misperceived as being responsible for the trauma or at least failing to repair it (whether repair is humanly possible or not). So the trauma has a negative impact on the existing attachment relationship.

When the secure attachment relationship is disrupted in childhood, instead of a secure attachment, the child develops an insecure attachment which may be of various types that tend to fall into two major categories: "resistant" to separation and reunion (in which the child is clingy) or "ambivalent" about separation and reunion (in which the child is dismissive of the need to attach). When the parent has a trauma history, and therefore cannot modify disruptions that occur, a disorganised and disoriented attachment occurs (Ainsworth, Blehar, Waters & Wall, 1978). Whichever attachment pattern results, the person will relate as an adult in ways governed by it, and will show the attachment style in relation to the spouse eventually (Clulow, 2001).

When each member of a couple has a secure attachment style they will be better able to deal with any new trauma that befalls the couple. Even then, trauma can overwhelm and disrupt the couple relationship at least temporarily. But when one or both members of the couple have insecure or disorganised attachments it is hard for them to trust the other, and impossible to cope with any intervening trauma. Couples deal with new trauma in the light of existing trauma. The original pain comes back and augments the current pain. The couple's adult coping strategies in the present may be more relevant to the original source of trauma and inadequate to the current trauma.

Disrupted attachment is only part of the picture (D. Scharff & J. Scharff, 2012). Within that attachment context, we see the development of characteristic intrapsychic dynamics. To cope with trauma the individual self splits off the overwhelming experience and dissociates from it, just as the body goes into shock in response to an extensive burn. The dissociated mental contents clump together in traumatic nuclei that extract traumatic material from the endopsychic situation and wrap it up in a tightly sealed capsule, which is then buried (Hopper, 1991). This type of bundling of endopsychic contents leaves gaps in the psyche. As therapists we can sense these gaps when suddenly there is an impenetrable silence, or a feeling of a void into which we are falling, or a feeling of futility and emptiness inside ourselves. Traumatised individuals may or may not be aware of their splits. The splits in the self may by mutually exclusive so that the person may behave in a certain way at one moment and does not remember it at the next moment, may be delightful company ninety per cent of the time, but suddenly highly abusive in segments of experience, and not acknowledging of them. This makes it difficult for the spouse and the partner to understand what has activated the behaviour and work through it.

In some cases the trauma has been so severe, and the dissociation so complete, that the person has multiple selves with separate memory banks that do not communicate (J. Scharff & D. Scharff, 1994). The person may or may not know this, and even if he does know it, he may feel too ashamed to admit it. This is extremely difficult for the spouse to relate to because she does not know whom she is dealing with. More commonly we note an impaired capacity for fantasy and symbolisation, and a tendency to be literal and concrete, preoccupied with the mundane. The traumatised person is sometimes unable to put into words what she is feeling. Given that early traumatic experience is encoded in the iconic memory system, the traumatised person communicates in images that are realised in behaviour and bodily symptoms rather than in language. These bodily symptoms may be a source of hypochondriac preoccupation or may be expressed in sexual dysfunction that is highly frustrating to the individual and to the couple.

Let's think about the range of ways that the various types of childhood traumas show up in a couple relationship (see Table 2). Couples may show a preoccupation with aggression and damage, blame, and suffering. Symptoms such as infidelity, domestic violence, and incestuous sexual assault on a child may occur as a direct perpetuation of existing trauma. A conscious hatred of the existing trauma may lead to a life devoted to avoiding its repetition, which itself is constraining—for instance, in lieu of violence there is passivity that actually attracts a spouse's violence; in lieu of infidelity a suffocating devotion that drives the spouse away; in lieu of incest, sexual dysfunction or refusal—and so the trauma finds its expression anyway. This occurs because at the intrapsychic level, painful feared and fearful elements of self and internal object relationships are put into the spouse through projective identifications as if they could be deposited there and not have to be owned and dealt with in conscious memory. Some couples appear to be dealing with their trauma histories, but when fate deals them a blow, they experience the new trauma in the light of previous trauma that gets reignited and complicates working through. An earthquake, a house fire, an invasion, amputation of a treasured body part will traumatise the healthiest couples, but they will recover more quickly than the couple with a trauma history.

When a new trauma to a member of a couple or to the couple itself is severe, the capsule around the original trauma may thicken and stiffen in time and block unconscious communication between parts of the self at the individual level, and therefore between the partners at the level of the couple relationship. This leads to a rigid individual personality and deadly repetitive cycles of interaction in the marriage. The couple relationship is maintained by a projective identificatory cycle in such a way as to prevent the emergence of traumatic material that could reactivate the trauma. Nevertheless, it may drive the trauma by projective identification into members of the next generation, and they may then become symptomatic.

The traumatised couple with secure attachment is most likely to recover from the trauma without splitting up. The traumatised couple with insecure attachment faces violence, abandonment, threats of divorce, separation, and possibly murder. Their excessive aggression is an outgrowth of the rejecting object constellation writ large as a defence against over-excitement and unfulfilled longing for love and security. The spouses fear for their bodily integrity and reach for objects to support themselves—literal objects such as guns and knives and personal objects such as a best friend, family, and lover. They live as part-objects in a state of paranoid-schizoid anxiety, whether with or apart from each other, with no breathing room for the relationship to develop into a more mature one with depressive concern and a capacity for reparation to each other. Partners with preoccupied and fearful forms of insecure attachment style are more at risk than those with a dismissive insecure attachment since the dismissive ones are likely to leave the relationship. The fearful ones are least at risk for abuse since they are not demanding or assertive (Bartholomew, Henderson & Dutton, 2001). The stereotypical pattern of abuse features a man with a preoccupied style and a fearful woman, but there are more female perpetrators than has been recognised. The most common abuse relationship following trauma is one in which both spouses have a preoccupied style.

Analytic couple therapy for trauma

When traumatised couples come for therapy, they may seem to be avoiding the topic at hand, and we may feel tempted to call this resistance against dealing with the trauma. It is more useful to regard their avoidance as necessary. We have to remember that they do not have confidence in the value of talking, and they need time to establish trust before they can cooperate with treatment. As we do our analytic work we need at all times to monitor our provision of care and work to maintain a safe holding environment.

Traumatised couples may spend many sessions on the trivia of domesticity and deflect any attempt to deepen the conversation with reference to latent content. We need to think of this as their recreation of the time between, before, and after the traumatic events. Our therapeutic attitude is one of welcoming this going-on-being, to borrow a term that Winnicott used for infants' way of taking for granted the provision of a secure environment that is facilitating to their growth (1975). Occasionally they will dip down into the trauma like a kingfisher suddenly going for a fish, and just as quickly they emerge and stay quietly on the surface until the next foray. We value the opportunity to work directly on the trauma but we value equally the essential times of going-on-being. We hold a therapeutic stance of interest without intrusion. We are present as both an object for direct relating, as a context in which to relate, and as an absence. We will be perceived as the tormentor and as the void, painful countertransferences that are hard to bear (especially that of the void), and that is why both we and the couples require the periods of going-on-being to maintain the therapeutic relationship.

Trying to do analytic couple therapy with traumatised couples, we may become frustrated at the lack of dream material, which blocks one point of access to the unconscious. Instead we have to look at the projective identificatory system of the couple's relationship. How do they deal with each other? What do they see of themselves in each other? What has been split off and projected into the partner, or into us? If we look at the body language we may detect affect and projections that need to be named. If we look at how we are feeling, and what we are imagining, we may recover lost images that hold the memory of the trauma. Having done that, we can then put the images into narrative form—not necessarily a literally accurate recall but a working reconstruction that makes sufficient sense of experience to let it go and move forward. Our goal is to provide a treatment experience and model for reflection and discussion that allows the couple to recover its sense of itself as a healing, supportive environment for its members. By detoxifying the trauma and building good experiences the couple transmutes trauma to genera. As individuals, the partners take back their projective identifications and each of them re-finds the self as its own object.

Clinical example: working with traumatic nuclei and gaps in the psyche

Sometimes the couple presents for depression, anxiety, or sexual difficulty, with no hint of trauma, past or present. Trauma history emerges only after some time in treatment. The couple has successfully split off all awareness of traumatic experience and sequestered it inside the marriage in traumatic nuclei. An apparently satisfactory marital relationship may cover these traumatic nuclei but, as I explained earlier, the gathering of trauma into nuclei leaves gaps in the psyche. How do analytic couple therapists access the gaps as a way to reach the nuclei? They look at gaps in the treatment process (unplanned absence, lateness, silence) or their own instances of discomfort and mental blocking.

Tony and Theresa (briefly referred to in Chapter One and described more fully in J. Scharff & D. Scharff, 1994) had a happy marriage and family life. Both worked at the same company and shared domestic chores and child-rearing at home. Because of an unexpected medical trauma, Tony had a major infection that led to his having his right arm amputated. Tony could not recover from the trauma, refused help, and could not work. Theresa took over both jobs, but Tony did nothing at home except argue. In therapy, it became apparent that their previous contentment had been built on a faithfully respected promise to avoid any repetition of abuse. As children each of them in their own families had been the one who took the hit in order to protect the others from abuse. As spouses and parents, they both got angry but they never hurt each other: They hit the wall instead, sometimes even injuring their hands because, although they could avoid perpetrating abuse on others, they had not metabolised the hurt from early abuse and kept repeating it in this shared way. In so doing, they built a wall around their feelings of rage. The medical trauma burst through that wall, robbed Tony of his way of expressing anger, and left him full of rage and grief. Tony and Theresa's relationship was in chaos.

Tony and Theresa took to therapy, and spoke easily and with feeling about what had happened. They did not deal with dreams or symbolisation, but focused concretely on the events that had occurred. Sharing this information in therapy brought some relief. So the therapist was surprised when the couple fell into silences and began to skip sessions. Then he thought to himself that they were creating a gap that suggested the presence of another traumatic nucleus. He said to Tony and Theresa that they were avoiding another painful topic. It turned out that this previously happy couple had been unable to enjoy intercourse for some years. Tony had not been told that Theresa was avoiding it (and therefore him) because intercourse had become painful since her hysterectomy.

Now the therapist knew of trauma in the past and in the present. They had literally lost Tony's right arm and Theresa's uterus, and had functionally lost his ability to work and express aggression and her ability to respond in intercourse and express love and excitement. If they could recommit to analytic couple therapy, Tony and Theresa would need time to mourn their losses and re-find ways to express love and anger.

Some couples deal with trauma by repeating it. Let's say that an individual has been sexually abused in childhood, that individual may find a partner with whom to have sex compulsively apparently in order to release sexual tension and guilt by having sex with a non-incestuous object, but this way of coping actually continues the feeling of being used as a sexual object. Other sexually abused individuals may avoid sexuality, and the frustration this causes to the partner may lead to physical abuse or forced sexual interaction. Other couples who, like Tony and Theresa attempt to avoid repetition of abuse may avoid intimacy altogether and may inhibit their children's capacity for intimacy, sexuality, and the appropriate expression of aggression as well.

The process of analytic couple therapy enables us to recreate a transitional zone where the couple can begin to convert implicit memories contained in bodily symptoms or symptomatic behaviours into explicit thoughts and fantasies. Analytic couple therapy for trauma supports the growth of "genera", healing nuclei that gather good experience to repair and replace the traumatic nuclei of injury and self-destruction.

References

Ainsworth, M. D. S., Blehar, M. C. Waters, E., & Wall, S. (1978). *Patterns of Attachment: A Psychological Study of the Strange Situation*. Hillsdale, NJ: Lawrence Erlbaum.

Bartholomew, K., Henderson, A. J. Z., & Dutton, D. G. (2001). Insecure attachment and abusive intimate relationships. In: C. Clulow (Ed.), *Adult Attachment and Couple Psychotherapy* (pp. 43–61). London: Brunner Routledge; and Philadelphia, PA: Taylor and Francis.

Clulow, C. (Ed.) (2001). *Adult Attachment and Couple Psychotherapy*. London: Brunner Routledge; and Philadelphia, PA: Taylor and Francis.

Fairbairn, W. R. D. (1952). *Psychoanalytic Studies of the Personality*. London: Routledge and Kegan Paul. Also published as *An Object Relations Study of the Personality*. New York: Basic Books.

Hopper, E. (1991). Encapsulation as a defense against the fear of annihilation. *International Journal of Psycho-Analysis, 72*, 4: 607–624.

Scharff, D. E. & Scharff, J. S. (1987). *Object Relations Family Therapy*. Northvale, NJ: Jason Aronson.

Scharff, D. E. & Scharff, J. S. (1991). *Object Relations Couple Therapy*. Northvale, NJ: Jason Aronson.

Scharff, D. E. & Scharff, J. S. (2011). *The Interpersonal Unconscious*. Lanham, MD: Jason Aronson.

Scharff, J. S. & Scharff, D. E. (1994). *Object Relations Therapy of Physical and Sexual Trauma*. Northvale, NJ: Jason Aronson.

Winnicott, D. W. (1975). *The Maturational Processes and the Facilitating Environment*. London: Hogarth.

CHAPTER TWENTY-SEVEN

Treating intergenerational trauma: the bomb that exploded me continues to blow up my family

Hanni Mann-Shalvi

This chapter focuses on the unconscious processes that take place in families and couples who experienced loss from terror attacks. Over the years Israel has been exposed to different kinds of terror attacks that target civilian children and adults, in the most unexpected circumstances during everyday life. Experience has taught me that in such circumstances unique unconscious processes unfold.

Freud (1920) used the word "trauma" which means in Greek "wound", to emphasise how the mind can be wounded by events that overwhelm mental processes by being too sudden or extreme to accommodate and process (1916). Working for many years with families that experienced loss in terror attacks I realise that latent and overt aggression were the main emotional components that endangered the family members as individuals and as a family unit by accumulating continuous destructive energy in new, various, and different emotional patterns. Aggression is a known response to trauma. Freud (1920) explained it as a person's attempt to control the traumatic situation by turning the passive role into an active role. Anna Freud (1936) explained it as a defence mechanism of identification with the aggressor.

The psychoanalytic view on trauma holds that the impact of traumatic events upon the mind can be treated only through achieving a deeper knowledge of the particular meaning of those events for that individual, integrating it into the individual's conscious existence. The trauma touches and disrupts the core of the individual's identity, and may damage the individual's capacity to symbolise. Since the survivor can never be restored to a pre-trauma state, mourning is part of the therapeutic process, in addition to the mourning for the beloved dead family member. The need to face the extent of human destructiveness makes the task of therapy very difficult (Garland, 1998).

The "ball of fire" is uncontrollable in the family

According to Freud a "constancy principle" regulates the distribution of energy within an organism in order to keep the level of stimulation as close to zero as possible (Freud, 1895, p. 197, 1920, p. 9). When a bomb explodes and kills a family member, the deadly destructive energy penetrates the family system with its ongoing explosive quality and seeks a suitable container to host it, absorb it, and enable the release of its explosive material, "freeing" the other family members live.

Since containing excessive aggression means risking intra-psyche and interpersonal equilibrium the dreadful "ball of fire" is thrown between the family members in their efforts to push it away. Severely traumatic events stir up the unresolved pains and conflicts of childhood (Garland, 1998). In the case of terror attacks, it gets "magnetised" to existing unprocessed unconscious violent forces, hidden in the personality or in the relationships, and "uses" the surviving family members as anchors.

The intensified aggression breaks former organisations of defences, and can cause pathologic reactions like psychotic breakdown, suicide, divorce etc., even in families that had not suffered in the past from any emotional pathology. The symptomatic manifestations can be so removed from the origin that they can easily be misinterpreted as not being related to the death that had occurred earlier.

Thus, in addition to the difficult mourning processes, these families have to confront the intensified aggression that is locked-up within their family system, threatening to continue the experience of endless explosions from unexpected directions.

The therapeutic process

All the therapeutic functions that are relevant in object relations couple and family therapy can be applied to the treatment of families who have experienced a violent death of a family member:

- Opening the potential space for exploration
- Holding relationships
- Accepting individual and family projective identifications and feeding them back to the family (J. Scharff & D. Scharff, 2000, p. 15).

In extreme family trauma the explosive nature of the aggression shapes all of the above emotional processes. If the process is not identified (by the therapist and then re-experienced and detoxified in the therapeutic process), therapy is conducted under ongoing threats of explosions from innumerable unexpected sources and directions, preventing the evolvement of a therapeutic safe space.

The therapeutic process demands:

a. **Thorough family evaluation** of:
   1. The patterns of relationships and how they have changed because of the trauma.

2. The emotional personality structure of the family members in order to identify unresolved repressed conflicts that might allow discharge of the explosive aggression.
3. Tracking the elusive path that the aggressive energy has taken in each family member and in the family dynamics.

b. **Identifying vulnerable family members and relationship patterns** that are at risk to become the second-line "absorbers", once the first-line "symptom presenters" will be treated (the "weak link", the "scapegoat", etc.).
c. **Maintaining a therapeutic process** that enables working-through of the identified unresolved conflicts that put the certain person or relationship at risk.
d. **Allowing space for the mourning process**, bearing in mind that the aggressive forces in the family are still striving to be released.
e. **Containing the acute violent** forces. This makes it possible for family members to meet their extreme rage and work it through.
f. **Forming new patterns** of relationships and personality dynamics.

Treatment can never take away the pain of the violent death of a loved one. Nor will the family ever return to their past emotional dynamics. But treatment can safeguard the family from a chain-response of continuous intensive crises, and at the same time, allow them to experience a process of growth and development on their way to continuing their life in a new equilibrium.

The Buckle family

Avi, sixty-eight-years-old and Hadar sixty-six-years-old are the parents of two sons (Eran and Eli) and a daughter (Mia) and are grandparents of ten grandchildren. They have been married for forty years in what can be described as a quite "good tense" relationship. Disputes were part of their normal relationship pattern, and centred most of the time on his frequent business travels abroad. Avi's father had left the family when Avi was four. Avi never forgave him but did not talk about it.

Hadar came from a strict patriarchal family. When she was seven-years-old her mother was killed by an Arab sniper and she was raised by her father's second wife, whom she did not like. The Buckles appeared to be a mainstream family that led a rich economic, social and family life. Hadar was the centre of the extended family. The children fulfilled the parents' expectations; all were married to "the right" spouses, held respectable jobs and led "decent lives".

The idyllic picture was shattered when their first-born son Eran was killed. "One morning" Hadar told me: "I heard on the news that a suicide bomber exploded himself in a commercial center in Tel-Aviv. I knew immediately that Eran was killed, I called Avi and shouted: 'Let's go to the hospital!' I arrived and screamed 'I am Eran's mother, I want to see him', but it was too late."

From this moment their lives changed, "the destructive energy" penetrated the family attacking interpersonal relationships and internal equilibrium.

The therapeutic climate was constantly changing because of the burst of new centres of aggression which provoked life-threatening crises in the family. To begin dealing with this, we need a strong and resilient frame. As the Scharffs put it: "Family therapy offers the provision of a frame in which work can go on. By providing the time, space, and structure for the therapy, we give form to the provision of the holding space … the setup needs to be adequate and appropriate to the job to be done …" (J. Scharff & D. Scharff 1987, p. 170).

Thorough family evaluation

a. Patterns of relationship in the nuclear family

A closer look inside the "perfect family façade" revealed a passive—aggressive pattern between the parents. This pronounced itself through Hadar's ongoing accusations and Avi's complying, yet never satisfying, reaction.

The mother-child relational pattern was controlled by the mother's "victim" position. The children were always aware "how not to upset mother" who had endless reasons to be upset. The only exception was Hadar's relationship with her eldest son Eran, whom she loved the most and felt that he, and everything he did, was perfect. This caused his siblings to feel jealous, which was reversed to complying behaviour by trying to be "as good as Eran."

Hadar said, The minute he was born I looked into his big blue eyes and I knew that he was special. I love all my children but with him it was always something else …" Only after his death, in one of the individual sessions, the secret origin of this special love started to unfold and with it the multiple layers of the family jealousy.

b. Identifying vulnerable family members and relationship patterns

The most vulnerable family member who was at-risk to absorb the aggressive energy was Hadar who as a young child lost her mother in a similar situation and since then has carried a burden of suppressed unconscious, emotional conflicts that she had never dealt with. Probably her controlling relationship pattern with her family served as a defence against those feelings.

Indeed, shortly after Eran's death Hadar's relationship with her family deteriorated. She "fired" destructive aggression in all directions. Aggressive conflicts were exploding one after the other among different family members.

- During the individual sessions Hadar told me that she married Avi as a replacement for a relationship with an ex-lover her father objected to. It became clear that she transmitted her emotions for her ex-lover to her first-born child Eran. The blocked love flooded her uncontrollably. The ex-lover heard in the news that her son was killed and called her. The love between them burst forth again. She considered marrying him. This libidinal energy served as a "pain-killer" for her grief. But the combination of destructive aggression and unacceptable libidinal attraction was too much to handle at the same time.
- The tension between Avi and Hadar became more intense and aggressive.
- Being in a "symbiotic" relationship with her children Hadar penetrated their individual and married space carrying with her destructive aggression.
- New and old conflicts in the young couples reactivated, especially between the daughter who was identifying with her mother and her father. The daughter and her husband were considering divorce.
- The hidden conflict between Eran's "two wives": Naomi, his widow and Hadar, his mother, deteriorated to a point where Naomi did not allow Hadar to see her grandchildren anymore.

- The destructive aggression moved to the third generation, making them the next vulnerable candidates. The aggression was escalating to the level of suicidal thoughts in Eran's eldest son, who, in addition to the loss of his father, lost the connection to his father's family.
- Hadar's aggression which did not fully explode yet, was targeted towards herself and she became weaker, sicker, thinner, and angrier almost to a point where her life was in danger.
- Avi's unresolved anger towards his disappearing father was reactivated, flooding him and serving at the same time as a distraction from his son's death.
- Eli's anger toward his father who was not there for him throughout his childhood was reactivated. A tense gap opened between them, manifesting itself in sarcastic remarks from Eli toward his father on family occasions and with long periods of detached silence.
- Avi became more and more isolated within his own family and therefore a good candidate to become the next vulnerable aggression-absorber.
- Avi became involved in Mia's life. Mia's marriage crisis served as diversion from his grief and a solution for his emotional isolation in the family, since he "was called upon" to help his daughter and could not "indulge" himself in his own emotional crisis.

c. Unfolding, differentiating, and working through

It was clear that the whole family was at risk, with the aggressive energy moving from one generation to the other. The next disaster "was written on the wall". Since the multiple crises were chain reactions to the terror attack, not all the crises needed to be treated. I choose to treat four centres which I thought would stop the dangerous distractive process:

1. Hadar's emotional dynamics
2. Avi's emotional dynamics
3. Hadar and Avi's marriage
4. Mia and Uri's marriage.

Since the suicide threats were situated in the third generation, I felt that stopping the process in the first and second generation would "free" the grandchildren. In order to allow Hadar to work on her relationship with her ex-lover, I met Hadar and Avi separately and as a couple. I met Mia and Uri in couple therapy. The therapeutic process continued for three years.

Treatment process

1. In Hadar's individual psychotherapy she became aware that her love for her ex-lover was the origin of her special love towards Eran. Her ex-lover's return into her life made it possible to confront her genuine feelings, rather than fantasised feelings, towards him.
2. She re-lived the mourning for her mother including her anger towards her. This made it easier for her to go through a separation-individuation process from her mother and from her children as well.
3. Avi worked on his unresolved anger towards his father. A new space for relating opened in him. He could face his emotional difficulty in engaging in meaningful warm relationships with his sons. Consequently his relationship with Eli improved.
4. The above processes unchained Hadar and Avi's present relationships from the pull of past unconscious conflicts, and paved the way in couple therapy for the discussion old conflicts while allowing for different points of view and emotional needs. Towards the end of therapy, Avi's new intimacy with his son Eli began to raise new tensions in Hadar's

and Eli's relationship, pushing them back to their "good, but sometimes tense" familiar relationship pattern.
5. Mia and Uri's couple therapy was centred on boundaries at the different levels of family relations.
6. New norms of relationship: The expression of emotions, needs, wishes, and the exercising of boundaries around personal and shared space became legitimate and began to spread as a new style from the family members in therapy throughout the family.

d. Making space for the mourning process and containing the acute violent forces

During the therapeutic mourning process, the released destructive aggression meshed with grief, especially with anger. Bursts of extreme pain, torturous feelings, violent anger, grief, and much more flooded the family members, shaking them and leaving them helpless to these extreme uncontrollable forces.

In these stages I needed to function as a reliable container who could absorb the extreme intensity, and not be destroyed by it, and also to be able to allow feelings to be expressed in words. Once acknowledged these raw feelings became legitimate and could be digested. Understanding the underlying dynamics helped me to be able to do this. Once the destructive aggression could be released in the therapeutic safe space, a working-through process became possible. Stage by stage the grip of the explosive energy loosened and the family formed new equilibrium patterns.

Forming new patterns

Hadar decided not to leave her husband and they went back to their "normal-tense" relationship. Boundaries and personal space replaced the symbiotic relationship between Hadar and her children, making it possible for Mia and Uri to build their marriage. For the first time, Hadar permitted herself to tell her children when she was too tired to invite them for the weekend meals and when she did not want to babysit for her grandchildren. Hadar now calmer, made peace with her daughter-in-law and gained healthier relationships with her dead son's children. Her grandchild no longer had suicidal thoughts. With the widow's cooperation Hadar took upon herself the role of telling Eran's children stories about Eran's childhood, a role that gave her a new constructive status in their family. All the family members formed new patterns of more satisfying relationships.

Towards the end of the therapy the entire family engaged in Eran's memorial project.

Conclusion

Time did not allow for more detailed description of the therapeutic process, nor for detailing aspects of focused and contextual transferences and countertransference which organise the therapist's understanding (D. Scharff & J. Scharff, 1987).

I have tried to show special aspects of family and couple therapy under extreme trauma. This family, and with them their therapist, faced extreme levels of destructive aggression that expanded and overwhelmed all the intra-psychic and inter-relational levels. It overflowed into previous and future generations, and into internalised object relationships as it continued to explode.

These conditions of trauma create unpredictable strenuous crises. The therapist is required to perform complex therapeutic functions: throughout therapy an ongoing "diagnostic eye" must be open to assess the dynamics of individuals and family as a unit, including those who are outside the therapeutic circle and attentive to the route that the destructive energy takes, once its current hosts have been treated. At the same time a safe space for the therapist and the family, which enables undisturbed therapeutic work to take place, needs to be created. From this safe base, we can identify the focal points of life risks and intervene and stay alert to processes of transference and countertransference. The therapist cannot afford to retreat from the onslaught or adopt an omnipotent stance in order to feel as if she is coping. The work of containment places a high emotional demand on the therapist. Therapists need to do more work on identfying the different characteristics of families in extreme trauma and providing access to skilled therapy.

References

Freud, A. (1936). The ego and the mechanisms of defence. In: *The Writing of Anna Freud, Vol. 11*. New York: International University Press, 1966.

Freud, S. (1895). *Studies on Hysteria. S. E., 2*: 9. London: Hogarth.

Freud, S. (1916). *Introductory Lectures on Psychoanalysis, S. E., 16*: 275. London: Hogarth.

Freud, S. (1920). *Beyond the Pleasure Principle. S. E., 18*: 9. London: Hogarth.

Garland, C. (1998) [2007]. Why Psychoanalysis? In: C. Garland (Ed.), *Understanding Trauma a Psychoanalytical Approach* (pp. 3–8). The Tavistock clinic series. London: Karnac.

Greenberg, J. R., Mitchell, S. A. (2003). *Object Relations in Psychoanalytic Theory*. Cambridge: Harvard University Press. (First published in 1983).

Scharff, J. S., & Scharff, D. E. (1987). *Object Relations Family Therapy*. Northvale, NJ: Jason Aronson.

Scharff, J. S & Scharff, D. E. (2000). *New Paradigms for Treating Relationships*. Lanham, MD: Jason Aronson.

Schneider, S. (2005). The effect of trauma on the conductor of the group: A type of identificatory countertransference. *International Journal of Group Psychotherapy, 55*: 1.

CHAPTER TWENTY-EIGHT

But my partner "is" the problem: addressing addiction, mood disorders, and psychiatric illness in psychoanalytic couple treatment

Janine Wanlass

Frustrated, detached, and despairing, forty-two-year-old Catherine leaves a message on my answering machine: "I'm checking to see if you still do couples treatment, and if you might have time to see Brad and me. This is his last chance. If he doesn't stop drinking, I don't know if I can stay married. He's ruining our family, and it doesn't seem to matter. I can't deal with his problem, and he won't take it seriously."

Although couple therapists frequently encounter evidence of addiction and mood disorders in one or both partners engaged in couple treatment, severe mental health issues other than character disturbances have received limited focus in the analytic literature (Morgenstern & Leeds, 1993). Historically, such problems were treated almost entirely in the individual context. Recently, research coming from the Scandinavian studies on schizophrenia illuminates the benefits of systemic interventions, highlighting the role of family treatment in more favourable outcomes (Buksti, Munkner, Gade, Roved, Tvarno et al., 2006). Anecdotal evidence from addiction treatment centres supports the importance of educating family members about addiction and providing a forum for frustrations to be aired and collusive dynamics understood. Research addressing the interpersonal aspects of depression cites marital distress as a contributing factor in unremitting depressive episodes (Gupta, Coyne, & Beach, 2003; Kouras, Cummings, & Papp, 2008). Certainly, I am not advocating for the sole use of psychoanalytic couple treatment to combat serious mental illness; rather, I am suggesting that couple treatment has a role in conjunction with medication, periodic hospitalisations, support groups, and individual treatment.

Why consider couple treatment when one or both partners presents with a significant mental health concern? First, the illness exists in the couple context and dramatically influences the couple dynamic. Consider the unconscious couple fit, the polarisation of the couple into roles of "sick" and "well" (Vincent, 2007), and the disowned, projected, and displaced "madness" and dependency. As the "identified patient", one partner holds the unacknowledged psychotic, disorganised, destructive aspects of the couple relationship. Second, the symptomatology itself may express some aspect of the couple dynamic. For example, a husband's pull toward cocaine represents an attempt to bring liveliness into an emotionally deadened marriage. A wife's lack of sexual desire is attributed solely to her medicated depression, eliminating examination of relational contributions and preserving an idealised view of the marriage. A couple's difficulty with emotional closeness is mediated with alcohol, creating a tolerable emotional distance. In each example, the symptoms of the illness express a problematic aspect of the couple relationship in addition to their individual meaning.

In some instances, the diagnosed addiction or mental health issue serves as a couple defence. For example, I will discuss a couple where the wife attributes any marital disagreement to her husband's bipolar disorder. When he gets angry with her, she asks if his medication needs adjusting. Any problem in couple relating is simply evacuated into the bipolar illness, viewed as a biologically caused, medical problem. In other instances, the mental health issue drains the marriage, leading to complaints about "missing the woman I married" or expressions of grief and fatigue following repeated hospitalisations, much as we see with chronic physical illness. The appearance or exacerbation of mental health issues may signify a failure in the couple containment, an emergence of encapsulated trauma, or a repeat of intergenerational patterns. In essence, we do not know the dynamic meanings and functions of the illness to the couple unless we adopt a couple state of mind (Morgan, 2005) and create psychological space for the question to be explored.

For the therapist, treating these couples is complex and challenging. The therapist must maintain a dual focus, examining the couple dynamic while keeping in mind the individual meaning and management of the illness. To lose track of either focal point compromises the treatment, as a destructive couple dynamic will exacerbate the illness or the illness itself can defeat the couple treatment. This dual focus on couple and individual pathology, the challenges in maintaining a couple state of mind, and the value of couple treatment in psychiatric illness is illuminated in the following two clinical examples.

Adam and Diane

Adam and Diane are in their forties, married twelve years with two daughters, ages eight and ten. Both work full time in the legal field, although Adam is relatively more successful in his career than Diane. Adam reveals the story of their courtship, commenting that when they first met, Diane was caught in an emotionally abusive relationship with her boss. Both characterise Adam as rescuing Diane, who had struggled to extricate herself from this problematic relationship. Adam's overt caretaking role has continued, as Diane displays a helpless, needy, childlike quality, complaining about any minor separations requiring her to care for the girls alone. Adam resents Diane's complaining, noting that his job demands occasional travel and suggesting he periodically needs time to himself.

Adam and Diane grew up in impoverished circumstances, both physically and emotionally. With little education and few resources, Adam's parents worked long hours at low paying jobs. Their nine children were often left unsupervised. Adam's older siblings drank as teens, frequently skipped school, and pursued minor delinquent acts. Physical violence was common in his family, as Adam saw his older brothers beaten and was sexually assaulted himself by an older cousin. His younger brother was killed at fifteen in a car accident. Diane's mother was always "sick," more a reflection of her mental health problems than her physical frailties. Her parents divorced when Diane was five, creating a state of mental collapse in her mother from which she never recovered. The five children were left to care for themselves, pushed toward pseudo-autonomy to survive. All five children have struggled with depression and addictions, experiencing difficulties creating lasting intimate relationships. Determined to improve their life circumstances, both Adam and Diane independently pursued higher education. Adam's entry into college followed an early adulthood marked by alcohol and drug abuse, necessitating an extended stay in an alcohol rehabilitation facility. After discharge, he remained sober for ten years, meeting Diane and starting a family together. In retrospect, Adam places his first manic episode at about age twenty-one, obscured and possibly exacerbated by his drug use.

Adam and Diane's relationship gradually deteriorated. This was primarily evidenced in a relational deadness or emotional void (Vincent, 2007). The couple argued over money, Adam's work hours, parenting, and sex, but even their arguments lacked passion. Allegedly unknown to Diane, Adam had two brief sexual encounters while away on business. Adam felt excited by these secret liaisons, but also guilty. He started drinking occasionally, which progressed to daily drunkenness. Looking back, Adam views his drinking as a way to control the alternation between an over-stimulated mind and a deepening depression. Privately, he struggled with encroaching madness, expressed in a comment as he left my office the first time: "I think I'm going crazy." Indeed, he did seem paranoid to me at first meeting, while Diane appeared defensively oblivious to his difficulties.

Two weeks into treatment, Adam presented in my office in a clearly psychotic state. His drinking was entirely unchecked and combined with occasional abuse of prescribed anxiolytics, amplifying his mental health issues. I told Diane he needed hospitalisation. Initially infuriated and confused, she said he had simply been drinking "a little too much." Once hospitalised, the alcohol cleared from his system and his manic state was unquestionably evident. Over the next year, he was hospitalised three additional times. He required high doses of anti-psychotic medication and struggled to regain his cognitive functioning and pre-hospitalisation personality. Diane could now see his illness, necessitating a role reversal, as she became his caretaker and the primary financial provider.

Once Adam stabilised, he began to address his traumatic childhood for the first time. Although he worked hard in treatment on these issues and was compliant with his psychiatric medications, he began sneaking alcohol, undermining both the treatment and his marriage. Diane had been clear. She could accept his bipolar illness, but she would not tolerate any drinking, as she correctly surmised that alcohol had contributed to his destabilisation. In retrospect, I believe Adam wanted out of the marriage even at the onset of treatment. In a repeat of Diane's predicament with her boss when they first met, Adam could neither voice his desire to end the marriage nor extricate himself. Together, they proceeded to destroy the good in their relationship. Each blamed the other, and Diane blamed me. I felt frustrated, defeated, and terrified that Adam would self-destruct. At times, I identified with Adam's anger at Diane's projection into him of everything "sick" and "bad." She presented as the "good girl," insisting all the problems in their relationship were Adam's fault. Other times, I felt pulled toward Diane, angered by

Adam's hell-bent path toward self-destruction and narcissistic self-absorption. He seemed to forget that he was the father of two frightened daughters who felt they did not recognise their father. It was only as Adam's condition continued to deteriorate that I learned of Diane's past history of alcohol abuse and prior hospitalisation, an unprocessed trauma rekindled by Adam's repeated inpatient stays.

How had this couple relationship become so toxic? Could this relational course and outcome be predicted? What was the dynamic function of Adam's substance abuse and mood disorder in the couple relationship? On the surface, conscious level, Adam and Diane seemed an obvious match. They had similar values, interests, career paths, level of education and desire for children. Diane commented that Adam provided safety, predictability, and caretaking—factors that were absent in her childhood home. Adam felt valued, important, and competent in his caretaker role, affirming his masculinity and success as a provider. He was the kind, responsible father that had been missing from his own childhood. But what of the couple's unconscious fit, a match at a deeper level? Initially, Adam was able to deny his early traumatic victimisation, projecting into Diane the needy child to be rescued. Diane chose an emotionally unstable partner, mirroring early interactions with her parents. Adam's "breakdown" placed her in the same chaos and terror she had experienced with her mother and later in herself. Adam's illness held the psychotic aspects of Diane's personality and that of the couple, distancing her from her own "madness." Part of her fury over Adam's hospitalisation stemmed from the memory it evoked of her own psychiatric hospitalisation, a shameful secret like Adam's sexual abuse. This was a couple bound by early traumas and internalised persecutory objects, encapsulated and un-metabolised.

Adam's bipolar illness and addiction served a dynamic function for the couple. His alternating moods of deep depression and mania captured their relational deadness and periodic uncontained affective flooding. Drawing from Fairbairn's theory (J. Scharff & D. Scharff, 1998), we can see that Adam's bipolarity and addiction express both the rejecting and exciting bad objects that dominated the couple's childhoods, their internal self-constructions, and their couple relating. Haunted by rejection and filled with longing, Adam's illness enacted the deadly, unknowable couple dynamic. I am not suggesting that the relationship difficulties caused the bipolar illness and substance abuse; however, the couple conflict created an exacerbation of existing vulnerability and dominated the couple's destructive approach to managing Adam's illness.

What was the impact of Adam's illness on the relationship? Adam became the identified patient, demanding redistribution of relational power and responsibility. Diane, compelled toward more mature partner and parental functioning through Adam's breakdown, could no longer be the whiney child. Certainly, Adam's illness surfaced extensive childhood trauma for both partners, a dramatic return of repressed bad objects. Diane felt abandoned and betrayed, initially responding as the caretaking child of her childhood and progressing to a raging dismissal of "incompetent professionals". Like her parents, I became the transference source of harm and perpetrator of pain. I could not keep her safe from Adam's acting out, and my insistence that we consider the couple aspects of Adam's illness challenged her well-defended stance that he was the problem. For Adam, his descent into madness replayed the out-of-control, dangerous father of his childhood and the fragmentation of his mind during repetitive childhood traumas. He was both perpetrator and victim, abusively attacking himself and leaving his wife and children traumatised and unprotected.

Most significantly, Adam's breakdown anticipated the break-up of their couple relationship and eventual divorce. In a sense, the exacerbation of his illness conveyed in action what neither could face directly or openly discuss. Adam would later comment that he could not speak of splitting up, something he had wanted but feared. Instead, he acted it out in an internal mood split and by doing the one thing his wife would not tolerate—he drank and drank again. He refused to take his alcohol addiction seriously until the marriage ended. This allowed Diane to leave the marriage with her "good girl" status intact, the loving partner who stood by her ill husband until he made it impossible for her to remain. In this way we could say that Adam protected her through his destructive actions. For each partner, Adam's symptoms became a means of attacking the marriage and evacuating the couple problem. His psychiatric illness and addiction were the problem, not the marriage.

So, what was the role and value of couple treatment for Adam and Diane? For this couple, divorce was a positive outcome, as they were unable to disentangle their shared and individual pathology while remaining in the marriage. They could not face splitting up, but they could not live together either. The couple work exposed the deadly couple they did not wish to see, projected and hidden in Adam's illness. He could not get better and sustain the marriage, an incompatible combination. She could not claim her own individual and couple pathology while Adam carried it for her. Diane believes that couple therapy failed, because they are no longer together. But since the divorce, Adam has remained stable and sober, though he struggles with periodic exacerbations of his bipolar condition and is fearful of new relationships. Diane has moved through a series of relational pairings and eventually returned to individual treatment for her own depression. So while their marital coupling has ended, each now has the psychological space to address their own demons, hopefully leading to more successful future partnerships.

Brad and Catherine

Brad and Catherine, married twenty years, are in their mid forties. Brad is employed full time as the director of a high profile government agency, a job he enjoys and values. Catherine runs a half-day preschool from their home and attends to the needs of their three children ages eight, ten, and thirteen. The couple met in senior school, marrying some five years later over the objections of Brad's staunchly Catholic parents. Brad's decision to marry outside his faith was a source of contention and blamed entirely on Catherine, despite Brad's having refused to attend mass since age fifteen. Brad began drinking and smoking occasionally during high school, primarily as a hidden statement of rebellion against his parents. Brad's father was raised by a pair of abusive alcoholics. This difficult early experience led Brad's father to forbid any drinking in his home, and he consistently warned Brad about the dangers of alcohol. Brad and Catherine attended colleges in different states, excelling academically and pursuing their relationship at a distance. After graduation, the couple married, and Brad moved through a series of jobs he disliked, uncertain about his career direction. Brad and Catherine describe their early marital years as "happy," but the couple struggled to relate sexually. Brad began drinking more, and

Catherine experienced heightened anxiety in the form of panic attacks. Finally, she told Brad about a history of extensive sexual abuse by a neighbour, and Brad encouraged her to enter individual treatment.

Catherine grew up as the middle child of three. Her father emerged from impoverished circumstances to become a highly successful businessman, a poster child for the American dream. Still, he was a workaholic, and the task of raising the children was left to her mother. Her parents' relationship was somewhat distant, leaving her mother to meet her intimacy needs through her children, a pattern Catherine would repeat in her own marriage. Catherine was sexually molested and emotionally threatened from ages five to ten by an older neighbour boy who tended the children and was a frequent visitor in their home. She did not tell her parents until she reached adulthood, as the boy said he would hurt her developmentally challenged, mildly autistic younger brother should she disclose anything to anyone. She repressed most of the specifics of these abusive incidents until she began having sex with Brad shortly before their marriage.

Brad is the oldest son and third child in a family of seven children. His parents are devoutly religious, moralistic, and emotionally distant. His mother was "sick" during most of his childhood, suffering from self-medicated, vague somatic symptoms. His financially successful father worked long hours in the real estate business and was obsessively preoccupied with cleanliness and order. Due to the mother's health issues, preschool-aged Brad and his two older sisters spent periods of time with his grandparents. They became repeated victims of sexual abuse by his alcoholic grandfather. In retrospect, Brad wonders how his father who suffered the maltreatment of alcoholic parents would leave his own children in their care. We can speculate that Brad's father kept his trauma encapsulated, dissociated from the conscious awareness that would help him become a protective parent. This dissociative process within the family system allows for such unmetabolised trauma to be passed from generation to generation, carried forward and repeated rather than worked through.

Brad was popular and successful in senior school and college. In reflecting on their relationship, however, Catherine notes that a part of Brad was always inaccessible to her. Although friendly and outgoing, he has no close friends. Brad seems conflicted about his own sexuality, an observation made by Catherine and dismissed by Brad. His ambivalence about his phallic potency is evident in the contrast between his job where he holds an "all powerful" role, and his passive stance at home with his wife and children. His drinking has been a feature throughout their twenty-year marriage, with periods of greater and lesser intensity. At his wife's insistence, he completed three alcohol treatment programs, but initial successes quickly descended into relapse. Brad and Catherine made a brief attempt at couple treatment with me, but they left after about three months, a flight into health when Brad stopped drinking for three weeks.

Five years later, Catherine again called to request couple treatment, saying it was "Brad's last chance." When they came for the appointment, I was struck by physical changes in Brad's appearance. He looked as though he had aged twenty years. His gaze seemed lifeless and vacant, his tone irritable and dismissive. Weary, frustrated, and frightened, Catherine spoke directly about Brad's drinking. Brad minimised the severity of his alcohol abuse, while Catherine viewed it as their primary relational problem. The triggering event for the treatment request occurred while Catherine was away visiting her mother. Brad transported the children to their activities in a drunken state, reported both by the boys and by a concerned neighbour. When Catherine expressed anger and concern, Brad volleyed back a series of expletives and announced that her only real caring was for the children. As I listened, I could hear Brad's envy of his young sons, recipients of the mothering Brad seemed to crave. Catherine expressed her loneliness in both her parenting and spousal roles.

Initially, they blamed each other. Brad harped on Catherine's emotional and sexual distance, ignoring her comments about his drinking. Catherine attributed her emotional withdrawal to her hurt and distrust from Brad's drinking. Each seemed defensively entrenched in a position of moral rightness. During the next few months, I chipped away at their shared couple defences, with limited success. At times, Catherine could think about her contribution, aspects of their unconscious pairing, and her struggles setting limits and boundaries. Brad seemed less permeable and more resentful about being in treatment. Although he verbalised a wish to quit drinking, it felt disingenuous like the adolescent who accepts a curfew knowing he will sneak out later. I struggled to maintain a couple state of mind (Morgan, 2005), recognising Brad's addiction while considering its meaning in the couple context, as captured in the following session six months into treatment.

BRAD: Okay, so I've been going to my recovery group, even though I hate it. It's just that the group leader, he isn't the brightest guy in the world. (I think this is a message to me.) I mean, he's okay, and the group's fine, but we just end up talking about so much that's superficial. Janine, I took your suggestion about individual therapy. I doubt it will be helpful, but what the hell, it might be. So, Catherine, I'm doing everything I can in terms of treatment, and I'm not drinking. (He looks at his wife, who is attentive, but does not respond verbally.) I feel like a kid checking in with my parents.

CATHERINE: I was thinking something similar. I'm not the treatment police.

BRAD: You're the one who insisted on it. You have control.

CATHERINE: I don't know why you say that. I did insist we come here for couple therapy, but I haven't really told you what to do in terms of your alcohol treatment. I stopped doing that.

BRAD: Well, it's implied.

JANINE: Catherine, I noticed you shaking your head.

CATHERINE: He's making it sound forced, like treatment is court ordered or something. I don't even know if he wants to do it.

BRAD: Of course I want to do it. Of course I want to stop drinking. Don't you know that I'm an alcoholic? I'm just tired of your moral judgment. It's there all the time, even if you don't state it.

JANINE: Judgment?

BRAD: She thinks she married a loser. I have an alcohol problem. I get it. (He turns to his wife.) I just don't think you get it.

CATHERINE: I can tell you're mad at me about something. What is it that I don't get?

BRAD: I struggle with alcohol every single day. I don't think you get that for starters. Every day, I struggle with alcohol. I think, okay, I'm not going to drink. And for

	that day, I make a commitment. But it starts over again the next day, and the next. Every day, it's the same thing. You want me to promise you I won't drink, and I can't, because every day is a struggle. But you can't accept that. It's something you can't understand in your world of perfect control.
CATHERINE:	Perfect control?
BRAD:	I know you see me as weak, as inadequate, as less than. (They are both quiet for a few minutes.) Well, isn't that what you think?
CATHERINE:	You're right; I don't know what it's like to struggle every day with alcohol. But it's so strange, so weird that you think I'm Miss Control. I don't feel in control at all. I don't get to decide if you drink.
BRAD:	You get to decide if you trust me or not, and you've said you don't trust one thing that comes out of my mouth.
CATHERINE:	Because you've lied about drinking so many times. We agreed you'd tell me the truth, and you haven't. I know you're going to relapse some times, but I just want you to tell me. Instead, I always have to catch you at it, find an empty liquor bottle for you to own up. I believed you for years and years when you said you weren't drinking, and now you tell me you lied all along. So no, I don't believe you any longer, and I do start thinking, "What else is he lying about?"
BRAD:	Well, I'm not having an affair, if that's what you're implying. Okay, so I lied about drinking. That doesn't mean I'm lying about other things. Do you think I'm seeing someone else? Is that what you think?
CATHERINE:	I don't think that Brad. I did ask once, but only because you seemed so far away, so distant. (To me) I know I'm getting defensive, but I feel like I'm on trial. Maybe I'm not as understanding as I should be, but I can't trust him, not right now. (To Brad) I'm sure it doesn't feel supportive when you're trying to do this thing that's impossibly hard. I want to trust you, but I don't think I can.
BEN:	Because I'm such a loser, a disappointment.
CATHERINE:	Oh, this is so frustrating. (Exasperated) Yes, I guess that's right. I'm disappointed.
JANINE:	Brad, when Catherine says she doesn't trust you, you hear it as evidence that you're a loser and it feels unsupportive. But I think, Catherine, what you're trying to convey is that you're scared, afraid to trust him, only to discover that he's drinking again.
BEN:	Well, why didn't you just say that, tell me you're scared?
CATHERINE:	(crying now) I don't know. I guess because I don't want to feel about it either. You're not the only one who blocks things out. I get so scared that this is our life, that you'll keep drinking, and I'll have to choose—to stay with a drunk you or leave you—and that's not a choice I want to make. But honestly, it's not just the drinking. I mean, that's what got us here, but I keep trying to talk about how secretive you are. There's a part of you that you keep out of our relationship, and I don't know why. I don't know if it's something I'm doing. You keep a part of yourself away, unknown to everyone around you, including me.

The couple continues with an exchange about how each feels the other controls the future of their relationship. Brad complains that Catherine only cares about the children.

BRAD: Catherine is the most important thing to me in the world, more important than my kids, more important than my job. But I'm not important to her, not in that way. The kids always come first.

CATHERINE: (Angrily) And why is that Brad? Why is that? I think you have no idea what your drinking has done to us. No idea. Yes, I invest in the kids. That's where I get my intimacy needs met, and it's a problem. I want to get them met with you, but I stopped hoping. You're always checked out—mostly drunk I guess. You don't show up. You think the kids and I just dismiss you, like you have nothing to offer. But you're just vacant—you come home, but you're not really there. (She's crying again.) This is his problem, not mine. I'm not going to take responsibility for his problem.

JANINE: He's the one drinking, but it's a problem you both carry, a problem in your relationship.

CATHERINE: Brad's problem.

JANINE: There's no question that Brad is responsible for his drinking, but perhaps we can think about this in terms of your relationship—you each talk about a kind of painful distance between you that's longstanding. Brad's drinking just compounds it.

BRAD: (Angrily) Why did you marry me? Was I just a meal ticket for you, a way to have kids?

CATHERINE: No. (She pauses.) I married you because I loved you. I thought you were this great guy, and we had fun. We had the same values, some of the same interests. We were different in ways that were useful. Like you do get me to slow down, not over-schedule. I'm afraid to slow down, to sit with myself. I think we have to be honest, Brad. Part of the reason we got together was because of our histories. I don't think we knew it at the time. So, of course I was attracted to someone secretive, because I had a secret. We must have been drawn together in part because of our past abuse.

BRAD: And you've dealt with yours, you've reconciled it, but I can't.

JANINE: Perhaps that's where you feel a kind of judgment from Catherine—a sense that she's overcome her past, but you haven't.

BRAD: Well, that's the feeling I get. I mean, she does seem to have come to terms with her history, but I can't reconcile with mine. I can't let myself off the hook for it. I know I was just a kid, but I still feel responsible. Maybe I'm jealous of you Catherine. You seem so okay now, and I just feel broken. (He pauses.) You know what? I like to drink. It's a way of saying, "Fuck you." It's an act of defiance.

CATHERINE: Against me or against your family?

BRAD: All of you. I don't know; I get confused. I don't know who I'm mad at. All I know is that I want to matter to Catherine. I don't care what happens to me, not really. I wouldn't care if I drank myself to death, except for Catherine. I don't mean to be dramatic, but she's the only thing that makes life worth it.

CATHERINE: But I don't want that.
BRAD: That's pretty obvious. You don't want me.
CATHERINE: No, I mean I don't want me to be the only reason you're alive. I want you to live for you and for our family. I want you to care about you. I want you to be the person I can count on.

What is the unconscious fit for this couple? What role does Brad's addiction play in their couple dynamic? As Catherine commented, this pairing emerged within a shared history of encapsulated trauma. Each had a traumatic sexual secret, kept from each other and from themselves. In her marriage to Brad, Catherine recreated her parents' marriage—a distant, workaholic husband married to a lonely, overwhelmed stay-at-home mother. Although Brad feels powerful at work, he feels impotent in his marriage, projecting into Catherine the phallic potency he fears. Catherine colludes with Brad's projection, defending against intrusive males who penetrate her vulnerability. The couple's view of their sexual difficulties as "Catherine's problem" protects Brad from facing his conflicted sexuality. Is he gay? Brad is uncertain and cannot even think about it. In her rejection of his Catholic faith, Catherine becomes the scapegoat for Brad's family, a repetition of abuse taken to protect her younger brother. Brad is furious with Catherine for standing up to his parents in a way he cannot. Both Catherine and Brad share contempt for and an avoidance of emotional dependency, fended off with aggression, projection, and alcohol.

Brad's drinking helps maintain the emotional distance required by the couple and becomes the container for the couple's unexpressed desire and longing. The alcohol down-regulates Brad's fear and rage, creating an absent, numbed, dissociative-like response much like the mother he knew as a child. McDougall (1989) contends that addiction is a psychosomatic representation for something that cannot be thought about, a displaced discharge of affect in action. This couple struggles to process past abuse and present sexuality. Childhood rage finds neither voice nor healthy containment. Brad's addiction illuminates unresolved trauma, located in Brad but true for both partners. Brad feels guilty for his secret pleasure in drinking, an exciting but shameful feeling he associates with sexual arousal during his childhood abuse. Brad silences his anger through his drinking, and the drinking in turn provides a safe target for Catherine's anger. As a "victim" of Brad's drinking, Catherine finds an outlet for her anger that hides all other targets. She does not have to be angry with her parents or others, because Brad gives her an alternate, "safer" target.

Just when this couple seems entrenched and untreatable, Catherine makes a shift. Through the couple work, she begins to recognise that the lying she hates in Brad is present in her own protection of a family secret. When the children have suspected Brad's drinking, she has denied any difficulty, negating their reality. Despite knowing Brad is a heavy drinker, she has allowed him to transport and care for the children. Horrified by her own neglect of her children's welfare, Catherine sets a clear limit, telling Brad she no longer trusts him with the kids. With conviction, she announces that she will leave him if he continues to drink. "I won't watch you self-destruct." In standing up *to* him, Catherine is standing up *for* him as well. Catherine sets the boundary with Brad that she could not set during her childhood abuse. "This must stop. We can't continue to live like this, and I'm not just talking about your drinking." When she can acknowledge their shared difficulties with emotional intimacy and sexuality, the problem moves from being just about Brad to being about the couple. The diagnosis shifts from Brad's alcohol addiction to include their shared trauma-induced fear of intimacy. Both give up their use of Brad's alcoholism as a destructive means of playing out yet hiding their difficulties in relating.

In the couple treatment, Brad is faced with a clear limit around his drinking. If he continues to drink, Catherine will leave. Additionally, I explain in very clear terms what combination of treatment will provide the most help—Alcoholics Anonymous, medication, individual therapy, and consistent couple work. He has been resistant to this in the past, insistent that he can stop drinking on his own, but never really motivated to quit. Once Catherine takes ownership for her part in the couple difficulties and in Brad's addiction, he is freed from his death grip on the bad object. For the first time, I feel I have a couple in treatment working on the couple's problems. Initially, Brad rages against Catherine's limit setting, but then he hears her genuine offer of support, not just around the drinking, but also in creating the kind of spousal partnership that has been missing. Brad begins to take his addiction seriously—to invest in himself, in his children, and in the potential for a healthy spousal partnership. While the outcome is uncertain, a therapeutic shift has occurred. The couple is now the patient, instead of just Brad and his addiction. Over the next three years, Brad remains sober and the couple explores their intimacy problems and parallel traumatic histories. From my view, Brad would not have stopped drinking without the couple treatment. Brad's drinking was a means of moving the couple to treatment, where we then had the opportunity for addressing both couple and individual issues.

What do we learn from these examples about the importance of couple treatment in situations where one or both partners suffer from clearly diagnosed psychiatric difficulties? In each example, the illness became the receptacle for the unacknowledged destructive couple dynamics. The problems of the couples were located in an "identified patient," entangled in the "sick" partner's symptoms in a way that defeated treatment of either the illness or the relational problems. For each couple, the illness became a shared means of attacking the marriage. It evacuated the pathological parts of the "non-afflicted" partner and the couple into an individual symptom set. Since the couple problems were injected into the illness, the illness could not be effectively treated. Because the illness hid the couple problems, the actual relational difficulties remained undetected and unresolved.

For Adam and Diane, couple therapy became a road to divorce. Adam's illness was a vehicle to end a destructive pairing that could only be understood after a traumatic parting. While together, Adam and Diane could not see their individual contributions to the problem, how they repeatedly played out earlier trauma, and the destructive ways their individual and couple pathology destroyed their creative couple potential. But at least the couple therapy allowed them to say in words that they wanted to split up, and to acknowledge that their deadly coupling allowed Adam to disengage from his self-destructive path. What the couple treatment illuminated was the need to de-couple in order to find insight, stability, and hope. Once separated, Adam was able to manage his bipolar illness and addiction in a responsible way, and Diane was able to get treatment for her own disavowed depression.

In contrast, Brad and Catherine used couple therapy to find their generative couple potential. This provided support and motivation for Brad to treat his addiction, particularly once

Catherine could see her own contribution to maintaining its potency. Together, they were able to face the ways they used Brad's alcoholism to avoid central difficulties in relating sexually and emotionally. Before this, neither had resolved their childhood trauma. This set up an unconscious fit that drew them together, but then became a barrier to their creative couple potential. When Brad felt less alone in the couple relationship, he was able to take in the support of others to help him stop drinking. No longer the perpetrator of destruction in his marriage, he could address his own victimisation and the confusion associated with the sexual abuse. Catherine became accountable for her own wellbeing, moving herself from a victim stance by standing up for the marriage she wanted rather than passively accepting the one she had. The changes made by each partner moved their marriage from a state of deadness to an alive, vibrant connection.

When addiction and other psychiatric issues appear in couple treatment, what are the challenges for the couple therapist? Perhaps the most central is having the dual focus of acknowledging the illness while maintaining a couple state of mind (Morgan, 2005). The therapist must look within and beyond the symptoms to access the underlying problematic couple dynamic. Viewing the illness from a shared lens allows the couple to understand how it functions within their relationship, providing greater potential both for better management of the psychiatric difficulty and for improved couple relating. A psychiatric diagnosis is a powerful message, however, and may overshadow the need for the couple to also focus on themselves as a couple. Containment is difficult, given potentially life threatening risks, affective flooding, frequent trauma histories, and intense transference/countertransference reactions. Due to the need for a wraparound treatment approach utilising multiple conjoint services (e.g., medication, hospitalisation, recovery groups, individual and couple therapy), the therapist must establish working relationships with other mental health professionals who may not share a psychoanalytic perspective. In both couples presented here, their avoidance of the issues compounded the problems. We cannot afford to share their blind spots by pretending, like them, that addiction and psychiatric illness do not enter our work with couples. We need to find a way to discuss, understand, research, and write about these difficult treatment issues that require us to acknowledge and understand the complexity of interacting factors that create and perpetuate individual and couple frailty.

References

Buksti, A. S., Munker, R., Gade, I., Roved, B., Tvaro, K., Gotze, H., & Haastrup, S. (2006). Important components of a short-term family group programme. From the Danish Multicenter Schizophrenia Project. *Norway Journal of Psychiatry*, 60: 213–219.

Gupta, M., Coyne, J. C., & Reach, S. R. H. (2003). Couple treatment for major depression: Critique of the literature and suggestions for some different directions. *Journal of Family Therapy*, 25, 4: 316–345.

Kuoros, C. D., Cummings, E. M., & Papp, L. M. (2008). Interrelations and moderators of longitudinal links between marital satisfaction and depressive symptoms among couples in established relationships. *Journal of Family Psychology*, 22, 5: 667–677.

McDougall, J. (1989). *Theaters of the Body*. New York: W. W. Norton.

Morgan, M. (2005). On being able to be a couple: The importance of a "creative couple" in psychic life. In: F. Grier (Ed.), *Oedipus and the Couple* (pp. 9–30). London: Karnac.

Morgenstern, J. & Leeds, J. (1993). Contemporary psychoanalytic theories of substance abuse: A disorder in search of a paradigm. *Psychotherapy, 30*, 2: 194–206.

Scharff, J. S. & Scharff, D. E. (1998). *Object Relations Individual Therapy*. Lanham, MD: Jason Aronson.

Vincent, C. (2007). Touching the void: the impact of psychiatric illness on the couple. In: M. Ludlam & V. Nyberg (Eds.), *Couple Attachments: Theoretical and Clinical Studies* (p. 133–144). London: Karnac.

CHAPTER TWENTY-NINE

The ending of couple therapy with a couple who recovered joy

Pierre Cachia and Jill Savege Scharff

In the assessment process prior to beginning analytic couple therapy, the spouses or partners outline what they expect and what they hope to achieve in therapy. From that moment on, as therapists embarking on an open-ended, analytic couple therapy, we keep those expectations in mind as we work through the various phases of the treatment process. We aim for a reasonably satisfactory conclusion in which the partners feel that they have accomplished their goals, or have adjusted to a more realistic outcome for their couple relationship. We do not arrive suddenly at the day of termination. Instead we keep it in mind and prepare for it from the beginning (Blum, 1989; Sabbadini, 2007). We do this by dealing with reactions to parting at the end of each session and before every holiday, and we address them both before the departure and after the reunion. In this way we rehearse for the eventual separation that will occur when the couple is ready to finish with us. How do we know when that time is? We arrive at it in discussion, reaching a compromise between the couple's goals and our goals.

Sometimes we have to be satisfied to have helped the couple achieve life goals that fall short of the resolution of infantile conflicts that we would prefer to have accomplished (Ticho, 1972). We prefer to think in terms of a good enough ending, rather than a supposedly ideal termination (Gabbard, 2009). Lack of perfection is not a reason to analyse a couple interminably. When we are disappointed in the outcome of treatment, our attitude can actually block progress. As Freud (1937) said of the goals of individual psychoanalysis, "Our aim will be not to rub off every peculiarity of human character for the sake of a schematic 'normality'" (Freud, 1937, p. 250). Freud had come to understand that "a normal ego is, like normality in general, an ideal fiction" (Freud, 1937, p. 234). We must learn to accept what is possible, deal with our disappointment, and let the couple get on with their own way of doing things. We have done all we can.

A couple may feel ready to end therapy but the therapist may feel ambivalent and uncertain. This cause for hesitation can hold the couple back from getting on with life, but more often it proves useful in supporting a thorough contemplation of the ending process.

A couple who has worked well with the therapist and progressed considerably may be so relieved to feel better that they bound away from treatment before they get worse again. This joyful but ill-considered "flight into health" might well be of a manic reparative nature (Segal, 1986) and may need to be challenged. We need time to consider the possibility that a couple like that, who having made good use of treatment, may have retreated from what might be usefully stirred up and examined as part of the process of ending. On the other hand, the wish to leave behind the discomforts inherent to couple psychotherapy may represent a desire for a more "secluded" reparative playfulness (Klein, 1975) imbued with genuine concern for one another and a real desire for intimate connection. Matters are complicated by the fact that such reparative, developmentally driven processes at times co-exist with more defensive ones that may inhibit reparative aims. The stress of ending can stir defensive and destructive forces in the couple relationship, giving us a second chance at analysing them. Then the couple's desire to move beyond therapy may be met with curiosity, validation, and genuine support.

We always hope that termination of therapy allows for a creative process of closure, integration, and consolidation of the couple's gains in treatment. Experience suggests, however, that endings take many forms. A harmonious, collaborative ending is pleasant and less stressful for all concerned and in many ways seems desirable, but we must be wary of an idealising conclusion that excludes negative aspects still in need of work. Endings that are somewhat more combative in nature may still lead to a good outcome and may indeed prove pivotal to a couple's recovery. Sometimes we recommend that a couple delay termination so as to allow for a planned closure. Sometimes we recommend continuing in treatment for an extended period. Couples may accept our recommendation or they may insist on finishing because they feel ready and want to play with autonomy and dependency. Those couples who end treatment against our recommendation may well be engaged in a developmentally driven process towards mastery of anxieties concerning the manner in which they relate to the world around them. The therapist who may not agree will try to avoid collusion with infantile needs while at the same time supporting the couple's emerging capacity to manage relational anxiety. Whether or not a couple will accept a recommendation about readiness to terminate is determined by the therapist's capacity to appreciate and acknowledge these developmental needs rather than simply oppose the couple's decision.

Readiness to end couple therapy

There are criteria that may help us to assess the readiness to end treatment when working with spouses or partners, but total cure is not one of them: we do not expect a total absence of suffering, and we do not seek to eliminate all sources of conflict. We do expect an improved ability to recover from setbacks and feel care and concern for the partner. We look for relative freedom from internal unconscious blocks, differentiation, and growth—not radical personality change. We hope for a reduction in the narcissism that lies at the root of failure to collaborate in partnership (Scharff & Bagnini, 2003). We expect an improved ability to deal with castration anxiety arising from hostile feelings and reactions to and from the partner.

We look for the partners' capacity to deal with separation from each other when work, social life, or family obligations interfere with their time together, and with their therapist. We look for less splitting and more integrated perceptions of each other, of family members, and of their therapist, as projections are owned and re-integrated inside the self (D. Scharff & J. Scharff, 1991). We want to see better individual regulation of affect and at the same time increased sensitivity to the moods and feelings of the partner. We look for increased containment of self and other, so that more respect is shown to the other, more gratitude and reparation for mistakes and hurts. We are looking for the presence of a stronger, experience-processing marital container (Colman, 1993) and the emergence of creative couple functioning (Morgan & Ruszczynski, 1998).

We hope it will be true of each partner that he or she has rehabilitated his or her own internal objects, especially allowing the images of their parents in mind in a creative union. When the couple's experience of their respective parental couples was traumatic, severely damaged or altogether absent, we hope to draw on other, less toxic couples as a better foundation for an internal couple on which the couple can build in treatment. Perhaps each of the partners can reflect on the relationship between siblings, grandparents, or a couple they admire. Most central to therapeutic action, they also draw on the relationship each of them creates with the therapist, and they take in the experience of the therapist as a third party relating to the couple. Their experiences in therapy often facilitate the establishment of a more hopeful phantasy around the viability of dyadic relating which, as the therapy progresses, comes to be imbued with curative hope. This re-establishment of the internal couple, in whatever form it may take in each individual, is the crucial element that promotes the establishment of a couple state of mind.

We want to see that the partners, as a couple, can bear the losses they face, mourn them, and help each other with them. We like to see an improved capacity for reflecting and analysing difficulties. We feel most assured that the time for ending has come when we see that the analysing function of therapy has become installed. They have grown and do not need us anymore. They are ready to face the next phase of life able to cope with the developmental strain brought on by the challenges of moving forward through the life cycle.

The pre-ending phase

The couple in the late phase of treatment enters a pre-termination phase, introduced perhaps by a dream, by a successful response to a holiday break, by a new-found capacity for work, by the welcome conception of a child. We notice a freer atmosphere. We look for evidence that the criteria listed above are met, and if we find it, we begin to think of the end of therapy. As soon as a termination date is agreed upon, we often see a regression back to old ways of relating and dealing with conflict. Therapists may be tempted to think of this as proof that the therapy must continue, but experience shows that the presenting symptoms are simply returning for a last hurrah. The therapist should not hang on and get in the way of progress. The alternation between regression and progression gives the forward looking therapist a chance to recapitulate the learning and consolidate the gains of treatment. If the couple is ready to terminate, the regressions will be short-lived and of less intensity than early in the treatment.

It is a relief for couples to be ready to move on, and a pleasure for their therapist to feel that the work has been effective. But it is sad too. Just when spouses or partners become engaging, reflective, flexible, and resilient, it is time for their therapists to acknowledge their growth and prepare for departure. The last piece of work of analytic couple therapy is to review the good and bad parts of the treatment process and mourn the impending loss of the experience.

Clinical example: the couple who recovered joy

We will now present an example of termination in analytic couple therapy drawn from the late phase of treatment with the couple who lost joy and whose mid-phase session was the subject of Chapter Eighteen. In the following account the therapist, Pierre Cachia, summarises his impressions of the couple and the course of therapy in the mid-phase (which we presented in detail in the earlier chapter). He then provides a summary of the sessions over the last few months of treatment before presenting the process of one of the penultimate sessions.

The couple and their history

When I first met them, Catherine and Edmund were the essence of pure human joylessness. They were sullen and burdened by life. Their relationship was flat and deadened. Catherine's mounting frustration led her to pursue Edmund who retreated into a stony silent anger which drew yet more pursuit. They had tried simple instruction on life skills, but it did not help move them forward because they knew that their unhappy family life had its genesis in the couple relationship and in their histories. A much fuller and complex story would emerge over time.

Central to Catherine's experience were hurt over her mother's indifference to her father while making her career a priority (the opposite of what Catherine has done), puzzlement over her father's professional breakdown, and sadness about his imminent death. Edmund's parents were on again and off again until they finally parted ways when Edmund was twelve. Edmund distances himself from his father whom he perceives as hedonistic and hurtful to his mother, and yet his mother will not allow Edmund to express any negativity about him.

Catherine and Edmund are successful professionals who used to enjoy being together. Their safe haven grew deadly with the arrival of their first child, a boy whose birth was traumatic because Catherine became ill at that time, later discovered to be due to an allergy. Catherine increasingly attended to the children while Edmund worked at securing their livelihood. The transition to parenthood had thrown them into a downward spiral from which they had never recovered. In reaction to this, the couple created a defensive structure that was functional but joyless.

The couple in therapy: the emergence of the couple dynamic over time

The analytic couple therapy with Catherine and Edmund had three rather distinct phases. In the opening phase, a seven month period, Catherine described the unbearable, coldness and distance in their relationship, and Edmund spoke of his anger at Catherine for undermining his confidence and joy in his fathering. The stories were, in some ways ordinary, the pain and sadness intense. In this opening phase, I provided containment for their transition from a tentative engagement with each other and with me around these ordinary dissatisfactions and long standing complaints through to the development of a more creative space in a thinking, feeling partnership with me.

In the mid-phase, a nine-month period, important experiences emerged concerning early sexual abuse, neglect, and humiliation. Working through led to a new capacity to enjoy a family holiday. The session from the sixteenth month (presented fully in Chapter Eighteen) proved to be a turning point to the next phase.

In the late phase, another nine-month period, Edmund and Catherine realised that they failed to celebrate their achievements and downplayed their new closeness. As they began to open up about their needs and their love, I felt that they symbolically invited me home: they told me that they found intimacy in sharing a love of food, which was like sharing intimacy in sex, in that both allow the satisfaction of need and are therefore aspects of a very intimate and private matter. Edmund and Catherine could enjoy good experience without feeling too threatened that I might destroy it for them, or indeed, that they might destroy it for each other.

Our work usefully became more confrontational, a change made possible because our relationship had become more robust and the couple less fragile. At various points along the way, the couple had suggested ending treatment, but not as an accomplishment. After I interpreted their suggestion variously at these times as a threat of quitting, a retreat, or a signal of hopelessness, they agreed to remain in treatment. In the final months of the late mid-phase, I became able to talk more directly about their aggression, depression, and desire, and they seemed more willing to voice dissent when my interpretations failed to accurately grasp their experience. This is when the possibility of ending started to become real, not as a retreat, but as an accomplishment of their goals—some five months before we did end.

The couple in the end-phase

Four months to ending

Edmund and Catherine were in disagreement as to whether to end therapy. They both expressed disappointment: Edmund wanted Catherine to be more accepting of his upset; she wanted him to accept her being upset with him being upset. He was apologetic about complaining, emphasising that things were now a thousand times better and hoping this meant they were ready to finish. On the other hand, they expressed anxiety and turmoil in connection to the Easter break coming up, that being a time when fears were stirred up—this time especially as it would be the first anniversary of Catherine's father's death. Because of that, Catherine's mother would be feeling vulnerable (as they all would feel). Catherine realised that her fear of losing her father echoed her fear of losing therapy as a couple space for thinking and mending difficult threads of experience.

Catherine voiced anxiety about being without therapy whereas Edmund associated continuing therapy with a sense of deficit, a feeling of something being wrong. I said that Edmund was anxious about allowing care to come his way should he need it, as if having needs is felt to be necessarily a bad thing. I likened this to how, when depressive feelings loom large, Edmund struggles to admit he needs Catherine's help. He was intrigued by the idea that perhaps, when distressed, he could approach his wife for care, perhaps in a romantic manner. The couple was able to share a moment of close emotional contact as Edmund allowed his desire for comfort to become apparent.

As Edmund and Catherine's focus stayed on recovering intimacy and physicality, shared anxiety about ending emerged. Having explored it, the couple linked that anxiety to fear that without my support their new-found closeness would shrivel. Edmund expressed, in a very spontaneous manner, a desire that they would again start holding hands when they walked side by side. Catherine was confused and unsure as how to respond to this desire. She expressed disbelief that he would really want this, because "he really hates such things."

Edmund came alone the next week, saying that he wanted Catherine to rest before an audition that would be coming up the following day. I saw him alone, even though this is not ideal, as individual sessions may cause split transferences, create unworkable secrets, and intensify paranoid feelings. However, because of this couple's life circumstances I had found it necessary to have an individual session from time to time in order to sustain continuity. Edmund told me that the last session was "the best ever" because since talking in that session, they had been holding hands as they fall off to sleep. I felt that his enthusiasm had many layers, including that he wanted to communicate to me his gratitude and excitement that he had managed to make his desire known to Catherine and to me and that it had been responded to by her. I saw his attending the session alone as a request for recognition as a specially responsive and grateful patient and as a demonstration of his appreciation for my work and what the couple had achieved.

Three months to ending

Edmund and Catherine arrived together and sat down. Immediately the room was again somewhat filled with tension. Edmund returned to his belief that things had been getting much better now that they are holding hands. This grateful appreciation of improvement triggered intense anger in Catherine who confronted Edmund for all the times he did not acknowledge her efforts and was angry at her instead. Edmund froze, unable to respond, unable to acknowledge his previous cruelty. He countered with a reminder that he was at the receiving end of her nastiness as well. He then deflected his anger at some students for making lots of noise in the corridor outside my office as they were leaving the lecture room.

Catherine was angry that Edmund had prohibited her from visiting her father during the last Christmas before he passed away. Edmund was unable to offer anything that reduced the pain of this. We contemplated the difficulty of making reparation in the face of such overwhelming feelings and a history with so much hurt. I noted that they were still struggling with feeling dropped out of mind over the past years. Both now angry about it, they remained in a state of passionate engagement that is tiring but does not lead to a feeling of utter separation, as would have happened earlier in treatment.

Two months to ending

After a three-week Easter holiday break, Edmund and Catherine reported that they had a good time, even though they had to deal with the loss of friend. They felt the upset, but they shared it, held on to one another for support in the face of great sorrow, and had not become polarised. They associated this improvement with their improved capacity to plan and enjoy their holiday away from home. This time in agreement they raised the issue of ending therapy. After a sustained discussion, we agreed on a date for ending the couple therapy in two months. They immediately began to speak of Edmund's mother as a woman who does not allow need, which was true of Catherine's mother as well. Did they see me as now rejecting of need because I had agreed to a planned ending? Edmund then began to consider taking up individual therapy after a few months—perhaps with me. I had a distinct sense that now, as they approached ending, this request was really a way of holding on to me together and individually to ensure my continuing availability. I did not answer, but left it open for exploration. We discussed Edmund's request and the consequences to the couple if I were to accede to that request and exclude Catherine, or refuse it as their internal mother figures do. My hope was that they had internalised the capacity to think about shared experience and that they would have continuing access to this capacity without my presence.

Final month

Edmund and Catherine told me that they felt ashamed of the need they had revealed, a need for contact with a nourishing, responsive other. Their histories have made them thin-skinned about criticism or refusal of their needs. Even so, Edmund and Catherine have become able to think together as a couple. A more creative manner of relating has emerged, and has allowed Edmund and Catherine to start believing they could make a good life for themselves eventually. Towards the latter part of their therapy they had started to allow me to know of the better parts of their experience. Conversations in this late phase often centered on the pleasures of physical contact and food: they had become able to enjoy not only holding hands affectionately and cuddling companionably but also finding joy in sexual interaction. They both longed to leave behind years of difficulty and move on to a better place, even if the prospect of ending continued to stir up considerable anxiety and ambivalence. Now, joy in the face of shared good experience left them vulnerable to shame. Their capacity to think about what was stirred up within them gave testimony to the journey they had been through.

An unexpected twist to the planned ending

Reception called to let me know that Catherine had arrived on time, and that her husband would be ten minutes late. I was informed that she was asking if she could come to my office and start the session anyway. I acceded because Edmund and Catherine have had numerous disruptions and, unlike some other couples, they are able to make use of these irregularities creatively.

Catherine now enters my office, walks to her armchair, and as usual takes off her coat, and throws it in a pile over her rather large leather bag, as if to be free of its bulkiness. The therapy room is a place where they can offload their many layers. She tells me that she has been successful in an audition she had mentioned some weeks ago, and so she has been offered a job which would take her away from London. I realise that this will mean that the couple therapy will have to come to an end the following week, two weeks earlier than anticipated. We will have only one more session, rather than the two sessions that we had planned for and counted on.

My mind races as I calculate the number of months we had contemplated ending, only to find the actual ending rather abrupt anyway. I recall that, the previous year Catherine had refused a job offer that would have taken her away from London and so would have spelled the end of therapy. A year ago ending would have been certainly premature. Now, I think, the couple feels more resilient.

This time, Catherine says, she really wants to take on this assignment. She thinks they could manage the challenge of her being away and ending the therapy. This seems to her to confirm the possibility we had been working towards, namely that therapy should come to an end. Edmund knocks on the door. He apologises for having been delayed on the way to the clinic, says something to Catherine, takes off his coat, and throws it over his bags by the wall. Catherine turns and, addressing us both, tells Edmund she has told me about the job. He joins in with some excitement about this work being a good thing for Catherine to take on. This reminds me of how excited Edmund was the previous summer (or was it two summers ago?) when Catherine took on a major piece of work, and that had been a source of anxiety and conflict.

Nevertheless Edmund assures me that they will cope really well, and Catherine expresses confidence that all will be well, even if she still feels bad about being away from the children. She knows the children will be fine, but she cannot stop herself from worrying that her decision will deprive them in some way or other. Edmund offers some reassurance. He says that the children really enjoyed their time with him the last time she was away, and he would make it a point to be home early to spend some enjoyable time with them. I enquire whether Catherine might be away for longer spells than before, and Edmund explains that she might be caught up for a couple of days on set, but she would be commuting back home most days.

I comment on the sense of comfort with which they were discussing being away from each other and coping with the demands of two young children. Edmund affirms that he is excited about having to make the time to attend to the children's needs. He did a good job the last time, he says, and so he feels confident that things will work out better this time around. The children had survived and they had such a good time. Catherine reminds Edmund of some rather stupid thing he once did trying to fit his older child into the smaller uniform of a younger child, and they both laugh about it.

I note that Catherine is not dwelling on the more problematic exchanges they had back then. She does not address his difficulty with maintaining communication with her while she was gone, cutting her off and pushing her out of the picture. Here is evidence that their confidence in each other has grown, but I think I should not speak of this positive aspect again in case it might shield subtle avoidance of difficulty. It then dawns on me that what is not being spoken about at all is the fact they will have to tolerate being away from each other. Having reconsidered the work we have recently been doing about their improved ability to express their need for connection in terms of food, hand holding, cuddling, and sex I say that they again seem to be finding it easier to connect with their children's need of mother and father than to speak of missing each other. They both respond with a softer look and a knowing nod, as they turn towards each other. I see their sadness in the way they look at each other and at me. Perhaps I am looking for affirmation that I have done good enough work with this couple to justify terminating, but I look at this connecting gaze as another little confirmation that the couple has really come a long way to a better place. I begin to consider the story leading up to, and the reactions about, the ending, as saying something about the couple's experience of therapy.

I say that the end of therapy is happening around a story that represents new possibilities. The couple is dealing with the active re-launch of Catherine's career and Edmund's having another opportunity to be a hands-on father. This welcome sense of opportunity and challenge involves the management of a real loss, not only of the couple relationship and family time, but also of their relationship with me. Catherine immediately responds: "Sometimes I am afraid about how it will be without this weekly meeting. Coming here means we always speak about difficult moments, but this will not be there then. Still, things are better between us." Edmund responds to her with his characteristic phrase: "It will never be perfect." This stirs up my anxiety about his capacity to hold claim to a decent enough life for himself. He then moves on to a more considered and thoughtful comment: "Still, we have become better at getting unstuck." Besides, he adds, staying on would mean that they are still unwell, and they cannot be unwell forever. I highlight the real paradox—therapy essentially exists to render itself redundant. Seeking help from therapy is important but the real goal is that the partners keep on creating a good experience for themselves—meeting each other's needs from shared resources. I say that perhaps they have finally come to a place where they feel they have enough goodness within themselves to nourish both them and their children.

I recall (but do not mention, because I feel that I am saying a bit too much) that over the course of treatment they stopped thinking of themselves as inadequate parents and, on the contrary, often report positive changes in their children's behaviour and levels of attainment.

Edmund reaffirms that he is sure they will manage and if things do get impossibly difficult again, they know they can find me. I say that this is something we can discuss. Ideally they would not need to return, but who knows how their circumstances might change. However, I realise that we have come to the end of the hour, and I call time. The couple leaves, repeating the familiar ritual of putting on their coats, picking up their respective bags, and Edmund leaving the room trailed by his wife. Both of them smile and nod. As they leave, Catherine tells me that they will be seeing me again the next week.

As they leave, I feel both satisfied and apprehensive. I have grown fond of the couple, and they will soon be leaving me. Have I done enough? Where will they be in six months' time? Will they be able to find me if need arises? What if this would be the last session? I have to make haste, jot down a few brief clinical notes, and make my way home. I push my worries to the side and do what I have to do.

The last session

In their final session Catherine and Edmund told me that they had been alternating between states of security and anxiety about not having their therapy sessions to return to. To their relief they were able to find within themselves a reliable capacity to tolerate such feelings, contain anxiety, and not allow fear to paralyse or agitate them. Catherine's new work contract would present new challenges, and therapy would have been hugely disrupted if they had stayed in treatment. We discuss how, having contemplated the approaching end for some months, at the final session the termination feels somewhat forced upon us. We silently share a moment of sadness. The rest of the time was spent in reviewing the process of the therapy. We said our farewells, asking ourselves: What will this ending mean?

Tying theory and case example together

As we reflect on the clinical material in the light of the theory that we presented earlier, we agree that the first glimpse of the possibility of being able to end therapy some say came from the couple's positive reaction to a good holiday, which was the first time they had recovered a bit of joy in their life together. Each break from therapy reflects earlier separations and prepares the way for the eventual end of the therapeutic relationship. We note that, working with them on elements of abandonment and neglect in their histories, reactions to Catherine's father's impending death, and later the anniversary of that death, the therapist associated to the couple's difficulty in separating from him during breaks. The therapist first became aware that ending Edmund and Catherine's analytic couple therapy had become a real possibility when he became more able to talk directly about their aggression, depression, and desire, and when they became more able to correct his understanding of them. The couple was less fragile and the therapy more robust. This development occurred after he had felt symbolically invited into their home to hear of the pleasures of food, affection, and sexuality.

As soon as ending became a real possibility, the couple expressed disappointment and disagreement. Ambivalence about ending was split and projected into each member of the couple and into the therapist—Edmund eager to finish a thousand times better, and Catherine upset and anxious that Edmund would not be able to meet her needs, and the therapist worried if he had done enough to sustain them for the future. Improvement unleashed rage at how bad things were between them before treatment. The ensuing hurt and difficulty in making reparation for it could have made the therapist quite despairing. But it is his task to contain this, reminding himself that this is an inevitable regression, a last chance to express complaint and find containment.

Even when Catherine is angry and Edmund is feeling accused, the couple is able to remain connected and intimate. They are able to contain their difficulty within their couple relationship. It is not that everything is smooth between them. It is simply that they are "better at getting unstuck." Their anger is communicative, not distancing, and they operate from a depressive position that is lively and hopeful. Facing the death of a friend, Catherine and Edmund manage to support each other and stay connected as they face another loss. Even while mourning they are able to enjoy their relationship and their family. Again, while making tremendous progress as a couple, there is a movement back to Edmund as an individual with needs that Catherine could not meet. During the end-phase we are not surprised to see the couple regress to earlier ways of behaving, but when they are ready to end, this regression is temporary, and the relationships can recover.

As couple therapy is ending, it is not uncommon for one member of the couple to request individual therapy, as Edmund did. It may be a sign of progress, as the couple is able to differentiate among the needs of both partners and plan to meet those needs responsibly and without assigning blame. It may be a sign of longing, regression to narcissistic preoccupation, dependent clinging to a therapist viewed as an ideal object. It may be thought of as an aggressive attack on the creative couple and on the therapist's tenet of the couple relationship as the patient. In short, the therapist does not accept or deny the request. As with everything else the couple and the therapist discuss the meaning of the request and its implications.

If the couple therapist agrees to become an individual therapist for one member of a couple, a problem can arise if the other partner wants to return to couple therapy and then feels that the previously neutral couple therapist seems to be hostage to just one point of view. Another problem occurs if a husband in individual therapy grows out of pace with his wife and moves towards separation and divorce. If the wife is upset and wishes to return to therapy, but the husband wishes to continue his individual therapy, the wife is shut out. She has no trusted therapist who knows her and her husband. This is the kind of implication that the therapist asks the couple to consider before making the request actual. At that point, the therapist needs to assess his ability to deal with the ethical dilemma that he may face. In this case, Edmund's request has not materialised.

Conclusion

Catherine and Edmund are ready to face the challenge of separation and differentiation posed by a job offer that could boost Catherine's career. Edmund is able to take pleasure in her success and to express confidence in providing childcare in her absence. Having developed enough trust in Edmund's capacity to care for the children and still stay connected to her during her absence, Catherine is able to accept the offer with his full support, each confident of relating across a separation and retaining their capacity for joy.

With a final review of the process and an acknowledgement of what it had meant to the couple and the therapist, the treatment comes to a close. The termination of this treatment has been contemplated and then planned, and yet, as so often happens, its actual end is brought forward, forced by a life circumstance. This does not spoil the termination or make the treatment incomplete. The goal is a fulfilling life as a couple, not a treatment concluded by the book. The treatment must be in the service of the couple's life outside the consulting room. Once a couple can detoxify bad experiences and create good experiences for themselves, the therapist is no longer needed, and it is time to end.

References

Blum, H. P. (1989). The concept of termination and the evolution of psychoanalytic thought. *Journal of the American Psychoanalytic Association, 37,* 2: 275–295.
Colman, W. (1993). Marriage as a psychological container. In: S. Ruszczynski (Ed.), *Psychotherapy With Couples: Theory and Practice at the Tavistock Institute of Marital Studies* (pp. 70–96). London: Karnac.
Freud, S. (1937). Analysis terminable and interminable. *S. E., 23:* 216–253. London: Hogarth.
Gabbard, G. (2009). What is a good-enough ending? *Journal of the American Psychoanalytic Association, 57:* 575–594.
Klein, M. (1975). *Love, Guilt and Reparation and Other Works 1921–45.* London: Hogarth.

Morgan, M. & Ruszczynski, S. (1998). The Creative Couple (Unpublished paper). 50th Anniversary Conference the Tavistock Marital Studies Institute. London.

Sabbadini, A. (2007). On the open-endedness of psychoanalysis. *Psychoanalytic Review, 94,* 5: 705–713.

Scharff, D. E. & Scharff, J. S. (1991). *Object Relations Couple Therapy*. Northvale, NJ: Jason Aronson.

Scharff, J. S. & Bagnini, C. (2003). Narcissistic disorder. In: D. K. Snyder & M. A. Whisman (Ed.), *Treating Difficult Couples* (pp. 285–307). New York: Guilford.

Segal, H. (1986). *Delusion and Artistic Creativity and other Essays*. London: Free Association Books.

Ticho, E. (1972). Termination of psychoanalysis: treatment goals, life goals. *Psychoanalytic Quarterly,* 41: 315–333.

EPILOGUE

Being a member of a couple is central to the lives of many people who seek our help, whether for therapy as an individual, in a group, or in couple or family therapy. The theory of couple dynamics provides the base, and our own experience of the unique unconscious dynamics of each individual and each couple yields the specifics needed to conceptualise problems and approach solutions in any treatment modality. The pressure of trying to express ourselves clearly and helpfully about couples' problems through therapeutic interventions sharpens our thinking, both in the office with a couple, in videoconference teaching sessions, and at the computer writing about our work.

Equally, it can trigger anxieties that make it harder to think as we would like to, so that we do not always get things right in the therapeutic moment. We may make missteps and outright gaffs. Mistakes or slights are inevitable in delicate situations such as couple therapy or supervision, so making reparation is as important in therapy and training as it is in all relationships. Since therapists are not immune from mistakes, how we repair them with couples is crucial to what we convey. Intimacy always makes partners vulnerable to slights and misunderstandings. They need to develop a shared capacity to recover from such missteps and repair rifts between them. Therapy works largely because it strengthens that fundamental skill for couples. That lesson emerges clearly in therapy with couples, and gives us humility in the face of the complexity of our work.

Contributors from the International Psychotherapy Institute and the Tavistock Centre for Couple Relationships have come together in teaching and writing to offer in depth explorations and examples that illustrate how we think—or at least how we aspire to think in practice. We have reached for a comprehensive coverage of the basics of analytic couple therapy. Many topics remain for future consideration: The differences in the experience of working as a single therapist or in co-therapy, sexual addiction, hypersexual demands, internet addiction, occupational problems and the impingements of the global economy, pre-marital adjustment, and problems in pregnancy, infancy, and parenting throughout the life cycle. Much of our therapy has to do with what a couple's children's behaviour stirs up for them and what personality characteristics of their children represent for the couple relationship. For middle-aged couples, the provision of care for aging, physically disabled and mentally depleted parents is a rapidly growing problem as longevity increases. It is humbling to see how much remains undone, and yet it is exciting to contemplate new frontiers to explore.

What we hope we have done with this assemblage is to outline the basic ideas, to explore some of them in depth, and to give encouragement to the novice and food for thought to the veteran practitioner. Working with couples is an ever intriguing field, at times frustrating, at times deeply satisfying, but always interesting. Desiring, seeking, and maintaining a couple relationship is deeply embedded in our genes and our psychology, even as the specific ways to form couples continue to expand and differentiate in our modern world. Being part of a couple relationship is an aspect of being human that is richly, infinitely complex. Faced with the myriad ways that couples relate, we are always challenged to expand our understanding. The contributors to this volume have conveyed their enthusiasm for analytic couple therapy. We hope that you will feel encouraged to learn more, invest in couple therapy, and be inspired to offer new ideas yourself to the richly rewarding field of psychoanalytic work with couples.

INDEX

abortion 246–247, 253
    case example 247–252
Abraham, Karl 159
addiction 310–311, 319, 321. *See also*
    alcohol abuse; cocaine addiction
Adelson, E. 271, 277
adhesive identification 165
    clinical examples 165–168
Adult Attachment Interview (AAI) 55
affair(s) 30–31, 224–225, 254
    and divorce 282–288
    assessment 261, 261t
    case examples 282–288
    developmental causes
        individual causes 259
        marital strain 259
    effects on family 260
    factors leading to 256, 256t
    in homosexual marriages
        and partnerships 260
    Internet 258
    non-sexual, emotional 31, 257–258
    secrets and secrecy 257–258, 261–262
    shared fear of intimacy after 262–264
    the other man or woman 260–261
    treatment 261–265
        the course of 262
    types of 255–257
    unconscious collusion 258–259
    unconscious factors in 256–257, 256t
    working with the couple when there is an
        21–22
affect, following 13
affect regulation 45–48, 63–64
    and couple psychotherapy 49–50
    and the adult couple 48–49
    attachment and 63–64
    clinical example 50–52
affective ruptures, therapist as repairer
    of 53–54
aggression 59, 71–74
    and narcissism in couples with cocaine
        addiction 182–185 (*see also* cocaine
        addiction)
    assessing couple 66–67
    attachment theory and 74–76
    benign/normal *vs.* malignant/reactive
        59–62, 69
    clinical example 68–69
    countertransference and 69

defences against 67
    failure to connect and 76–79
    mental representation of 67
    origins 60–61
    social attitudes and 65
    Winnicott's synthesis 61–62
aggressive partnerships, types of 64–65
aggressive relationships, internalisation of 60–61
Ainsworth, Mary D. S. 10, 48, 295, 298
alcohol abuse 311
    case examples 185, 271–272, 312–321
Alexandrov, E. O. 55
Allen, J. 72
amygdala 62, 64
analytic couple therapy. *See* psychodynamic couple therapy
anger 73, 79
    attachment theory and 74–75
    case example 76–79
    healthy *vs.* unhealthy 72–73
    See also aggression
Anzieu, D. 106
archetypes 32
"as if" phenomena *vs.* "what if" ideas 27
assessment, couple
    example of 15
    technique in 13–16
attachment
    and affect regulation 63–64
    and sexuality 216–217
    defined 45
    early-life parental 216
attachment security 45–48
    clinical example 50–52
    therapist as "safe haven" and "secure base" 52–53
attachment style(s) 10–11
    assessment of couple's 15
    trauma and 298–300
attachment theory 44–45
    aggression and 74–76
    couple therapy and 10–11
attachment trauma 296t
Atwood, George E. 95
Augustine of Hippo, Saint 73
Avni, N. 196–197

Bagnini, Carl 325
Balfour, A. 48
Balint, Enid 4
Bannister, K. 28–29
Barden, N. 82
Bartholomew, K. 5, 11, 75, 79, 300
Basson, Rosemary 234
Bate, W. J. 42
Beach, S. R. H. 310
Beebe, Beatrice B. 50
Bernstein, A. E. 196–197
Bion, Wilfred R. 39, 67, 118, 120, 134, 153, 165
    container/contained model 63, 122, 134, 165, 168
    on alpha function 122
    on attacks on linking 118, 187
    on dreams 106–107
    theory of projective and introjective identification 7–8
Birtles, E. F. 60
Blechner, M. J. 197, 298
Blehar, M. 10, 48, 295
Blum, Harold P. 323
Bollas, Christopher J. 161–162, 171
Bowlby, John 10, 44, 47, 53, 74–75, 216
Brandchaft, B. 95
Britton, Ronald 126
Brotto, L. 234
Buksti, A. S. 310
Bunston, W. 72

Campbell, D. 79
Caruso, Norma J. 191
Chadwick, H. 73
child therapists 269–270, 277
    referring children to 289
children
    divorce and 284–289
    See also parents in couple treatment
Clark, C. L. 75
Cleavely, E. 173, 177
Clulow, Christopher 29, 45, 48, 54, 71, 73, 91, 177
    on attachment styles 216, 298
    on attachments of couples 5, 10–11
cocaine addiction, couples with 181
    aggression and narcissism in 182

case vignette 185–187
  narcissistic motives and strains on
    containment in 185–188
  technique with 182–185
collusion, unconscious 258–259
Colman, W. 28, 37, 53, 87, 117
coming out 84
"communication cure", psychoanalysis as 55
complementariness, unconscious 93
complementary identification
  (countertransference) 5
concordant identification (countertransference) 5
condensation 104
confusion, fear of 103
Connolly, C. M. 82
constancy principle 304
container, marital 177, 325. *See also* containment:
  couple
containment 13, 134, 168, 176–177, 305
  Bion's container/contained model 63,
    122, 134, 165, 168
  couple 37, 148–149, 311
    and triadic transference in supervision
      154–156
    case vignette 185–187
    containment issues with collusive couples
      150–151
    narcissistic motives, addiction, and strains
      on 185–187
    See also container, marital
  curiosity and 121–122
  triangular 148–149
  See also affect regulation
contextual holding 9f, 11–12
contextual transference 11–12, 175–176
countertransference 11–12, 12f
  aggression and 68–69
  case example 146
  fears 103
  focused 11, 175
  neurobiology and 54
  types of 5
  working with 13, 15–16
  See also triangular field
couple
  as the therapist's patient 53

working with the difficult 20–21
couple state of mind 325
  and the physical, practical, and psychological
    setting 126–130
  case example 119, 316
  challenges in maintaining 311–321
  creative 117
  of therapist 119, 125–131, 254, 311, 316, 321
couple therapy
  assessment of suitability for 204
  development of 3–4
    in America 4–5
    in Great Britain 4
  handling acute couple distress 22
  initial stage 205
  value in psychiatric illness 311–312
  See also specific topics
Cowan, Carolyn Page 48, 55
Cowan, Philip A. 48, 55
Coyne, J. C. 310
Crandell, L. 5, 10, 49
creative couple relationships 116–118
  clinical vignettes 118–122
Crowell, J. A. 49, 55
Cudmore, L. 29
Cummings, E. M. 310
curiosity
  containment and 121–122
  defence against 119
custody agreements 289–291

daydreams *vs.* imagination 27. *See also* phantasy:
  vs. fantasy
death 225–226
death instinct
  Fairbairn on 61
  Freud on 60, 73–74
  Klein on 60–61
defence(s)
  against aggression 67
  against catastrophe 30
  against curiosity 119
  moral 61
  omnipotent 27, 38–39
  shared 29, 31–32, 146, 155, 251
  See also resistance

defensive patterns in couples 163–164
depressive position 152, 168, 183, 186, 195, 257, 332
D'Ercole, A. 83
Derogatis, L. 234
development, childhood
    trauma and 298t, 299
    See also specific topics
developmental transitions, adult 219
Dicks, Henry V. 4–5, 8, 134, 158, 160, 173
    hypotheses 160–161
    Marital Tensions 4, 93
    model of sex and marital dynamics and therapy 4, 8, 93, 237–239
    on affairs 256
    on "complete marriages" 176
    on interactional field 151
    on joint marital personality 4, 95
    on projective identification 4
    on unconscious complementariness 93
dissociation 299
divorce 225, 279–280
    and the legal system 293–294
    children and 284–289
    clinical examples 282–288, 291–292
    cohabitation before the split 286–287
    couples in treatment contemplating 280–281
    disbelief, begging, and the initiator's response 281–282
    exploring next steps following 288–289
    referring the couple to attorney or mediator 289
divorced parents, work with
    managing the re-emergence of the marital dynamic 291–292
    post-separation co-parenting "counselling" 290–291
    See also divorce
Doll's House couples 163–164
domestic violence 71–72, 79
    attachment styles in 75
    case example 76–79
    clinical management 68
    social attitudes and 65
    See also aggression
Dora, Freud's case of 104
"double dosing" 41

"downloading" of affect regulating capacity 47–48
dream construction, mechanisms of 104–107
    composition and identification to create composite/collective figure(s) 105
    condensation 104
    displacement, distortion, and disguise 105
    dramatisation 106
    reversal 105
    symbolisation 105–106
dream work 13–14, 17
    dynamic approaches to 107
    example of dream analysis in sex therapy 17–20
    in analytic couple therapy 101, 108–109, 114, 190–192
        clinical examples 109–114, 192–199, 264–265
        resistance to 102
    principles of 104
    therapists' resistances to 102–103
dreams
    fears in 103
    Freud on 101, 104–106, 191, 195
    from before Freud to object relations 101–102
    functions 106–107
    of therapist 195–198
    projective identification in 190, 196–198
Drescher, Jack 88
drives
    Freud on 60, 73–74, 159
    Klein on 60–61
drug abuse. *See* addiction; alcohol abuse; cocaine addiction
Dutton, D. 5, 11, 75, 300
dyspareunia 233–234

Ehrlich, F. M. 173
Ellis, M. L. 81
environmental mother 9, 134, 175
erectile dysfunction 234
Erikson, Erik H. 93
evacuation, experience of 120–121
expectations, mismatch over
    as presenting problem 165–166
extramarital affairs. *See* affair(s)
Ezriel, Henry 30

Faimberg, H. 271, 277
Fairbairn, W. Ronald D. 67, 96, 134, 180, 237, 295, 313
    model of psychic structure and organization 5–6, 6f, 134
    on aggression 60–61
    on dreams 106–107
    on moral defence 61
    on sexuality 238
Falco, K. L. 88
family evaluation 304–308
family therapy 305–306. *See also* parent work
family trauma 296t
fantasies
    triangular field of fantasy (*see* triangular field)
    types of 27
    working with 13–14
    See also phantasy
fears
    related to dreams 103
    See also safety
fee in couple therapy 127, 132
Feeney, B. C. 75
Ferro, A. 107, 278
Fisher, James 5, 10, 29–30, 49, 122, 165
focused relating 9f
focused transference and countertransference 11, 175
Fonagy, Peter 10, 50, 52, 55, 63, 216
Fourcroy, J. 234
Fraiberg, S. 271, 277
frame, therapeutic 13, 120, 129, 207
    in family therapy 305–306
    interpretation of reactions to 11, 133
    "safe haven" and "secure base" functions 53, 134
    therapeutic relationship and 131–134
    See also couple state of mind: and the physical, practical, and psychological setting
Freud, Anna 26, 303
Freud, Sigmund 4
    on constancy principle 304
    on dreams 101, 104–106, 191, 195
    on drives 60, 73–74, 159
    on fantasy 25–26
    on goals of analysis 323
    on loss and mourning 247
    on normality 323
    on phylogenetic inheritance 32
    on projection 158–159
    on trauma 303
    on Wolfman 26
    terminology 25–26
Friedman, R. 191–192
Fugl-Meyer, K. 234
fusion 154, 156, 187. *See also* merger; self/other confusion

Gabbard, Glen O. 323
Gade, I. 310
Gallese, V. 39, 63
Gamill, J. 106
Garland, C. 303–304
gay and lesbian marriages and partnerships 81, 89
    affairs in 260
    case examples 85–88, 287–288
    challenges to psychoanalytic thinking and practice 81–82
    gender roles in 86–87
    respecting difference 82–83
    separation and children of 287–288
    therapist factors 88–89
    working with unconscious processes 83–85
George, C. 55
Gergely, G. 10, 50, 55, 63, 216
Glasser, M. 62
going-on-being 300
Gottman, J. M. 49
Gotze, H. 310
Green, André 271, 274
Green, R. J. 83
Greenan, D. E. 86–87
Greenson, Ralph R. 102, 107
Grotstein, James S. 171
Guan Daosheng (Kuan Tao-sheng) 35
Gupta, M. 310
Gus, J. R. 81

Haastrup, S. 310
Halliday, K. S. 182
Heimann, Paula 171

Henderson, A. 5, 11, 75, 300
Herrick, L. 293
Hertzmann, Leezah 83–84
Hesse, E. 48
Hewison, David xiii, 32
history, gathering 13
history taking, individual 230–231
Hobbes, Thomas 73
holding 9f, 11–13
holding environment 296, 297f
    collapse of 296, 297f
Holmes, J. 50, 55
homophobia 82
    internalised 82–84, 88
Hopper, E. 298
hypoactive sexual desire disorder 234

"I" statements 154
Ibsen, Henrik 164
identified patient 310–311
illness 223–224
imagination *vs.* daydreams 27. *See also* phantasy:
    vs. fantasy
impotence, fear of 103
infertility 221–222
infidelity. *See* affair(s)
internal object 37
internal working models 47
International Psychotherapy Institute (IPI) xiii, 92
Internet affairs 258
Internet pornography 154
intersubjectivity 65
intimacy
    components of 36
    developmental transition from isolation into
        93
    journey from self/other confusion to real
        42–43
    married love and 35–39
    models of 36
    sexual, asking about 16
    shared fear of, after infidelity 262–264
introjection 159. *See also* introjective identification
introjective identification 19
    projective identification and 7, 8f, 164, 171–174
intrusive identification 165

invasion, fear of 103
Isaacs, Susan 26–27

Jacobs, Theodore J. 172
Johnson, S. 55
Johnson, Virginia 5, 17, 240
joint marital personality 4, 12, 93–95
joint transference. *See* transference: joint
Jones, S. 72
Joseph, Betty 171
joy, a couple who lost 201–212
    recovery of joy 326–333
Jung, Carl Gustav 27, 168
Jurist, E. L. 10, 55, 63, 216

Kantzian, E. J. 182
Kaplan, Helen Singer 5, 17, 237, 240
Kaplan, N. 55
Katz, S. C. 196–197
Keats, John 42
Kerig, P. K. 48
Kernberg, Otto F. 61
Kichli, Tamar (TKB) 197
Killepsy, H. 88
King, M. 88
King, P. 26
Klein, Melanie 171, 173, 324
    Controversial Discussions and 26
    on depressive position 168, 195
    on drives 60–61
    on omnipotent phantasy 39
    on paranoid-schizoid position 39, 168
    on phantasy 26, 153
    on projective identification 4, 7–8, 39, 134,
        164–165, 237
Kline Pruett, M. 48
Knudson-Martin, K. 82
Kohut, Heinz 94–96
Kouras, C. D. 310
Kron, T. 196–197
K-state-of-mind (Bion) 122
Kuan Tao-sheng 35

Lachmann, Frank M. 50
Laplanche, J. 25–26
Laughlin, M. J. 82

Leeds, J. 182, 310
Leiblum, S. 234
lesbian couples. *See* gay and lesbian marriages and partnerships
Lesser, R. C. 86
LoPicollo, J. 239
loss 225. *See also* mourning
love, married 35–39
Lowen, L. 87
Ludlam, M. 270

Madonna/Whore split 256, 259
Main, Mary 10, 55
Malin, A. 171
marriage, sexuality, and commitment 220–221
Marsh, S. 173
Masters, S. 83, 88
Masters, William H. 5, 17, 240
mate selection 219–220
Mattinson, Janet 163
maturational reorganisation 215–216
maturity of couples 168
McAuliffe, W. E. 182
McDougall, Joyce M. 319
McGilchrist, Ian 45, 55
meaning-making relationship, couple as 168
Meltzer, Donald W. 29, 102, 126–127, 165
mentalization 55, 152
merger 38–39, 41–42, 164. *See also* fusion; symbiosis
mirror neurons 63
mirroring 50–52
    maternal 49–51, 54, 95
    therapist as mirror 54
misunderstanding 118–119
Mitchell, Stephen A. 81–82
Mitchell, V. 83
Money-Kyrle, Roger E. 27
Monguzzi, F. 59, 64, 72
Monin, J. K. 75
monogamy *vs.* open relationships 86–87. *See also* open relationships
moral defence 61
Morgan, Mary 37, 48, 119, 126, 321, 325
    on couple state of mind 125, 311, 316
    on creative couple relationship 116
    on projective gridlock 164
Morgenstern, J. 182, 310
Morris, S. 31
mother–infant relationship. *See* parent–infant relationship
mourning 247, 305. *See also* loss
Munkner, R. 310

narcissistic couples 180–181
    case vignette 185–187
    strains on containment in treatment of 185–188
    technique with 182–184
    See also cocaine addiction
narcissistic rage 96
narrative builder, therapist as 55–56
Nazareth, I. 88
negative therapeutic reaction 182
Neri, C. 191
neuroscience
    affect regulation, attachment, and 45–46, 54–55, 64
    interpersonal aspects of development and 62–63

object mother 9, 175
object usage 153–154, 186
Ogden, Thomas H. 106–107, 172, 174, 187
old age and death 225–226
omnipotent defence 27, 38–39
omnipotent phantasy 37–39, 41–42, 47–48
open relationships 86–87, 185–187, 255
orgasmic disorder, male 234
Osborn, D. 88

Palombo, S. R. 106
Papp, L. M. 310
paranoia 158
paranoid-schizoid anxiety 300
paranoid-schizoid position 39, 152, 168, 183, 186, 257, 293
parent–infant relationship, Winnicott's theory of 8–9. *See also* Winnicott, Donald W.
parent work
    vs. couple work 269–271

post-separation co-parenting "counselling" 290–291
See also parents in couple treatment
parenthood 223
parents in couple treatment 271
    challenges for couple therapists 277–278
    clinical vignettes 271–277
    See also parent work
Parke, R. D. 48
partner abuse. *See* domestic violence
Patrick, B. C. 36
personality disordered couples 151–152
    with sado-masochistic features, theory of 180–181
    See also cocaine addiction
Peters, M. J. 173
Peters, T. C. 173
phantasy 37–38
    shared 28–29
        how to understand a couple's 31–33
    vs. fantasy 25–27
    when it arises 26–28
Pincus, Lily 28–29
Pines, M. 191
Pontalis, J. -B. 25–26
pornography
    Internet 154
    secret use of 258
Poulton, James L. 56
pregnancy 222–223
prermature ejaculation (PE) 155, 232
presenting problems 229–230
    history of 230
projection 159–160
    Freud on 158–159
    troublesome patterns of spousal 162–165
projective-gridlock couples 163–164
projective identification(s) 8, 28, 39, 93–94, 134, 164–165, 220
    couple therapy and 184, 279, 300–301, 304
    definition and nature of 171, 218
    in dreams 190, 196–198
    introjective identification and 7, 8f, 164, 171–174
    joint marital personality and 4, 12, 95
    Klein on 4, 7–8, 39, 134, 164–165, 237
    mutual 238, 270, 293
    of parent onto child 218
    "one-person" 171–172
    onto therapist 196–197
    taking back 301
    trauma and 299–301
    "two-person" 171–174
projective identificatory system of couple 15, 148, 198, 280, 293. *See also* projective system
projective system 41–42. *See also* projective identificatory system of couple
psychodynamic couple therapy 3
    theoretical basis 5–7
    See also specific topics
psychosexual therapy 235
psychosomatic partnership 9
psychotherapeutic strategies 91
psychotherapy, defined 44

Quinodoz, J. M. 101

Racker, H. 4–5, 273
Reis, H. T. 36
Relate 72
repetition compulsion 302
resistance
    to couple therapy, managing 21
    to dream work 102–103
return of the repressed 98
reverie approach to dreams 107
Rilke, Rainer Maria 42
Ringstrom, P. A. 95
Rosenfeld, Herbert 60, 180–181
Roved, B. 310
Rustin, M. 270
Ruszczynski, S. 29, 56, 59, 65, 82, 125–126, 165, 325

Sabbadini, A. 323
sado-masochism in relationships 62, 65–66, 151, 180–181
safety
    lack of 119–120
    See also fears
same-sex couples. *See* gay and lesbian marriages and partnerships
Sandler, Anne-Marie 26, 32

Sandler, Joseph 26, 32
Scarf, M. 215
Scharff, David E. (DES) xiii, 3–4, 15–16, 60, 65, 91, 94, 171, 237, 251, 255, 296, 301, 313, 325
  assessment with a couple 15–16
  developmental object relations approach to sexuality 17
  dream analysis in sex therapy 17–20
  dream work with a couple 109–114
  on contextual *vs.* focused transference 174–175
  on countertransference 11, 21, 308
  on disrupted attachment 298
  on dissociation 295, 299
  on dreams 101, 107, 191, 197
  on family therapy 305–306
  on infidelity 262
  on interpersonal unconscious 56, 191
  on narcissistic disorders 182
  on projective identification 11, 218, 304
  on sexual symptoms and sex therapy 216–218, 240–241
  on sexuality 5, 9, 17, 20, 101, 197, 220, 238
  on transference 174, 308
  on trauma 20, 101, 299
Scharff, Jill Savege 3–4, 16, 21, 65, 94, 219, 237, 296, 301, 313, 325
  assessment with a couple 15–16
  on contextual *vs.* focused transference 174–175
  on countertransference 11, 21, 308
  on disrupted attachment 298
  on dissociation 295, 299
  on dreams 101, 107
  on family therapy 305–306
  on infidelity 262
  on interpersonal unconscious 56, 191
  on intimacy 255
  on narcissistic disorders 182
  on projective identification 11, 171–172, 218, 304
  on sexual symptoms and sex therapy 216, 218, 240–241
  on sexuality 5, 9, 17, 20, 101, 220
  on transference 11, 174, 308
  on trauma 20, 101, 299
Scharff, Kate 293

schizoid pathology 181. *See also* paranoid-schizoid position
Schore, Allan N. 46–48, 55, 62
Schulz, M. S. 48
Searles, Harold F. 171
secrets
  affairs and revelation of 258, 261–262
  and secrecy 257–258
Segal, Hanna 27, 106, 171, 246, 324
self language 154
self/other confusion 39, 94
  journey to real intimacy and healing from 42–43
  See also fusion; merger; symbiosis
self psychology 94–99
self regard, attachment patterns and 75
selfdyad
  and a case of sexual dysfunction 97–99
  and a model for treatment 96–97
  as bridge between the individual and couple 92–94
  as expansion of joint marital personality 94–95
  defined 93
selfdyad fracture 96
Semlyen, J. 88
separation, marital 284
  couples who have decided to separate 284
  post-separation co-parenting "counselling" 290–291
  See also divorce
sex and marital therapy 237, 240–241
  case illustration 238–239, 244
    couple therapy 240–243
    dynamic formulation from object relations framework 239
    evaluation 239
    feedback and recommendations 239–240
  model of 237–238
  See also psychosexual therapy
sex therapy, example of dream analysis in 17–20
sex therapy techniques, integration in couple therapy 16–17
sexual abuse 218–219
sexual intimacy, asking about 16
sexual relationship, assessing the 228–229
  a typical sexual encounter 232

diagnosis and further treatment 232–233
individual histories and 230–231
maintaining factors 232
precipitating factors 231
predisposing factors 231
presenting problem 229–230
history of 230
sexual symptomatology
aversion to sex 238–244
development of 217–219
See also sexual relationship
sexual trauma 296t
sexuality
attachment and 216–217
commitment, marriage, and 220–221
Seymour, Jane 325
Shapiro, R. 5
Shapiro, V. 271, 277
shared defences 29, 31–32, 146, 155, 251
shared narrative 285
Sharpe, Ella F. 102, 108
Shaver, P. 36, 75
Siegel, J. 277
social attitudes, aggression,
and violence 65
Solomon, J. 10
Solomon, L. 173
Spears, B. 87
Spillius, E. B. 182
Steger, J. 239
Steiner, R. 26
Stern, Daniel N. 46
Stewart, R. H. 173
Stolorow, Robert D. 95
Storr, Anthony 74
Strachey, James 25
Strange Situation 10
Sutherland, John D. 10
symbiosis 37–39, 47, 154, 194, 251, 306, 308.
See also merger
symbolic equation 246–247, 252–253

Target, Mary 10, 50, 52, 55, 63, 216
Tavistock Centre for Couple Relationships (TCCR)
xiii, 4, 10, 32, 92, 145. *See also* Tavistock Marital Studies Institute

Tavistock Marital Studies Institute 10–11, 29. *See also* Tavistock Centre for Couple Relationships
technique(s) in couple therapy 13–16, 14f
Temperley, J. 128
termination 22, 332–333
clinical example 326–333
criteria for 22t
pre-ending phase 325–326
readiness to end couple therapy 324–325
therapeutic alliance 53. *See also* therapeutic relationship
therapeutic jurisprudence 293
therapeutic relationship, establishing 131, 157
beginning with the phone call 131–134
clinical example 135
assessment 145–147
conflict over work and intimacy 135–137
object relations history 140–145
problems in relationship 137–140
therapist, couple
attributes and roles in affect regulation 52–56
therapist as "corpus callosum" 54–55
therapist as decoder 55
therapist as narrative builder 55–56
therapist as part of couple's environment 56
therapist as "safe haven" and "secure base" 52–53
challenges to 20–22
dual focus on couple and individual pathology 311–321
working between the individual and couple 176–178
See also specific topics
third, analytic 174
third, symbolic 117, 121, 129
third position 117, 121, 126–127
Ticho, Ernst 323
transference 11–12, 12f, 126–127, 133
case example 146
contextual and focused 11–12, 174–176
infidelity and 262
joint 170–177
multiple 170–171, 176–178
neurobiology and 54
"one-person" projective identification and 171–172 (*see also* projective identification)

origins 171
triangular 148–150, 154, 156–157
working with 15–16
transference field. *See* triangular field
transitional space 9f, 38, 302
trauma 295, 303
    analytic couple therapy for 300–302
        example of working with traumatic nuclei and gaps in psyche 301–302
    Freud on 303
    individual effects 296–300
    repeating 302
    sexual 218–219
    terror attacks and intergenerational 303, 308–309
        and the therapeutic process 304–306
        clinical example 305–308
        family evaluation 306–308
        forming new patterns 308
        uncontrollable "ball of fire" in family 304
    types of 295, 296t
    working with 20
    See also aggression; domestic violence
Treboux, D. 49
triadic transference in supervision of a couple case 154–156
triangular field 148–153
triangular space and oedipal dynamics 127
triangular theory 151
triangulation, fantasy, and containment
    clinical example of 153–154
Tuch, R. 260
Tunnell, S. C. 86–87
Tvaro, K. 310

unconscious phantasy. *See* phantasy
unconscious relating, a couple version of 28–30
unconscious, working with the 13

vaginismus 16, 233, 235
Vaughan, Susan C. 83
Vincent, Christopher 48, 71–72, 310, 312
violence. *See* aggression; domestic violence; trauma
Viorst, Judith 215

Walby, S. 72
Wall, S. 10, 48, 295, 298
Wanlass, Janine 69
Waters, E. 10, 48, 55, 295, 298
Watson, J. 50
Wilner, W. 196–197
Winnicott, Donald W. 95
    in mirroring 49–50
    on aggression 61–62, 72–73
    on false self 128, 180
    on going-on-being 300
    on parent–infant relationship 8–9, 38, 134, 175
Wolf, E. S. 95
Wolfman, Freud's case of the 26
Woodhouse, D. 28
Wright, K. 50

Zavattini, G. C. 173
Zeitner, Richard M. 91
Zilbach, J. J. 173
Zinner, J. 5